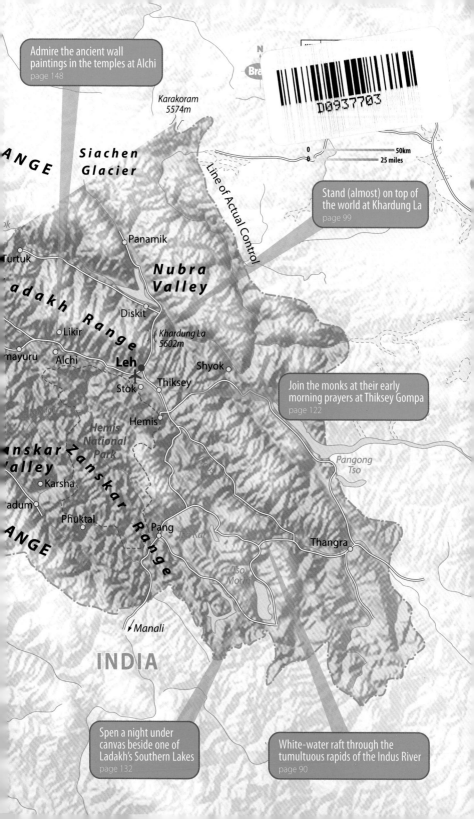

Admire the ancient wall
paintings in the temples at Alchi
page 148

N

Bre

D0937703

0
0
50km
25 miles

Stand (almost) on top of
the world at Khardung La
page 99

Karakoram
5574m

Siachen
Glacier

ANGE

Line of Actual Control

Panamik

Nubra
Valley

Turtuk

adakh Range

Diskit

Likir

Khardung La
5602m

mayuru

Alchi

Leh

Shyok

Stok

Thiksey

Join the monks at their early
morning prayers at Thiksey Gompa
page 122

Hemis

Hemis
National
Park

nskar Zanskar Range

Pangong
Tso

alley

Karsha

adum

Phuktal

Pang

Thangra

ANGE

Tso
Morii

Manali

INDIA

Spen a night under
canvas beside one of
Ladakh's Southern Lakes
page 132

White-water raft through the
tumultuous rapids of the Indus River
page 90

Ladakh
Don't
miss...

Houseboats of Srinagar
Relax for hours in one of India's floating palaces on Dal or Nagin lakes (l/S)
page 190

Thiksey Gompa
Join the monks in their early morning prayers at this monastery in Ladakh (sp/S) page 122

Chadar Winter Trek

This six-day hike along a frozen river is the ultimate challenge for visitors to Zanskar (SC/S) page 178

Amarnath *yatra*

Join Hindu pilgrims making the annual journey to the Amarnath Cave, one of their religion's most sacred shrines (ZA/A) page 184

Khardung La

Stand (almost) on top of the world at this pass along the earth's highest motorable road (AS/D) page 99

Ladakh in colour

above   The colourful interior of Matho Gompa, one of
Ladakh's least-visited monasteries
(PA/AWL) page 124

left   Carved deep into the rock, the 9m-tall Maitreya
Buddha is Mulbekh's most spectacular site (MT/S)
page 154

below   Founded in 1515, the mud bricks of Basgo Gompa
are sadly 'melting' from the elements (N/S)
page 143

above   Diskit's vast Maitreya Buddha was inaugurated by the Dalai Lama in 2010 (t/S) page 105

above right   Perched like a crow's nest atop a hill above the Indus River, Stakna has one of the most photogenic locations of any monastery in Ladakh (mS/S) page 125

below   Monastery festivals provide the best chance to witness Ladakhi cultural tradition, such as here at Hemis (mt/S) page 127

<table>
</table>

above   The Martand Sun Temple near Mattan was built in the 8th century AD and contains a number of well-preserved carvings (MEP/S) page 207

left   The Jamia Masjid in Srinagar has 370 pillars built from wood from around the city, while the pagoda-like design reflects the regional influence of Tibetan-Buddhism (PL/S) page 195

below   Jammu's Shri Raghunathji Temple is the largest complex of its kind in northern India (S/S) page 224

AUTHOR

Sophie Ibbotson first arrived in central Asia in 2008 when her auto-rickshaw (tuk-tuk) got snowed in en route from Darjeeling, India, to London. Forced to overwinter, she fell in love with the region and became excited by the opportunities it offered, opening the Kyrgyz office of her investment promotion company, Maximum Exposure Productions (MEP), the following year. Sophie now runs Maximum Exposure Ltd, providing tourism and culture consultancy and PR services, and is the co-founder and managing editor of *Panorama: The Journal of Intelligent Travel.*
She is also a member of the Royal Society for Asian Affairs (**w** rsaa.org.uk).

UPDATER

Stuart Butler (**w** stuartbutlerjournalist.com) is a writer, award-winning photographer and guidebook author specialising in the Himalaya region and Africa. He has authored over 40 guidebooks, including Bradt guides to Benin and Bhutan, as well as two trekking guides to the Himalayas. Having travelled extensively throughout India and the greater Himalaya region, he has also written on subjects as varied as conservation in the Himalayas, trekking, festivals and nomadic life. When not in the Himalayas he lives on the beautiful coast of southwest France with his wife and two children.

UPDATER'S STORY

I was sitting inside the dark, yak-hair tent of a nomad family in southern Ladakh. Outside, scruffy sheep searched for greenery among the barren moonscape and raptors circled in the thermals. Somewhere, just over the pass, were the sparkling waters of Tso Moriri. As we huddled around the hearth the old man handed me a small glass of salty, yak butter tea. 'There were wolves here two nights ago', he told me. 'This time I chased them away, but they will come back again and try and get at my sheep. It's happening more and more. Everything about being a herder is getting more difficult. Maybe my sons won't want to continue this life. My wife and I might be among the last of the nomads here.'

Although the conversation was a little on the depressing side, I felt happy in this family's tent and could have sat there chatting about the past and future for hours. It is encounters like this that are the reason I love the Himalayas. I have been travelling around these mountains for some 25 years, and although every corner of the region has its own special magic, the cold deserts of Ladakh are a place that call to me with more force than most. So, when Bradt asked me if I could update this book, I could hardly refuse. Unlike some guidebook updates I have done elsewhere, researching the extraordinary diversity of Ladakh, Zanskar, Kashmir and Jammu didn't feel like work – it was pure pleasure. I hope you enjoy exploring this area as much as I have.

In the introduction to the first edition of this book, Sophie observed that the landscapes and people of Kashmir linger on your mind long after you leave. I couldn't agree more. I visited a few years ago (trekking into the Ladakh range to write a newspaper piece on efforts to protect the snow leopard) and it's a trip I still think about often. The shifting colours of the mountains are extraordinary, as is the sight of golden eagles spread against the sky and blue sheep leaping among rocks high on the slopes. I remember staying a night with a local family in a remote village; they spoke no English, but we spent a happy evening together sitting on the floor, drinking butter tea and making pasta for our dinner. The region's pleasures might be simple, but they are vivid and life-enhancing. This new edition – updated by Stuart Butler – will help you bank a treasure of memories.

Second edition published November 2019
First published July 2014
Bradt Travel Guides Ltd
31a High Street, Chesham, Buckinghamshire, HP5 1BW, England
www.bradtguides.com
Print edition published in the USA by The Globe Pequot Press Inc,
PO Box 480, Guilford, Connecticut 06437-0480

Text copyright © 2019 Bradt Travel Guides
Maps copyright © 2019 Bradt Travel Guides Ltd; includes map data © OpenStreetMap contributors
Photographs copyright © 2019 Individual photographers (see below)
Project Manager: Laura Pidgley
Cover research: Pepi Bluck, Perfect Picture

ISBN: 978 1 78477 095 2

British Library Cataloguing in Publication Data
A catalogue record for this book is available from the British Library

Photographers Alamy.com: ZUMA Press, Inc. (ZA/A); AWL Images: Peter Adams (PA/AWL), Paul Harris (PH/AWL); Dreamstime.com: Abhishek Singh (AS/D); J&K Tourism (J&KT); Maximum Exposure Productions (MEP); Shutterstock: AJP (AJP/S), Vivek BR (VB/S), Siriwatthana Chankawee (SC/S), Kobby Dagan (KD/S), Natalia Davidovich (ND/S), Francesco Dazzi (FD/S), Ajith Everester (AE/S), ImagesofIndia (I/S), khlongwangchao (k/S), srbh_graphy (s_g/S), Pius Lee (PL/S), Maximum Exposure Productions (MEP/S), Niraelanor (N/S), NaughtyNut (NN/S), Dmitry Rukhlenko (DR/S), chris piason (cp/S), Martin Pelanek (MP/S), suchitra poungkoson (sp/S), Ondrej Prosicky (OP/S), saiko_3p (s/S), szefei (sz/S), martinho Smart (mS/S), tscreationz (t/S), THONGCHAI.S (T/S), Mai Tram (mt/S), Mazur Travel (MT/S), Zzvet (Z/S); SuperStock (SS)
Front cover Ladakhi women standing in front of Lamayuru Monastery (FB/AWL)
Back cover Dal Lake, Srinagar (s_g/S)
Title page Stakna Gompa (mS/S); Masked dancer at a monastery festival (Z/S); Sonamarg (VB/S)

Maps David McCutcheon FBCart.S

Typeset by D & N Publishing, Baydon, Wiltshire
Production managed by Jellyfish Print Solutions; printed in Turkey
Digital conversion by www.dataworks.co.in

Acknowledgements

STUART BUTLER Thank you first and foremost to my wife Heather and children Jake and Grace for all their patience while I indulged myself in this Himalayan project. Thank you to all at Bradt for the chance to work on such an exciting title and for patience throughout the project. In J&K, thank you to Ajaz Khar at Chicago Houseboats in Srinagar, Mr Kakpori at Caravan Centre hotel in Leh, Lobzang Visuddha from Ancient Tracks in Leh, and the staff at the Horizon Camp, Nubra Ecolodge and the Hotel the Kargil. Thank you also to Tashi at the Dragon Guesthouse in Lamayuru, Mohmad Azharudin from Heevan Hotels in Kashmir, Captain Prasenjit Biswas from the Desert Himalaya Resort and Norboo Gailtsan in Alchi.

STOP PRESS

In the week that this book went to print, the Indian government unexpectedly revoked Article 370, which guaranteed Kashmir its special semi-autonomous status. Kashmir and Jammu are to become Union Territories (administrative units controlled and governed by the union government), while Ladakh was made a totally separate Union Territory and will no longer be politically connected to Kashmir. While the news was generally met with joy in Ladakh, in J&K the opposite is true. A near total media and communications blackout was in force across the state and a curfew had been imposed. Although it cannot be predicted how this will play out, it's very likely that protests and perhaps violence will follow. Do check on the current situation before travelling to J&K.

HOW TO USE THIS GUIDE

AUTHOR'S FAVOURITES Finding genuinely characterful accommodation or that unmissable off-the-beaten-track café can be difficult, so the author has chosen a few of his favourite places throughout the country to point you in the right direction. These 'author's favourites' are marked with a ✳.

MAPS Maps include alphabetical **keys** covering the locations of those places to stay, eat or drink that are featured in the book. Note that regional maps may not show all hotels and restaurants in the area: other establishments may be located in towns shown on the map.

Several maps use **gridlines** to allow easy location of sites. Grid references are listed in square brackets after the name of the place or site of interest in the text, with page number followed by grid number, eg: [78 C3].

Contents

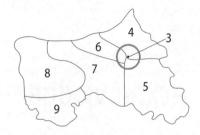

WHAT'S IN A NAME?

The first edition of this guidebook was titled *Kashmir including Ladakh and Zanskar*, but we chose to name this second edition *Ladakh, Jammu & the Kashmir Valley*. The reason for this change is simply to reflect that the greater part of this book is dedicated to Ladakh and that this is the most popular region of J&K with both domestic and international tourists. Otherwise, you will find that the book still contains comprehensive coverage of Srinagar, the Kashmir Valley and Jammu.

Introduction

Gar firdaus ae baruhe zamin ast
Hamin astu hamin astu hamin ast.

If there is heaven on earth,
It is here, it is here, it is here.
Emperor Jahangir, 17th century

Whether you were fortunate enough in times gone by to be a Mughal emperor, a civil servant of the Raj, a hippie on the hippie trail, or are a modern visitor discovering Kashmir, Ladakh, Zanskar and Jammu now for the very first time, you cannot fail to be impressed by this region. The incredible beauty of the natural landscapes, the richness of the history and the warmth and diversity of the people get deep under your skin and linger in your mind long after you have had to leave. Sitting on the terrace of a colonial-style houseboat as the dawn mists rise off Srinagar's Dal Lake and the sunlight glints on the water can bring a lump to your throat and make you contemplate the possible truth behind Emperor Jahangir's Kashmir-inspired poetry.

The geographical scope of this guide is the Indian state of Jammu and Kashmir (J&K), a vast stretch of northern India encompassing lands from the plains of Jammu, up through the Kashmir Valley to Srinagar, and east through the mountainous landscapes of Ladakh, where apricot desert dunes mingle with the snows of massive Himalayan peaks to create a landscape that will simply take your breath away (if the altitude doesn't first!). With epic moonscapes, atmospheric cliff-top Buddhist monasteries, incredible Himalayan trekking opportunities, breathtaking turquoise lakes and vibrant Tibetan Buddhist culture, Ladakh, and neighbouring Zanskar, are two of the most alluring parts of the Himalayas that are attracting an ever-growing number of domestic and international tourists.

However, although Ladakh and Zanskar are safe and stable, the beauty of this far corner of India comes with a thorn in its side. India and Pakistan are at loggerheads over ownership of the Kashmir Valley and international borders in this region vary depending upon who is doing the talking. This simmering dispute means that Srinagar and the Kashmir Valley has been plagued with unrest and violence for decades, and while there was an air of optimism over the region's future when the first edition of this book was published, since then the situation in the Kashmir Valley has deteriorated significantly. In 2019 India and Pakistan came very close to war over Kashmir and at the time of going to print much of the Kashmir Valley was not safe to visit. Check the security situation first and if you're uncertain then just head to Ladakh and Zanskar, where the biggest danger you'll face is a persistent itch to return again and again. There is no other part of the Himalayas quite like it.

Part One

GENERAL INFORMATION

Location Jammu & Kashmir (J&K) is a state of India located mostly in the Himalayan mountains. International border with China in the north and east; the Line of Control (LoC) separates it from Pakistani-controlled territories in the west and northwest.

Area 222,236km² (85,806 square miles)

Climate Varies from subtropical to mountain desert depending on altitude

Population 12.54 million (2019)

Life expectancy 70.9 (male), 74.9 (female)

Capital J&K: Jammu (winter), Srinagar (summer); Ladakh: Leh

Other main towns Kargil, Leh

Main exports Agricultural produce, handicrafts

GDP US$25 billion (2018–19 estimate)

Official language Urdu. English, Hindi, Ladakhi and Kashmiri are also widely spoken.

Religions Islam, Hinduism, Buddhism

Currency Indian rupee (Rs)

Exchange rate UK£1=Rs87, €1=Rs79, US$1=Rs72 (Sep 2019)

National airline Air India

International dialling code +91

Time GMT +5½ hours

Electric voltage 220v

Weights and measures Metric

Flag Orange, white and green horizontal stripes with a *chakra* in the centre

National anthem 'Jana Gana Mana'

Major sports Polo, cricket, skiing

Public holidays* 26 January (Republic Day), 21 February (Maha Shivaratri), 9 March (Holi), 1 April (Bank Holiday), 14 April (Dr Ambedkar Jayanti), 30 April (Buddha Purnima), 21 May (Jumat-ul-Wida), 23 May (Eid al Fitr), 30 July (Eid al Zuha), 11 August (Janmashtami) 15 August (Independence Day), 21 August (Muharram), 30 September (Bank Holiday), 2 October (Mahatma Gandhi's Birthday), 25 October (Dussehra), 14 November (Diwali), 30 November (Guru Nanak Jayanti), 25 December (Christmas Day)

* These dates are correct for 2020. As some of the religious festivals are calculated according to the lunar calendar, dates will change from year to year.

Background Information

GEOGRAPHY

When talking about the political geography of Kashmir as a whole, there are two things to consider: the geography of greater Kashmir, and the more limited geography of Jammu and Kashmir (J&K) state.

Greater Kashmir (also known as the Princely State of Kashmir and Jammu) includes territories administered by India, Pakistan and China. In the west are the provinces of Azad Kashmir and Gilgit-Baltistan (Pakistani-administered); to the north and east are the Trans-Karakoram Tract and Aksai Chin (Chinese-administered); and the south and central parts are the regions of Ladakh, the Kashmir Valley and Jammu (Indian-administered), which are the focus of this guidebook. Local maps of the region are likely to depict different international borders depending upon which country produced the map.

Historically, nomads, traders and the population at large could move back and forth across Kashmir (and beyond) at will. This mobility ended with the solidification of borders following conflicts between India and Pakistan, and India and China, in the 20th century (page 15), and Kashmir has been fractured ever since.

J&K , however, is a state of the Republic of India. The United Nations refers to it as Indian-administered Kashmir, while the government of Pakistan calls it Indian-occupied Kashmir. The semantics are politically charged. J&K is made up of three divisions – Jammu, the Kashmir Valley and Ladakh – and is further divided into 22 districts, most of which take their name from their major town. The state has two principal cities, Jammu and Srinagar, and a number of smaller towns including Kargil and Leh.

The state's physical geography is diverse due to its varied elevations: the biogeography varies from barren deserts to subtropical pine forests, alpine meadows to scrub and steppe. The 70km-long Siachen Glacier (which is today a battleground, with India controlling the glacier in full and Pakistani troops based just below them on the Pakistani side of the Line of Control) is the longest in the Himalayas, and the waters of the Chenab, Indus, Jhelum, Ravi and Tawi rivers have cut valleys through the rock and continue to irrigate the land. Much of the landscape is mountainous thanks to the Himalayan, Hindu Kush, Karakoram, Ladakh and Pir Panjal ranges; the highest peaks in the state are the 7,135m Nun and the only slightly smaller Kun at 7,077m, both of which lie in the Suru Valley south of Kargil.

GEOLOGY The Indian Himalayas, which cover the vast part of J&K state, were created by the collision of the Indo-Australian and European tectonic plates, a process which has been ongoing for the past 50 million years. The edges of both of these plates are low-density crust, which is why they have thrust up and folded

NATURAL RESOURCES IN J&K

J&K has no oil, but there are small reserves of natural gas and semi-bituminous coal near Jammu. Seams of low-grade coal are also found further north in the Kashmir Valley.

More interesting than its fossil fuels, however, are the mineral resources. There are significant bauxite and gypsum deposits around Udhampur, substantial quantities of thorium and uranium in Ladakh, and small amounts of copper, granite, halite, iron, marble, sulphur and zinc elsewhere in the state. It is also possible to find gemstones, including precious stones such as sapphires and rubies.

J&K's greatest natural resource is undoubtedly water. The Himalayan glaciers and meltwater feed the rivers of the subcontinent, providing water for more than a billion people, and not only irrigate the crops but can also be harnessed for hydro-power. There are at least 11 such dams and hydro-power projects either already functioning or under construction throughout Indian J&K.

into the mountain range we see today. The Himalayas continue to grow at a rate of around 5mm per year, leading to intense seismic activity in the area.

Earthquakes Earthquakes are an ongoing concern in J&K due to the fact that the state straddles this tectonic fault line. Although most of the tremors are small and cause relatively minor rockfalls, there are eight to ten quakes each year measuring 4.0 magnitude or more on the Richter scale. Major earthquakes of 7.6 and 7.2 magnitude shook the state in 2005 and 2008 respectively, the former causing an estimated 86,000–87,000 deaths (mostly in Azad Kashmir) and displacing more than 2.8 million people.

Avalanches A feature of Himalayan life are avalanches, which occur day in and day out but largely go unnoticed by most people as they normally occur high up on the peaks. However, they can prove deadly for mountaineers or occasionally even trekkers, and can cause problems for road maintenance crews. Many mountain routes throughout the Himalayan region are hit by regular avalanches or landslides (particularly during the southwest monsoon season and spring thaw in March) and roads are frequently blocked with the debris of such events (fortunately vehicles are rarely hit in them). Normally these take a day or two to clear, but sometimes roads can be blocked for much longer.

CLIMATE

J&K has a varied climate due to the state's size and its variation in altitude and topography. Jammu has a humid, subtropical climate with summer temperatures well into the 40s (°C); a substantial drop in winter sees lows just above freezing. The area receives monsoon rains between June and September, and annual rainfall averages 693mm for Srinagar, 102mm for Leh and 1,238mm for Jammu (which gets hit by the bulk of the Indian monsoon). Srinagar is also subtropical and humid, though due to its increased altitude (1,585m), temperatures are generally lower. Summer days touch a pleasant 30°C, but in winter there can be deep snow, and temperatures hover around freezing during January and February. There is less rainfall here than in Jammu, though the spring can still be wet, and we've been caught in storms and hail in September.

The climate up in Leh is dramatically different: it's a desert. Winters are long and harsh with months of deep snowfall and the bitter temperatures can get as low as −28°C. There's little rainfall here – just a few millimetres each month – and for much of the year the days are warm and bright, albeit cooler at night.

Over the last decade or so, however, Ladakh has experienced a marked shift in its weather, most likely due to climate change. Much less snow is falling, leading to concerns about the availability of water (though saying that, when we updated this edition of the book we experienced unseasonably heavy snowfall in mid-September). In the same timeframe, however, there have also been huge and unanticipated cloudbursts: in August 2010 four inches of rain fell in just 30 minutes. Floods washed away villages, as well as homes in Leh, and more than 250 people were killed. Further heavy floods (but without the loss of life) occurred in July and August 2015.

NATURAL HISTORY AND CONSERVATION

PALEONTOLOGY The Tibetan plateau and the northern side of the Himalayas were once the bottom of a prehistoric ocean and today parts of J&K are rich in marine fossils. One of the oldest fossil beds, discovered by a British palaeontologist in 1886, is the Permian-period (approximately 260 million years old) Guryul Ravine to the south of Srinagar. The fossils found here, which are the remains of creatures that were wiped out during a period of mass extinction between the Permian and Triassic periods, are those of therapsids (large, reptilian land animals), small invertebrates and primordial corals and plants. Though theoretically a protected site, the Guryul Ravine is allegedly mined for limestone and stone chips used in local cement factories.

Not far away, in the saffron fields of Pampore, Indian geologists excavated one of the largest elephant fossils in the world in 2001: the skull alone measures 1.2m by 1.5m. Carbon dating has shown the fossil to be some 50,000 years old, revealing Kashmir must at that time have had a significantly different climate from the present day, as elephants are no longer found in these mountainous foothills.

The fossil record of Ladakh is particularly well preserved due to the dry climate and limited human impact. Ostracods and avian fossils have been found in large numbers around the southern lakes and Nubra Valley; palm leaf fossils in the Nidar Valley show there was once a tropical climate here; and fossilised woods have been found on both sides of the Indus River.

The Palaeontological Society of India (w palaeontologicalsociety.in) publishes detailed reports on fossil sites in the country, as well as field guides, and occasionally delivers public lectures.

FLORA Partly owing to the low population density, but also the diversity of climates, altitudes and ecosystems, J&K has the greatest biodiversity of any state in India. The varied natural environments are known to support 3,054 species of plant, of which 880 are found in Ladakh, though this does not include species of fungi and algae.

J&K's flora can be roughly split into three categories, reflecting the principal phyto-geographic regions. **Alpine desert vegetation** is found in Ladakh, typically at heights above 4,000m where there is little soil, little water and extremes of temperature. Trees are exceedingly scarce (and hence such areas are often referred to as being 'above the tree line'), and much of the flora you do see is either in small oases on riverbanks and surrounding springs, or is artificially irrigated and cultivated by man. Ladakh is known for its medicinal plants, however, and practitioners of *sowa rigpa* (traditional Tibetan medicine) will travel for days on foot to pick plants such as Himalayan larkspur (*Delphinium cashmerianum*), Himalayan mayapple (*Sinopodophyllum hexandrum*), Himalayan rhubarb (*Rheum australe*), tarragon (*Artemisia dracunculus*), atis (*Aconitum heterophyllum*) and manjistha (*Rubia cordifolia*). WWF India produces a detailed field guide to Ladakhi flora, which can be downloaded for free from w http://awsassets.wwfindia.org/downloads/field_guide_floral_diversity_of_ladakh.pdf.

In the Kashmir Valley, where temperatures are less extreme but rainfall is more frequent, there is **temperate vegetation** that abounds around the lakes and lagoons, and also in the Pir Panjal forests. Here there are plentiful fruit and nut trees, including pomegranate (*Punica granatum*), walnut (*Juglans regia*) and almond (*Prunus dulcis*). Many of the varieties found in this region are broad-leafed. There are both coniferous and deciduous forests, though the cedar forests (*Cedrus deodara*) in particular have been over-cut, a problem that dates back to at least the 1500s. Reforestation programmes are important for the state's future, and consequently sites such as the hill beneath Hari Parbat have been replanted and protected by the Department of Forestry.

In this temperate zone you will also find numerous aquatic plants, such as those that comprise the floating gardens in Srinagar (known as *Rad* in Kashmiri; page 194). In addition to the many beautiful varieties of water lilies (*Nymphaeaceae*) and lotuses (*Nelumbo nucifera*), cucumbers (*Cucumis sativus*), tomatoes (*Solanum lycopersicum*) and members of the melon family (*Cucurbitaceae*, which includes gourds as well as the sweet melon fruit) grow particularly well in the nutrient-rich gardens.

Saffron (*Crocus sativus*) grows particularly well in the fertile soil around Pampore and is an important export for the state (see box, page 204).

Further south around Jammu, where year-round temperatures are much warmer, **subtropical vegetation** is to be found. Trees and plants here are typically deciduous and require little water, though in higher areas (such as around Patnitop) you will again find evergreen forests of deodar cedar (*Cedrus deodara*) and also pine (*Pinus*). At a slightly lower altitude, in the foothills, the forests are of fir (*Abies pindrow*); there are also pockets of oak trees (*Quercus*) east of Batote, and large, mixed forests to the southwest of Udhampur.

FAUNA J&K is home to a vast range of animals, and as Ladakh lies at the confluence of three zoogeographic zones, it is a superb place for spotting wildlife.

Mammals One of the most ubiquitous creatures in the mountains is the fat and fluffy **Himalayan marmot** (*Marmota himalayana*), a close relative of the steppe marmots of Mongolia. They might look cute but keep in mind that the bubonic plague first made the leap to humans from infected marmots! Equally cute (but with rather less of a nasty surprise) are the **flying squirrels** (*Eoglaucomys fimbriatus*), which are relatively common in the west of J&K towards the Line of Control (LoC; border between India and Pakistan).

In all parts of the state you will see large numbers of **herbivores**, in particular domesticated sheep, goats, yak and dzo (a cross between a cow and a yak). The nomad flocks are nothing unusual – most of them will be slaughtered at Eid and eaten – but now and then you'll come across a changthangi, or Pashmina goat, with its highly sought-after fleece that is used to make pashmina shawls.

SNOW LEOPARD CONSERVATION

The protection of snow leopards in Ladakh is spearheaded by the Snow Leopard Conservancy India Trust (SLC-IT), a local NGO founded in 2000. The SLC-IT believes that community participation, combined with ecotourism, is the best way to protect snow leopards' habitats and ensure their future. The core components of the conservation programme are scientific research (including surveys); initiatives such as building predator-proof enclosures to reduce the impact of snow leopards on local communities and their livestock; and training local guides so that the presence of wildlife can become beneficial to the local economy.

Equally important for the long-term success of the project is education and outreach: workshops and public meetings can teach people the value of leopards to the ecosystem and understand ways in which people and leopards can live harmoniously side by side. The SLC-IT works in government schools and encourages field trips to Hemis National Park and other areas of ecological importance.

More information on the SLC-IT, its work and how to get involved can be found at w snowleopardindia.org/index.php.

The rarest of the wild herbivores is the critically endangered but stunningly beautiful **hangul** (Kashmir stag; *Cervus elaphus hanglu*). It is a subspecies of European red deer but has been hunted almost to extinction on account of its impressive antlers. The exact number of animals surviving in the wild is a little uncertain, though a survey in 2015 estimated that there were no more than 186 of them surviving and that they lived mainly in the Dachigam National Park (page 198). With a good guide, patience and a little luck, you may also be fortunate enough to see Tibetan antelopes (*Pantholops hodgsonii*), Tibetan gazelles or goas (*Procapra picticaudata*), markhor (*Capra falconeri*), Himalayan musk deer (*Moschus chrysogaster*) and wild yaks (*Bos grunniens*).

Easier to spot on account of their larger populations and frequent apathy towards the presence of humans are J&K's **primates**. The Rhesus macaque (*Macaca mulatta*) is a large and clever creature that is happy to live in close proximity to humans and, at times, can become an urban pest. They can occasionally be aggressive, especially if they think they're being challenged, so don't try to get too close. In J&K they are found in areas of Kashmir and Jammu below 2,500m altitude. Far rarer is the tree-dwelling **Kashmir grey langur** (*Semnopithecus ajax*), which lives in alpine forests above 2,200m. Urban development has encroached on much of its natural habitat, and populations have consequently fallen to the point that this langur is sadly now considered an endangered species.

J&K is home to several species of large **carnivores**, and if you are fortunate enough to see one it will be a highlight of your trip. In Ladakh, particularly in the Hemis National Park (page 10), there are majestic **snow leopards** (*Uncia uncia*), and you can increase your chances of spotting one, albeit at a distance, by taking a winter snow leopard trek to parts of Ladakh and Zanskar (page 165). They are painfully shy of people (and rightly so, given that they're attractive to illegal hunters), so be sure to carry binoculars, but sightings on these leopard-spotting tours are becoming increasingly common. You might also see the strange-looking Pallas's cats (*Otocolobus manul*) with their distinctive markings. They are indigenous to highland areas of central Asia and are very occasionally caught on camera traps in Ladakh's Changthang region.

1

There's a greater variety, and larger numbers, of **large carnivores** in the quieter parts of the Kashmir Valley, especially in mountainous areas towards the LoC where food is plentiful but the human population is still relatively small. Here you can hope to see Himalayan brown bear (*Ursus arctos*), Himalayan black bear (*Ursus thibetanus*), Indian wild boar (*Sus scrofa cristatus*), leopards (*Panthera pardus*), golden jackals (*Canis aureus*), jungle cats (*Felis chaus*) and Indian wild dogs (*Cuon alpinus*). If you are travelling by car you're unlikely to see a thing, so be sure to plan at least a short trek on foot to get away from the roads and out to quieter locations where the wildlife will be more at ease.

The J&K Wildlife Protection Department (w jkwildlife.com) produces an informative brochure on the state's endangered species, which includes close-up photos and advice on where and when the animals might be spotted. It can be downloaded for free from w jkwildlife.com/pdf/wild_species.pdf. An equally useful resource, this time produced by WWF India and focused on Ladakh's mammals, can be downloaded from w awsassets.wwfindia.org/downloads/field_guide_mammals_of_ladakh.pdf.

Birds Around 150 species of avifauna have been spotted in J&K. Some of them are resident year round, and many more are seasonal visitors as the state lies beneath migration paths. The official state bird is the **black-necked crane** (*Grus nigricollis*); there are just 5,000 of these birds worldwide and its only breeding ground outside of China is Tso Moriri in Ladakh.

Perhaps surprisingly, despite the fact that large parts of J&K are high-altitude desert, nearly a quarter of the birds in J&K are **aquatic**, favouring either muddy riverbanks or pristine waters of the high-altitude lakes. Very common local residents include the little grebe (*Tachybaptus ruficollis*), the red-wattled lapwing (*Vanellus indicus*) and the common moorhen (*Gallinula chloropus*), which in Kashmiri is called the *tech*. The pheasant-tailed jacana (*Hydrophasianus chirurgus*) is a common summertime visitor, as is the whiskered tern (*Chlidonias hybridus*), while in the winter months you can expect to see common teals (*Anas crecca*) and northern pintails (*Anas acuta*) with their attractive, if rather unusual, bright blue beaks.

In the mountainous areas you will find J&K's **birds of prey**. Common kestrels (*Falco tinnunculus*) reside year round near Gulmarg, and the Eurasian hobby (*Falco subbuteo*), a kind of falcon that migrates vast distances, spends its summers in the mountains around Pahalgam, where it is also possible to see Himalayan griffons (*Gyps himalayensis*). The state is also home to black kites (*Milvus migrans*), bearded vultures or lammergeiers (*Gypaetus barbatus*) and, occasionally, long-legged buzzards (*Buteo rufinus*).

J&K also has birds in glorious, bright colours that are a pleasurable sight for amateur and aficionado bird spotters alike. The Eurasian golden oriole (*Oriolus oriolus*), or *posh nool* as it is called in Kashmiri, is canary-yellow with a fetching black stripe; there's no prize for guessing the striking colouring on the blue throat (*Luscinia svecica*); the long-tailed minivet (*Pericrocotus ethologus*) is flame red and black; and the slaty-headed parakeet (*Psittacula himalayana*) has a plumage predominantly in gorgeous pistachio green.

Reptiles and amphibians Living in India you quickly become friendly with **geckos**, and visiting J&K is no different. The Ladakhian or bow-fingered frontier gecko (*Cyrtodactylus stoliczkai*) is a small, stripy creature with a disproportionately large head. It's mostly found in the area around Dras. If you have a gecko in your room then you should count yourself lucky, as they like to munch on the flies and

BIRDING IN KASHMIR   *With thanks to Ben Tavener (w bentavener.com)*

Although the overall fauna of the Kashmir region has much in common with that of central Asia and the Tibetan Plateau, the birdlife of the region includes species from an even wider area, both due to migration routes, for example from warmer parts of India to Ladakh, and the fact that the area bridges both Oriental and Palaearctic avifauna regions, even incorporating species from the Mediterranean. All this offers the chance for highly rewarding birding.

Some regional specialities to look out for include the Kashmir flycatcher, Kashmir nuthatch, Tibetan snowcock, Tibetan sandgrouse, Tibetan blackbird, Himalayan jungle-crow, Himalayan (white-tailed) rubythroat and Himalayan woodpecker, as well as the stunning iridescent Himalayan monal. Other birder favourites include the red-fronted serin, black francolin, brahminy (ruddy) shelduck, long-tailed shrike, blue rock thrush, blue-cheeked bee-eater, and fire-capped and rufous-naped tits, while summer visitors include the hoopoe and the charismatic black-necked crane, which breeds in parts of Ladakh. Two other species of crane – demoiselle and Siberian – can also be found here. The brown-flanked bush warbler, Tickell's leaf warbler and variegated laughingthrush will likely be on keener birders' target lists.

Globally important populations of raptors, including the Indian peregrine falcon, lammergeier, Himalayan griffon, white-eyed buzzard, crested honey-buzzard and steppe and golden eagles, are resident here.

Multiple species of finch (including plain mountain-finch, spectacled finch, pink-browed rosefinch), accentor (including robin accentor), bunting (such as white-capped bunting), redstart and wheatear reside here, helping birders to healthy list totals and a flurry of lifers. Take time to record all European species you have seen before, as some of the region's subspecies will likely be candidates for future splits.

For an up-to-date list of birds in Kashmir, see w kashmirnetwork.com/birds. The site is curated by amateur naturalist Dr Bakshi Jehangir.

other insects that would otherwise bother you. There are also four different species of **agama**, including Theobald's toad-headed agama (*Phrynocephalus theobaldi*) and the indigenous Kashmir rock agama (*Laudakia tuberculata*).

A variety of **snakes**, both venomous and non-venomous, are found across J&K, though fortunately they avoid people as much as they can. The poisonous ones (and so the ones you really should try not to step on) include the Indian cobra (*Naja naja*), which is considered sacred in Hindu mythology and, despite protection under the 1972 Indian Wildlife Protection Act, is still sometimes used by snake charmers; and the pit viper (*Hypnale hypnale*), a species endemic to India and Sri Lanka. Another fairly common snake is the Aesculapian snake (*Zamenis longissimus*), a very long constrictor that feeds principally on rodents and birds and is harmless to humans.

Of the amphibians, J&K has lots of **frogs and toads**. Ladakh has its own high-altitude toad (*Scutiger occidentalis*) and plateau frog (*Nanorana pleskei*), while lower down you'll find the Himalayan toad (*Bufo himalayanus*), green toad (*Bufo viridis*), the Indian skipper frog (*Euphlyctis cyanophlyctis*) and the ornate narrow-mouthed frog (*Microhyla ornata*).

Fish With its many rivers, lakes and reservoirs, numerous species of fish are found in J&K, though not all of them are indigenous; brown trout (*Salmo trutta*), for example, was introduced by the British, who thought it would be good for fishing. The brown trout flourished in its new environment, as did the rainbow trout (*Oncorynchus mykiss*), introduced at the same time, and we're still eating their descendants today.

For those who understand the categorisation of fish, four orders are represented in J&K: *Cypriniformes*, *Siluriformes*, *Salmoniformes* and *Cyprinidontiformes*. Unique to the area is the algaad (*Schizothorax niger*), though its survival is threatened by pollution caused by the dumping of fertilisers and pesticides into the water courses. Other species of fish that are similarly endangered include the rama gurun (*Botia birdi*), chirruh snowtrout (*S. esocinus*), chosh (*S. labiatus*), khont (*S. plagiostomus*) and sater gaad (*S. curvifrons*).

Information on angling in J&K is available from the Department of Fisheries (w jkfisheries.in).

NATIONAL PARKS There are currently three national parks in J&K with a combined area of nearly 5,000km². A remarkable 90% of this land is within the confines of a single reserve: the huge **Hemis National Park**, which was established in 1981 and, at 4,400km², is the largest national park in India. Bounded to the north by the Indus River, Hemis is on the Karakoram-West Tibetan Plateau and so has an alpine steppe ecosystem with a varied landscape of pine forest, alpine shrub and tundra, and meadow. The park is home to a recorded 16 species of mammal (including an estimated population of 200 snow leopards, as well as the Tibetan wolf, Eurasian brown bear and small numbers of shapu and ibex) and 73 types of bird, including birds of prey. It is a prime location to spot golden eagles and the Himalayan griffon vulture.

J&K's two other national parks are the small **Dachigam National Park** (141km²) near Srinagar, and the larger **Kishtwar National Park** (400km²) in Kishtwar district. There used to be a fourth park, the tiny Salim Ali National Park in Srinagar, but this was converted into the Royal Springs golf course in the late 1990s. The name Dachigam means 'ten villages' and is said to refer to the ten villages that were relocated when it was formed. Located in the Zabarwan mountain range, the park is set on the mountain slopes with terrain varying from bare, rocky cliffs to much lusher

SNOW LEOPARD SAFARIS

Known as the 'Ghost of the Himalaya', the beautiful yet highly elusive snow leopard is the focal point of almost as many myths as the yeti – and until a couple of years ago it was almost as hard to spot. Today, in certain Ladakhi valleys, spying snow leopards is starting to get much easier. In fact, in the past few years snow leopard sightings have become commonplace enough for certain specialist tour companies to start offering snow leopard safaris. Taking place only in the frozen winter months (leopards move lower down the mountains then and are easier to track at this time), these tours have surprisingly good success rates at spotting this elusive creature. One of the original – and best – companies offering such tours is Ancient Tracks (page 77), who offer a whole variety of excursions, including ones that take in festivals as well as snow leopard safaris. They also offer bear- and lynx-watching tours.

For more on snow leopards and snow leopard conservation, see the Snow Leopard Conservancy website (w snowleopardindia.org/index.php).

grassland. Leopards and leopard cats, Himalayan black and brown bears, musk deer, jackals, jungle cats and otters all live here in sizeable numbers, as well as the critically endangered hangul, or Kashmir stag, J&K's state animal. Kishtwar National Park is criss-crossed with rivers that cut narrow valleys through the landscape and are fed by the glaciers above. The extensive forests include silver fir, cedar, blue pine and spruce, and these provide an ideal habitat for Himalayan brown bears, hangul, markhor, langur, leopards and Himalayan snowcocks (a type of pheasant).

Though not technically a national park, the **Gulmarg Biosphere** (180km²) is also a haven for wildlife. Snow-covered in winter but lush and green by late spring, the reserve is largely dominated by conifer forests, which support populations of musk deer, brown and black bears, leopards, red foxes and hangul.

HISTORY

The history of Kashmir, and in particular its history since 1947, is a highly sensitive subject about which many different and often mutually incompatible views are held. No account, however bland, is going to satisfy everyone, and so our approach in this section is to present our own, personal understanding of, and opinion on, the region's past. It is reflective of our own experiences, readings and conversations and is not aligned with any particular school of thought.

The history of Ladakh and Zanskar is, at least until the 19th century, quite separate from that of Kashmir, and so we have dealt with it separately in the box on page 12.

EARLY HISTORY Origin myths are one of the earliest forms of oral history; they are the stories passed down from one generation to the next about who people are and where they come from. Though they do not always tally with geological and archaeological records, they give us insight into the beliefs of early peoples.

In **Hindu legend**, Kashmir was once a lake (which does in fact agree with the geological record) that was drained when the *rishi* (sage) Kashyapa, a son of the god Brahma, cut the hills at Baramulla in two, allowing the water to flow out (this part has a little less historical evidence backing it up!).

There has been human habitation in the Kashmir Valley since at least 3000BC, and archaeologists have found the remains of mud houses and stone tools dating from this earliest period in the Neolithic site at Burzahom, a little to the north of the Shalimar Gardens in Srinagar. These early people would principally have been hunter-gatherers, though there is some suggestion they may also have grown wheat and lentils. They produced primitive pottery and also expressed themselves artistically: in the 1960s archaeologists working here uncovered a stone slab depicting a hunting scene.

It is not until the Classical period that we have written sources to supplement the archaeological record: we start to get a clearer picture of the area from the 4th century BC onwards, when the Greeks and other chroniclers make mention of Kashmir's rulers and their battles. The kings of Kashmir and Paurava (now in Pakistan) fought together against Alexander the Great (or Alexander the Accursed as he's known across vast swathes of western Asia) at the **Battle of Hydaspes** (the Hydaspes River is now known as the Jhelum and flows through the Punjab) in 326BC, and when they were defeated, the Kashmiris sent Alexander tribute. The Paurava king Porus became a Macedonian *satrap* (provincial governor).

Shortly after this, Kashmir became incorporated into the mighty **Mauryan Empire** (322–185BC), an empire which grew up in the vacuum left by the retreat of

1

Petroglyph rock carvings show that Ladakh has been inhabited since **Neolithic** times. The area's population has always been sparse, however, and the majority of inhabitants were either nomadic or passing through en route to elsewhere, so little else from this early period remains.

Like with Kashmir, our earliest historic records about Ladakh come from the pens of outsiders: the Mons and Dards, the two principal tribes of Ladakh at the time, are referenced in the writings of Herodotus, Megasthenes and Ptolemy, among others.

In the 1st century AD Ladakh was part of the **Kushan Empire**, which spread from Bactria (around the Oxus River in central Asia) south to what is now Karachi on the Arabian Sea, across northern India and as far north as Turfan in Xinjiang, China. It was during this period that Buddhism arrived here from elsewhere in India, though the local people were mostly still followers of Bon (see box, page 96).

China and Tibet were both expanding their influences in the 8th century, and consequently Ladakh was a hotly contested territory. When the Tibetan Empire broke up in AD842, a court official called Nyima-Gon was able to take control of Ladakh and establish for himself the first **Ladakhi dynasty**. The local population was by now predominantly Tibetan, and the dynasty spread Buddhism widely.

As the Islamic conquests sped through south Asia in the 1300s, Ladakh aligned itself closely with Tibet, helping it preserve its Buddhist identity. Some Ladakhis did convert to Noorbakshi Islam, but they were in the minority.

Ladakh's most famous royal lineage, the **Namgyal dynasty**, emerged in the late 15th century. Lhachen Bhagal Namgyal (the Namgyal suffix meaning 'victorious') of Basgo overthrew the King of Leh to unite Ladakh under his rule, and his successors built numerous fortifications to expel central Asian raiders and expand their territory into Zanskar, Spiti and, albeit briefly, Nepal. The dominance of the Mughals prevented expansion further west into Kashmir.

The Namgyals were doing well until they decided to side with Bhutan in a war against Tibet. When the Tibetans then invaded Ladakh, the Namgyals were forced to ask the Mughals for assistance in repelling the invaders. Help was granted, but the 1684 **Treaty of Tingmosgang** severely restricted Ladakh's independence and required the king to convert to Islam, as well as to build Leh's first mosque.

In 1834, the Dogra general Zorawar Singh annexed Ladakh on behalf of Gulab Singh and, despite a rebellion in 1842, Ladakh was incorporated into the **Princely State of Jammu and Kashmir**. The Namgyal family were awarded the *jagir* (a feudal land grant) of Stok, but were otherwise stripped of their power.

Alexander's forces. It is during this period that Buddhism spread from its homeland in what is now the north Indian state of Bihar to Kashmir, first introduced under the auspices of the Emperor Asoka (304–232BC), a man still greatly respected for his military prowess, skill as an administrator and Buddhist teachings. The Asokan column, with its finial of three realistically carved lions, is the national emblem of India and appears on all of the bank notes. Kashmir remained a centre of learning for both Hindus and Buddhists until the early 6th century AD.

The quiet and cultured civilisation that had emerged in Kashmir came to an abrupt end with the **Hephthalite invasion** in the late 5th century AD. Known also as the White Huns, the Hephthalites were central Asian warriors who led an aggressive campaign across the Sogdian Empire, western China and then northern India. When the Hephthalite Emperor Mihirakula (rAD515–30) was eventually driven back from Malwa (in what is now the central Indian state of Madhya Pradesh), he fled to Kashmir, where he was at first welcomed by the local king but then led an armed revolt, overthrowing his host and generally leaving destruction in his wake. Buddhist shrines were particularly vulnerable to his wrath, and he caused untold damage to religious structures both in Kashmir and, further west, in Gandhara.

Kashmir did recover, fortunately, and in the following centuries the region became known once again for its religious scholars, philosophers, artists and poets. The 8th-century Karkota emperor Lalitāditya Muktapīda (rAD724–60) oversaw a Kashmir-centred empire that stretched from Iran in the west to Tibet in the east and reached well up into Turkestan. He was able to defeat incursions from the Turks, Tibetans and Dards, and even to resist the Arabs. He was a noted patron of the arts, and actively encouraged trade. The Karkotas' regional dominance was not to last, however: by the 10th century the kingdom was increasingly unstable politically and hence vulnerable to attack.

MUSLIM RULE The invaders came from the west and took their name, the Shah Miri (King of Commanders), from their leader, Shams-ud-Din Shah Mir (r1339–42). Also known as the **Sayyid dynasty**, these possibly Afghan kings claimed descent from the Prophet Muhammad, and their invasion was motivated by religious zeal as much as by the possibility of territorial acquisition. They would rule Kashmir from 1339 until 1561.

The Shah Miri dynasty brought with them relative stability, and political, trade and cultural connections that spread across central Asia and Persia. They also oversaw the conversion of many of Kashmir's Hindus, though more through the work of missionaries than by the sword. There were a number of revered Islamic preachers in Kashmir during this period, most notably Sheikh Nooruddin Noorani, who combined Shaivism with Sufi mysticism in his discourse, making his teachings accessible to local people through their familiarity. The rulers were generally tolerant of non-Muslims (with the exception of Sultan Sikander, an iconoclast who encouraged forced conversions) and the transition to Islam in the valley was evolutionary rather than revolutionary.

It could rightly be argued that this medieval period was a golden age for Kashmir: it was a wealthy, cosmopolitan place, and people travelled vast distances to appreciate its beauty. Persian replaced Sanskrit as the court language, introducing a rich new literary canon; artisans were invited from across central Asia and Persia to come to the court and practise their crafts, including papier mâché, wood carving and weaving; and many of the architectural masterpieces we admire today, such as the Jamia Masjid and Makdoom Sahib shrine in Srinagar, date from this period too.

Having such a jewel on his northern borders inevitably captured the attention of the **Mughal emperor Humayun** (1508–56), who sent his general, Mirza Muhammad Haidar Dughlat, to seize the kingdom in 1540. The Mughals were central Asians, claiming descent from the infamous Timur (known in the west as Tamerlane), and had come to India under Humayun's father, Babur (1483–1530). Babur considered the country uncivilised and a mere shadow of what he had left

1

behind, and as Humayun had also spent significant periods in exile at the Safavid Court in Iran, it is likely that he too would have felt a certain nostalgia for high Persian culture. In many ways closer in its natural and cultural environments to the Timurid world than to other parts of India, Kashmir would have felt wonderfully familiar. Possessing it was the next best thing to going home.

Though Humayun never came to Kashmir in person, his son, **Akbar the Great** (1542–1605), arrived in 1589, and it was only then that Kashmir came under direct Mughal rule. Akbar was responsible for the construction of the heavily fortified wall that surrounds the Hari Parbat Fort in Srinagar, and it is for this reason that it is often referred to as a Mughal fort, even though the actual fort dates from much later. Akbar and his descendants also built the stunning series of Persian-style gardens, the so-called Mughal Gardens, taming the natural landscape and re-shaping it in the style of gardens in Kabul, Lahore, Samarkand and beyond. The gardens they created must have been close to perfect as Akbar's grandson, the emperor Jahangir (1592–1666), saw Kashmir and proclaimed, 'If there is a heaven on earth, it is here, it is here, it is here.' Emperor Jahangir certainly knew a few things about beauty: he himself was responsible for the building of the Taj Mahal.

The Mughals were strong administrators as well as able military commanders, and Akbar in particular was renowned for his religious tolerance, inviting the leaders of all faiths to debate with him in the Ibadat Khana (Debating Hall) at his palace at Fatehpur Sikri (close to modern-day Agra in the Indian state of Uttar Pradesh). Major restriction on religious freedom, including iconoclasm and an excessively heavy tax burden for non-Muslims, did not return until the last of the Great Mughals, Emperor Aurangzeb (1618–1707), murdered his brothers and seized the throne with support from the Islamic orthodoxy in 1658.

Though the influence of the Mughals declined in Kashmir after Aurangzeb's death, Islam was here to stay. The Mo-i-Muqqadas (the hair of the Prophet) was brought to Srinagar in 1700 and housed at the Hazratbal Shrine (page 195), making Srinagar a major place of pilgrimage for Muslims from across the Indian subcontinent.

When the Persian Nadir Shah invaded India in 1738–39, he fractured what was left of the Mughal Empire, and Kashmir once again was seized by Afghans. Ahmad Shah Durrani (1722–72), founder of the Durrani Empire and often regarded as the father of modern Afghanistan, took control of Kashmir in the mid-1700s, adding it to an empire that already stretched north to the Bukharan Khanate (now in Uzbekistan) and south to the Arabian Sea. Ahmad Shah's son, Timur Shah Durrani (1748–93), was not a statesman of the same calibre as his father, however, and so by the end of the 18th century the Durrani Empire was already starting to disintegrate.

SIKHS AND DOGRAS Maharaja Ranjit Singh (1780–1839), founder of the Sikh Empire, wrested control of Kashmir from the Afghan Durranis in 1819. His army was generally less destructive than those that had come before him, and the Sikhs were relatively tolerant of other faiths, though their blanket ban on cow slaughter did not go down well with Kashmir's meat-loving Muslims. A state-wide famine in 1832 shook Kashmir severely, but the Sikh rulers cut taxes and made loans available to enable a swift recovery. Jammu, though still with its own ruler, was a vassal state to the Sikh Empire, and Ladakh and Baltistan (now in modern-day Pakistan) were annexed by General Zorawar Singh in the 1830s and early 1840s.

The **First Anglo-Sikh War** broke out in 1845: the British were terrified that the Sikh Empire, which by this time was seen as both corrupt and unstable, was still a military threat to British territory. Diplomatic relations between the Sikh court and the East India Company (the principal British entity in India prior to the start of direct rule in 1857) broke down. An East India Company force (comprised of Bengali and British units) began marching on Ferozepore, and Sikh forces crossed the Sutlej River to meet them. The British interpreted this move as an act of war.

The war was to last just three months but included the **Battle of Mudki** and the **Battle of Aliwal** (both in the Punjab), as well as smaller encounters. The Sikhs were finally defeated after British artillery fire destroyed bridges behind their lines, preventing troops from retreating. Refusing to surrender, they were slaughtered.

The **Treaty of Lahore**, the peace treaty, was signed in March 1846. It required the Sikhs to surrender the Jullunder Doab (the land between the Beas and Sutlej rivers) and pay an indemnity of Rs15m. When the Sikhs were unable to raise this sum, they forfeited Kashmir and the Hazara region on the borders of what are now Pakistan and Afghanistan.

The British promptly sold Kashmir to the Raja of Jammu, Gulab Singh (1792–1857), for Rs7.5m, and the **Princely State of Jammu and Kashmir** was born. Thanks to Zorawar Singh, it already included Ladakh and Baltistan, as well as Jammu and the Kashmir Valley.

Gulab Singh's son and successor, Ranbir Singh (1830–85), had remained loyal to the British in the 1857 Indian Mutiny (also known as the Rebellion or the First War of Independence) and so was able to maintain a good relationship with the British government, which was by now the dominant political and military power in India. He added to the Princely State's territory the fort at Gilgit, and his son, Pratap Singh (1848–1925), incorporated the kingdoms of Chitral, Hunza and Nagar, all of which now lie on the Pakistani side of the Line of Control (LoC).

POST-INDEPENDENCE British India gained independence on 15 August 1947 and was divided into two new countries: India and Pakistan. The Maharaja of Kashmir, Hari Singh (1895–1961), like other princely rulers, was given the option of acceding to either country or, at least in theory, heading an independent kingdom. The expectation was that those states with Muslim-majority populations would join Pakistan, and those with a Hindu majority would accede to India.

Kashmir had a Muslim-majority population but was ruled by a Hindu king. The local working party took the decision to support accession to India, but Maharaja Hari Singh preferred for Kashmir to remain independent and so offered a **standstill agreement** to both countries to retain the status quo. Pakistan accepted the suggestion, but India declined it.

Following an **uprising** in Poonch and Mirpur, backed by Pashtun tribesmen who then started advancing on Srinagar, Hari Singh called for support from the Indian army. The Indian government agreed to support him, but only if he acceded to India. Hari Singh agreed, signed the **Instrument of Accession** on 26 October 1947, and volunteers from the Jammu and Kashmir National Conference supported the Indian army to drive back the incursion.

Pakistan believed Hari Singh had no right to call in the Indian army, but despite receiving orders to send troops to the front, General Sir Douglas Gracey, commander-in-chief of the Pakistani army, initially refused to do so. By the time Pakistani troops were finally dispatched, Indian forces had occupied the eastern two thirds of Kashmir, though Gilgit and Baltistan were secured for Pakistan by the Gilgit Scouts. This was the start of the **First Kashmir War**, in which both sides grabbed territory in Kashmir, and the conflict only ended with a UN-negotiated ceasefire in 1948 that required Pakistan to withdraw its forces but allowed it to retain around 40% of the territory, with India occupying the remaining 60%.

The UN resolution also required a plebiscite to be held to determine the future of Kashmir (as of 2019, the referendum has still not taken place).

It is from this point on that we can discuss J&K as a state of the Republic of India, and Pakistan was by no means the only regional power pressing at its borders. Indian and Chinese troops clashed in the 1962 Sino-Indian War, leading to the swift annexation by the Chinese of Aksai Chin, and the demarcation of the Line of Actual Control (not to be confused with the Line of Control, page 181) between Pakistan, India and the Trans-Karakoram tract, now also claimed by China.

Two further conflicts broke out between India and Pakistan in 1965 and 1971. The first of these, the **Second Kashmir War**, erupted after the discovery of Operation Gibraltar, in which Pakistani insurgents were infiltrating J&K to destabilise the state from within. Some 30,000 Pakistani troops crossed the LoC on 5 August 1965, and the war began in earnest. Pakistan's principal attack, code-named Operation Grand Slam, aimed to capture Akhnoor in Jammu, breaking India's supply lines, and for the next five months both sides tore into each other with air strikes, tank battles and, albeit on a far smaller scale, naval hostilities. Independent sources estimate 6,800 soldiers died (3,000 of them Indian), and both the US and the USSR brought diplomatic pressure to bear to end the conflict and negotiate a ceasefire.

The 1971 **Indo-Pakistan War** began when Pakistan launched pre-emptive strikes on 11 Indian air bases during Operation Chengiz Khan, prompting India to join forces with nationalists in East Pakistan (today Bangladesh) fighting for their independence. Although the focus of the conflict was principally East Pakistan, Kashmir was drawn into the conflict too. The war ended with Pakistan's defeat and the creation of the new sovereign state of Bangladesh. The **Simla Agreement** was signed by both India and Pakistan in July 1972. It committed both sides to settling future disputes, including those in Kashmir, by bilateral negotiations and effectively solidified the LoC that divided the Indian- and Pakistani-administered areas of Kashmir into a de facto border.

MILITANCY PERIOD State Assembly elections took place in J&K in 1987. There were widespread allegations of election fraud, and this gave impetus to a pro-independence insurgency spearheaded by the militant Jammu and Kashmir Liberation Front (JKLF). The JKLF stated that theirs was a nationalist, not Islamist, cause, but the Indian government believed the unrest was being fomented by Pakistan. The Indian army killed 100 demonstrators at Gawakadal Bridge in 1990, after which the insurgency escalated.

Several additional militant factions emerged, including the **Hizbul Mujahideen**, which allied itself closely with Pakistan and projected the conflict as a holy war. Mujahideen fighters who had been battling the Soviets in Afghanistan turned their attentions to Kashmir, and their existing training camps produced a new generation of militants, this time to fight the Indian army. Both sides deployed hundreds of thousands of troops, mostly in the Kashmir Valley, and the civilian population bore the brunt of the pain: ethnic cleansing caused Hindu pandits to flee; those who remained (both Hindu and Muslim) suffered mass killings, disappearances, arbitrary imprisonment, torture and rape. Both the Indian army and the militants were responsible for these crimes.

Militants crossed into the Kargil district in 1999. India believed the Pakistani government was behind this incursion, and this sparked the Kargil War (see box, page 156). There was serious concern that the conflict would escalate into nuclear war, as the previous year Pakistan had carried out successful atomic tests, and India had been testing its nuclear weapons since 1974. Both countries were therefore nuclear powers. The war lasted three months and included heavy shelling and air strikes. A memorial stands near Kargil to those Indians who died in the war.

The early 2000s were marked by a number of terror attacks in J&K, including an assault on the state legislature in Srinagar in 2001 that killed 38 people, and the killing of a further 30 people, mostly the families of Indian servicemen, in an attack in May 2002. The latter caused tensions to escalate, with Pakistan implying it might use nuclear weapons to counteract any Indian attack. The situation was defused, in part, by the intervention of US diplomats.

In general, security improved in J&K in the late 2000s, though there were still several incidents of concern: major protests took place in 2010 after a demonstrator was killed by the Indian army, and the following year the Indian State Human Rights Commission (ISHRC) confirmed the discovery of 2,000 bodies in an unmarked grave near to the LoC. Many of the victims are thought to have been Kashmiris who disappeared after being arrested by security forces. In a rare positive step, in 2013 the prime ministers of both India and Pakistan agreed to try to reduce the number of violent incidents along the LoC, and for a short time things looked hopeful for an easing of tensions. However, within a year that glimmer of hope had been erased as India accused Pakistan of interfering in its internal affairs and a flare-up in violence along the border (which left 18 dead) led to strongly worded warnings being exchanged between the governments of Indian and Pakistan.

J&K TODAY In 2015 India's right-wing Bharatiya Janata Party (BJP) was sworn into power in J&K in a power-sharing deal with the People's Democratic Party (PDP). Almost immediately, tensions increased as the BJP enforced a colonial-era ban on eating beef. In July 2016 huge demonstrations took place after the popular young militant leader, Burhan Wani, was killed by Indian security forces. A curfew was imposed in most parts of Kashmir, but, despite this, at least 70 people were killed and 9,000 injured in some 50 days of violence. In September 2016 India announced that it had carried out 'surgical strikes' against suspected militants along the India–Pakistan border.

In July 2017 demonstrators and security forces engaged in violent clashes on the anniversary of the killing of Burhan Wani. Later that month militants killed at least seven Hindu pilgrims in the worst of such attacks in 17 years. Throughout the rest of 2017 and 2018 the security situation continued to deteriorate, and 2018 claimed the dubious title of 'most deadly year' in the entire Kashmir conflict.

Events continued to develop in 2019. On 14 February, a convey of vehicles carrying Indian security forces was attacked by a suicide bomber in the Pulwama district of Kashmir. At least 40 people were killed and the attack was claimed by the Jaish-e Mohammed militant group. India immediately blamed Pakistan for the attack – despite the fact that the Pakistani government strongly denied the allegations – and went on to revoke Pakistan's 'most favoured trading nation' status, meaning that all Pakistani goods coming into India had customs duty raised by 200%. In the days after the attack, Kashmiris living in other parts of India (especially Kashmiri students) reported cases of violence and harassment and some were reportedly evicted from their homes. On the other side of the coin, many non-Kashmiri Indians offered lodging and food to those who had been evicted.

On 26 February, Indian air force jets bombed the Balakot area of Pakistani Kashmir. The Indian government claimed that they struck a Jaish-e Mohammed training camp and that large numbers of militants were killed, but Pakistani authorities say that no such camp ever existed and that the Indian jets missed their intended targets. The following day a dog fight occurred between Indian and Pakistani fighter planes over the Line of Control and in the process an Indian jet was shot down and the pilot captured. Much of the Indian media (and some politicians) went into a frenzy calling for retaliation and war, and for a time the two nuclear-armed nations appeared to be on the brink of conflict. However, Pakistani President Imran Khan played an expert diplomatic role and, calling for calm, released the captured pilot as a good-will gesture and arrested a number of suspected militants. The move was enough to calm tensions in the region and the threat of all-out war was averted.

The 2019 skirmish aside, one of the big problems the Indian authorities face in Kashmir is that as Indian politics turn ever more Hindu right-wing and countrywide anti-Muslim sentiment increases, so the players in the conflict in Kashmir change. Increasingly, it's not Pakistani militants fighting against Indian security forces but home-grown Indian militants fighting the Indian security forces. To make matters worse, the Indian government's heavy-handed response to protests has turned huge swathes of Kashmir's population against India.

For the moment there's no end in sight to the troubles Kashmir faces, and anyone travelling here should keep abreast of the latest developments and avoid public demonstrations.

GOVERNMENT AND POLITICS

Until August 2019, J&K had special status within India: **Article 370** of the Indian Constitution granted the state special autonomy. However, in the week that this book went to print, the Indian government unexpectedly revoked this and decided that Kashmir and Jammu were to become Union Territories (administrative units controlled and governed by the union government). Ladakh was made a totally separate Union Territory and will no longer be politically connected to Kashmir. What this will mean for the government and legislation of the state remains to be seen, as India's Supreme Court has agreed to hear petitions against the federal government's decision.

As of 2019, though, J&K has a multi-party, democratic system of governance. Representatives are elected to the **J&K Legislative Assembly** on six-year terms, one year longer than in other state assemblies in India. The last assembly elections took place over five phases in November–December 2014, after which a coalition government was formed by members of the PDP (People's Democratic Party), which operates on the ideology of self-rule for J&K, and the right-wing BJP (Bharatiya Janata Party), whose ideology reflects Hindu nationalist positions. Despite calls for a boycott from hard-line separatist groups, the turnout was an impressive 65.23%, the highest it had been in 25 years. **Mufti Mohammad Sayeed**, leader of the PDP, was chosen as Chief Minister, but after his death on 7 January 2016 was succeeded by his daughter, Mehbooba Mufti. However, her tenure only lasted from April 2016 until June 2018, when she resigned after the BJP withdrew its support of the coalition. At the time of writing, the position of Chief Minister remains vacant, and the state is under the national president's rule. The president, whose position is largely ceremonial with the prime minister (Narendra Damodardas Modi) holding the real power, is Ram Nath Kovind.

In 2019, a country-wide general election was held over seven phases between April and May. With over 900 million people eligible to vote and a turnout of 67%, it was the largest general election ever held anywhere in the world. The elections were won by a clear margin by the BJP and Narendra Modi was returned to power.

HUMAN RIGHTS Since the start of the militancy in 1989, numerous well-founded allegations of severe human rights abuses have been made by various international organisations, including Amnesty, Human Rights Watch and the US State Department, against both the Indian security forces and militant groups. Recorded abuse includes ethnic cleansing, disappearances, extra-judicial killings by security forces, and the massacre and rape of large numbers of civilians. Atrocities have been committed both by militants belonging to the Jammu Kashmir Liberation Front (JKLF) and by the Indian armed forces and police.

Amnesty International, Human Rights Watch and the UN have all raised serious objections to the Indian government in the past, and it is generally considered that troops and police continue to commit such crimes with the tacit acceptance of their superiors. They are able to do so thanks to the 1958 **Armed Forces (Special Powers) Act** (AFSPA), which permits, among other things, firing on civilians for the maintenance of public order, arresting without warrant those who are suspected of an offence, and legal immunity for army officers.

ECONOMY

Since the end of the militancy in the early to mid-2000s, J&K's economy has been expanding rapidly: the state's GDP is US$25 billion (2018–19 estimate) and the economy has grown by at least 10% year on year for the past five years. Poverty levels have been falling steadily since the early 1990s (the poverty rate currently stands at around 10.35%, as opposed to 21.9% in India as a whole), with the vast majority of those falling below the poverty line living in rural areas.

Tourism was the staple of J&K's economy for much of the 20th century, and in the last few years the partial recovery of the tourism industry has been a major contributor to the growth in GDP. Some 14.32 million tourists came to the state in 2017, but almost all of them (14.24 million) were domestic visitors, with only 79,770 being foreign tourists. The majority of tourists, whether domestic or foreign, went only to Ladakh and Zanskar. Visitor numbers to the Kashmir Valley had been steadily rising, but the troubles of 2017 and 2018 have seriously curtailed these numbers. Hindu pilgrims visiting the Vaishno Devi shrine alone contribute more than US$75 million to the local economy each year.

The other significant economic sector is **agriculture**. Kashmir is known for its high-grade timber, especially cedar and willow (used in cricket bats), its fruits, grain, nuts and, of course, its saffron. Sericulture, handicrafts production and the manufacturing of consumer goods are also important.

The main economic activity in Ladakh is small-scale farming (barley, wheat, peas, buckwheat and animal husbandry), which employs around 90% of the population. Tourism is becoming increasingly important to the local economy, though, and in big tourist centres such as Leh it is by far the biggest income generator.

Improvements to **infrastructure**, in particular the transport infrastructure, are key for enabling economic development in the state. As it stands, moving goods and passengers by road is expensive and time-consuming, and many areas are completely inaccessible in the winter months. The completion of the Kashmir Railway project, which will ultimately connect Srinagar to the rest of the Indian Railways network, will be hugely beneficial, as will an increased number of road tunnels.

The state may also look at harnessing its **natural resources**, specifically its rivers, to generate power that could both be used locally and exported to other parts of India. There are currently at least 11 such dams and hydro-power projects either already functioning or under construction throughout Indian J&K and more are likely to follow.

According to 2011 census data, the population of J&K state is around 12.5 million, just over 1% of India's total. The population density is 56 people per square kilometre, which is about one sixth of the national average, and there are 889 women for every 1,000 men, a nationwide problem that results from a preference for, and preferential treatment of, male children. The population of J&K has increased by just over 23% in the past decade, which can be attributed to the returning home of refugees as well as a greater life expectancy for residents.

Given its location, Kashmir's history is one of human migration, in some cases from places as far away as Iran, Iraq and the Caucasus. Some people just passed through; others chose to stay. Many of them left their genetic mark. The largest ethnic groups you are likely to encounter are mentioned here, though their genetic identities are by no means separate due to centuries of inter-marriage with other communities.

DARDS The Dards have been known in the West since at least the time of Ptolemy, who refers to the community as the *daradrai* in his 2nd-century treatise the *Almagest*. Most Dards live in Dardistan in the northern part of the Kashmir Valley, as well as in Gilgit and Chitral in Pakistan-administered Kashmir, but a smaller number also live in parts of Ladakh, and they are thought to be descended from Aryan-speaking tribes. They were historically followers of Buddhism and animism, and this is still evident in the practices of Dards in Dha-Hanu (known as the Brokpa), though now many Dards are Muslim.

The Dards are one of India's Scheduled Tribes (officially designated groups of historically disadvantaged people in India) and therefore benefit from positive discrimination when applying for higher education and government jobs.

DOGRAS The Dogras are mostly Hindus who inhabit Jammu region and also parts of Punjab. A dynasty of Dogra kings ruled Kashmir in 1846–47, and they continue to hold prominent positions in politics, business and as military officers. The British categorised the Dogras as a martial race, and hence they are still well represented and respected in the armed forces.

Social anthropologists are unsure as to the origins of the Dogra people: the *Imperial Gazetteer of India* suggests, however, that the word is a corruption of *dwigart desh* and refers to the land between the two lakes of Mansar and Surinsar, the Dogra's traditional territory. Clan identity remains strong, and many families take Dogra as a surname.

GUJJARS The nomads that you see driving their flocks of sheep, goats and cattle in the southwestern parts of J&K are the Gujjars. Again, their origins are unclear: there is some evidence that they came from the Caucasus and Iran, though many Gujjars believe that their forefathers migrated here from Gujarat and Rajasthan. In any case, it seems they have been present in Kashmir since the 5th or 6th centuries AD.

The community is loosely divided into two: those who practise settled agriculture, and those who are transhumant. In traditional mud-brick houses, families share their living quarters with the cattle, which keeps them warm in winter. Their language has no written form, and so stories and information are instead passed down through song.

HANJIS The Hanjis are the boatmen you see on the lakes around Srinagar. Some Hanjis claim descent from the Prophet Noah (and hence, one would hazard, a strong desire to keep their feet dry); others believe them to have come originally from Sri Lanka. Though most of the Hanji population are Muslim, prior to this they were probably *kshatriya* Hindus.

Most Hanjis make their living from trades connected to the lakes: they are the vegetable growers and sellers, the fishermen and the men who punt the *shikaras* (a type of wooden boat unique to Srinagar). Incomes and literacy rates are low by local standards, and the return of tourism will be of great benefit to the community.

KASHMIRIS Kashmiris are widespread in the state but concentrated in the Kashmir Valley. The community, which is thought to include ancient immigrants from Afghanistan, central Asia, Iran and Turkey, is predominantly Muslim, having converted to the faith from the 14th century onwards. A sizeable population of Kashmiri Hindus does, however, survive.

The majority of Kashmiris belong to familial clans, and the clan name denotes their place of origin and business: the Wain or Wani are thought to have come from the Persian Gulf and are traditionally traders; the Lone are an agricultural clan whose members are concentrated in the north of the Kashmir Valley; and the Maliks are descendants of Hindu Rajput clans that have long since converted to Islam.

The modern Kashmiris are a settled population: those in the villages depend on agriculture (in particular orchards and saffron fields) for their living, while the urban population makes its money from handicraft production and business activities. Kashmiri families are active players in the tourism industry, often running hotels, restaurants and shops. For information on the Kashmiri language, see below.

LADAKHIS The Ladakhis are not actually a single ethnic group: it's a catch-all term used to describe the various ethnic groups (including Tibetans, Monpas and some Dards) that inhabit the Leh and Zanskar districts. Many of them are descended from Mongoloid tribes from the Tibetan Plateau (including more recent Tibetan refugees who fled Tibet around the same time as the Dalai Lama) and they are predominantly followers of Buddhism.

The total population of Ladakh is tiny: just over 250,000 people. Many of the inhabitants live in remote villages, growing the few crops that can survive at such high altitude and herding sheep and goats. Although Ladakhis do work in the tourism industry, particularly as trekking guides, many of the people you see around Leh in the summer are in fact migrant labourers who have come for the tourist season.

LANGUAGE

The official language of J&K is **Urdu**, an Indo-Iranian language that is mutually intelligible with Hindi but is written from right to left in the Perso-Arabic script (Hindi is written from left to right and in the Devanagari script, showing its Sanskritic roots). Urdu is closely related to Persian, and indeed many of the canonical works of literature are shared. It also includes many loanwords from Arabic.

There are over five million speakers of **Kashmiri** in India, and most of them live in the Kashmir Valley. Another Indo-Aryan language, but in this case in the Dardic sub-group, it is a compulsory subject in local schools for primary age children. It has been written at different times in the Sharada, Devanagari and Perso-Arabic scripts, but still it preserves many grammatical features that are present in Sanskrit but have been lost in Hindi and Urdu.

Ladakhi is a Tibetic language, though not mutually intelligible with Standard Tibetan. It can be further broken down into five regional dialects: Lehskat, which is spoken in the Leh region; Shamskat, spoken to the northwest of Leh; Stotskat, spoken in the Indus Valley; Nubra, which is spoken in the Nubra Valley; and Purigi/Balti, which is spoken in Kargil district. Those dialects spoken in northern Ladakh and in Zanskar are similar to those from central Tibet. Ladakhi is written using the *uchen*, or Tibetan, script, and pronunciation is similar to that of Classical Tibetan.

BUDDHISM IN LADAKH AND ZANSKAR

With thanks to Tanzin Norbu (**w** *mountaintribalvision.com)*

The early religion of Ladakh and Zanskar was the animistic **Bon** (see box, page 96), worshipping spirits and mountains. Even these days at New Year, people give recognition to these spirits as Protector deities and in the Dard regions people still celebrate Bono-Na festival every two in three years.

It is believed that Buddhism was introduced to Ladakh before it arrived in Tibet, during the **Third Buddhist Council** in Kashmir (272–232bc), when Emperor Asoka sent a Buddhist missionary to Ladakh. Evidence for this includes an early Kushan-period stone cave in Sani, Zanskar, which dates from somewhere between 100bc and ad500. Contemporary rock carving can be seen at Khalatse and Mulbekh, and also in the giant Buddha at Kartse Khar.

Conversely, early Mahayana stone carvings may in fact have travelled here from Tibet: statues of Buddhas and bodhisattvas from these periods can be seen in the Zanskari villages of Karsha, Padum, Tong-de and Mune.

During this period, however, though the Tibetan emperors were at the height of their reign, Tibet still had a somewhat limited knowledge of Buddhism. Around ad600–800, **Tibetan Buddhism** started to travel from India towards Zhang-Zhung in western Tibet. Around ad842, after the assassination of the Lang-dharma, the last emperor of Tibet, his descendants moved further west to establish a new kingdom which included the provinces of Rudok, Purang and Guge.

As Buddhism started to find its niche, one of the kings of Guge, Ye-shey-Od, became a monk. In order to improve the quality of Buddhism and to propagate the new religion, he invited Atiśa, a scholar and a professor of Nalanda University, to be his teacher. He also sent a group of young students to study Buddhism in India so they could return as learned men and help to spread Buddhism in Tibet. Only two students returned, one of whom was **Rinchen Zangpo**, a great translator and artist. He established the monastery at Alchi and, later, Sumda and Mangyu monasteries, which were built with the help of Kashmiri artists. These are some of the oldest monasteries in Ladakh.

Although Buddhism may have taken root in Ladakh and Zanskar earlier, Tibet was the country that introduced the Mahayana form of Buddhism here. Travelling Buddhist hermits, scholars and teachers influenced and gave shape to Ladakhi and Zanskari Buddhism. Padmasambhava, known as **'the Second Buddha'**, visited Baltistan, Kargil, Phokar-Zong and Sani, meditating in caves along the way. In Sakti village, the Urgyan rock bears imprints of his body, and the Thagthog Gompa was

In Ladakh, the principal language of instruction in government schools is Urdu, followed by English. Ladakhi and Tibetan are only taught as additional subjects, though they are understandably given greater priority in monastery schools.

For helpful phrases and a guide to pronunciation, see page 225.

RELIGION

Though J&K is home to followers of all manner of faiths, including Zoroastrianism, Sikhism and Christianity, the majority of people follow Islam, Hinduism or Buddhism (listed in order of number of adherents).

built in a cave where he meditated. This monastery still follows the Nying-ma-pa school of Buddhist thought, founded by Padmasambhava and Santaraksita, and it is the only one to do so in Ladakh.

Around AD935–1045, the great yogi and pandit **Naropa** meditated in Dzongkhul cave in Zanskar (the site of the Dzongkhul Gompa). His teachings were based on oral traditions, and he passed on his wisdom to disciple Lama Marpa, who in turn passed it on to Milarepa. This lineage later became known as the Kagyu (or Kagyupa) tradition. Similarly, Stongdey Gompa was founded by Lama Marpa (it is also known as the Marpa Ling).

Roughly at the time of Rinchen Zangpo, a famous Zanskari translator called **Phagspa Sherab** (also known as Zanskar Lotsawa) translated parts of the 200-volume *Bstan-gyur*. It is said that he founded Karsha and Phugthal gompas in Zanskar, monasteries that now follow the Gelugpa school (page 105).

After Rinchen Zangpo, the school of Bka-dam-pa founded by Atiśa and Bromton flourished in Ladakh. In the 13th century, however, Je Tsongkhapa founded the somewhat more austere and scholarly **Gelugpa** (Yellow Hat) school of Tibetan Buddhism. It is said that one of Tsongkhapa's main disciples, Sharap Zangpo, founded the monastery of Diskit in the Nubra Valley and Stagmo Lhakhang in Stagmo, travelling to Zanskar to set up the Gelugpa lineage at Karsha and Phugthal gompas. He died in Phugthal, where a stupa containing his relics remains, and is known as Sharap Zangpo's Stupa. Later, his nephew Paldan Shera founded the monastery of Thiksey.

King Sengge Namgyal, the Lion King, ruled Ladakh between 1590 and 1620, and during this period Ladakh enjoyed an excellent relationship with Bhutan. The Lion King sent his son there to become a disciple of Lama Stag-tsang-ras-pa, a renowned Tibetan monk known as the Tiger Lama. The lama became teacher to both father and son, and together they founded the gompas at Hemis, Chemde and Hanley.

While the mountains of Ladakh and Zanskar connect earth and sky quite literally, the ancient monasteries provide a spiritual bridge between worlds past and present. The culture and tradition of Ladakh and Zanskar promote the notion of interdependence and sustainability, two reasons why people have thrived for thousands of years in such a harsh environment. Ladakh, which is also known as Little Tibet because of its religious, cultural and architectural resemblance to Tibet, has prompted the Dalai Lama to state that Ladakh and Zanskar are two places beyond the borders of Tibet where the future of Tibetan Buddhism may thrive.

ISLAM J&K is a Muslim majority state: somewhere in the region of 68.31% of the total population is Muslim, although most of them reside in the Kashmir Valley. In Jammu and in Ladakh, they are in the minority.

Though Islam first came to Kashmir sometime in the 8th century AD, it was not widely adopted for the next 500 years. The end of Hindu rule in 1339 gave way to a succession of Muslim sultans, some of whom were tolerant of other faiths and others less so, and Kashmir's trading prowess meant that the valley was a melting pot of mostly Muslim traders from Afghanistan, central Asia and Iran, as well as from elsewhere in India.

The majority of Muslims in J&K are **Sunnis**, the branch of Islam who followed Muhammad's companion, Ali Bakr, and not his son-in-law Ali, following the Prophet's death. Sunnis make up the majority of the world's Muslim population. Many Kashmiri Muslims are **Sufis**, a mystical branch of Sunni Islam that teaches its followers that they can grow close to God in this life, as well as in the next. They believe that by purifying themselves (and in particular their spirit), they will be rewarded with an esoteric knowledge of God.

HINDUISM A little under 30% of J&K's population is Hindu. Kashmir traditionally had two main Hindu populations: those around Jammu; and the Kashmiri Pandits, Brahmins of the Kashmir Valley. Most Kashmiri Pandits fled during the militancy (page 16), either to refugee camps around Jammu, or elsewhere in India.

Jammu is known as the City of Temples, and here Hindus are in the majority at around 81.19% of the total population. The city's population swells during important festivals, however, with Hindus from other parts of India visiting Jammu's shrines and also passing through en route to the Amarnath and Vaishno Devi shrines.

Hinduism is a polytheistic religion, the amalgamation of numerous and diverse regional belief systems. The word Hindu was not historically used by followers but entered into European languages from the Arabic *al Hind* (the land beyond the Indus) and then into Indian languages also. The three principal strands of Hinduism are Shaivism (followers of the god Shiva), Vaishnavism (followers of the god Vishnu) and Shaktism (those who worship the goddess Shakti).

EDUCATION

State-wide, **literacy** in J&K stands at 68%, an increase of more than 10% in the past decade. Access to basic education is unequal, however, with a gender gap of slightly more than 20% (more men are literate then women), and children in urban areas are far more likely to be in school than their rural counterparts. Though this is in part due to cultural and economic reasons, corruption also plays a part: state schools in remoter areas are frequently underfunded and understaffed, with teacher truancy high. Many teachers have had no formal training. The militancy period seriously disrupted the education of many in the Kashmir Valley, with schools closed and many children sent away for their safety.

State education in J&K is provided by the Jammu and Kashmir State Board of School Education (JKBOSE). There are ten years of compulsory schooling in primary, middle and high schools, and a minority of students continue on to college or university education.

There are a number of well-regarded **universities** in the state, including the University of Jammu, the University of Kashmir and the Islamic University of Science and Technology.

The rich and diverse cultures of J&K are one of the principal reasons for coming here: whether you want to immerse yourself in meditation at a Buddhist monastery in Ladakh, watch carpet making and woodwork in Srinagar, or sing and dance on the set of a Bollywood movie on an alpine pasture, J&K has it all.

MUSIC Each of J&K's regions has its own distinctive style of music, which reflects their diverse cultures and historical influences: Jammu's music is closely related to other classical styles of northern India; the Kashmir Valley takes inspiration from Persia and central Asia; and Ladakh's music is similar to that of Tibet. Your best opportunities to hear traditional music are at weddings and during festivals.

Indian classical music is well represented in J&K and two of India's most famous *santoor* (a trapezoid hammered dulcimer) players hail from the state: Shivkumar Sharma of Jammu, who has recorded three platinum-selling albums, and Srinagar's multi-award-winning *Bhajan Sopori*. The *santoor* has its roots in Persia, but the version played in India today was developed in Kashmir. It is used along with harmonium, *saz* (a long-necked lute), *setar* (a four-stringed lute with moveable frets) and *tabla* (a goblet drum) to perform **Sufiana Kalam**, the music of Kashmir's Sufi mystics, which arrived here from Persia sometime in the 15th century.

There are many varieties of **folk music**, often based on songs that tell stories or are linked to specific events such as a wedding or the harvest. **Chakri** – played with the harmonium, *rubab* (a short-necked lute originating in Afghanistan) and *sarangi* (a short, stringed instrument played with a bow) – is used to accompany epic love songs and may also feature **rouf**, traditional dancing at a wedding.

Also fitting into the folk category is **ladishah**, humorous and sometimes rude songs performed by travelling musicians. The lyrics of each song are tailored to the village in which they are being sung.

Ladakhi music is, not surprisingly, influenced by that of Tibet, though it does have some unique characteristics. Here the music is frequently linked to religious events, drum beats and rhythmic chanting being an ancient way of reciting holy texts. This music often accompanies dances by masked and costumed figures. The dances symbolise the triumph of good over evil and are given as offerings to the monastery's protective deity. The main instruments you will see in the orchestra are the *nga* and *damaru* (two types of drum), *drilbu* (bells), *dungchen* (long horn), *dung* (conch shell) and *silnyen* (cymbals).

LITERATURE Kashmir has a rich literary canon, with fine works of poetry and prose in Sanskrit, Persian, Urdu, Hindi, English and Kashmiri.

Kashmir was a centre of Shaivism in the early medieval period, and so the earliest surviving works are on religious topics. **Vasugupta's** *Shiva Sutras* date from the 9th century AD; the 10th-century philosopher and mystic **Abhinavagupta** wrote more than 30 works, including *Tantrāloka* and *Abhinavabharati*; and his disciple, **Rajanaka Kṣemarāja**, compiled the Pratyabhijna *Hridayam*. These works were in Sanskrit, a more-or-less dead language comparable to Latin and Greek in which many canonical texts of Hinduism and Buddhism were written.

The use of the Kashmiri language in literature began in the middle of the 13th century with **Shitikantha**'s writing of the *Mahanayakaprakash* (Light of the Supreme Lord), a text that popularised the esoterics of Shaiva Tantra. The Kashmiri language was well suited to producing religious poetry, and so some of the finest literary works of this period are poems: the *Vakhs* of the poetess **Lal Ded** are particularly revered, as are those of the poet-saint **Sheikh Noor-ud-din Wali**.

The 16th to 19th centuries were particularly fruitful for Kashmir's writers and poets. The beautiful **Habba Khatoon**, 'the Nightingale of Kashmir', wrote melodious love songs that twist between joy and the sorrow of separation. Her songs remain popular today. Other prominent mystic poets, many of them female, include **Rupa Bhawani**, **Arnimal**, **Mahmud Gami** and **Rasool Mir**.

Since independence, J&K has also produced notable poets, writers and playwrights. The contemporary playwright **Moti Lal Kemmu**, recipient of the Padma Shri award (an Indian honour similar to the OBE), writes in both Kashmiri and Hindi; **Amin Kamil** is known for his poetry, short stories, novels and literary criticism; and **Ghulam Nabi Firaq** has published dozens of works, including his own poems in various styles, and translations of great English poems into Kashmiri.

FILM Bollywood loves Kashmir. Though there is not a major indigenous film industry, the romantic lakes of Srinagar and the spectacular surrounding hills, not to mention the ski resort at Gulmarg, are familiar to any devotees of Indian films. Two of Shammi Kapoor's classics, *Jaanwar* (*Animal*) and *Junglee* (*Wild*) were shot partly in Kashmir, as was one of our personal favourites, the artistically shot but terribly sad *Pakeezah* (*Pure*), in which the heroine floats one night on a houseboat on Dal Lake in Srinagar.

The troubles in Kashmir have also provided plenty of fodder for Bollywood's scriptwriters, sometimes with great success. If you're new to Bollywood and can't stand the thought of too many syrupy song and dance numbers (though you can't avoid them entirely), you might want to watch the 2006 tear-jerker *Fanaa* (*Destroyed in Love*, or *Annihilation*), the tale of a Kashmiri girl who falls in love with a terrorist, and in which both lovers must choose between their love for each other and what they believe to be right. Roles are reversed in *Dil Se* (*From the Heart*), and this time it's the hero who falls for a female terrorist.

ARTS AND CRAFTS J&K is famed for its handicraft production, and especially for its fine silk carpets and valuable pashmina shawls. In addition to some superb shopping opportunities, you can also see artisans following traditional production methods. You'll learn most about these crafts and the families who produce them by taking a Heritage Walk in Srinagar (page 188).

Kashmir's jewel-like **carpets** are rightly famous around the world and, if you have the budget, are one of the most beautiful souvenirs you can take home from your trip. This kind of carpet making was introduced from Persia, and the finest examples are made from pure wool or a mixture of wool and silk. Synthetic materials feature only in the 'lower-grade' carpets. Kashmiri carpets are hand-knotted on a loom. Production typically takes place in people's homes rather than a factory, and even a small carpet takes months to complete. Many members of the same family may contribute to the process, and the skills required are passed down from one generation to the next. Popular patterns include the 'paisley' motif (inspired by the shape of an almond or mango stone), the Chinar tree and the tree of life.

Far more portable and accessible on a greater range of budgets is locally made **jewellery**. Sapphires and rubies are both mined in J&K, but they're usually cut, polished and set in Rajasthan before being shipped back to the shops in Jammu and Srinagar. Arguably more striking, and certainly more affordable, are pieces of Ladakhi jewellery, with coral, turquoise and lapis lazuli set into silver or made into hundreds of beads. Although antique pieces are available, and attract a premium price, modern replicas are often just as attractive and the craftsmanship, in many cases, is fine.

Kashmir has always been renowned for its artists, and they paint in a variety of styles. Largest in scale are the **mural paintings** that decorate many of the Buddhist monasteries in Ladakh. Frequently depicting scenes from the life of the Buddha, or of guardian figures and demons, the conservation of these ancient works and, in some cases, production of new paintings is keeping yet another generation of artists in business.

Far smaller but produced with no less skill are the *thangka*, paintings on silk that are frequently surrounded by a rich brocade border. These lustrous wall hangings were originally teaching tools and so depict scenes such as the Wheel of Life (the explanation of Buddhist cosmology). Originally a Nepalese art form, *thangkas* were exported to monasteries in Tibet from the 11th century onwards. They could be easily rolled up and carried and hence quickly became popular.

Kashmir also has its own schools of **miniature painting**. Though often small in size, the word miniature actually comes from *minium*, the Latin for red lead. These paintings were produced to illustrate valuable manuscripts, both secular and religious, and became particularly popular from the 15th century onwards. Often removed from their original bindings for display, you can see a large collection at the Dogra Art Museum in Jammu (page 223).

Papier mâché is thought to have been introduced to Kashmir by the Seljuk dynasty of Iran, whence it spread across central Asia and into Kashmir. It was produced in and around Srinagar from the 14th century onwards, and although no examples from this period survive, we do have manuscript descriptions of its existence.

The interest in papier mâché was revived in the 19th century, as French merchants wanted their pashmina shawls wrapped and shipped in papier mâché boxes. Though costing almost nothing in Srinagar, the boxes fetched a high price in Paris, and so a separate trade in the boxes developed, with production being targeted towards European tastes. Papier mâché items produced in Srinagar today can be made of either pulped paper or, more frequently, paperboard sheet or another substructure that has been painted and covered with lacquer.

Kashmir is also known for its exquisite **wood carving,** and a number of carpentry workshops survive in Srinagar in particular. These artisans once produced the intricate cedar-wood panels for the houseboats, and indeed they continue to restore them and produce replacements, but now most of their output is carved furniture, screens and decorative items for the home.

SPORT The national sport of J&K is undoubtedly **polo**, and games draw vast crowds of spectators. Although variants such as running polo and even elephant polo can be seen elsewhere in India, here the original horse variety is king. This is a particularly apt phrase as, given the royal lineage of many of the top players, polo is still often referred to as the sport of kings. The best place to watch professional polo matches is at Drass (page 163), where families are proud of producing generations of polo players and see the game as a key part of their heritage. At around 3,350m, the polo field at Gulmarg is the highest in India, and you'll occasionally catch games there too.

Owing to the mountainous terrain, J&K is a hub for **adventure sports**. The state offers the best **trekking** opportunities in the Indian Himalayas, although road construction is increasingly eating away at trekking trails, and trek lengths on the standard routes can be quite short (rarely more than a week). **Mountaineers** will find peaks for all levels of ability, and there are numerous pleasant **walks** for those with less energy. **Mountain biking** and **climbing** are perennially popular among visiting tourists, as is **motorcycling**.

Various **watersports** are already on offer, and more activities are being added each season. White-water rafting is well developed across Ladakh in particular, and a boat club in Srinagar teaches sailing and rents out boats, and you can also hire jet-skis, kayaks and windsurfs. In the summer months, fishing for brown trout is possible in some of the Kashmiri rivers.

India's premier **ski** resort is at Gulmarg, so in the winter months you can ski and snowboard at a fraction of the cost of European and American resorts. It's also possible to snow shoe, heli-ski and ice skate. There's even a growing interest in ice hockey, with popular teams in Leh and Kargil and players drawn from several army regiments and police forces.

SEND US YOUR SNAPS!

We'd love to follow your adventures using our *Ladakh, Jammu & the Kashmir Valley* guide – why not tag us in your photos and stories via Twitter (🐦 @BradtGuides) and Instagram (📷 @bradtguides)? Alternatively, you can upload your photos directly to the gallery on the Ladakh, Jammu & the Kashmir Valley destination page via our website (w bradtguides.com/ladakh).

2

Practical Information

WHEN TO VISIT

The state of J&K is a year-round destination: there are major attractions in every season, although if you want to visit a specific place or undertake a particular activity you will need to take the extremes of weather into consideration.

In **winter** Ladakh is only accessible by air, as the roads are closed due to snow. Be warned: getting around at this time can be very difficult and most accommodation is closed. Nevertheless, this is the best time to spot snow leopards on one of the growing band of snow leopard safaris (see box, page 10), as well as undertake the Chadar Winter Trek along the frozen Zanskar River, accompanying local teachers returning to Zanskar's remote villages after their winter break. It's also the time to catch Ladakhi Losar, the New Year, which is celebrated in late December or early January (although the exact date is set by the lunar calendar), and the cold weather means that few other tourists will be around. The snow itself is an attraction at this time of year, as the wintry landscapes make for some dramatic scenery. Srinagar in the snow is a picture-perfect scene. You can keep warm with a *kanger* (an earthen pot filled with hot embers, which is kept close to the body in order to keep warm in winter) beneath your *phiran* (a long cloak or robe worn in Kashmir), tucked up toasty warm on a houseboat, or use the city as a springboard for the ski resort at Gulmarg. This is the most developed resort in the Himalayas; ski passes, kit hire and lessons are exceptionally cheap, and you can even try your hand at heli-skiing.

Spring is when the snows begin to melt, and the alpine meadows erupt into rainbows of colour, with wild flowers everywhere you look. In Srinagar the magnificent tulip fields also come into bloom, and though the domestic tourists have begun to arrive, there are still relatively few foreigners to be seen. Everything is lush, green and fresh, and the lower trekking routes start to beckon.

In the **summer** months, it's time for trekking. The snow has retreated to the uppermost peaks, and the roads are clear enough to drive to Leh and even down to Zanskar. While Leh itself is busy, there are plenty of quiet village retreats in the surrounding valleys where you can explore walking trails or biking and bridal routes (you can even ride a camel if you wish), and few things are more beautiful than sitting out around a campfire beneath the stars. Even the rivers and lakes look enticing in July and August. There are plenty of opportunities for kayaking and white-water rafting on the rivers of Ladakh, while to the west the lakes of Kashmir offer opportunities for a variety of watersports, leisurely boat trips and trout fishing.

The greatest draw in **autumn** is the Ladakh Festival, which runs for two weeks at the start of September (see box, page 85). A wonderful celebration of Ladakhi culture, it's a prime opportunity to see traditional costumes and masked dance, archery competitions and polo. Come November, the saffron fields of Kashmir are riotous purple; the crocuses are harvested and the saffron is dried.

Jammu is different again to Kashmir and Ladakh. Its lower altitude means that, like much of India, it's at its best from October to March. April to June can be uncomfortably hot and steamy, as the summer heat builds up and the monsoon brews. Come July, the heavily pregnant clouds finally let go of their precious water and the monsoon rains fall. This is a bad time to be in Jammu (but Ladakh and Zanskar are great at this time of year).

HIGHLIGHTS

It is often said that a place has something for everyone, but in the case of J&K that is actually true. Thousands of years of history sit side by side with vibrant modern communities, and spectacular natural landscapes ripe for exploration are dotted with all manner of architectural curiosities. Whether your idea of heaven is heli-skiing in Gulmarg or joining monks for their early-morning meditation, trekking along frozen mountain trails to Zanskar, white-water rafting on the Indus or simply lazing on a houseboat with a good book, you won't be disappointed.

BUDDHAS OF KARGIL Far less famous but no less impressive than the ill-fated Buddhas of Bamiyan in Afghanistan, which were destroyed by the Taliban in 2001, is the 7m-tall rock-cut Buddha at Kartse Khar. Dating back to the 7th/8th centuries AD, this statue was carved by early missionaries and the depiction of the body, jewellery and hair are typical of the Kashmiri style. Four other Buddha carvings, including the standing Buddha at Mulbekh, are also found within the district.

THE MUGHAL ROAD When the Mughal emperors travelled to their Kashmiri paradise in the 1600s, the road they took was far west of the current National Highway. Their route has recently been paved, making it an epic and accessible drive through the spectacularly beautiful mountain scenery.

MUBARAK MANDI At first glance, Jammu's Mubarak Mandi is a crumbling wreck, a pitiful place of neglect. Look closer, however, and this 19th-century palace complex has remarkable wedding-cake architecture and is overrun with monkeys.

TREKKING IN ZANSKAR The vast majority of trekkers head to Ladakh as the routes are more easily accessible from Leh, but it's well worth the effort of travelling further afield to Zanskar. The landscapes are more striking, there are fewer people on the trails and there are fantastic opportunities for spotting flora and fauna, including the elusive snow leopards. In winter, you can join local teachers on the Chadar Winter Trek as they brave the snow and ice to return to their rural schools after the winter break.

MEDITATING AT THIKSEY MONASTERY Joining monks in their early-morning prayers here will send shivers down your spine. The room, dark save for candlelight, resonates with sonorous chanting and the atmosphere is spellbinding. Though other monasteries such as Hemis are better advertised, the laidback atmosphere of Thiksey allows you to feel a part of the community rather than simply a spectator.

MUGHAL GARDENS Described by the Mughal emperors as 'Heaven on Earth', the Shalimar Gardens, or the equally beautiful Chashma Shahi, are at their best early in the morning. At this time you'll not only be able to explore these divine gardens before the crowds but also see the mist rising eerily off the lawns and water channels. Heavenly indeed.

- Run the Ladakh Marathon and prove your endurance at altitude (see box, page 86)
- Mountain bike from Khardung La down one of the world's highest motorable roads to Leh (page 99)
- White-water raft through the rapids of the Indus River (page 139)
- Fish for trout in the high-altitude lakes around Kashmir (page 193)
- Complete the Chadar Winter Trek across frozen rivers to Zanskar (see box, page 178)
- Ski off-piste at Gulmarg, India's top winter sports resort (page 199)
- Horse trek to the Thajiwas Glacier (page 183)
- Try heli-skiing at a price you can afford (page 203)
- Sneak up on an elusive snow leopard on a winter-only safari (see box, page 10)

HOUSEBOATS OF SRINAGAR If you take home one image of Srinagar, it'll be of India's floating palaces, the houseboats of the Dal and Nagin lakes. Stay just one night floating on the water and you'll see why the colonial British hired boats for months on end; ride a *shikara* (a type of wooden boat unique to the lakes and waterways around Srinagar) among the lotus gardens and you'll probably never want to leave.

KHARDUNG LA There's a certain draw to visiting places with superlatives attached to them, and Khardung La, one of the highest motorable roads on earth, is no exception. Yes it's touristy, yes it gets crowded, but without climbing Everest it's probably the closest you'll get to standing on the roof of the world, and that makes it worth the effort.

SUGGESTED ITINERARIES

Your itinerary is inevitably going to depend on a variety of factors: the time you have available, how far you want to travel, the time of year and, if time is short, whether you're going to focus on Srinagar or Leh. We've therefore suggested a mixture of options in the hope that there's something here for you, wherever and whenever you're going.

A WEEKEND With just two days based in **Srinagar**, book yourself on to a pampered colonial-style houseboat to see life as the other half once did. On the first day take a ride on the gondola to the shrine of Makhdoom Sahib, then continue up the hill to Hari Parbat Fort and have a picnic in the surrounding eco-reserve, looking out across the city. After lunch, pay a visit to the Hazratbal Shrine with its sacred hair of the Prophet, then return to Dal Lake via the Jamia Masjid, making sure you're back on the boat in time to watch the sun set across the water.

On day two, rise at dawn and take a *shikara* ride to the floating vegetable market, admiring the patchwork of floating islands as you go. Buy some honey macaroons to keep hunger pangs at bay, and then return to land for a tour of the Mughal Gardens. Chashma Shahi and the Shalimar Gardens are a must, as are the tulip gardens if you're visiting in April. Finish up your day with a drink at the Vivanta Dal View hotel, the entirety of Srinagar laid out at your feet.

If your two days are in **Leh**, prepare yourself for immersion in Ladakh's Buddhist culture. Start your visit with a walk in the Old Town, climbing up the narrow streets from Main Bazaar to the LAMO centre for an introduction to Leh's history, before continuing up to Leh Palace and then Tsemo Fort. If you're feeling less than fit, or haven't yet acclimatised to the altitude, you might need to take a taxi between the two.

On day two, go to the Shanti Stupa before breakfast so you can explore it before the crowds arrive. Drive back into town via the far older Tisseru Stupa, and have a bite to eat at one of the many cafés in Changspa. If you're an adrenaline junkie, spend the rest of your day descending from Khardung La by mountain bike, or enjoy a leisurely few hours exploring some of the nearby villages by hired taxi.

A WEEK With a week in **Ladakh**, use Leh as your hub for exploring the district. Travel first to the south of Ladakh, visiting the monasteries of Thiksey and Hemis en route to Tso Moriri and the Tso Kar lakes. Stay in a tented camp, admire the reflections of the sky and mountains in the ice-blue waters, and take the opportunity to do some walking in the surrounding hills.

Pass through Leh again as you drive back north, continuing on to visit Phyang and Likir monasteries, where you can spend the night with boy monks at their school and admire the impressive, gilded Maitreya Buddha. There are finely preserved wall paintings at Alchi and, if you have time, the lunar landscapes just before Lamayuru are a fascinating geological feature.

If time allows, scoot down along the Nubra Valley, checking out oases villages, sand dunes and ice-coated mountain vistas as you go.

In a week you also have time to drive the length of the **Vale of Kashmir** from Srinagar to Jammu. Having explored Srinagar itself, travel to the relaxing hill resort of Pahalgam via the saffron fields at Pampore and the two remarkable temples at Avantipore. If it's winter and Pahalgam is inaccessible, go to Gulmarg instead for a rewarding (and affordable) day on the slopes at the premier ski resort in the Himalayas.

The drive southwards through the valley is spectacular: the hairpin bends clinging to the mountainside are an attraction in their own right, if a little hair-raising. Take time to visit the stunning Sun Temple at Martand and, if you've not yet had your fill of horticulture, the Mughal Garden at Verinag.

Approaching Jammu, the Hindu shrine at Katra is an important pilgrimage site, and quite a contrast from the Muslim ones further north. End your trip staying at Hari Niwas, the former palace of Maharaja Hari Singh, sipping gin and tonics on the lawn overlooking the Tawi River.

TWO OR MORE WEEKS A fortnight or longer is sufficient to travel across larger parts of the state and/or to do an extended trek. If your interest is primarily in **Ladakh**, start in Leh, exploring the town and the monasteries between Leh and Lamayuru. Take the short (two-day) trek from Lamayuru through the mountains to Rangdum, and then allow yourself seven to ten days in Zanskar. Don't miss Karsha Gompa or the 12th-century rock-cut monastery at Phugtal, the latter of which is accessible only on foot. In Padum there are superb Buddha carvings down by the river, which are unfortunately often overlooked. On your return, be sure to drive through the Suru Valley to see the Buddha at Kartse Khar.

The trekking opportunities in **Kashmir** are also under-appreciated, and two weeks is ample time to get up into the mountains and away from other foreigners. From Pahalgam to Sonamarg it's a four-day trek via the Amarnath Cave, and your companions will be Hindu devotees visiting the cave's Shiva ice *lingam*. For a quieter, tougher and majestically scenic hike, you could lace up your boots and do the week-long Great Lakes Trek. It's one of the best treks in the Himalayas and yet surprisingly it is often neglected.

TOUR OPERATORS

International tour operators, many of which cover destinations across India and further afield, are listed below. For local tour operators, see individual chapters.

UK

Exodus ☎020 3811 4158; e sales@exodus. co.uk; w exodus.co.uk. Multiple escorted tours to Ladakh, including adventurous options such as searching for snow leopards & several trekking options. They also have a Canadian office.

Explore! ☎01252 883 743; w explore.co.uk. Their escorted 17-day Little Tibet tour takes in all the major monasteries in Ladakh then returns to the plains overland via Dharmsala & Amritsar.

✳ **Indus Experiences** ☎020 8901 7320; e holidays@indusexperiences.co.uk; w industours. co.uk. Tailor-made & luxury tours to the Indian subcontinent & Indochina. The 9-day 'Kashmir: The Secret Garden' tour includes cultural interaction with local communities & sightseeing in Srinagar & Gulmarg, while the 14-day 'Hidden Ladakh' tour takes in Leh and the Nubra Valley.

Mountain Tribal Vision m 07950 517 068; e tanzin.norbu@gmail.com; w mountaintribalvision.com. If you want to travel with a Ladakh & Zanskar specialist, look no further than Mountain Tribal Vision. Owner Tanzin Norbu, a fellow of the RGS, was born in Zanskar & studied in India & the UK. His organised treks can be epic in scale, snow leopards & other fauna in the winter, & wild flowers, photography & local culture in the summer. Tanzin is also an expert on Buddhism. His passion for his homeland is infectious.

Native Eye ☎01473 328 546; e info@ nativeeyetravel.com; w nativeeyetravel.com. Small adventure travel company with a personal touch; specialises in unusual destinations. Offers a 14-day tour taking in Leh, Shey, Thiksey, Hemis, the Nubra Valley, Diskit, Kargil, Zanskar & Srinagar & elsewhere in the wider region.

✳ **Nature Trek** ☎01962 733 051; e info@ naturetrek.co.uk; w naturetrek.co.uk. Highly regarded wildlife specialist tour company offering a quality snow leopard tour of Ladakh, where the chances of seeing the 'ghost of the Himalayas' are surprisingly high.

On the Go Tours ☎020 7371 1113; e info@ onthegotours.com; w onthegotours.com. Private & group tours of both Kashmir & Ladakh, including mini breaks (4 days) in Ladakh. Trips to Kashmir can also be combined with the Golden Triangle.

Responsible Travel ☎01273 823 700; e rosy@ responsibletravel.com; w responsibletravel. com. A huge array of Kashmir, Ladakh & Zanskar tours from this agency acclaimed for its socially & environmentally aware travel ethos.

Steppes Travel ☎01285 601 770; e enquiry@ steppestravel.co.uk; w steppestravel.co.uk. Respected, upmarket tour company that offers a superb (but pricey!) 2-week winter snow leopard tour led by expert Ladakhi & European guides.

TransIndus ☎020 8566 3739; USA ☎+1 866 615 1815; w transindus.co.uk. Asia specialist TransIndus offers spectacular tailor-made tours of Ladakh, Zanskar & Kashmir (or you can combine all). They also have a US office.

Travel Local w travellocal.com. A UK-based website where you can book direct with selected local travel companies, allowing you to communicate with an expert ground operator without having to go through a third-party travel operator or agent. Your booking with the local company has full financial protection, but note that travel to the destination is not included. Member of ABTA, ASTA.

Undiscovered Destinations ☎0191 296 2674; e travel@undiscovered-destinations.com; w undiscovered-destinations.com. Running exciting & often one-of-a-kind exploratory trips to some of the world's lesser-known corners, this well-regarded agency offers a Ladakh itinerary timed around the Hemis Festival.

✳ **Wild Frontiers** ☎020 8741 7390; e info@ wildfrontiers.co.uk; w wildfrontiers.co.uk. Well-run group & tailor-made tours to both Kashmir &

Ladakh. Choose from wild walking, extended boat trips & mountain camping. Their 10-day Kashmir Walking Adventure is a highlight of their tour list.

ELSEWHERE

Adventure Associates ☏+61 2 6355 2022 (Australia); e mail@adventureassociates.com; w adventureassociates.com; see ad, 2nd colour section. Accompanied small-group tours to destinations around the world, including Ladakh.

✳ **Kamzang Journeys** m +977 980 341 4745 (Nepal), +91 941 998 1715 (India); e kim@kamzang.com; w kamzangjourneys.com. American Kim Bannister knows the Himalayas like few other westerners. She puts her experience to good use by running exclusive treks across the Himalayas from her base in Kathmandu. These include mammoth Ladakh cycle adventures & trekking trips which are sometimes along previously untested – and very exciting – routes. Kim brings her own team on every trek, ensuring the standard of catering, portering & customer service is second to none.

Sawadee ☏+31 20 420 2220; e info@sawadee. nl; w sawadee.nl. Renowned Dutch tour operator offering comprehensive tours of Ladakh. The itinerary includes trekking from Lamayuru & returns to Delhi overland via Manali & Dharamsala.

RED TAPE

The Indian government loves red tape. Some claim this is a legacy of the British, but the bureaucrats have taken it one stage further. Photocopies, permits and triplicates rule the roost; though slowly – *slowly* – things are going digital.

VISAS All foreign nationals (excluding Nepalese and Bhutanese) need a visa for entering India. For tourist visas there are two different options: the easiest and cheapest to get is the e-visa, while the longer, more versatile one is the standard 180-day tourist visa.

E-visas are by far the quickest and cheapest to get (UK and US passport holders pay US$102.50; most EU passport holders and Australian passport holders pay US$82.50). The application is made completely online (see w indianvisaonline. gov.in) and on average takes two days to process (though in our experience they're frequently ready by the following morning). You can apply for three e-visas per year, which are valid for 60 days and allow two entries into India. You will need a PDF of your passport photo page, plus a scanned photo of the correct size (this can be a bit of a pain to get right!). However, there are two problems of note to keep in mind when applying for an e-visa. The first is that the website is quite difficult to use, and numerous people report problems when it comes to the online payment. Secondly, and far more importantly in the case of J&K, is that technically you are not allowed to travel anywhere in J&K including Ladakh with an e-visa. In reality, many people do travel on such a visa (especially to Ladakh) but it's entirely possible that airlines could refuse you boarding, or police could send you back to Delhi with a stern telling off. Whether you choose to risk it is up to you.

If you're going to be in India for more than two months, you want to make multiple entries or – sensibly – don't want to risk trying to visit J&K on an e-visa, then you'll have no choice but venture down the headache-inducing 180-day **tourist visa** path. The price of the visa depends on both your nationality and where you apply: UK passport holders applying in London currently pay £113 plus £7.44 service charge. Visa fees are payable at the time of submitting your application and are non-refundable, even if your visa is refused.

In the UK, Indian visa applications are handled by a private contractor, VFS Global. You should download the application form from here and then either submit it by post or in person at one of the visa centres in London, Birmingham,

Cardiff, Edinburgh, Glasgow and Manchester, for which you can book a timed appointment. Take a good book to read as they frequently run late.

In addition to your printed and signed application form, you must submit two recent 50x50mm passport photos (NB: this is not the same size as a standard UK passport photo), your passport, any supporting paperwork and a self-addressed Special Delivery Envelope (SDE; this applies to postal applications only). Occasionally, an applicant will be asked to take a biometric test, for which they will have to visit one of the aforementioned VFS visa centres.

If you apply in person, it typically takes five working days to process your visa, though Pakistani, Sri Lankan and Bangladeshi nationals should allow significantly longer. Those applying by post should allow a minimum of ten working days and send their documents by recorded delivery.

REGISTRATION If you are travelling on a tourist visa, you do not usually need to register in India: this is a requirement for long-term visa holders only. However, special requirements are in place for J&K due to the security concerns. If you arrive by air, you will be registered at the airport on arrival. Coming by road, you will need to fill in a registration form at a police checkpoint. There are no charges for this kind of registration, and you do not need to show any documents other than your valid passport and visa.

PERMITS For those travelling from Leh to the Nubra Valley, Dha Hanu or the southern lakes, it is necessary to get an Inner Line Permit. You can either try to get this yourself once on the ground in Leh or you can apply online at w lahdclehpermit.in (though the system can be a bit temperamental!). If you decide to apply for the relevant permit yourself, you will need to find at least two other people to apply with you.

If doing it in person, take your passport, photocopies of your passport, a print-out of your intended itinerary and a covering letter addressed to the **Deputy Commissioner's Office** in Leh (\ 252 010; ⊕ 09.00–15.00). The permit itself costs Rs20 per day, with an additional one-off Rs300 environmental fee and Rs100 compulsory contribution to the Red Cross. The permit will be issued usually on the same day. If you are short of time or need additional people with whom to apply, give your paperwork to a local travel agent (page 76), as they seem to be able to rustle up the requisite additional people and can get the permits at great speed, sometimes even at the weekend.

Mountaineering permits are required for some ascents. If the peak is under 7,000m you can apply yourself via the Indian Mountaineering Foundation's office in Leh (see box, page 89). Permits for higher peaks require prior authorisation from Delhi. Full information is available on the IMF website (w indmount.org).

EMBASSIES

There are no foreign embassies in J&K itself, and foreign governments typically warn that they can provide little consular support here. You should apply for visas for onward travel and refer consular enquiries to the appropriate embassy in Delhi (see w embassypages.com/india for a list).

GETTING THERE AND AWAY

India is well connected to the rest of the world, particularly in terms of flights, and onward transport connections from the main hubs to Jammu, Srinagar and Leh are

India's chaotic capital is a love-it-or-hate-it city. What is certain is that if you can't tick a monkey, a naked holy man and a cross-dressing *hijra* off your I-spy list before lunchtime, you're probably not making the most of Delhi.

GETTING AROUND Delhi is a mega-city, with all the transport problems that moniker infers. The best way to get around is by **metro**. Six lines cover central Delhi and outer suburbs; trains are efficient, air conditioned and clean, and fares are just Rs10–60 depending on distance.

Alternatively, you can take a **taxi** or **auto-rickshaw**. These are supposed to charge by the meter, but you may prefer to agree a price before you set off. Auto-rickshaws are about half the price of taxis (expect to pay Rs100–130 for a 20-minute journey as opposed to Rs250). Taxis with air conditioning charge more.

WHERE TO STAY By Indian standards, Delhi is an expensive city, and this is reflected in the room rates.

Hotel Imperial (200 rooms) Janpath Lane, Janpath; 2334 1234; e luxury@ theimperialindia.com; w theimperialindia. com. The award-winning Imperial is considered one of India's finest hotels & is the place to stay if money is no object. Built in 1931 in a striking colonial style, it has previously hosted the likes of Gandhi & Earl Mountbatten. The service is impeccable & there's a world-class art collection. **$$$$$**

Hyatt Regency (507 rooms) Bhikaiji Cama Pl, Ring Rd; 2679 1234; e delhi. regency@hyatt.com; w hyatt.com. Delhi's premier business hotel. Staff are highly professional, every need is catered for & the hotel has some of the best restaurants in the city. **$$$$$**

Bloomrooms @ New Delhi Railway Station 8591 Arakashan Rd, Paharganj; 4122 5666; w staybloom.com. Opposite New Delhi railway station & on the edge of the hectic traveller quarter of Paharganj, Bloomrooms is a bright-yellow, super-clean, well-equipped budget chain hotel with a reasonable in-house restaurant. **$$$**

De Holiday Inn (39 rooms) 22/18 Raj Guru Rd, Chuna Mandi, Paharganj; 2356 2690; e info@affordablehotelsandresorts.com; w deholidayinternational.com. As students we spent many happy months at De Holiday Inn & still go back when we want a lemon pancake. Staff are warm & helpful & it's by far the cleanest option in the backpackers' area of Paharganj. **$$$**

affordable and frequent. Bear in mind, however, that in the winter months Leh is accessible only by air, and that Jammu is currently the only major city in the state to have a rail connection to the rest of India.

As there are no international connections to J&K, this section is arranged as follows: international flights to Delhi and travel information on that city; domestic flights connecting J&K to other parts of India; train connections to Jammu; and road connections to J&K via Himachal Pradesh and the Punjab.

BY AIR India has superb flight connections around the world, and you'll generally be able to choose from a range of departures from your place of origin. If the primary focus of your trip is J&K as opposed to other parts of India, opt to fly into Delhi to maximise your onward travel options. Other major international airports in the country include Bangalore, Kolkata and Mumbai.

✗ **WHERE TO EAT AND DRINK** Delhi has probably the best restaurants in India, and whether you're craving doughnuts or *dosas*, samosas or sushi, you won't be disappointed. For international food, **La Piazza** and **TK's Oriental Grill** (both at the Hyatt Regency, opposite; $$$$$) are expensive but worth the splurge. **Lodhi, The Garden Restaurant** (1 Lodhi Rd; ✆ 3958 5266; $$$$$) has both indoor and outdoor tables in a romantic setting and, for something more laidback, you can't beat **Turtle Café** (Shop 23, 2nd Flr, Middle Ln, Khan Market; ✆ 2465 5641; $$$–$$$$) and **The Big Chill** (A-68, Prithviraj La, Khan Market; ✆ 4175 7588; $$$–$$$$). The latter two also do excellent coffee and cakes.

For north Indian cuisine, we like the opulent **Veda** (H-27, Tropical Bldg, Connaught Circus; ✆ 4151 3535; w vedarestaurants.com; $$$$$) or, for traditional Mughlai dishes in more rough-and-ready surroundings, the Old Delhi institution that is **Karim's** (16 Matia Mahal Bazar, Nr Jama Masjid; ✆ 2326 4981; $$$). The best parathas ($–$$) are from the stalls in Old Delhi's **Paratha Gali** (Paratha Alley), a stone's throw from Karim's.

WHAT TO SEE AND DO Delhi has some 1,200 heritage buildings and more than 200 monuments of national importance. Standard tourist itineraries include the **Qutb Minar** (Mehrauli; ⊕ dawn–dusk daily; admission Rs30/500 local/foreigner), the world's tallest brick-built minaret; **Humayun's Tomb** (Mathura Rd; ⊕ dawn–dusk daily; admission Rs30/500 local/foreigner, one of the architectural models for the Taj Mahal; the impressive **Red Fort** (Netaji Subhash Marg; ⊕ dawn–dusk Tue–Sun; admission Rs30/500 local/foreigner; and the **Jama Masjid** (off Netaji Subhash Marg; ⊕ 07.00–noon & 13.30–18.30 daily, closed to tourists during prayers; free admission).

Lesser known but no less interesting sights include the crumbling **Purana Qila** (Mathura Rd; ⊕ dawn–dusk daily; admission Rs20/200 local/foreigner), a large and wild site with thick ramparts, impenetrable gateways and a library, from the roof of which Emperor Humayun fell to his death, probably in an opiate-induced haze. **Lodhi Gardens** (Lodhi Rd; ⊕ dawn–dusk daily; free admission) contain a large number of tombs from the Lodhi and Sayyid periods, including the octagonal tomb of Sikander Lodhi; and the **Jantar Mantar** (Connaught Pl; ⊕ dawn–dusk daily; admission Rs25/200 local/foreigner), the 18th-century astronomical observatory of Maharaja Jai Singh, is worth an hour of your time if you're not going to see its larger sister observatory in Jaipur.

Note that you are usually required to have both a print-out of your ticket (even for e-tickets) and your passport in order to gain access to the departure terminal.

International flights via Delhi
Indira Gandhi International Airport (DEL) is the busiest airport in India and handles around 65 million passengers every year. The international terminal is modern and easy to navigate, and getting through immigration and baggage collection is usually very fast and painless.

The following airlines operate international flights to Delhi.

✈ **Aeroflot** w aeroflot.com. Daily departures from Moscow.

✈ **Air China** w airchina.com. Regular departures from Beijing.

✈ **Air France** w airfrance.com. Daily departures from Paris.

✈ **Air India** w airindia.com. The national airline has regular departures to Delhi from Europe,

37

The town of Manali lies in the Himalayan foothills of Himachal Pradesh, close to the northern end of the Kullu Valley. The River Beas is the local focal point, and domestic tourists flock here throughout the year to explore the surrounding countryside. It makes a natural – and very welcome – stop for those travelling the route from Delhi to Leh.

GETTING THERE AND AROUND The **airport** serving Manali is 50km away at Bhuntar (KUU), and Air India operates a daily flight here from Delhi (1hr 20mins).

The majority of visitors to Manali come by **road**. NH1 goes as far as Chandigarh, after which the Kullu Highway (NH21) continues on to Manali. The drive from Delhi to Manali is 540km and takes at least 12 hours.

Volvo coaches leave Delhi's Kashmiri Gate bus stand for Manali each evening between 20.00 and 21.00, reaching Manali 15 hours later. Tickets cost Rs1,668 per person and can be booked via the Himachal Road Transport Company's website (w hrtc.gov.in). Ordinary buses depart regularly throughout the day and cost Rs777.

Buses shuttle between Manali and Kullu every 15 minutes and cost Rs40 per person. **Motorbike hire** (try Manali Bike Rental; m 981 602 4288; e info@ manalibikerental.com; w manalibikerental.com) is popular and a day's hire will set you back around Rs800 for a Bullet or Honda bike.

WHERE TO STAY Manali is a popular destination for domestic tourists, so book accommodation well in advance if you plan to stay here during holiday periods.

Span Resorts (20 rooms, 6 cottages) 14 Mile, PO Katrain, Kullu–Manali Hwy; m 981 609 2413; e info@spanresorts.com; w spanresorts. com. Manali's only 5-star property is 15km from the town centre beside the River Beas. Serving mainly domestic tourists on package tours, it has everything from a swimming pool to mini golf & can arrange horseriding & paragliding. All rooms have AC & heating; if your budget allows, request one with a river view. **$$$$$**

John Banons Hotel (18 rooms) Manali Orchards; 252 335; e rsvn@banon. in; w banonhotel.com. Family-owned hotel in downtown location. Pleasant setting in an orchard. Restaurant serves Indian & continental cuisine. **$$$$**

Hotel New Adarsh (12 rooms) The Mall; 250 693; m 988 243 7750; e hotelnewadarsh@gmail.com; w hotelnewadarsh.com. Behind Adarsh

the Middle East & southeast Asia, plus the USA.

✈ **British Airways** w britishairways.com. 2 direct flights a day from London Heathrow.

✈ **Cathay Pacific** w cathaypacific.com. Daily departures to Bangkok & Hong Kong.

✈ **China Airlines** w china-airlines.com/en. Daily flights from Taipei with good connections across China & southeast Asia.

✈ **Drukair** w drukair.com.bt. Bhutanese national carrier. 4 flights per week from Paro.

✈ **Emirates** w emirates.com. 2–4 flights a day from Dubai with good connections worldwide.

✈ **Finnair** w finnair.com. Daily flights from Helsinki flying the shortest route from Europe to Delhi.

✈ **Jet Airways** w jetairways.com. India's best airline has direct flights from Canada, Europe, the Middle East & southeast Asia.

✈ **KLM** w klm.com. 5 flights a week from Amsterdam.

✈ **Lufthansa** w lufthansa.com. Daily departures from Frankfurt & Munich.

✈ **Malaysia Airlines** w malaysiaairlines.com. Daily departures from Kuala Lumpur.

✈ **Oman Air** w omanair.com. 3–5 flights daily from Muscat.

✈ **Pakistan International Airlines** w piac. com.pk. Pakistan's national carrier. Daily flights from Lahore. Frequently sold out so book early.

Restaurant, rooms here are simple & clean & unusually good value. It's in a convenient location & staff are generally helpful. **$$–$$$**

🏠 **Sarthak Resorts** (54 rooms) Khakhnal, Left Bank, Naggar Rd; ☎ 259 323; e booking@

sarthakresorts.com; w sarthakresorts.com. Well-maintained resort hotel with good views. Many rooms have balconies. Best rates are through online booking agents rather than the hotel directly. **$$**

✗ **WHERE TO EAT AND DRINK** The majority of Manali's hotels offer meal plans, as all-inclusive packages are preferred by Indian tourists. However, if you want to eat out, **Casa Bella Vista** (Log Huts Rd; m 98 154 44488; **$$$$$**) and **Il Forno** (Hadimba Rd; m 98 1604 0144; **$$$$**) both serve authentic Italian food, and **Johnson's Bar & Restaurant** (Circuit House Rd; w ilforno.co.in; **$$$**) does affordable Indian and continental cuisine with a great ambience and efficient service.

For a quick snack, **Manali Sweets** (off Mall Rd; **$–$$**) serves divine *jalebis* and *rasgullas* (traditional Indian sweets dripping in honey) and excellent chickpea samosas.

WHAT TO SEE AND DO The attraction of Manali is its natural environment and, for many Indian visitors, their first opportunity to see snow. Trekking and picnicking within the **Van Vihar** and the **Pin Valley national parks** are perennially popular, as is hiking to the **Jana** or **Rahala falls**. The **Rohtang Pass**, 50km north of Manali, will leave you literally and metaphorically breathless due to the altitude (3,978m). Getting to the pass from Manali by taxi takes 4–5 hours and costs Rs2,000.

If you prefer something cultural, there are a number of attractive religious buildings: the **Hadimba Devi Mandir** (off Hadimba Temple Rd; ⊕ 08.00–18.00; free admission) is a striking 16th-century Hindu temple set on a hilltop and best reached on foot along a steep track through the peaceful surrounding woodland. Elsewhere, the **Gadhan Thekchholking Gompa** (off Mall Rd; ⊕ 06.00–18.00; free admission) gives you a small taste of what is to come if you're heading on to Ladakh; and the **Raghunath Temple** (Kullu Town; ⊕ 06.00–20.00; free admission) has a striking façade, albeit in a poorly maintained setting. Although entry to these sites is free, you may be asked to make a donation. You should also observe any dress and behavioural requirements.

✈ **Qatar Airways** w qatarairways.com. 2 flights per day from Doha.

✈ **Singapore Airlines** w singaporeair.com. 2 daily departures from Singapore.

✈ **Swiss** w swiss.com. Daily flight from Zürich.

✈ **Turkish Airlines** w turkishairlines.com. Daily flights from Istanbul.

✈ **Virgin Atlantic** w virgin-atlantic.com. Daily flights from London.

Domestic flights Jammu, Leh and Srinagar all have airports with regular commercial flights to other parts of India. Flying into the state is certainly the easiest way to get here, though if you head straight to Leh you will need to allow several days to acclimatise to the altitude.

The flight-booking portals of Yatra (w yatra.com) or Make My Trip (w makemytrip.com) display – and allow you to book – the prices and schedules of all the airlines serving Srinagar and Leh. Alternatively, flight tickets can be booked from the airlines' own websites, offices, at the airport counters or from a local travel agent. Details of local ticketing offices and the airports' contact details are given in the relevant city chapters.

The main domestic airlines serving airports in J&K are Air India (w airindia. com), Go Air (w goair.in), IndiGo (w goindigo.in), SpiceJet (w spicejet.com) and Vistara (w airvistara.com).

Note that due to concerns that J&K flights might be targeted by terrorists, security on flights to and from destinations in the state is particularly tight. Additional baggage checks are common, and you may not be able to carry hand luggage on the plane. Please check with your airline prior to flying for up-to-date baggage requirements.

To Srinagar Srinagar (SXR) is the best connected of the state's airports. It's possible to fly here from Delhi, Mumbai, Amritsar, Bangalore, Chandigarh, Kolkata and Lucknow. The direct flight from Delhi takes around an hour and tickets start at Rs4,500. Before booking, check that you are looking at a direct flight, as some of the options route via Jammu.

To Jammu You can fly to Jammu airport (IXJ) from Delhi, Chennai and Mumbai, among others, and there are also occasional connections from Jammu to Leh and Srinagar. Flights from Delhi cost from around Rs5,000 each way, and most of the options leave Delhi early in the morning. The flight takes 1 hour 20 minutes. Flights from Leh to Jammu also take 1 hour 20 minutes and cost from around Rs5,000.

To Leh There are regular flights to Leh airport (IXL) from Delhi, Chandigarh, Jammu, Mumbai and Srinagar. The flight from Delhi takes about 1 hour 15 minutes and costs around Rs4,500 in the winter months but up to twice as much in summer. Tickets in high season can be in short supply, so book ahead to ensure you get the date you want and be aware that even in August bad weather can cause flight delays and cancellations.

BY TRAIN The only major city in J&K to have a railway station is Jammu, and though the line is being extended to Srinagar, this part of the route is unlikely to be operational for some years to come.

Travelling by train in India is a memorable experience, and if you buy a first- or second-class ticket it's a pleasurable one. Don't underestimate the value of travelling in an air-conditioned compartment. Trains run more or less on time and when you buy a ticket (which must be done in advance), you automatically get a seat reservation.

Train timetables and fares are available from the Indian Rail website (w indianrail.gov.in), though you might find private sites such as w erail.in easier to use. Once you've found out the times of the trains, the next problem is actually buying a ticket. Technically, if you have an Indian SIM card in your phone and an IRCTC train registration number you should be able to book them online. However, in reality it's very complicated for foreigners to even get the IRCTC number, and normally when you try to pay using a non-Indian credit card the payment will be rejected. Almost all potential foreign train travellers quickly give up with the system and instead buy their tickets through a travel agency, who will take a small commission (a couple of hundred rupees is the standard) for their assistance. You can either buy a ticket for a single journey, or buy an IndRail Pass, which is valid for up to 90 days. The latter is only available to foreigners and must be paid for in foreign currency: more details are available at **w** indianrail.gov.in/international_Tourist.html.

There are at least seven trains daily from Delhi to Jammu (station code JAT). Note that Delhi has several railway stations, so make sure you know which one you're leaving from. There are also regular trains between Amritsar (station code ASR) and Jammu, as well as from Rajasthan (see page 219 for details of all the above services).

BY CAR The journey from Delhi to J&K by road is long but perfectly feasible. Very few foreign tourists drive their own vehicles in India and it's impossible to hire a self-drive car to venture all the way to J&K. Cars always come with a driver. While the roads themselves are generally in good condition and ever more expressways are opening across the north Indian plains, the same compliments cannot be applied to Indian drivers. Road travel in India can be a hair-raising experience and at times is positively dangerous. The worst roads are the busy main roads linking the big cities of north India, and the road from Delhi to Jammu can be very scary. Quiet country roads are much more relaxing.

Via Himachal Pradesh Visitors heading to Ladakh by road from Delhi will probably come up from the plains via Himachal Pradesh, although do note that this long and arduous road is closed in winter. The section from Delhi to Chandigarh and the popular hill resort of Manali (see box, page 38), the usual point at which travellers break their journey, is not too bad (though it's busy and there can be some dangerous drivers sharing the road with you).

It is the 490km Manali–Leh Highway that is the most challenging section of the route, as it crosses a number of high passes: Rohtang (3,979m), Baralacha La (4,890m), Lachulung La (5,060m) and Taglang La (5,328m) among them. There is significant risk of altitude sickness at these points, and snowfall and ice frequently close the passes even in late spring. A tunnel is under construction beneath the Rohtang Pass, which is due to open at some point late in 2019. You should allow two days for the journey: the going is very slow. The buses break the journey at Keylong or Sarchu, and those in private vehicles are advised to do likewise.

Via Punjab If you are travelling to the western part of J&K (Jammu and Kashmir districts, as opposed to Ladakh and Zanskar), it is more appropriate to drive up from the Punjab. It's just 203km from Amritsar to Jammu and the journey takes around 3 hours. Continuing on from Jammu to Srinagar, the road is far slower and prone to landslides and closures during bad weather.

The main route between Jammu and Srinagar is the National Highway 1A (NH1A). Driving this road takes 8–10 hours depending on the weather, though as there are plenty of interesting things to see on the way it would be a pity to just drive straight up the valley without stopping. Note that at the time of going to print the governments of some Western countries were advising against travelling this route due to the ever-changing security situation in the Kashmir Valley, so do check before travelling this way.

BY BUS The Himachal Pradesh Tourism Development Corporation (**w** hptdc.nic.in) runs daily tourist coaches from Manali to Leh between 1 July and 15 September, as well as an onward connection to Delhi from Manali in air-conditioned Volvo coaches (Rs2,900; 2 days with overnight in Keylong).

BEFORE YOU GO

Travel insurance Comprehensive travel insurance should be the first thing on your shopping list when you contemplate visiting J&K. Choose a policy that includes medical evacuation (MedEvac) and make sure that you explicitly state your destination when getting quotes: many policies will not cover you for travel to places about which the FCO advises against all, or all but essential, travel. Even if the insurance policy covers India in general, it may not include all of J&K.

Check the small print carefully for terms and conditions relating to claims resulting both from acts of terrorism and natural disasters (sometimes referred to as acts of God or *force majeure*). If you plan to mountaineer, trek at high altitude, ski, horseride or engage in any other activity that may be perceived to have additional risks attached, ensure you are fully covered. The moment you call the insurance company to report you've broken your leg skiing off-piste in Gulmarg is not the time you want to discover your policy does not include winter sports cover.

Leave a copy of the policy documents at home with someone you trust, email them to yourself as a PDF attachment, and keep a copy of your policy number and the emergency contact number on you at all times just in case you need them.

Vaccinations Your GP or a specialist travel clinic (see opposite) will be able to check your immunisation record and advise on any extra inoculations you might need for travelling to J&K. It is wise to be up to date on **tetanus**, **polio** and **diphtheria** (now given as an all-in-one vaccine, Revaxis, that lasts for ten years), typhoid and **hepatitis A**. Immunisations against rabies, hepatitis B and Japanese encephalitis may also be recommended depending on the duration of your stay and the sort of activities you will be undertaking.

Hepatitis A vaccine (Havrix Monodose or Avaxim) comprises two injections given about a year apart, though you will have cover from the time of the first injection. The course typically costs £100 and, once complete, gives you protection for 25 years. The vaccine is sometimes available on the NHS. **Hepatitis B** vaccination should be considered for longer trips (one month or more) and by those working in a medical setting or with children. The vaccine schedule comprises three doses taken over a six-month period, but for those aged 16 or over it can be given over a period of 21 days if time is short. The rapid course needs to be boosted after one year. For those aged 15 or younger, the course takes a minimum of eight weeks. A combined hepatitis A and B vaccine, 'Twinrix', is available, though at least three doses are needed for it to be fully effective. The schedules used are similar to those for hepatitis B vaccine alone.

The injectable **typhoid** vaccines (eg: Typhim Vi, Typherix) last for three years and are about 75% effective. Oral capsules (such as Vivotif) may also be available for those aged six and over. Three capsules taken over five days last for approximately three years but may be less effective than the injectable version depending on how they are absorbed. Typhoid vaccines are particularly advised for those travelling in rural areas and when there may be difficulty in ensuring safe water supplies and food.

Rabies is present across India and vaccination is highly recommended for those travelling more than 24 hours from medical help or who will be coming into contact with animals. Any mammal can carry rabies, though dogs and monkeys are the most likely culprits. It can be transmitted through a bite, scratch or even a lick on skin. A pre-exposure course of vaccines ideally given over 21–28 days (but can be done over 7 days if time is short) is advised for everyone. Having

While there are reasonably well-equipped pharmacies in towns across J&K, it is still highly advisable to prepare your own first-aid kit and to carry it with you wherever you travel. A minimal kit should contain:

* A good drying antiseptic, eg: iodine or potassium permanganate
* A few small dressings (Band-Aids)
* Suncream
* Insect repellent
* Aspirin or paracetamol
* Imodium and rehydration salts
* Ciprofloxacin or norfloxacin (for severe diarrhoea)
* A pair of fine-pointed tweezers (to remove thorns, splinters, ticks, etc)
* Alcohol-based hand sanitiser or bar of soap in plastic box
* Clingfilm or condoms for covering burns
* Tampons (highly absorbent and excellent for nose bleeds)
* Sterile needles, scalpel and surgical thread
* Water purification tablets (essential for trekkers)

pre-exposure rabies changes the treatment needed after an exposure and makes it more available in J&K.

There is a small risk of **Japanese encephalitis**, a viral infection spread through the bites of infected mosquitoes. There is no treatment for the disease once you are infected, and about 30% of those who develop the disease will die. Approximately the same proportion will have permanent neurological damage. If you are planning to spend time in areas where infected mosquitoes may be present (rice paddies and piggeries are their favourite breeding grounds), have the inoculation and take the usual precautions against being bitten (see box, page 45). The highest risk of the disease is during the rainy season of May to November. The course of Japanese encephalitis vaccine (Ixiaro) is two doses a month apart but can be given more rapidly over seven days if time is short.

The risk of **malaria** in J&K is considered low enough for most travellers not to need to take malaria tablets. Those over the age of 70 or with complex health problems would be advised to seek individual advice regardless of destination as their risk of malaria is increased.

Travel clinics and health information A full list of current travel clinic websites worldwide is available on w istm.org. For other journey preparation information, consult w travelhealthpro.org.uk (UK) or w wwwnc.cdc.gov/travel (USA). Information about various medications may be found on w netdoctor. co.uk/travel. All advice found online should be used in conjunction with expert advice received prior to or during travel.

COMMON MEDICAL PROBLEMS
Travellers' diarrhoea Diarrhoeal diseases and other gastrointestinal infections are incredibly common in all parts of the Indian subcontinent. Travellers' diarrhoea and more serious conditions such as typhoid (of which there are not infrequent outbreaks in J&K) come from getting bacteria in your mouth. To minimise the risk, you should ensure that you observe good hygiene practices, such as regular hand washing,

ALTITUDE SICKNESS

Acute mountain sickness (AMS or altitude sickness) can occur at any altitude above 3,000m, so visitors to almost any part of Ladakh and Zanskar, as well as the higher peaks in Kashmir, are at risk. Symptoms include headache, nausea and confusion and can herald the onset of high-altitude cerebral edema (HACE) and high-altitude pulmonary edema (HAPE), both of which can result in death. Further information on AMS is available from the Academic Unit of Respiratory Medicine (w altitude.org), the British Mountaineering Council (w thebmc.co.uk) and Medex (w medex.org.uk).

SYMPTOMS OF AMS If you spend more than six hours at an altitude of 2,500m or more, you may start to experience headaches, nausea and vomiting, loss of appetite, fatigue, breathlessness and inability to sleep. Those with asthma, diabetes, epilepsy and existing heart and lung conditions, or who are pregnant, are at particular risk of developing these symptoms.

PREVENTION OF AMS The single most important piece of advice is to take time to acclimatise. If you are travelling by land, increase your altitude steadily, and if you are flying straight to a high-altitude destination such as Leh, spend at least two to three days acclimatising there before going any higher. Get lots of rest, drink plenty of fluids (but avoid alcohol), eat lightly and do only gentle exercise while you are acclimatising. If gradual ascent is not possible, you may also consider taking acetazolamide (Diamox), which can be prescribed by your GP or at a travel clinic.

TREATMENT OF AMS If you are suffering the early symptoms of AMS, stop and do not go any higher. Always seek advice. You may be advised to rest for 24 hours, drink plenty of fluids and to take ibuprofen or paracetamol to treat your headaches to see if your symptoms improve. You may also be advised to descend 500m straight away.

HACE AND HAPE Left untreated, AMS can develop into the far more serious HACE (gathering of fluid on the brain) and HAPE (gathering of fluid in the lungs). Both of these conditions are medical emergencies and can be fatal if not treated quickly. Sufferers would need to be rapidly evacuated to lower altitude by stretcher or helicopter, as continued physical exertion would worsen their condition.

using bottled water (including for cleaning teeth), and avoiding foods of doubtful provenance. Many travellers use the following maxim to remind them what is safe:

PEEL IT, BOIL IT, COOK IT OR FORGET IT

This means that fruit you have washed and peeled yourself, and hot foods, should be safe but raw foods, cold cooked foods, salads, ice cream and ice are all risky, and foods kept lukewarm in hotel buffets often harbour numerous bugs. That said, plenty of travellers and expatriates enjoy fruit and vegetables, so do keep a sense of perspective: even street food, if deep fried in front of you and eaten then and there, can be perfectly safe.

If you are struck down with diarrhoea in spite of your precautions, remember that dehydration is your greatest concern. Drink lots of clear fluids. Sachets of oral rehydration salts give the perfect biochemical mix to replace all the fluids you are losing. If you don't have rehydration salts, or can't stand the taste, any dilute mixture of sugar and salt in water will do you good: try Coke or orange squash with a three-finger pinch of salt added to each glass (if you are salt-depleted you won't taste the salt). Alternatively you can add eight level teaspoons of sugar (18g) and one level teaspoon of salt (3g) to one litre (five cups) of safe water. A squeeze of lemon or orange juice improves the taste and adds potassium, which is also lost if you have diarrhoea. Drink two large glasses after every bowel action, and more if you are thirsty.

These solutions are still absorbed well even if you are vomiting, but you will need to take small sips at a time or you will bring it straight back up again. Even if you are not eating you need to drink three litres a day plus whatever is pouring into the toilet. If you are in any doubt, look at the colour of your urine. If it is anything other than clear and colourless, you need to drink more, and this is a helpful reminder even when you're feeling perfectly healthy. If you feel like eating, take a bland, high-carbohydrate diet. Plain rice, dry bread or digestive biscuits are ideal.

If the diarrhoea is bad, or you are passing blood or slime, or you have a fever, you will probably need antibiotics in addition to fluid replacement as you are likely to have dysentery. Consult a doctor as soon as possible. There is a lot of resistance in India to ciprofloxacin so this is not recommended in J&K. If you do want to take something with you then azithromycin (a stat dose of 2 x 250mg) would be suitable for both dysentery and travellers' diarrhoea. If you think you have dysentery you should always seek medical advice before taking the antibiotics unless you are more than 24 hours from help.

Prickly heat All parts of J&K, including mountainous areas such as Ladakh, can become exceptionally hot in summer: temperatures well above 40°C are not unknown. A fine pimply rash on the chest or forearms is likely to be heat rash;

AVOIDING INSECT BITES

Although J&K is not an area with a high risk of malaria, mosquitoes can carry other diseases such as dengue fever, Zika virus and Japanese encephalitis, and their bites are, in any case, an irritation and liable to become infected in the heat. As the sun is going down, put on long clothes and apply repellent on any exposed flesh. Pack a DEET-based insect repellent: roll-ons or stick are the least messy preparations for travelling, though, providing you can find a way of stopping them leaking, the sprays have best coverage. Repellents should contain between 50% and 55% DEET and can still be used for children and pregnant women.

Insect coils, battery-operated devices and fans reduce rather than eliminate bites. Travel clinics usually sell a good range of nets, treatment kits and repellents.

Mosquitoes and many other insects are attracted to light. If you are camping, never put a lamp near the opening of your tent, or you will have a swarm of bloodsucking bedfellows waiting to join you when you retire. In hotel rooms, be aware that the longer your light is on, the greater the number of insects will be sharing your accommodation.

LONG-HAUL FLIGHTS, CLOTS AND DVT

Any prolonged immobility, including travel by land or air, can result in deep-vein thrombosis (DVT), with the risk of embolus to the lungs. Certain factors can increase the risk and these include:

- History of DVT or pulmonary embolism
- Recent surgery to pelvic region or legs
- Cancer
- Stroke
- Heart disease
- Inherited tendency to clot (thrombophilia)
- Obesity
- Pregnancy
- Hormone therapy
- Older age
- Being over 1.83m (6ft) or under 1.52m (5ft)

A DVT causes painful swelling and redness of the calf or sometimes the thigh. It is only dangerous if a clot travels to the lungs (pulmonary embolus). Symptoms of a pulmonary embolus – which commonly start three to ten days after a long flight – include chest pain, shortness of breath and sometimes coughing up small amounts of blood. Anyone who thinks that they might have a DVT needs to see a doctor immediately.

PREVENTION OF DVT
- Wear loose comfortable clothing
- Do anti-DVT exercises and move around when possible
- Drink plenty of fluids during the flight
- Avoid taking sleeping pills unless you are able to lie flat
- Avoid excessive tea, coffee and alcohol
- Consider wearing flight socks or support stockings, widely available from pharmacies

If you think you are at increased risk of a clot, ask your doctor if it is safe to travel.

it is caused by sweat becoming trapped beneath the skin and causing a histamine reaction. Cool showers, dabbing dry and talcum powder (usually available in local pharmacies) will help. Treat the problem by wearing only loose, 100%-cotton clothes and, if it is at all possible, sleeping naked under a fan. An antihistamine tablet may help reduce the itching, as will hydrocortisone cream or Sudocrem.

Sunstroke and dehydration The sun in J&K can be very harsh, even in the mountains where the lower temperatures may suggest otherwise. Sunstroke and dehydration are serious risks.

Wearing a hat, long loose sleeves and sunscreen helps to avoid sunburn. Prolonged unprotected exposure can result in heatstroke, which is potentially fatal. Try to stay out of the sun between noon and 15.00 when the rays are at their strongest.

In the heat you sweat more, so dehydration is likely. Don't rely on feeling thirsty to tell you to drink – if your urine is anything other than colourless and odourless then you aren't drinking enough. Carry bottled water with you at all times and make sure you stop to drink it. For advice on rehydration, see page 45.

Tetanus Tetanus is caused by the *Clostridium tetani* bacterium and though it can accumulate on a variety of surfaces, it is most commonly associated with rusty objects such as nails. Cutting yourself or otherwise puncturing the skin brings the bacteria inside the body, where they will thrive. Clean any cuts thoroughly with a strong antiseptic.

Immunisation against tetanus gives good protection for ten years, and it is standard care practice in many places to give a booster injection to any patient with a puncture wound. Symptoms of tetanus may include lockjaw, spasms in any part of the body, excessive sweating, drooling and incontinence, and the disease results in death if left untreated.

Mild cases of tetanus will be treated with the antibiotic metronidazole and tetanus immunoglobulin, while more severe cases will require admission to intensive care, tetanus immunoglobulin injected into the spinal cord, a tracheotomy and mechanical ventilation, intravenous magnesium and diazepam.

SAFETY

Ladakh, Zanskar and Jammu city are all safe areas in which to travel (altitude issues aside), but Kashmir and the rest of Jammu can be a different matter. The security situation in this part of India is fluid, and it is particularly important to check the situation before venturing to Srinagar. Due to a recent upsurge in violence at the time of going to print (see box, page iii), most Western governments were advising against all but essential travel to Srinagar, Gulmarg and other areas within the Kashmir Valley. Ignoring this advice could make your travel insurance invalid. Note, too, that some Western governments were also warning about travelling to areas outside the city in Jammu.

When violence does occur in the state it is not targeted at foreign tourists, though two British nationals were killed during a grenade attack on a minibus in Bijbehara, a village in Anantnag district, in July 2012.

The three greatest threats to the safety of tourists in J&K are natural disasters, being caught up in local protests and road accidents.

NATURAL DISASTERS The area suffered a major earthquake in 2005 which measured 7.6 on the Richter scale and killed between 86,000 and 87,000 people. Smaller earthquakes occur frequently, often causing loss of life due to collapsed buildings and landslides on mountain roads. Flooding, caused both by glacial meltwater and heavy rains, is equally commonplace. If you plan to travel in mountainous areas in particular, you should pay attention to the weather forecast and avoid travelling during bad weather. The same applies whether you are driving or on foot: numerous pilgrims die each year trying to complete the Amarnath *yatra* or pilgrimage (see box, page 184) because they ignore weather warnings and are caught by the snow and ice.

LOCAL PROTESTS AND RIOTS These occur frequently, especially in Srinagar and the Kashmir Valley. Though they are frequently publicised in the media as clashes between the police and terrorists, local people often disagree, citing police brutality, corruption or communal issues as the real causes. In any case, such incidents can and do turn violent, and so you should avoid getting too close to either protestors or uniformed officials. Avoid areas where there is a strike, and if there is a curfew imposed, remain in your hotel.

ROAD SAFETY Driving in India instils fear in even the most seasoned travellers, and hence hiring a car and driver together is far more common than elsewhere in the world. Roads in J&K are frequently poorly maintained, especially in more remote areas, riddled with pot-holes and at risk of flooding and landslides. Street lights are a rarity, and other people on the roads may not have lights on their vehicles (or herds of goats, which they seem to like moving after dark). Plan your journeys so that you can leave and arrive during daylight hours. If you are hiring a taxi, check the vehicle yourself (see box, page 56), and make sure the driver is both competent and sober. If you are in any doubt, find another taxi, as you will need all your wits about you to keep a car on the road even when the weather is fair.

WOMEN TRAVELLERS Women usually travel in India trouble-free: people are typically conservative but are used to seeing both local and foreign women travelling independently, working in all occupations and taking prominent roles in both politics and the media. It is often possible for females to get a seat in women-only compartments on trains, join women-only queues and, where the latter are not available, queue-jump straight to the front to avoid waiting among unfamiliar men. Privately, however, attitudes towards women are more old-fashioned: many families expect their daughters-in-law to give up working after marriage and to look after elderly relatives. Dowry payments are still often required when a girl gets married, despite the practice being illegal, and violence against women, particularly in the home, is high. Friendships between men and women are not encouraged and, thanks to years of damaging stereotypes in the Indian media, foreign women who are open and friendly towards Indian men, even in a solely platonic way, are seen to be 'easy'.

Some foreign women do report verbal and occasionally physical harassment, particularly when wearing clothing that shows their shoulders or legs, or when visiting bars and clubs. This kind of abuse is more common in larger cities such as Delhi.

In recent years there have been a number of more high-profile attacks on women in India, including serious sexual attacks on tourists. If you are attacked, the police number to call is ☎ 100 (112 from mobile phones). You should also contact your embassy (page 35) for consular assistance and support.

LGBTQ+ TRAVELLERS India decriminalised homosexuality in 2009 and Delhi's first Pride Parade (now an annual event) took place the same year. However, in December 2013 the Supreme Court overturned the legislation, re-criminalising gay sex, leading to protests around the world and a backlash in the Indian media. After five years of debate and legal challenges, in September 2018 the country's Supreme Court unanimously ruled to decriminalise homosexuality.

There is a burgeoning gay scene in many of India's larger cities (Mumbai is the undisputed gay capital) and there are now a number of LGBTQ+ travel agents in India that are part of the International Gay & Lesbian Travel Association (w iglta. org). That said, regardless of the law, most of India's LGBTQ+ community continue to keep their sexuality very private. Most people remain deeply conservative on the issue and coming out is generally considered to bring shame on a family. While two men holding hands or sharing a room will not raise eyebrows, open displays of affection most certainly will. Verbal harassment is common (though more likely to be suffered by locals) and police harassment is also a possibility.

Kashmir in particular is more intolerant of LGBTQ+ travellers than many other parts of J&K and the rest of India in general.

TRAVELLING WITH A DISABILITY
While it is possible to travel in India if you have a disability, it certainly isn't easy. Poor infrastructure and health-care facilities pose difficulties for all visitors, and the challenges are undoubtedly magnified if you have a physical disability. Hotels, tourist sites and public places are rarely wheelchair accessible and little if any assistance is provided for those with hearing or sight problems. There is widespread discrimination against those with disabilities, with many people believing that a disability is the result of wrongdoing in a previous life. India has no welfare support for those with disabilities and consequently many disabled people resort to begging on the streets.

If you do travel to Kashmir, you will need to plan ahead and make sure all transport and accommodation providers are briefed about your needs well in advance. Airlines and upper-end hotels are generally helpful provided you give them time to prepare and are explicit about what you need. For tips about travelling with a wheelchair, and for details of wheelchair-accessible hotels, contact **Accessible Journeys** (35 West Sellers Av, Ridley Pk, PA 19078, USA; ☏ +1 800 846 4537; e sales@accessiblejourneys.com; w accessiblejourneys.com). The UK's **gov.uk** website (w gov.uk/guidance/foreign-travel-for-disabled-people) also provides general advice and practical information for travellers with disabilities preparing for overseas travel.

TRAVELLING WITH CHILDREN   *With thanks to Hilary Stock*
Because of the dangers of altitude mountain sickness (AMS), this destination is not recommended for babies or children too young to communicate symptoms (really anyone under the age of about nine or ten). For older children and teenagers, though, it is a dream destination. There are abundant homestays, allowing families to gain unprecedented access to the local culture. Accommodation is cheap, the food is more child-friendly in Ladakh and Kashmir than in much of the rest of India and activities abound: cycling, river rafting, camping, trekking, sightseeing, shopping in markets.

There has been little research into the effects on children of the popular drug Diamox, which counters the effects of AMS. Better to do a gradual, drug-free ascent if possible, or if you fly in, be sure to block off at least three days on arrival to do nothing but acclimatise.

Teenagers are said to suffer more from AMS than younger children or adults. Try to be clear of any international jet lag before travelling to the region as it can muddle symptoms. AMS can sound frightening and should be taken seriously, but it's the only health hurdle you have to deal with in order to access one of the most beautiful and welcoming areas in the world. (And some children don't suffer at all.)

High-altitude desert in summertime is a good climate for travelling with children as long as you're equipped properly. Travel light and efficiently, but be warned: appropriate clothing might not be a teenager's idea of fashion. The sun is extreme, so pack good sunglasses and wide-brimmed hats, and the very highest factor suncreams and lipsalves. Take any children's medicines with you. Dehydration is a challenge. Children are particularly vulnerable and need to be reminded constantly to drink water.

WHAT TO TAKE

You may wish to consider taking the following items, in addition to your usual packing.

- **Plug adaptors** Sockets across India are the twin round pin, continental European type. The voltage is 220v. Look for an adaptor that fits close to the wall as sockets are often loose and the weight of plug plus adaptor may frustratingly pull out of the wall.
- **A torch** Many parts of Kashmir, including city streets, are unlit at night, and pavements may conceal dangers such as uncovered manholes and other trip

TREKKING KIT

There are numerous online and high-street retailers selling hiking and winter sports wear, though some of it definitely veers more towards fashion than functionality. If you don't know exactly what you need, or simply want advice on how your boots, rucksack, etc should fit, the following companies have knowledgeable staff and will take the time to talk you through what's right for you and your trip.

Blacks w blacks.co.uk. High-street brand with enthusiastic staff. Wait for the sales when prices are heavily discounted.
Keela w keela.co.uk. Brightly coloured fleeces & affordable base layers & socks.

Mountain Warehouse w mountainwarehouse.com. Cheap & cheerful outdoor clothing and accessories.
Rohan w rohan.co.uk. High-quality outdoor clothing & footwear. Ideal for trekking. UK supplier of Eagle Creek products.

In our experience, the two items that make the biggest difference to your trekking experience are your boots and socks. Boots need to be strong and give support to your ankles but still flexible enough to be comfortable as you move. Choose a pair with good grip and ideally with a fully waterproof upper, as tromping around with sodden feet is miserable. Pick socks with a high percentage of natural fibres so that your feet can breathe. Specialist hiking socks (as opposed to general sports socks) are reinforced in just the right places and so reduce the chance of blisters. You should also pack:

- Breathable base layers
- Fleeces (one thick, one thin)
- Thermals (one or two thermal tops and at colder times of year thermal under-trousers)
- A waterproof (and ideally windproof) outer layer
- Sunscreen and sunglasses
- A durable water bottle with internal filter and/or purification tablets
- High-energy snacks such as dried fruits, nuts and energy bars
- A map, compass and GPS unit
- First-aid kit (see box, page 43)

However long or short your intended trek, always tell someone where you are going, the route you plan to take and how long you expect it to take.

hazards. Power cuts are commonplace too. If you are planning to camp, or stay in rural areas, you'll need a torch to navigate to the latrine at night. A head torch is especially useful as it leaves your hands free.

- **Mosquito repellent** Kashmir may not be a malarial area, but the swarms of mosquitoes you may encounter in summer among its lakes and forests can still impair enjoyment of your holiday. Make sure you pack long-sleeved shirts (you'll also need these for visiting conservative areas and religious places).
- **Warm clothing** If you are going anywhere other than Jammu, pack plenty of warm layers, whatever time of year you are travelling. The weather can turn quite unexpectedly in the mountains, temperatures often plummet at night, and even in Srinagar September rains can turn to biting hail. Several thinner layers are better than one thick layer.
- **Good footwear** In winter, wear rubber-soled boots, preferably lined with fleece. If you are trekking, good hiking boots are essential (see the box opposite for more detailed kit advice).
- **Flip-flops** You'll need these if you're planning to visit temples and mosques, as unlacing and removing boots every time you want to step across the threshold is a faff. They also come in useful in less than savoury bathrooms, which are numerous.

If you will be staying in bottom-range accommodation, a **sheet sleeping bag**, of the kind used by youth hostellers, can help save you from grubby bedding. A **universal sink plug** is also worth packing.

Good **suncream**, **lipsalve** and **sunglasses** are essential in the mountains: the glare of the sun is harsh, and you will burn quickly. **Toilet paper**, **wet wipes** and **hand sanitiser gel** are highly advisable and will make staying clean infinitely easier. **Dental floss** and a **needle**, a roll of **gaffer tape** and a packet of **cable ties** will enable you to fix almost anything while you're on the go. A small **penknife** or **multi-tool** also comes in handy, but don't forget to pack it in your hold luggage before flying.

Small **gift items** related to your home country make ideal presents for hosts: consider taking tea towels featuring cathedrals, boxes of fudge, snow globes with castles, and a few snapshots of your family and home.

What you pack your gear into will depend in large part on the sort of activities you'll be undertaking. If you're taking a leisurely trip with hotel accommodation and a car and driver, a standard suitcase will be fine. If you're travelling more by public transport, a strong duffle bag (with or without wheels) or rucksack will be easier to manhandle on and off buses and jeeps, and will squish under seats or lie across laps more comfortably.

MONEY

India's currency is the rupee (Rs). Each rupee is made up of 100 paisa. Paper notes come in denominations of 5, 10, 20, 50, 100, 500 and 1,000, and the standard issue (ie: non-commemorative) coins are Rs1, 2 and 5. These days it is very rare to actually see coins of less than Rs1 in face value as they are virtually worthless, and only the 50 paisa coin remains legal tender. On the rare occasions that your shopping does not come to an exact number of rupees, the vendor will either round the figure to the nearest whole number or give you a sweet with your change.

The rupee is currently reasonably stable against foreign currencies. The exchange rates given here were correct at the time of going to print (September 2019), but you are advised to check the latest rates online, in the newspapers or with the banks before changing money.

£1 = Rs87   €1 = Rs79   US$1 = Rs72

WHAT TO CARRY Currency controls prevent you being able to exchange Indian rupees abroad. Consequently, you will not be able to buy rupees from a bureau de change before you go.

There are several ways to get rupees once you have arrived in India: withdraw them from an ATM; get a cash advance on your Visa or MasterCard in a bank; or change foreign notes with a local bank or money agent. ATMs are widespread in almost all towns and usually well stocked. Many of them are inside small booths but are accessible 24 hours a day if you swipe your bank card in the lock on the door. Before you leave home, check with your bank as to their charges for accessing funds from abroad as these can mount up quickly.

Hotels and travel agents are increasingly able to process card payments, which reduces the amount of cash you will need to carry. That said, the card machines are dependent on the electricity and phone lines working, and you will always need cash on hand for taxis, meals and buying small items in shops.

Although travellers' cheques were popular in the past, they are increasingly difficult to change. It is normally only possible to process them in the larger banks, and even then you will usually get a poor exchange rate. Our advice is to forget about travellers' cheques.

CHANGING MONEY Money changers are as omnipresent as mosquitoes, and every town has a wealth of places where you can change foreign currency, from banks to travel agents to cyber cafés. US dollars, euros and sterling are all easily exchanged; other currencies are exchangeable, but you may have to haggle harder for a fair rate.

Changing larger denomination notes (fifties and hundreds) tends to be easier than fives and tens as they are considered less likely to be forged. For the same reason, money changers also have a preference for dollar bills printed after 2010. Try to keep your foreign currency notes flat and clean: those that are torn or marked (even with a cashier's pen) may not be accepted.

BUDGETING

Whether you are scraping by on a backpacker's budget or have a king's ransom to spend, J&K has plenty of options for you.

Although India, and J&K in particular, is not as cheap as it was just a few years ago, backpackers can still survive on Rs1,500–3,000 per day. For this you'll be able to get a dorm bed or share a basic twin room in a guesthouse, eat simple, vegetarian meals and travel by public buses. Now and then you'll be able to have a beer, and you'll have change to make donations when sightseeing in gompas and temples. With a daily budget of Rs4,000–8,000 you can travel comfortably, sharing a room in a mid-range hotel, eating varied meals in restaurants (where tipping is typically 10%) and travelling in a mixture of buses and shared taxis. If you keep your costs down in the towns, you'll then be able to afford to do some trekking, especially if you have your own equipment and are happy joining a group.

Costs start to rise if you want to get away from the main towns. Taxi rates are relatively high but are frequently your only means of getting somewhere. Tented camps in the Nubra Valley and southern lakes charge disproportionate sums for what you actually get, and as there's an absence of food shops and restaurants you'll probably have to pay for a hotel meal plan.

At the upper end of the scale, Leh, Srinagar and Jammu all have hotels with rooms of upwards of Rs10,000 per night. Hiring a car and driver maximises your flexibility, and you may consider taking a domestic flight if time is of the essence. Genuine pashminas and silk Kashmiri carpets are more affordable here than elsewhere in the world, but they still come with a hefty price tag, and of course you have to pay to ship the latter home.

To give you a sense of small spends, the following prices were accurate for basic items at the time of writing.

Bottle of water (1 litre)	Rs15
Bottle of beer (½ litre)	Rs120
Fresh juice (0.3 litres)	Rs50
Genuine pashmina	Rs4,000+
Papier mâché box (small)	Rs200
Petrol (1 litre)	Rs77
Phone call (local)	Rs5
Phone call (international)	Rs10
Plate of *momos* (vegetarian)	Rs120
Postcard	Rs15
Stamp (international)	Rs25
Tailor-made shirt	Rs1,000
Tailor-made suit (three-piece)	Rs8,000
Wi-Fi (1 hour)	Rs40

GETTING AROUND

J&K is a large state and transport infrastructure is relatively poor. Journeys by road are often long and uncomfortable, regardless of your means of transport, as even the national highways are narrow and badly maintained. Accidents and road closures are frequent. Take local advice on the latest journey times, depart early in the morning if you have a long way to travel and make sure you've got a really good book (other than this one, obviously) to help pass the hours.

BY AIR Jammu, Leh and Srinagar all have civilian airports and domestic flights link them together, as well as to other parts of India. Flights are most regular in the summer months when customer demand is highest (and prices also increase), so you may need to book well in advance to guarantee a seat. The flight from Srinagar to Leh takes an hour and costs from Rs4,000 each way; flights between Jammu and Leh take 1 hour 20 minutes and tickets start from Rs5,600. There are around five to six flights daily from Srinagar and Jammu (around an hour), with prices starting from Rs2,300 and flights taking from 30 minutes to just over an hour. See individual chapters for more information on flights between Jammu, Leh and Srinagar.

Tickets can be booked online via the Indian travel portals of w yatra.com and w makemytrip.com (both of which include tickets for India's budget airlines) and the individual airline websites (see page 37 for contact details), as well as from airport ticketing desks and through local travel agents.

Security is particularly strict on flights originating in J&K due to terrorism fears, so check airline baggage regulations before travelling. Note that you are usually required to have both a print-out of your ticket (even for e-tickets) and your passport in order to gain access to the departure terminal.

BY ROAD The best roads in J&K are the national highways: NH1A in the west between Jammu and Srinagar, and NH1 from Srinagar to Leh via Kargil. These roads carry a mixture of trucks, taxis and private vehicles, as well as frequent military convoys driving between the different military bases. Though mostly covered with tarmac, the surfaces are far from smooth, with pot-holes a common hazard. In the narrowest sections there is not enough space for a vehicle to overtake, and high passes are forced to close when it snows.

Away from these highways, the road conditions deteriorate further. Many roads are unmade, making for very slow progress, and some quite important routes, including the main road from Kargil to Zanskar, are closed completely throughout the winter months, reopening again only in late spring.

By bus The JKSRTC (w jksrtc.co.in) operates a reasonable network of buses between J&K's main towns, and they typically stop in the larger villages en route too. Public buses are the cheapest way to travel and depending on the type of bus (standard, deluxe, coach, etc) you might even get your own seat. Larger items of luggage (and occasionally additional passengers) travel on the roof, so buy a small padlock for your rucksack or case and keep valuables inside the bus with you.

Given the winding roads and tendencies of the bus drivers, you may consider taking anti travel-sickness medication, even if you don't normally feel nauseous in the car. It may also come in handy for other passengers, as will wet wipes and tissues, and given your close proximity to them it's in your own best interest to share.

Details on individual bus routes, journey times and ticket prices are given in the *Getting there* sections of each chapter in *Part Two*. However, as a guide for a standard coach or bus ticket (one way), prices start from:

HOW FAR IS...?	
Jammu to Kargil	497km
Jammu to Leh	727km
Jammu to Padum	737km
Jammu to Srinagar	293km
Leh to Kargil	234km
Leh to Padum	474km
Leh to Srinagar	434km
Srinagar to Kargil	204km
Srinagar to Padum	444km
Padum to Kargil	230km

Gulmarg to Srinagar	Rs146
Katra to Jammu	Rs44
Jammu to Srinagar	Rs230
Kargil to Padum	Rs350
Kargil to Srinagar	Rs357
Leh to Srinagar	Rs737
Pahalgam to Srinagar	Rs153
Sonamarg to Srinagar	Rs153
Srinagar to Yusmarg	Rs146

By taxi Leh, Kargil and Zanskar all have their own taxi unions, which set rates and other taxi-related regulations, including which taxis can go where. The regulations are designed to protect local drivers from outsiders stealing their business but can be infuriating for visitors forced to change taxis to continue their journey or prevented from using their original car and driver for both outward and return journeys.

That said, you quickly get used to the system, and the fixed rates remove the usual hassle of haggling over price. Taxis can be either cars or minivans, and drivers have to be registered. The drivers frequently speak a few words of English, and some are knowledgeable about local sites and culture, acting as informal guides for their passengers. They know where to stay and where to eat and, on the whole, we consider their standard of driving to be high by regional standards.

If you have a car and driver for several days, it is appropriate to tip the driver at the end of your trip, even if you've prepaid an agent for a package. We work on the basis of Rs400 tip per day and it's always gratefully received.

Full details on the routes, driving times and prices are given in the *Getting there* sections of each chapter in *Part Two*. For hiring a small car or van, minimum one-way prices on the inter-city routes are given below. Note that due to the fact fares are set by the individual taxi unions, prices sometimes change depending on the direction you are travelling.

Jammu to Srinagar	Rs5,000
Kargil to Padum	Rs14,000
Kargil to Srinagar	Rs6,400
Leh to Kargil	Rs7,749
Srinagar to Leh	Rs14,828

Self-drive Though it is possible to hire just a car in India, more often you get a car and driver together (page 41). If you do get a self-drive hire car then it would only be through a big international agency in a city like Delhi, so you won't be able to venture much beyond the city with the car. The reality is, for all intents and purposes, car hire means car and driver hire and this is available in almost every tourist town across the entire country. It is likely then that if you are driving yourself you have bought or imported your own vehicle, or are driving the car of a friend.

EU driving licences (which currently includes UK photo-card driving licences, but things might change if and when the UK leaves the EU) are valid in India, though you may wish to get an International Driving Licence before leaving home. In the UK these are available from the RAC and some larger post offices.

If you are bringing your vehicle into India from another country, you will need to purchase a *carnet de passage en douanes*, or 'carnet' for short. This document, also available from the RAC, is a waiver for import duty and guarantees you will remove the vehicle from India at the end of your trip. The cost of the 'carnet' is

- Drive a car that is common in the local area: you won't stand out and if you break down the parts and expertise to repair it are more likely to be available.
- Check you have a spare tyre, jack and wheel wrench. Spare oil and water, a tow rope, a jerrycan of fuel and a shovel are also highly advisable.
- If you have the option, get central locking, electric windows and air conditioning: they give you greater control over what (and, indeed, who) comes into the vehicle with you.
- Make sure you know the rules of the road and have a good idea about where you are going. Tell someone you trust your route and your expected time of arrival.
- Carry your driving licence and any vehicle documentation with you at all times. Photocopies are useful for handing to police and other interested parties.
- Ensure there is a first-aid kit, food and plenty of drinking water in the boot in case of emergencies.
- A mobile phone is essential in the event of an accident or a breakdown you can't fix by the side of the road. Unless you have a garage's number already, your best bet would be to call a large hotel in the nearest town or city and ask them for a recommendation.
- If you're planning on heading into remoter areas or along quieter backroads, check with locals first as to where fuel is available.

determined by the value of your vehicle and full details are available on the RAC's website (w rac.co.uk).

The rules of the road are theoretically very similar to those in the UK, and vehicles are supposed to drive on the left. The reality is that people drive wherever there are fewest pot-holes and rules are typically observed only when a policeman is watching. Driving anywhere in India, and especially in the mountainous parts of J&K, is not for the faint-hearted.

By bike You would have to be exceptionally fit and not just a little bit mad to consider cycling in Ladakh and Kashmir. The roads are badly maintained, the motorists homicidal and the altitude is an additional hurdle. In spite of all this, you will still see cyclists on the road – all of them are foreigners, and most of them undertaking epic bicycle journeys across India, Asia or around the world.

It is possible to hire bicycles in Leh (page 76). These are mountain bikes rather than road bikes, and rentals are typically by the day, though you can request longer packages. Demand and wear a helmet, regardless of how silly you think you look, and make sure you have spare inner tubes and the tools required to fix a punctured tyre. Do not, under any circumstances, cycle at night or be tempted to undertake other vehicles, regardless of how slowly they are moving.

If you are considering bringing your own bike to Kashmir, take all spare parts with you. The boneshaking roads take their toll on bikes as well as bodies, and replacement parts are not always available locally. If you forget something or something breaks, it would have to be couriered to you from Delhi or even from abroad.

There are one or two tour companies running cycling trips in Ladakh. The best are probably those organised by Kathmandu-based Kamzang Journeys (page 34).

MAPS J&K has been well mapped. The majority of the roads appear on national road atlases, free tourist maps show the major towns and tourist sites, and specialist trekking maps show the topography and trekking routes.

General maps of the area are available in bookshops in Leh and to a lesser extent in other big towns, as well as in souvenir shops elsewhere. If you require a specific map (and in particular large-scale trekking maps) you would be advised to order them before leaving home to ensure you can get the ones you want. If you plan to do extreme trekking beyond the established routes, military-grade maps produced by cartographers from the Soviet Union are held in some national libraries and can be scanned or photocopied, though they are not commercially available.

When looking at state-wide maps, be cognisant of the fact that many of those published in India do not show the Line of Control (LoC) with Pakistan. All parts of Greater Kashmir, including the states of Azad Kashmir and Gilgit-Baltistan,

---

HITCHHIKING IN LADAKH AND KASHMIR   *Steve Dew-Jones*

'Nothing comes for free in India – you'll never hitchhike there!' These were the words of encouragement I received as I prepared to leave Lahore in Pakistan to make for the Indian border.

But in fact hitchhiking in India's mountainous north proved rather straightforward. This may in part have been down to the advantage of having a white face and thus becoming an object of interest to many who picked me up. But beyond that, in India there seems to be a general appreciation for the concept of hitchhiking.

Perhaps the practice doesn't exist in quite the same way as in Europe but standing by the side of the road with thumb outstretched seems to do the trick, and Indians seem to translate the enterprise through the use of the word 'lift' – pronounced 'leafed'.

There were a few occasions when the driver seemed bemused by the concept of a 'lift' without payment, but it is always a good idea in Asia to clarify before the start of the journey whether you expect to pay.

If you do not, the phrase 'rupee nahi' (literally: money none) will clarify your intentions and cause the driver either to speed off in a bemused rage (seemingly indignant that someone could envisage being given a ride without wishing to pay for the service) or to invite you in with a welcoming shrug of the shoulders.

Beyond this, the same rules and advice apply to Kashmir as to anywhere else in the world. Top tips include standing in a visible position (not the middle of the road), making sure there is space for drivers to pull in on either side of where you are standing, and having a few words of the native language under your belt (20 words can get you a surprisingly long way) to ease negotiations over direction and any monetary contribution you do or do not wish to make.

Patience, as ever, is a virtue when hitchhiking. Try to make sure your driver takes you to a helpful spot, although this may be hard to communicate. Where possible, aim for petrol stations or main roads leading out of town (in the direction you wish to travel), and make sure you have a map.

It is never possible to recommend hitchhiking without a word of caution, due to the inherent risks involved, but this writer believes it is both possible and a lot of fun, wherever you are in the world.

You wake up in a tent, under a bridge or in a bush and think, 'Where shall I go today?' Mounting your steed, bags loaded behind you and only a map in front, all you have to do is choose. Overland travel by motorbike is quite possibly the most liberating form of travel: there's something about being able to reach out and touch what's around you.

Kashmir is wild country and driving here in or on anything is not to be underestimated. Forging these roads from mountains that are constantly trying to reclaim them is an ongoing task and as such many areas are not metalled. At the time of research, many roads, including key stretches such as the Zojila Pass between Kargil and Srinagar, were still unsurfaced. Trepidation is advisable, but if historic and frankly amazing-sounding names mean that you just can't help yourself, then here's some advice.

Take care with the seasons. Some parts of J&K are affected by the monsoon, and large parts of the state are under thick snow in winter. When the snow begins to melt, the roads all around Leh as well as many other areas churn into mud. Rain adds weight to the soil and this season often sees the most landslides, which can stop your journey for days. Last time I rode in Kashmir it froze, then snowed hard, and I had trouble escaping Manali with my fingertips intact, so avoid the winter months too.

Few local bikes are safe in this region so it is best to source a suitable bike and fly it (or, even better, ride it) to Kashmir. If you have to buy or hire locally, look for something with long suspension, a front disc brake, a big front wheel and a rack or some other way of carrying your kit, as keeping it on your back is not a good idea. Before you leave, make sure you check the lights and horn (the louder the better), the front and back brakes (it's a long way down those precipices), the suspension (you're going to need it) and that the chain is in good condition with plenty of oil. Make sure the wheels are round (seriously) and, if you're going on broken roads, that you have knobbly or new tyres with lots of tread. If the bike looks too old, is making particularly odd noises or rattles on tarmac, find something better. Traffic is rare and mechanics are only to be found in big towns. There are more fulfilling things than finishing an epic journey with your bike in the back of a truck.

Before you leave, ask yourself lots of questions. What's my fuel range? Do I know how to repair a puncture? How will I navigate? What if it snows? Do people know where I'm going and what time I'll check in with them? Do I have more than enough clothes to be warm and dry? Will I need a sleeping bag?

Be aware of the distances and the time it takes to travel between them. Kargil to Padum is only 230km but can easily take a motorcyclist two, or even three, days to

are shown included within India's borders, causing confusion for visitors who would in reality not be able to cross the LoC, but would have to travel south to Wagah, enter Pakistan with a Pakistani visa, and again travel north from there.

ACCOMMODATION

J&K offers all manner of accommodation, from mats on dirt floors to luxury hotels, monastic cells and floating palaces. In peak season the best options can get booked up well in advance, but you'll always be able to find a room somewhere at a price you can more or less afford.

travel safely, especially as you should be off the road before it gets dark. En route you can be struck by anything from falling debris to a herd of goats. If that sort of thing excites you, get to it.

ESSENTIAL EQUIPMENT
Spare key
Puncture repair kit
Engine oil
Covers for baggage rack
Basic tools (spanners, pliers, screwdrivers)
Emergency food and water
Reliable map and compass (1:500,000 or less)

EXCEPTIONALLY USEFUL EQUIPMENT
Duct tape
WD40 and grease
Zipties
Spare throttle and clutch cables
Spark plugs
Spare bulbs

CLOTHING
Helmet with visor, goggles or sunglasses (for dust)
Thick bike gloves (& thin inner gloves for when cold)
Hardwearing jacket
Jeans (or similar) with over-trousers
Sturdy walking boots or biker boots
Thermal layers
Fleece jacket

The kit listed here is the absolute minimum for a short ride. Anyone wishing to go a long distance should read *The Adventure Motorcycling Handbook* by Chris Scott for practical information on bikes, preparation and maintenance, as well as known trips and overland adventure stories. The website w horizonsunlimited.com is an unparalleled resource for up-to-date overland information, and w advrider.com offers plenty of inspiration.

Don't drive after dark, and keep it rubber side down.

If you're travelling on a **shoestring**, find a buddy so you can split the room rates. The cheaper guesthouses and many homestays offer rooms, often with breakfast included, for less than Rs800, and many of the monasteries have space where visitors can stay in exchange for a small donation. Look out too for the hotels aimed at domestic pilgrims: in Jammu in particular there are a number of hotels with dormitories as well as private rooms. Most won't allow foreigners to stay in a dorm, but some will. Providing you have your own tent, camping is usually free or at a minimal charge.

In the **budget** and **mid-range** sections you have a great deal of choice. The majority of guesthouses and small hotels fall into these brackets, as do the smarter homestays. You will frequently get one or more meals included with the price of your room and can expect to have electricity and an attached bathroom with running water, although the hot water may come from a geyser. Rooms in these price brackets can vary spectacularly, so do look around at your options before making a final decision.

In the **upmarket** category you'll find larger hotels, tented camps and also many of the houseboats. J&K offers visitors the opportunity to stay in places they would not normally be able to afford, and the houseboats in particular offer great value for money. The tented camps, however, are generally overpriced: you pay a premium for the novelty value and some don't even have the facilities of a budget hotel.

Luxury accommodation is typically only available in the largest towns and cities. The best of Srinagar's houseboats are certainly luxurious and the likes of the Vivanta Dal View and Fortune Inn Riviera hotels are replete with all mod cons. Here you are paying not only for the surroundings but also for professionally trained, English-speaking staff who anticipate your every need.

EATING AND DRINKING

Food and drink varies between districts. In Ladakh and Zanskar the local diet is heavily influenced by Tibet, and Tibetan *thukpa* (soup with noodles) and *momos* (steamed dumplings filled with vegetables, yak meat or cheese) are common. Although in Leh your options are diverse and there are many restaurants serving international dishes, in smaller towns and villages you will be limited to what is produced locally.

Moving west to Kargil and Kashmir, the Muslim population eats a far richer diet with plenty of lamb and chicken. Indian take-away favourites such as *rogan josh* (braised lamb cooked in a gravy of shallots, yoghurt, garlic, ginger and flavoured with spices) is a Kashmiri signature dish, and Kashmiri naan (flatbread stuffed with raisins and nuts) will also be familiar to curry fans.

EATING OUT Leh and Srinagar, and to a lesser extent Jammu, have a wide range of restaurants serving all manner of international and Indian cuisines. Many of these restaurants are targeted at tourists and business travellers, although there is an increasing trend for middle-class locals to eat out too.

The smartest restaurants tend to be in the top-end hotels, and they are open to non-residents as well as hotel guests. You may need to book a table at weekends but can expect well-presented, tasty food and good service. You may also be able to drink alcohol with your meal (see opposite).

In other restaurants you'll find a huge range in quality, from the sublime to the horrific. The restaurants listed in this guide were reasonable or good when we visited, but do still take up-to-date recommendations from other travellers and look out for places that are packed with diners, as that tends to be an accurate indication of quality.

Even where the food is delicious, service may be slow. Be patient initially, but if things are getting ridiculous, do prompt the manager or kitchen staff as it's not uncommon for orders to be forgotten or for customers to be queue-jumped by later but more pushy arrivals. Service is rarely included, except in the more expensive establishments. If you have received good service and want to leave a tip, 10% or rounding up the bill to the nearest Rs100 is standard.

DRINK Alcohol is not widely available in J&K. Drinking isn't forbidden by law, but neither the Buddhist populations of Ladakh and Zanskar nor the Muslim majority of Kashmir drink heavily. You are unlikely to see much alcohol for sale in the shops, but some of the tourist-orientated restaurants do serve bottled beers, and the larger hotels have bars with a range of wines and spirits. Being drunk in public is culturally unacceptable and in any case makes you vulnerable to accidents, mugging and other misfortunes. Driving under the influence of alcohol is illegal.

Do not drink the tap water anywhere in the region without filtering or treating it first. The full range of soft drinks that you'd be used to at home are available pretty much everywhere.

Many Indians have an almost reverential approach to **tea**. The two most popular local types are *noon chai* or *sheer chai*, which is green tea with milk and salt, and *kahwah*, a delicious and light green tea made with saffron and almonds. In Ladakh

ACCOMMODATION AND RESTAURANT PRICE CODES

The price codes used in this book are given for guidance only, as during the lifespan of this edition prices will inevitably increase.

ACCOMMODATION These rates are for a standard double room in high season. Substantial discounts may be available in the winter or for longer stays, so be sure to ask when booking.

Luxury	$$$$$	Rs7,000+
Upmarket	$$$$	Rs3,500–7,000
Mid-range	$$$	Rs1,700–3,500
Budget	$$	Rs800–1,700
Shoestring	$	up to Rs800

RESTAURANTS The price codes used in this guide indicate the average price of a meat-based main dish, excluding vegetables and any service charge. The price of a full meal is likely to be several times higher.

Expensive	$$$$$	Rs700+
Above average	$$$$	Rs400–700
Mid-range	$$$	Rs250–400
Cheap and cheerful	$$	Rs150–250
Rock bottom	$	up to Rs150

and Zanskar you might come across Tibetan tea (also known as butter tea) made from yak butter, tea leaves, water and salt – be warned, it's an acquired but not wholly unpleasant taste.

PUBLIC HOLIDAYS AND FESTIVALS

India has a vast number of public holidays, but many of them are only celebrated in particular states or by one religious community. The three main secular holidays are **Republic Day** (26 January), **Independence Day** (15 August) and **Mahatma Gandhi's Birthday** (2 October), which are celebrated nationwide. Banks and government offices will be closed, and the sale of alcohol on these days is forbidden.

In J&K various religious occasions are also celebrated as public holidays. Dates are typically set according to the lunar calendar and so change from one year to the next. Prominent Hindu festivals include **Holi** (spring festival when coloured dyes are thrown in the streets), **Dussehra** (Hindu festival dedicated to worshipping the goddess Durga, usually in September or October) and **Diwali** (the autumn festival of lights).

The dates of the Muslim festivals of **Ashura** (Shi'a Muslim day of mourning for the martyrdom of Husayn ibn Ali), **Eid al Fitr** (the end of the holy month of Ramadan) and **Eid al Adha** (the feast of sacrifice) are calculated according to the Islamic calendar.

SHOPPING

J&K is a paradise for handicraft shopping, with some of the most beautiful (and, frequently, affordable) handicrafts anywhere in India made and sold here. In J&K, even budget travellers can afford to purchase papier mâché boxes and decorations, painstakingly painted by hand with intricate patterns. Scarcely more costly are the hand-carved wooden boxes and small statues crafted in Srinagar's backstreet workshops, and, of course, the tiny packets of dark-red saffron, grown, picked and dried at Pampore. Brightly coloured cotton or wool scarves and Buddhist trinkets from the Tibetan markets are similarly affordable and take up little room in your suitcase.

If you have a little more to spend, consider buying a unique piece of Ladakhi silver jewellery set with coral, turquoise or lapis lazuli. Antique pieces command a premium, but modern replicas are often just as attractive. Fake pashminas are

MONASTERY FESTIVAL DATES

The monastery festivals offer what is by far and away the best opportunity to see Ladakhi traditions such as masked dances, sacred dances, processions and oracle predictions. If you do have flexibility in your travel dates, plan ahead to be able to incorporate a visit to one of the larger monastery festivals such as Hemis, Thiksey or Lamayuru.

The dates of festivals are based on the Tibetan lunar calendar and so change from one year to the next according to the Western calendar. The following are the expected festival periods, but it's wise to check in advance with local tour companies; although even then they won't know the exact dates of all the festivals until very shortly beforehand.

Amarnath *yatra*	Jul–mid-Aug
Chemre	mid–late Nov
Dakthog	late Jul–mid-Aug
Diskit	late Oct
Galdan Namchot	Dec
Hemis	mid-Jun–early Jul
Karsha	mid-Jul
Korzok	late Jul–early Aug
Ladakh Festival	late Sep
Ladakhi Losar	Dec
Lamayuru	mid-Jun
Leh	Feb
Likir	Feb
Markha	mid-Dec
Matho	Mar
Nyoma	late Nov
Padum	late Nov
Phyang	mid–late Jul
Sindu Darshan	mid-Jun
Shikara	early May
Spituk	mid-Jan
Stok	Feb–Mar
Tingmosgang	Jun
Thiksey	early–mid-Nov
Tibetan Losar	Feb–Mar
Tulip Festival	Apr
Vaisakhi	mid-Apr
Yargon	late Feb–early Mar

everywhere (you'll learn to spot them from their coarser texture and garish colours), but reputable retailers do have authentic cashmere shawls with prices starting from around Rs4,000. They naturally come only in shades of cream, grey and beige (the colours of the goats), though it is possible to get other colours if they've been dyed. Many of the more expensive pashminas are decorated with very fine embroidery sewn by hand. If you are concerned that you don't know what you're looking at and might be cheated, the J&K government arts emporiums in Leh, Jammu and Srinagar have a small selection of real pashminas and the prices are fixed.

Kashmir is famed for its hand-knotted carpets made from wool and/or silk. Prices for quality pieces start from around Rs25,000 and the sky really is the limit. If you are contemplating buying one, take time to learn to differentiate between the varying qualities and to get a fair idea of prices. Village Arts and Crafts in Leh (page 86) and NCE Carpets and Pashminas in Srinagar (page 192) both have highly knowledgeable staff and a wide range of quality carpets. They can also arrange to ship your carpet home.

ARTS AND ENTERTAINMENT

Unlike other parts of India where music and dance spectacles and other forms of entertainment are laid on for tourists, in J&K this is less common: you can see masked dances during festivals in Ladakh's monasteries, but these retain their spiritual meaning and are for the benefit of monks and pilgrims as much as for casual spectators.

In high season there may be concerts and other performances laid on for visitors in J&K's larger towns, so look out for advertising posters and ask around. These are typically one-off, ticketed events and are sometimes set in splendid surroundings such as the Shalimar Gardens in Srinagar. Although international performers rarely make it to J&K, you may well be able to see leading Indian musicians perform. If you are attending such events in Srinagar, expect security to be tight. In and around Leh, though, it's a little more relaxed.

The best entertainment, however, is usually to be found at weddings and other private parties: fortunately these are lively affairs with hundreds of guests, and you will frequently be invited to join in the revelry even if you've only just met the host (or indeed one of his distant relatives). Seize the opportunity with both hands, dress up for the occasion and enjoy the food, music and dancing. Kashmiris really know how to party.

Although cinema (and Bollywood) is an India-wide obsession, there are relatively few cinemas in J&K. If you want to watch the latest blockbuster, your best bet is Jammu, where there is a cinema (page 221). Cultural films and documentaries are sometimes shown at LAMO in Leh (page 91).

MEDIA AND COMMUNICATIONS

The legacy of Kashmir's troubles is seen most clearly in its strict control of communications infrastructure, especially the red tape surrounding getting SIM cards for mobile phones, restrictions on mobile phone use, and the regularity with which internet services are switched off by the government.

NEWSPAPERS India's main English-language newspapers, including the *Times of India* and the *Hindustan Times*, are all widely available in Jammu and Srinagar, and you can usually also get copies in Leh. The *Kashmir Times*, the oldest newspaper in the state, is published daily in Jammu, and *Greater Kashmir* (a daily publication) and the *Kashmir Observer* are both published and distributed in Srinagar. Newspapers are not typically for sale in smaller towns and villages in J&K due to the challenges and costs of distribution.

TELEVISION Televisions are widespread in hotels, restaurants and middle-class homes across J&K, but they only work when there's electricity so you might find yourself left stranded halfway through a film.

Most users have a satellite box for the television, giving access to a large number of Indian and international channels in English as well as regional languages. The most accessible local news channel for foreign viewers is CNN-News18, a collaboration between CNN and the Indian Broadcasting Network.

PHONES Making phone calls in J&K can be a source of great frustration. SIM cards from outside J&K (including those of international operators) are blocked from working in the state; getting a mobile phone SIM card is complicated and time-consuming; and pay as you go customers cannot send or receive text messages on their phones.

The easiest way to make a local phone call in J&K is to use a **standard trunk dialling (STD)** landline. Booths are plentiful in villages and towns and usually clearly marked with a sign; most are hand-painted on a yellow background that says 'Get STD here' or words to that effect, leading to no end of giggles. Calls will cost you around Rs5 a minute. Note that STD lines do not have the capacity to make international calls.

There are two main ways to make an international call. You can either use an **international subscriber dialling (ISD)** landline or, if there is an internet connection, a voice-over IP (VoIP) system that uses software such as Skype or WhatsApp.

It is possible to get a local **SIM card**, albeit with reduced functionality (page 87).

INTERNET The rugged terrain and security issues mean that J&K's access to the internet isn't as advanced as many parts of India. Even so, it's improving year on year. There are cyber cafés in all of the major conurbations (although as in almost all of the rest of the world these are becoming rarer). Almost all hotels and many better restaurants have Wi-Fi. That said, this is only of use when the broadband is actually working. The cables providing broadband to Kargil and Leh have been buried too close to the surface and so are sometimes damaged by rockfalls and inclement weather; and electricity blackouts knock out the local hubs in any case.

POST India's postal service, India Post, is a remarkable if bureaucratic institution with post offices in all towns and in many larger villages: look out for the dark-red signage. In the larger post offices, particularly those that serve a lot of tourists, you may find an English speaker.

The post office's principal role is to sell stamps: an international stamp for a postcard costs Rs25. Delivery is slow (you may well arrive home before your postcards do) but cards and letters do seem to arrive eventually. Parcels can also be sent through India Post, but this is a time-consuming process, as items have to be wrapped in cloth, stitched up and sealed with a wax seal, in addition to completing the usual customs paperwork. You are not permitted to stitch up your own parcel in advance of coming to the post office, but this does at least keep tribes of (mostly) affable old men in work.

J&K is, on the whole, a conservative state and lewd behaviour, revealing clothing and intoxication with drugs or alcohol are unacceptable. Although you may not be publicly chastised for such actions, they reflect badly on other visitors and will embarrass and offend your hosts.

Specific religious observances are required at the different places of worship and these should be observed out of respect: although you are visiting sites as a tourist, they are usually still active places of pilgrimage and prayer for devotees and should be treated as such. In all cases you should remove your shoes, dress conservatively (shorts are not acceptable attire for men or women, however hot the weather) and refrain from smoking, public displays of affection and using bad language.

BUDDHIST MONASTERIES Circumambulate a Buddhist gompa or temple in a clockwise direction. Bow your head towards the Buddha as a mark of respect when entering a temple, and when sitting do not point your feet at a monk, nun or statue. Do not touch statues or paintings, and do not walk between someone who is praying and the idol they are facing. Rather than shaking hands with a monk or nun, instead greet them by putting your hands together with the palms flat and bowing slightly with your hands near to your forehead. It is acceptable for non-Buddhists to pray, meditate and light candles in Buddhist temples, and it is polite to make a small donation for the upkeep of the monastery and its inhabitants when you leave.

HINDU TEMPLES Hindu places of worship should also be explored in a clockwise direction. Devotees will typically ring a bell as they step across the threshold to alert the gods to their arrival, and visitors are invited to do likewise. If you are offered a *tilak* (a red mark on the forehead that denotes a blessing) or a piece of *prasad* (food that has been offered to the gods), it is polite to accept whether or not you are a believer.

MUSLIM MOSQUES AND SHRINES Foreign visitors are often cautious about visiting mosques and shrines, but there is no need to be: guardians and congregations are typically welcoming, and if there is a restriction on the entry of non-Muslims (for example for logistical reasons during prayer time), you will be advised accordingly.

Women must cover their hair when entering a mosque. Any scarf will do, and you may be able to borrow one if you don't have something to hand. Do not disturb or photograph people who are praying, or walk in front of them. Keep noise to a minimum.

PRIVATE HOMES In private homes you will usually be expected to remove your shoes at the door. It is polite to take a small gift for your hosts (chocolates or other sweets are perennially popular), to chatter excitedly even if you don't share a word in common, and to tuck in enthusiastically to whatever food or drink is served. Do not touch food with your left hand as it is considered dirty.

If you see something that you don't understand, ask. People are generally open to explaining their religious and cultural practices and, in a place like J&K, they are used to dealing with people from different cultures. Be polite in your approach and genuine curiosity will more often than not be met with genuine answers.

TRAVELLING POSITIVELY

The single most important thing you can do for J&K is to visit, to explore, to spend your money, and to share your positive experiences with others when you return home.

If you are keen to volunteer, there are plenty of opportunities to do so. One particularly effective NGO in Ladakh is the **17000ft Foundation** (w 17000ft.org), which provides improved infrastructure, teacher training and volunteer teachers to schools in the remotest parts of the district. It is also occasionally possible to arrange teaching placements at many of the monastery schools, including at Likir (page 144).

Volunteering opportunities are also available on a variety of projects with the **Ladakh Women's Alliance** (w waladakh.org), the **Students' Educational and Cultural Movement of Ladakh** (w secmol.org) and at the **Mahabodhi International Meditation Centre** (w mahabodhi-ladakh.org).

J&K, and in particular the mountainous areas, has a fragile ecosystem and this needs to be recognised and protected by tourists as well as the local population.

There is little capacity for recycling waste and so heaps of plastic bottles, tin cans, etc already mar the landscape on the outskirts of towns and in some popular picnic spots. Do not add to the problem. Reduce the plastics that you use and carry your non-biodegradable waste away with you. Water and electricity are also in short supply, so be sparing with what you use.

LADAKH, JAMMU & THE KASHMIR VALLEY ONLINE

For additional online content, articles, photos and more on Ladakh, Jammu & the Kashmir Valley, why not visit w bradtguides.com/ladakh?

Part Two

THE GUIDE

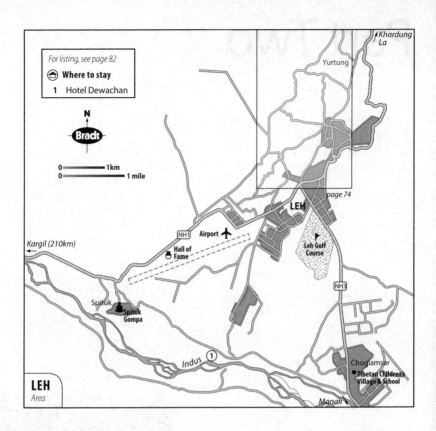

For listing, see page 82

Where to stay
1   Hotel Dewachan

N

Bradt

0 ▬▬▬▬▬ 1km
0 ▬▬▬▬▬ 1 mile

Khardung
La

Yurtung

page 74

LEH

NH1   Airport ✈

Hall of
Fame

Leh Golf
Course

Kargil (210km)

NH3

Spituk
Spituk
Gompa

Indus ①

Choglamsar
● Tibetan Children's
Village & School

Manali

LEH
Area

3

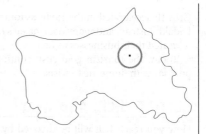

Leh

Telephone code: 01982

Life in Ladakh centres on the mountain town of Leh. The regional capital is a bustling hub with the rare combination of reasonably developed tourism infrastructure and a number of well-preserved tourist sites, but with the sensation that great wilderness adventures await just beyond the horizon. Most visitors to Ladakh start or finish their journey here, and the seasonal influx of both foreign and domestic tourists gives the area a cosmopolitan air.

If you arrive by air you'll need a few days to acclimatise to the altitude, but it's an easy place to spend time, especially during the summer months, and there are plenty of options for accommodation, food and entertainment.

The best way to get a feel for the city is to start out in the bustling bazaar and then climb the spaghetti-like tangle of streets between there and Leh Palace. The alleys are far too narrow for a car to traverse (though that doesn't seem to stop some trying …), which means visitors can get a glimpse into times gone by: men struggling uphill with handcarts laden high with vegetables; women baking flatbreads in ovens open to the street; and crowds of schoolchildren racing and shrieking along, excitable but good-natured street dogs in pursuit.

HISTORY

Leh was historically a small trading post on the southern spur of the Silk Road that linked Tibet and Ladakh with central Asia, and more southerly parts of the Indian subcontinent with China. Part of Greater Ladakh, it was an independent territory but a regular battlefield for Chinese, Mongolian and Tibetan forces from the 8th century onwards.

Leh was a relatively small and politically insignificant settlement when compared with neighbouring Shey (page 119), but the relocation of the Ladakhi royal residences here in the 16th century, first to the Tsemo Fort and then Leh Palace, put it on the map. The town's growing prestige was demonstrated in its new architecture, and particularly in the gompas and mosques. Large houses were built for officials and the aristocracy at the foot of the palace, and these structures, many of which date from the 17th century, form the heart of the Old Town today.

The first European to visit Leh was the Englishman William Moorcroft in the 1820s, who came here en route to Bukhara, now in Uzbekistan. Moorcroft signed commercial treaties with the local government, opening Ladakh up to British trade, and ultimately published an account of his travels under the wordy title *Travels in the Himalayan Provinces of Hindustan and the Punjab, in Ladakh and Kashmir, in Peshawur, Kabul, Kunduz and Bokhara, from 1819 to 1825*. After independence, foreigners were banned from travelling to Ladakh – restrictions that were not eased until 1974. However, Leh began to expand at great speed after the ban was lifted, with both the military and tourist sectors investing in infrastructure development.

Growth accelerated in the 1990s as tourists unable to travel in Kashmir headed for Ladakh instead, and many of Srinagar's hoteliers, souvenir sellers and restaurateurs relocated their businesses to Leh.

Today, the tourism gold rush continues apace as Ladakh becomes ever more popular with domestic tourists.

GETTING THERE AND AWAY

How you reach Leh will be dictated by your budget and the time of year. In the winter months (roughly mid-October to late April) all options are unreliable, as snow closes the road out of town in both directions and flights are frequently delayed, rescheduled or cancelled entirely. Even July and August are not immune to occasional bouts of inclement weather, so allow plenty of time for hold-ups.

BY AIR Leh's airport (IXL; ✆251 783) lies to the south of the city, situated between Leh town and Spituk. All flights into and out of Leh depart early in the morning, due to poor visibility and more generally unstable weather in the afternoons. Even so, flights are frequently cancelled due to bad weather, putting pressure on availability as passengers are bumped on to the next flight, sometimes displacing others who have bought tickets.

Several airlines, including Air India, Go Air, Jet, SpiceJet and Vistara, fly from Delhi daily. The flight takes 75 minutes and costs from around Rs5,000 one-way. Prices increase substantially in high season and flights get booked up well in advance. Air India also operates a direct service from Srinagar two or three times a week (1hr; from Rs5,000 one-way).

The airport terminal is a small and unprepossessing building, but the delivery of bags to the carousel is relatively efficient and foreigners' registration forms are handed out to fill in while you wait. Bring a pen, write in the usual details (passport number, visa number, etc) and hand the form in at the desk on the left as you leave.

Outside the terminal you'll find a small crowd of taxi drivers jostling fairly good-naturedly for your attention, but also a pre-paid taxi booth. The 3km ride into central Leh costs from Rs251 (depending on the kind of vehicle used).

BY CAR There are two roads linking Leh with the rest of the world, but they are open in the summer and autumn months only. The Srinagar–Leh road winds its way for 434km via Kargil and, until the opening of the Zoji La Tunnel at an as yet unspecified date, it is open only when there is no snow or rockfall. The tourist information centre in Srinagar (page 187) can advise you as to the current status of the road and any planned closures, as can the police station in Drass (page 163). In addition to Zoji La (3,540m), the road also crosses Fotu La (4,147m). You can also reach Leh by driving the 473km road from Manali in neighbouring Himachal Pradesh (page 41). This is the main overland tourist route but it's a hard road with four high passes, two of which, Lachulung La and Tanglang La, are over 5,000m. If you are driving your own vehicle, note that the last fuel pump on the road is at Tandi, 107km north of Manali. Ensure that you have sufficient fuel to complete the 368km drive to Leh.

Although categorised as national highways (NH1 and NH3), both of these access routes are slow. The tarmac is often broken, overtaking is difficult, and bad weather, avalanches and breakdowns frequently block the road. It is theoretically possible to drive between Srinagar and Leh in a day, leaving around 05.00 and arriving after 19.00, but it is better to break your journey in Kargil. Coming from Manali, you should spend the night around Keylong (page 41). It is another full day's drive from Manali to Delhi.

BY BUS Long-distance buses are the cheapest way to reach Leh, if not the fastest or most comfortable. The J&K State Road Transport Corporation (SRTC) (w jksrtc. co.in) operates standard and deluxe coaches on the Srinagar–Leh road from early June until mid-November. The standard coach (Rs925) departs from Srinagar at 07.30 and reaches Leh at 13.00 the following day, stopping for the night in Kargil. If there are enough passengers, the deluxe 18-seater coach (Rs1,330) runs along the same route. Accommodation in Kargil is not included in the fare.

Buses from Manali to Leh take around 19 hours and typically break the journey at Keylong or Sarchu. The Himachal Pradesh Tourism Development Corporation (HPTDC; w hptdc.in) runs daily tourist coaches between the two from 1 July to 15 September (Rs2,900 one-way inc dorm-style accommodation in Keylong). HPTDC also operates an onward connection to Delhi (Rs1,400) in air-conditioned Volvo coaches. At the time of going to press, HPTDC had launched a new bus route, which runs all the way from Manali to Leh in one long day. Buses leave Manali at 04.00 and arrive in Leh around 20.30 (Rs833). However, not only is this a very unsatisfactory way to travel to Leh, but it also potentially exposes you to a high risk of acute mountain sickness. Our advice is to stick to the slower buses.

HPTDC buses for Manali (with connections there for Delhi) depart from the HPTDC bus stand in Main Bazaar [78 C3]. Other long-distance bus and coach services, for example to Kargil and Srinagar, depart from the main bus stand by SNM Hospital [74 C5].

BY TAXI The taxi unions in Leh and Kargil dictate rates for long-distance taxis as well as local routes, and if you are travelling along the Srinagar–Leh road you may have to change taxis at Kargil in order to comply with taxi union rules. For the entire

LEH TAXI FARES

The following official taxi fares were published by the Ladakh Taxi Operatives Co-operative Ltd (LTOCL) in 2019. They are calculated from the main taxi stand on Fort Road [78 D3], differentiated by vehicle type and updated on a yearly basis. A copy of the latest rates list is available either from the LTOCL office by the taxi stand, or from the J&K Tourist Office. Taxi drivers tend to keep a copy in the front of their vehicle too.

The rates below are given in Rs.

Destination	Innova, Xylo Drop/return	Scorpio, Qualis Drop/return	Eco, Van, Sumo Drop/return
Changspa	138/180	132/170	125/162
Choglamsar	360/468	343/444	325/422
Gompa village	277/296	264/284	250/271
Leh Palace	213/277	202/264	192/250
Shanti Stupa	239/311	227/295	215/280
Skara	152/198	184/227	166/215
Sankar	152/198	184/227	166/215
Tsemo	260/336	247/320	235/303
Yurtung	201/261	191/248	181/236

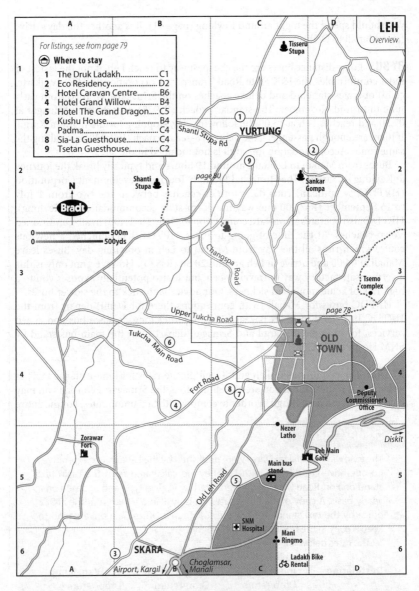

For listings, see from page 79

LEH
Overview

🛏 **Where to stay**
1 The Druk Ladakh..................C1
2 Eco Residency.......................D2
3 Hotel Caravan Centre..........B6
4 Hotel Grand Willow.............B4
5 Hotel The Grand Dragon.....C5
6 Kushu House.........................B4
7 Padma....................................C4
8 Sia-La Guesthouse................C4
9 Tsetan Guesthouse...............C2

Tisseru
Stupa

YURTUNG

Shanti Stupa Rd

Shanti
Stupa

Sankar
Gompa

page 80

N
Bradt

0 ____500m
0 ____500yds

Changspa Road

Tsemo
complex

Upper Tukcha Road

page 78

OLD
TOWN

Tukcha Main Road

Fort Road

Deputy
Commissioner's
Office

Nezer
Latho

Diskit

Zorawar
Fort

Old Leh Road

Leh Main
Gate

Main bus
stand

SKARA

Airport, Kargil

*Choglamsar,
Manali*

SNM
Hospital

Mani
Ringmo

Ladakh Bike
Rental

vehicle (actual price will be divided between the number of passengers), Leh-based drivers charge from Rs19,483 to Manali, Rs7,126 to Kargil and Rs14,122/16,606 to Srinagar (one day/two days). Return rates are available on some but not all routes: check the LTOCL list (see box, page 73) for the latest options.

If you want to pre-book your taxi, it's easiest to do so by contacting one of Leh's travel agents (page 77). If you are happy to share the vehicle, the travel agents are also proactive about finding other tourists travelling the same way on similar dates. This is particularly helpful if you have a limited budget but still want to get to remoter areas such as the Southern Lakes (page 132).

Leh is a reasonably compact town, and even if you decide to stay on its outskirts, you're never more than 15 minutes' drive from Main Bazaar. Journeys by bus and car often grind to a halt in traffic as badly parked vehicles cause bottlenecks in the already narrow streets, but the drivers are adept at squeezing through the tiniest of gaps.

ON FOOT It is often faster to get around the central parts of Leh on foot than by car, as the traffic creeps along and is frequently stationary. Indeed, in the Old Town walking can be your only option as many of the streets are too narrow for a vehicle to pass.

If you are spending a protracted period of time in Leh, it is worth getting to know the pedestrian cut-throughs as these will significantly shorten your walk. The alley running alongside the stream behind Rainbow Guesthouse [80 B4] links Karzoo to Changspa and shortens your walk by a good 15 minutes when compared with following the road. Likewise, the footpath opposite the Moravian Mission School [80 C5] cuts off three sides of a square if you are continuing to Zangsti. You can walk from Main Bazaar to Leh Palace faster than you can drive there and, providing you are fit, it is also just a short (albeit very steep) climb up the hairpin footpath from the palace to the Tsemo Fort.

It is generally safe to walk around central Leh, even after dark, although you should of course take standard precautions. The traffic moves slowly but at night you should carry a torch to make sure you can be seen by motorists and also so that you can see the drains, broken paving and other trip hazards that could easily break an ankle.

BY BUS A small number of minibuses run from the main bus stand [74 C5] to Main Bazaar, and also link the suburbs with central Leh. There is, however, little difference between these minibuses and the shared taxis. You are not guaranteed a seat and your baggage may have to travel on the roof, but you will typically pay less than a quarter of the taxi fare (see below).

BY TAXI Leh's taxis are mostly minivans that seat around five passengers comfortably. Drivers typically speak a few words of English and their vehicles are generally clean. Taxis congregate around Leh Taxi Union, the bus stand (see above) and the airport (page 72), and there are usually a handful on Changspa or up by the palace. If you prefer to call a cab in advance, you can contact the taxi union or speak to one of the below-listed taxi drivers directly.

The Leh Taxi Union [78 D3] (Fort Rd; \ 252 723) is a co-operative that regulates the town's taxi drivers and fares. It publishes an annual fare list (see box, page 73) and can arrange you a driver directly. Rates are charged from point to point, or you can hire a taxi for a half day (from Rs1,203) or full day (from Rs2,023) and take it wherever you please within the city.

For reliable and patient taxi drivers, we thoroughly recommend English-speaking Tsewang Rigzen (m 946 904 9347) with his large, jeep-like vehicle, and also Thinles (m 962 296 2197) and Hussein (m 990 698 3886). The latter two both have minivans, comfortably seating five and four passengers respectively, and they charge in accordance with the LTOCL rate list. Thinles and Hussein do not, however, speak English, so you'll either need to get good at charades or ask someone else to explain where you want to go.

Leh GETTING AROUND

3

BY MOTORBIKE Exploring Leh and its environs by motorbike is incredibly popular and other road users are generally used to the vagaries of bikers. Leh's bike-hire companies do not require you to show a bike licence but simply to answer in the affirmative the question 'Can you drive?'

It goes without saying, though, that there are significant risks associated with motorbikes. Hire rates include helmets and, in some cases, elbow and knee pads too. Wear them: your helmet is no use tied to the back of the bike. For general tips on biking in Kashmir, see the box on page 58.

Himalayan Odyssey [80 D5] Mentokling Complex, Zangsti Rd; m 946 920 6777; e himalayanodyssey@yahoo.in. Comes highly recommended & offers motorbike touring packages that include homestay accommodation.

Karmic Journeys [78 B1] Zangsti Rd; m 962 298 0973; e rinchen.wangail@gmail.com. Just 1 of a number of bike-hire firms along Zangsti, Rinchen & stocks Bullets (from Rs1,200/day), Pulsars (Rs800/day) & automatic scooters (Rs800/day).

Ladakh Bike Hire [80 B5] Tongspon Complex, Changspa Rd; m 959 692 8861; e info@

ladakhbikehire.com; w ladakhbikehire.com. Slick & professional operator hiring out motorbikes of various sizes from Rs1,000/day (Rs800 for a scooter).

Planet Himalaya [80 B5] Changspa Rd; m 962 296 442; e thabkas@gmail.com. Well established & professional, Planet Himalaya can supply Royal Enfields (Rs1,200/day) & Pulsars (Rs600–800/day) among other options. Rates include elbow & kneepad hire & a discount of Rs100/day is available for longer hire periods.

BY MOUNTAIN BIKE

Eco Travels [80 B4] Nr Wonderland Restaurant, Changspa Rd; m 985 880 6864; e ladakhecotravels@gmail.com. If you fancy the thrill of biking down Khardung La (page 99) but quite understandably cannot face the slog of getting up there, these guys will rent you a well-maintained mountain bike & drop you at the top for Rs800. The adrenaline-fuelled ride back down to Leh takes around 5 hours & is certainly not for the faint-hearted or those suffering from vertigo, but has some of the most impressive views around & a definitely unrivalled brag factor.

Himalayan Bikers [80 B5] Changspa Rd; m 946 904 9270; w himalayan-bikers.com. Offering a good selection of mountain bikes, this outfit charges Rs400–600/day for bike hire (depending on the bike chosen), including helmet & bike lock. They offer a similar trip down Khardung La for Rs1,400, Rs400 of which is the cost of the Inner Line Permit (not included in Eco Travels' price; see box, page 101).

TOURIST INFORMATION AND TOUR OPERATORS

TOURIST INFORMATION The state-run J&K Tourist Office [78 C3] (Fort Rd; ℡ 252 297; ☉ summer only 10.00–16.00 daily) is a nice idea but falls short of where it needs to be in terms of materials and even more so in regard to customer service. It's worthwhile popping in here for bus times, taxi rates and a photocopied map of central Leh, but if you want advice about where to go, what to see and where to stay, you'll need to speak to one of the local travel agents (see below). They all provide free advice and there's no obligation to buy their products or services.

J&K Tourism also has a tourist reception centre (℡ 252 297) on the Srinagar–Leh road close to the airport. Its location away from the town centre means that it is little used, however, and indeed is often closed.

TOUR OPERATORS Leh is reputed to have more than 400 registered travel and tour companies, from local boys chancing it in their front room to highly professional outfits capable of arranging world-class tours and expeditions. Though each company has its strengths and specialities, virtually all of them can arrange package tours, trekking, Inner Line permits and car and driver hire. Many of the travel agents have noticeboards outside, listing groups who need additional people to join them on a trek or to share jeep hire, and if your dates marry up (or can be altered to do so), this is an excellent way to cut your costs and share the experience with new friends.

Below we've listed some recommended companies. There are no doubt plenty of others who will provide excellent service: ask other tourists for their recommendations, and be sure to get in writing the details of what is included in any booking before handing over your money. Note that many of Leh's travel agents are closed during the winter months. In summer you will typically find them open from 08.00 until 21.00.

Ancient Tracks [78 C2] Opp SBI, Main Bazaar; m 941 986 2542; e lvisuddha@yahoo.com; w ancienttracks.com. Highly professional agency offering customised tours, inc bird & wildlife watching (May, Jun & Sep) & treks that include yoga & meditation sessions. If you want to try to see wild snow leopards, then these are your guys. Owner Lobzang Visuddha is a mine of helpful information & full of imaginative ideas for trips.

Dreamland Trek & Tour [78 A3] Fort Rd; 257 784; m 985 806 0607; e dreamladakh@gmail.com; w dreamladakh.com. Well organised & professional, these have been in business since 1996. Popular packages inc an 8-day Markha Valley trek & the 4-day Spituk to Stok trek, while in the winter months you can choose between the strenuous Chadar expedition along frozen rivers to Padum, or snow leopard spotting.

Ecological Footprint Travels [78 D2] Main Bazaar; m 990 697 7846; e stanzin@ecologicalfootprint.in; w ecologicalfootprint.in. Stanzin Odzer & his young team are passionate about Ladakh & its culture & keen to share it in a sustainable fashion. They focus primarily on climbing, trekking & homestays, encouraging even budget travellers to put their money directly into the local community & to get involved with natural farming & other eco-projects.

Exotic Travels [78 C2] LBA Complex, Old Fort Rd; m 941 917 8682; w exoticladakh.com. Francophone travel agent with more than 10 years' experience & a deservedly loyal following among French & Belgian tourists. Specialities include trekking, mountain biking & wildlife tours.

Glacier Travels [78 C4] Raku Complex, Old Fort Rd; 253 638; e jummaleh@yahoo.com; w ladakhglaciers.com. Glacier Travels is professionally run & the staff are proactive about

finding you travelling companions if you need to split the cost of a car or trekking guide.

The Ladakh Tours [78 C2] NAC Complex, Main Bazaar; m 962 297 5440; e info@theladakhtours.com; w theladakhtours.com. Attentive outfit offering personalised tours & treks for small groups. Highlights of its programme include the Chadar winter trek & motorbike expeditions to Pangong Tso.

Ladakh Yeti Travels [78 C1] Hemis Complex, Zangsti Rd; 225 3460; m 941 953 8256; e ladakh.yeti.travels@gmail.com; w ladakhyetitravels.com. This Ladakhi–Tibetan joint venture offers Ladakh's most adrenaline-hungry visitors programmes that include rafting, mountaineering, mountain biking & trekking. The owners are knowledgeable & enthusiastic.

Ladakhi Women's Travel Company [80 D6] Upper Tukcha Rd; 257 973; m 946 915 8137; e ladakhiwomenstc@gmail.com; w ladakhiwomenstravel.com. Owned & run by women, the company has all-female trekking guides but is happy to arrange treks & tours for men & women. It uses local homestays wherever possible & is focused on responsible tourism.

Moonlight Travels [78 C2] LBA Complex, Old Fort Rd; 202 332; m 941 921 9555; e info@ladakhtravels.com; w ladakhtravels.com. Director Nawang Lhundup is a bundle of energy, a charismatic individual who makes customer service a priority. In addition to trekking & expeditions he offers a number of more unusual options inc a springtime apricot flower tour popular with Japanese tourists.

Zanskar Thema Tour [78 C1] Hemis Complex, Zangsti Rd; m 946 972 7778; e vstobchazar@yahoo.co.in; @stobgyasTASHI. Specialist in Zanskar region offering ready-made & tailored packages. Options include trekking & mountaineering, horse trekking in both Ladakh & Zanskar, jeep safaris & cultural tours.

3

LEH
Old town

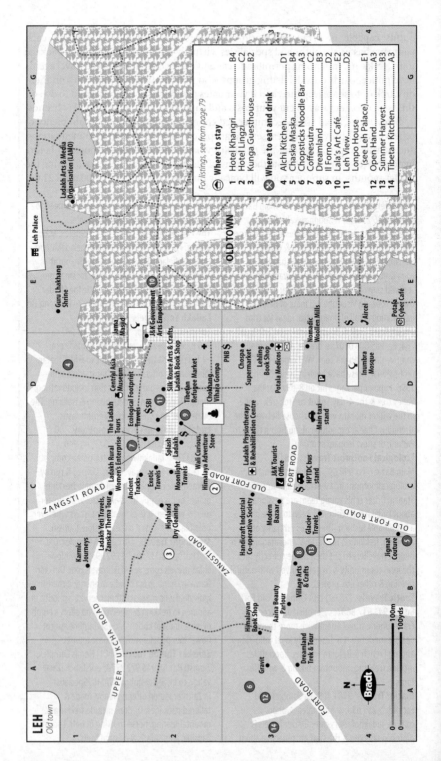

Leh Palace

OLD TOWN

ZANGSTI ROAD

UPPER TUKCHA ROAD

FORT ROAD

OLD FORT ROAD

FORT ROAD

Guru Lhakhang Shrine

Ladakh Arts & Media Organisation (LAMO)

Jama Masjid

Central Asia Museum

J&K Government Arts Emporium

Ecological Footprint

The Ladakh Tours

Silk Route Arts & Crafts, Ladakh Book Shop

Tibetan Refugee Market

Chokhang Vihara Gompa

SBI

Ladakh Rural Women's Enterprise Tours

Splash Ladakh

Wall Curious Himalaya Adventure Store

Chospa Supermarket

Lehling Book Shop

PNB

Potala Medicos

Nomadic Woollen Mills

Ladakh Yeti Travels, Zanskar Thema Tour

Ancient Tracks

Exotic Travels

Moonlight Travels

Ladakh Physiotherapy & Rehabilitation Centre

J&K Tourist Office

HPTDC bus stand

Main taxi stand

Inumbra Mosque

Aircel

Potala Cyber Café

Karmic Journeys

Highland Dry Cleaning

Handicraft Industrial Co-operative Society

Modern Bazaar

Glacier Travels

Jigmat Couture

Himalayan Book Shop

Aaina Beauty Parlour

Village Arts & Crafts

Gravit

Dreamland Trek & Tour

N

Bradt

0   100m
0   100yds

Where to stay
For listings, see from page 79

1 Hotel Khangri......................B4
2 Hotel Lingzi........................C2
3 Kunga Guesthouse.............B2

Where to eat and drink
4   Alchi Kitchen....................D1
5   Chaska Maska...................B4
6   Chopsticks Noodle Bar......A3
7   Coffeesutra.......................C2
8   Dreamland.........................B3
9   Il Forno.............................D2
10 Lala's Art Café...................E2
11 Leh View...........................D2
12 Lonpo House
    (see Leh Palace).............E1
    Open Hand.......................A3
13 Summer Harvest...............B3
14 Tibetan Kitchen................A3

Leh has a wide variety of places to stay, from homestays and basic guesthouses to upmarket hotels. Accommodation options at the upper end of the scale tend to have electricity round the clock (provided by a backup generator when the main supply goes out), both hot and cold running water in the bathrooms, and a restaurant on site. They offer meal plans should you wish to eat all your meals at the hotel.

The majority of cheaper guesthouses and hotels are situated in Changspa, Karzoo and around Main Bazaar. They are conveniently located if you're reliant on getting around on foot, with both sites and restaurants nearby. The downside of these properties is that they can be noisy, both due to traffic and other guests, and some of the rooms are cramped. You may want to have a look at several places before checking in.

All accommodation options listed below have free Wi-Fi unless otherwise mentioned.

AROUND MAIN BAZAAR
Main Bazaar is a bustling part of town, rather crowded & noisy but in the thick of the action & well located for both sightseeing & onward transport.

⌂ **Hotel Khangri** [78 B4] (35 rooms) Old Fort Rd; m 941 917 8207, 962 297 8077; e info@hotelkhangri.com. Though unassuming from the roadside, Khangri's internal courtyard is a pleasant enough spot for b/fast or a coffee. Rooms are unexciting but a decent size & with reasonable furnishings & clean linens. $$$$

⌂ **Hotel Lingzi** [78 C2] (24 rooms) Old Fort Rd; ☎ 252 020; m 962 231 8987; e lingzihotel@gmail.com; w hotellingziladakh.com. Very centrally located, this hotel has a wonderfully painted lobby that will put you in the mood to explore all the town's Buddhist temples. There's also a roof terrace with fort views & the large rooms (all with satellite TV) have pine-wood floors & furnishings. Staff are helpful & there's a small restaurant on site. $$$-$$$$

✳ ⌂ **Kunga Guesthouse** [78 B2] (27 rooms) Zangsti Rd; ☎ 250 726; m 979 767 3621; e kungahotel@rediffmail.com. Tucked back from Main Bazaar, Kunga is one of the best options in this part of town. The large sunny rooms have simple but tasteful decoration & Mr Simon, the manager, is a star. B/fast inc. $$$-$$$$

KARZOO
Some of Karzoo's hotels feel a little far from the town centre, but they're cheaper than those in Main Bazaar & less overrun with gap-year students than Changspa.

✳ ⌂ **Hotel Naro** [80 C2] (18 rooms) Karzoo Rd; ☎ 252 481; m 941 921 8214; e paldan.naro@hotmail.com; w hotelnaro.com. Superbly well-run, homely guesthouse with rooms painted in bold primary colours. There's a delightful garden & helpful staff. Located at the far end of Karzoo, it's in a quiet spot & is popular with motorcyclists due to the ample parking. Meals are available in the dining room. $$$$

⌂ **The Ladakh** [80 C3] (14 rooms) Karzoo Rd; ☎ 252 627; m 962 231 7125; e hoteltheladakh@gmail.com. Brilliant-value hotel with smart rooms containing dark-wood furnishings & Buddhist-red sashes on the beds. There's a pretty courtyard garden & a wealth of helpful travel-related information. $$$$

✳ ⌂ **Royal Ladakh** [80 D1] (27 rooms) Upper Karzoo Rd; ☎ 251 646; e hotelroyalladakh@gmail.com; w hotelroyalladakh.com. Definitely the smartest option in Karzoo, it's an attractive, well-kept hotel at the end of a quiet lane. Staff are attentive but not fussy; rooms are large, light & have fine views. Best option in this price bracket. $$$$

⌂ **Jigmet Guesthouse & Hotel** [80 B6] (25 rooms) Lden Malpak, Upper Tukcha Rd; m 962 296 5846; w jigmetladakh.com. Just 5mins' walk from Main Bazaar, Jigmet is a simple set-up in a quiet location. Guesthouse rooms are half the price of those in the hotel. Meal plans are available, though you're better off eating somewhere else in town. $$$-$$$$

⌂ **Naaz Guesthouse** [80 C4] (8 rooms) Karzoo Rd; m 946 970 2410. Right on the road, Naaz has the feel of a college hostel. There's no real outdoor space to sit & rooms are fairly bare-bones, but all have en-suite bathrooms. $$$

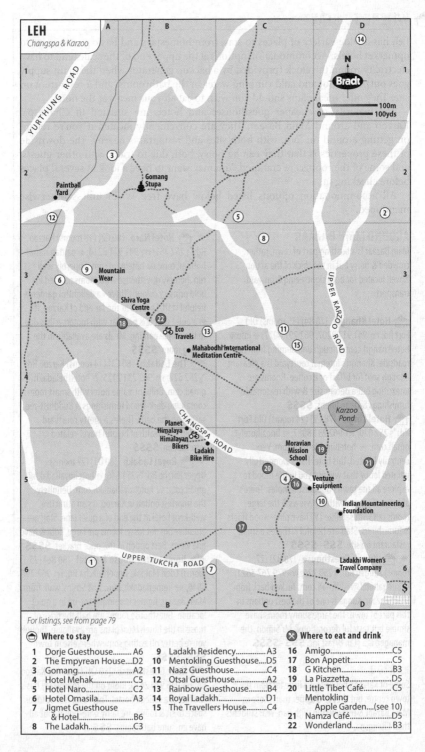

LEH
Changspa & Karzoo

YURTHUNG ROAD

UPPER KARZOO ROAD

CHANGSPA ROAD

UPPER TUKCHA ROAD

Paintball Yard

Gomang Stupa

Mountain Wear

Shiva Yoga Centre

Eco Travels

Mahabodhi International Meditation Centre

Karzoo Pond

Planet Himalaya

Himalayan Bikers

Ladakh Bike Hire

Moravian Mission School

Venture Equipment

Indian Mountaineering Foundation

Ladakhi Women's Travel Company

0 100m
0 100yds

For listings, see from page 79

Where to stay

1	Dorje Guesthouse	A6
2	The Empyrean House	D2
3	Gomang	A2
4	Hotel Mehak	C5
5	Hotel Naro	C2
6	Hotel Omasila	A3
7	Jigmet Guesthouse & Hotel	B6
8	The Ladakh	C3
9	Ladakh Residency	A3
10	Mentokling Guesthouse	D5
11	Naaz Guesthouse	C4
12	Otsal Guesthouse	A2
13	Rainbow Guesthouse	B4
14	Royal Ladakh	D1
15	The Travellers House	C4

Where to eat and drink

16	Amigo	C5
17	Bon Appetit	C5
18	G Kitchen	B3
19	La Piazzetta	D5
20	Little Tibet Café	C5
	Mentokling Apple Garden	(see 10)
21	Namza Café	D5
22	Wonderland	B3

🏠 **Dorje Guesthouse** [80 A6] (12 rooms) Upper Tukcha Rd; **m** 962 295 7511; **e** dorje_guesthouse@hotmail.com; **w** dorjeguesthouse.com. Charming Dorje & Konchok welcome guests to their family home in a quiet location. Split over 3 storeys, many rooms have views of the Shanti Stupa, Tsemo Fort or Stok Kangri range. A Ladakhi b/fast is served in the garden & Dorje can arrange trekking tours. **$$–$$$**

🏠 **The Empyrean House** [80 D2] (6 rooms) Upper Karzoo Rd; **m** 849 103 0355. One of the best guesthouses in Leh, this smart, tastefully decorated & cosy place has pine-tinged rooms with fresh flowers in vases & private bathrooms with rain showers & plenty of hot water. A group can rent the building in its entirety. Super friendly owners, free b/fast & a great location round out the package. **$$–$$$**

🏠 **The Travellers House** [80 C4] (8 rooms) Karzoo Rd; **** 252 048; **e** leosami@hotmail.com. Probably the friendliest of several guesthouses on this stretch of the road, Travellers comprises several buildings in a garden. The charming lady who runs it speaks good English. B/fast available on request. **$$**

🏠 **Kushu House** [74 B4] (8 rooms) Upper Tukcha Rd; **m** 981 199 6867. Friendly & well-run guesthouse a few mins' walk from the town centre, but far enough away to give a sense of rural peace. This is further enhanced by the traditional Ladakhi-style building having giant windows with views over an impressive veg patch & distant snow-sprinkled mountains. Rooms themselves are wood-lined & have modern bathrooms & the family who run the place can cook up a delicious dinner with advance request. **$–$$**

🏠 **Rainbow Guesthouse** [80 B4] (14 rooms) Off Karzoo Rd; **** 252 332; **m** 941 923 6792; **e** rainbowgh@rainbowghleh.com; **w** rainbowghleh.com. One of our favourite budget options in Leh, the Rainbow is tucked along a quiet side street & built around a lush garden. Rooms & bathrooms are basic but clean & there's running hot water round the clock. The English-speaking staff are friendly & helpful. A footpath gives swift access to Changspa Rd. **$–$$**

CHANGSPA
This is Leh's tourist hub: you don't come to Changspa so much to experience the local atmosphere as to share in the backpacker vibe.

🏠 **Ladakh Residency** [80 A3] (22 rooms) Changspa Rd; **** 258 111; **m** 941 917 8039; **e** info@ladakhresidency.com; **w** ladakhresidency.com. Changspa's smartest option is efficient if a little lacking in personality. There's no AC but rooms have fans, work desks, balconies, big, thick mattresses & colourful rugs. Plenty of secure parking. **$$$$$**

🏠 **Hotel Omasila** [80 A3] (40 rooms) Changspa Rd; **** 252 119; **e** hotelomasila@yahoo.com; **w** hotelomasila.com. With oodles of character, the Omasila is a true haven in what can be a hectic part of town. Rooms at the back of the property have striking mountain views. Mature fruit trees & patio plants give way to an organic vegetable garden that provides supplies for the kitchen. Central heating in winter. 24hr hot water. **$$$$**

🏠 **Mentokling Guesthouse** [80 D5] (10 rooms) Nr police station, Zangsti Rd; **m** 985 839 9142. This excellent budget guesthouse is housed within an attractive whitewashed building with carved wooden windows. There's a quiet orchard garden and it's in a convenient location. Rooms are large, modern in appearance & clean. The Indian Mountaineering Foundation (see box, page 89) has its office downstairs. **$$$**

🏠 **Hotel Mehak** [80 C5] (20 rooms) Opposite Moravian Mission School, Changspa Rd; **** 256 110; **m** 941 917 8664. Conveniently located but somewhat dark hotel on the eastern side of Changspa. Staff are pleasant & speak English. **$$**

🏠 **Otsal Guesthouse** [80 A2] (16 rooms) Past bridge, Changspa Rd; **** 252 816; **e** otsalguesthouse@hotmail.com. At the far end of Changspa is this large, popular guesthouse & its neighbouring restaurant. Rooms are large & reasonably clean. The secure courtyard is convenient if you need to lock up your bike overnight. **$**

FORT ROAD
Accessible & tourist-orientated but slightly quieter than Main Bazaar, Fort Rd is a good option if you plan to get around on foot.

🏠 **Hotel Grand Willow** [74 B4] (36 rooms) Fort Rd; **** 251 835; **m** 941 917 8242; **e** grandwillow@yahoo.co.in; **w** hotelgrandwillowleh.com. Large, traditionally styled hotel spread across 3 floors with quiet rooms facing away from the street & overlooking the garden. Note that some of the rooms are a bit too small for comfort. The central heating is a godsend if you are visiting Leh in the winter months. **$$$$**

🏠 **Padma Hotel** [74 C4] (15 rooms) Fort Rd; m 941 917 8171; e padmaladakh@gmail.com; w padmaladakh.net. Tucked back on a pedestrian alley running parallel with Fort Rd, this guesthouse has pleasant staff & a laidback feel. Rooms are warm & cosy, if a little dark. B/fast is served in the garden. **$$$$**

✳ 🏠 **Sia-La Guesthouse** [74 C4] (13 rooms) Fort Rd; ☎252 821; m 941 917 8100. Superb, upmarket guesthouse with big, bright rooms with good heating, thick rugs on the floor & private hot-water bathrooms. We were particularly taken with the dining room, which was like a museum of old Tibet. There's a big organic garden & views over Stok Kangri. **$$$**

OTHER AREAS

Some of Leh's pleasantest hotels are in the slightly outlying area. If you have your own transport (or are happy to walk further or take a cab), they offer better value for money &, in many cases, attractive surroundings.

🏠 **The Druk Ladakh** [74 C1] (26 rooms) Shanti Stupa Rd, Yurtung; ☎251 724; m 941 917 8448; e reservation@thedrukladakh.com; w thedrukladakh.com. Conveniently located for Shanti Stupa but sadly not much else, the Druk is on the very edge of Leh in an attractive setting. Staff are polite & attentive & the rooms are grand, but rather old-fashioned. **$$$$$**

✳ 🏠 **Hotel Caravan Centre** [74 B6] (30 rooms) Skara; ☎252 282; m 941 918 1260; e caravan@yahoo.co.in; w hotelcaravancentre. com. One of Leh's oldest hotels, Caravan Centre has been updated to keep in step with modern expectations. In a quiet location amid pleasant gardens, it's a good spot to relax away from the bustle of the town. Rooms are warm & comfortable, the bathrooms immaculate & the staff are attentive & can help to organise onward travel & treks. Buffet meals served in the

attractively painted dining room. Friendliest option in this price bracket. **$$$$$**

🏠 **Hotel The Grand Dragon** [74 C5] (47 rooms) Old Leh Rd; m 962 243 3776; e hotel@thegranddragonladakh.com; w thegranddragonladakh.com. Leh's most upmarket hotel mixes traditional Tibetan colours & design touches with modern hotel facilities to create a highly impressive place to stay. It's an especially good option if you happen to be in town during the frigid mid-winter when the heat & comfort of this place will prove irresistible. Facilities include a shop, restaurant & 24hr café. **$$$$$**

✳ 🏠 **Eco Residency** [74 D2] (12 rooms) Nr Sanskar Gompa; m 990 697 7846; e stanzin@ ecologicalfootprint.in; w ecologicalfootprint.in. Leh's 1st eco hotel is owned & run by the Ecological Footprint Travels team (page 77) & needless to say the ecological credentials are to be applauded. The rooms are bright & have pine panelling lining the walls, which gives the rooms a warm & inviting appeal. Customer service is spot on. Highly recommended. **$$$$**

🏠 **Gomang Hotel** [80 A2] Upper Changspa Rd; m 941 912 9157; e hotelgomang@gmail. com; w gomanghotelleh.com. Worthy of praise is the Gomang, which claims, with some justification, to be Leh's 1st boutique hotel. The interior boasts disco-pop colour schemes, lots of space & 1st-rate facilities. **$$$$**

🏠 **Hotel Dewachan** [map, page 70] (13 rooms) Ag Ling; m 962 297 4547; e tanzin. norbu@gmail.com. South of the city, not far from the airport, is this quiet haven where you can while away days in the garden looking out across fields. Rooms are simple but comfortable & the home-cooked meals are delicious. Highly recommended for anyone seeking peace. **$$**

🏠 **Tsetan Guesthouse** [74 C2] (11 rooms) Upper Changspa; ☎224 9125; e tsetan_n@yahoo. com; w tsetanguesthouse.com. A little away from the centre, Tsetan is quiet & set among beautiful gardens. It's clean, friendly & the slightly more expensive rooms have attached bathrooms. **$–$$**

✘ WHERE TO EAT AND DRINK

You won't find haute cuisine in Leh but, as the majority of foreign visitors are either backpackers on a budget or carbohydrate-hungry trekkers, that should come as no surprise. Both of these groups are well catered for, with a high concentration of cheap and cheerful, if slightly scruffy, restaurants serving all manner of meals along Changspa and around Main Bazaar. If you're looking for somewhere a little more upmarket, your choices are somewhat limited.

The restaurants listed below cater almost entirely to the tourist trade and so are open from May to October only, unless otherwise stated. They open for breakfast (muesli, porridge and banana pancakes are the not terribly imaginative menu staples) around 07.00 and remain open throughout the day, closing as the last patrons leave sometime after 22.00. Once the daylight fades you might be dining in the dark if the power fails, although a few of the larger restaurants are able to run their lights off a generator if need be.

As Ladakh's local population is predominantly vegetarian, as are many of the Indian tourists, all of the restaurants listed here have both vegetarian and non-vegetarian (i.e. meat) dishes on their menus. In many cases the vegetarian options outnumber the non-vegetarian, and the meals they offer are almost always delicious.

RESTAURANTS
Around Main Bazaar
For a really cheap, fast snack, check out the kebab stands (⏰ evenings only; $) on the corner of Main Bazaar & Old Fort Rd.

✘ **Alchi Kitchen** [78 D1] Old Town; ☎ 227 129. A branch of the stunningly good restaurant of the same name in Alchi (page 147), this suave place serves creative takes on Ladakhi classics. The *chutagi* (pasta stew) is a triumph. Easily one of Leh's best. **$$$$**

✘ **Il Forno** [78 D2] LBA Complex, Old Fort Rd. Rooftop restaurant with great views of Leh Palace & the Old Town. It's always packed with people just returned from a trek & desperate to get their lips around one of the wood-fired pizzas. Lavazza coffee is available. **$$**

✘ **Leh View Restaurant** [78 D2] Next to SBI, Main Bazaar. Serving reasonable Punjabi dishes, the Leh View has 2 floors: an inside restaurant & the roof terrace above. Head for the latter for an uninterrupted view straight up at the palace. Tables on the Old Town side are the best. In daytime enjoy the set b/fasts from Rs150 & take your camera. After dark it's no less atmospheric as the muezzin calls the faithful to prayer from the neighbouring Jama Masjid. **$$**

✘ **Chaska Maska Restaurant** [78 B4] Old Fort Rd. The only restaurant we've found in Leh serving south Indian food. Pop in for delicious crispy dosas stuffed with spiced potatoes & pretty passable idli & uttapam. It's also known for its sizzlers. If you haven't had enough of them yet, you can also get a plate of steamed momos. **$-$$**

Changspa and Karzoo
✘ **La Piazzetta** [80 D5] Changspa Rd; m 962 295 2080. Popular, if rather overpriced, pizza joint. 11-inch pizzas cost Rs210–390 depending on the toppings & salads, lasagne & cannelloni also make a welcome appearance on the menu. Most dishes use organic products. **$$$–$$$$**

✘ **Bon Appetit** [80 C5] Off Changspa Rd; ☎ 251 533; ⏰ lunch & dinner only. Some of the best continental cuisine in Leh. Dishes vary from well-done classics to slightly more unusual variations: think pizza margarita with sundried tomatoes or a caramelised onion & mutton burger. There's a strong line-up of mocktails (from Rs150) & cocktails (from Rs170) & you can also try local specialities like the delicious, vitamin-rich sea buckthorn juice. Follow the red signpost down the footpath from Changspa Rd. **$$$**

✘ **Amigo** [80 C5] Opp Moravian Mission School, Changspa Rd; m 946 970 9455. Authentic Korean restaurant with rooftop setting. Korean staples such as ramen noodles cost Rs170; dishes such as backsook (Rs470) & jimdak (Rs360) are for 2 people to share. Check out the daily specials board. **$$–$$$**

✘ **G Kitchen Restaurant** [80 B3] Changspa Rd; ☎ 253 670. An old timer of a restaurant, the G Kitchen has a relaxed roof-terrace restaurant with a varied menu & young backpacker clientele. The staff are friendly & the food, though a little bland, is pleasant enough. **$$**

✘ **Mentokling Apple Garden Restaurant** [80 D5] Nr police station, Zangsti Rd; m 985 839 9142. Pleasant garden restaurant tucked behind the Mentokling Guesthouse. Service is slow but the banana pancakes are worth the wait.

There's plenty of shade beneath the fruit trees, parasols & canopy, so it's a prime spot to sit with a Kingfisher beer & read or wait for friends. It's a real social centre, with frequent film nights & major sporting events shown on a big screen. $$

✳ ✗ **Namza Café** [80 D5] Zangsti Rd; m 941 929 9111; w namza-cafe-designer-store. business.site. A classy, boutique restaurant & clothing shop, this garden restaurant has a limited but carefully crafted menu of Ladakhi classics given a modern make-over. The setting & service is exquisite & if you're not in the mood for a full meal just pop by for a fresh juice or a tea. $$

✗ **Wonderland** [80 B3] Changspa Rd; m 962 297 2826. Though rather unprepossessing at street level, the interior staircase ascends to a large roof terrace where gentle Himalayan flute music sets the laidback scene. The extensive menu incorporates everything from excellent Italian bruschetta laden with garlic & olive oil to Tibetan *thukpa* (noodles in soup). Nothing happens in a hurry but the dishes are tasty & prices are fair. $$

Fort Road

✗ **Dreamland** [78 B3] Above Dreamland Trek & Tour, Fort Rd; ☎ 255 089; w dreamladakh. com. Upmarket inside restaurant & open-air roof terrace serving a range of international dishes but specialising in Kashmiri *waazwaan* (see box, page 62) & delicious momos & *thukpa* (Tibetan noodle soup). Free Wi-Fi. $$–$$$

✗ **Summer Harvest** [78 B3] Behind Dreamland, Fort Rd; m 990 698 6556. Though it describes itself as a Tibetan restaurant, you should come to Summer Harvest for its Indian dishes, which are quite possibly the best in Leh. Our favourites are the shahi paneer & malai kofta, accompanied by plenty of garlic naan. The vegetarian dishes here are highly recommended. $$–$$$

✳ ✗ **Tibetan Kitchen** [78 A3] Fort Rd; m 979 765 7181. Set back from the street behind a row of buildings, this is rightly Leh's most popular restaurant. The garden tables are invariably packed & if you don't arrive early you'll have to stand & wait. The building is influenced by traditional Tibetan architecture & the menu ranges from fresh trout to succulent Afghan

kebabs, but, as the name suggests, the real specialities are upmarket versions of traditional Tibetan classics. $$–$$$

✗ **Chopsticks Noodle Bar** [78 A3] Raku Complex, Fort Rd; m 941 917 8652. Chopsticks serves excellent Chinese & Thai dishes as well as superb momos (do the right thing & order a chocolate momo for dessert), plus other local favourites. It's spotlessly clean & service is efficient. The large tables outside may be shared by several groups of guests. $$

CAFÉS

▢ **Coffeesutra** [78 C2] NAC Complex, Main Bazaar. Homemade cakes & proper coffee served at tables on the 1st-floor veranda. For a bit of a treat, try one of the muffins. The bookshelf of secondhand titles is worth a browse too.

▢ **Lala's Art Café** [78 E2] Old Town. From the outside you'd be forgiven for thinking you're in the wrong place, but climb the crumbling stone staircase & you'll reach a Leh institution. A standard menu of teas & coffees is supplemented by the opportunity to try Tibetan butter tea, served in a miniature wooden churn, accompanied by traditional Ladakhi breads. The people behind the café do much to promote the restoration of heritage buildings in & around Leh.

▢ **Little Tibet Café** [80 C5] Changspa Rd. Tiny & very basic café serving locally bottled fruit juices (inc apricot & sea buckthorn) as well as tea & coffee. The staff are happy to share their extensive knowledge on all tings Tibetan & you can get a water bottle refill for just Rs10.

▢ **Lonpo House** [78 E1] Below Leh Palace. Right at the top of the steep climb if you come to the palace on foot, Lonpo House is run by the Himalayan Cultural Heritage Foundation (m 941 921 8013; e office.hchf@gmail.com). Situated in an atmospheric old building, the roof of which is held aloft by 4 hefty wooden pillars; guests sit on carpets on the floor & are served tea, coffee & soft drinks at low tables.

▢ **Open Hand** [78 A3] Library Rd; w openhand.in. If after weeks of rice & dal you cry at the sight of lettuce, this is the place for you. Decent coffee, juices & divine homemade cakes, salads & wraps, all served in a laidback atmosphere with indoor & outdoor space & free Wi-Fi. While you're there, be sure to check out the Open Hand shop (page 86).

ENTERTAINMENT AND NIGHTLIFE

Weekly **film showings** take place at LAMO (page 91) each Friday at 16.00. The programme is composed predominantly of documentaries, primarily shown in English, and usually with a social or environmental angle.

Other than this, there are no formal entertainment and nightlife options. What you will find during the high season, however, are locally advertised party nights and other such events, especially in the restaurants on Changspa. Look out for posters and chat to other travellers to find out what's happening where.

SHOPPING

With the exception of locally produced handicrafts, all of the goods for sale in Leh are imported either from other parts of India or from China: even basic foodstuffs and household items frequently come all the way from Jammu. For this reason prices are typically higher than elsewhere in India and you may see only a limited selection of items, though shops here are still better stocked than in other parts of Ladakh.

SOUVENIRS

There is no shortage of souvenir sellers in Leh, though the range, quality & prices are distinctly variable. We've selected the retailers below because they have stock that is a little out of the ordinary or their profits support local NGOs.

Handicraft Industrial Co-operative Society [78 C3] Old Fort Rd; ⏱ 11.00–19.30 daily. Simple selection of locally made stock inc sea buckthorn textiles & low tables finely carved or brightly painted with Tibetan dragons. A large, hand-carved table that packs flat for ease of transport costs from Rs7,000.

J&K Government Arts Emporium [78 D2] Main Bazaar; ⏱ 10.30–18.30 daily, closed 13.00–14.00. Next to the Jama Masjid, this small state-run emporium has fixed prices, giving you a good idea of what maximum amount you should be paying elsewhere. There's limited stock but they do have some attractive papier mâché pieces & genuine pashminas in natural colours from Rs4,000.

✳ **Jigmat Couture** [78 C4] Old Fort Rd; m 969 700 0344; w jigmatcouture.com; ⏱ 10.00–20.00 daily. Jigmat Couture really demands a category all of its own: encompassing both high-end fashion & family heirlooms, its artistic textiles are quite simply priceless. Their accessories have featured in photo shoots for French *Vogue* & every line can be customised to ensure it is not only unique but has the perfect fit. Even if you're not in the market to buy, go in & take a look.

Ladakh Rural Women's Enterprise [78 C2] NAC Complex, Main Bazaar; m 990 699 1375; ⏱ 10.00–20.00 daily. Tiny shop stuffed with knitted hats & socks, felt toy yaks & Bactrian camels, colourful slippers & other woollen items. Everything is made by local women & profits go back to them.

Nomadic Woolen Mills [78 D3] Opp Noor Complex, Main Bazaar; m 962 299 5456; w nomadicwoolenmills.com; ⏱ 09.00–19.00 daily. Elegant cashmere scarfs & hats woven by nomadic women.

Open Hand [78 A3] Library Rd; m 962 205 5896; w openhand.in; ⏰ 07.30–21.30 daily. Large & friendly shop & accompanying café selling fair-trade clothes, toys & other gift items. Products are made by marginalised & rescued women who receive training & a living wage for their work. We couldn't resist the gorgeous, brightly coloured toy elephants or the more unusual monk & nun dolls made by nuns at the Dolma Ling nunnery in Dharamsala.

Silk Route Arts & Crafts [78 D2] Next to SBI, Main Bazaar; m 962 293 6736; ⏰ 08.30–20.30 daily. Small, well-organised shop selling a selection of high-quality carpets, embroidery & shawls from Kashmir & central Asia. The pashminas are authentic & the owners not too pushy.

Tibetan Refugee Market [78 D2] Next to SBI, Main Bazaar; ⏰ 08.00–21.00 daily. This open-air market has numerous stalls selling colourful beads, turquoise & silver jewellery, prayer wheels & other nicknacks. The vendors are usually open to negotiation over price. There are several similar sites within Leh, including on Fort Rd close to the Tibetan Kitchen restaurant & in the southern part of Main Bazaar. In all cases the stock & prices are similar.

Village Arts & Crafts [78 B3] Fort Rd; m 990 656 6330; e wangnoomuzafar@gmail.com; ⏰ 10.00–21.30 daily; see ad, page 98. The best selection of Kashmiri carpets in Leh. Both wool & silk carpets available. Designs can also be made to order. Owner Muzafar Wangnoo speaks excellent English & French & has an intimate knowledge of carpet making. Payment can be made by Visa & MasterCard. Highly recommended.

Wali Curious [78 D2] Opp NAC Complex, Main Bazaar; ☎ 257 015; e walicurious@yahoo.co.in; ⏰ 09.00–21.00 daily. An Aladdin's cave of Ladakhi jewellery (antique & modern) inc beautiful pieces of lapis lazuli, turquoise & coral.

TREKKING GEAR

If you would rather buy than rent your trekking gear, **Venture Equipment** [80 C5] has a tiny shop at the eastern end of Changspa Rd.

Himalaya Adventure Store [78 D2] Goji Complex, Main Bazaar; ☎ 258 609; m 990 699 7072; e himadvstore@yahoo.com; ⏰ 11.00–22.00. If you're in need of serious trekking equipment, from 4-season sleeping bags & trekking poles to GORE-TEX jackets & hiking boots, come here. It keeps a wide range of stock in different sizes & at least some of the branded items are genuine.

Mountain Wear [80 A3] Changspa Rd; m 969 722 9434; ⏰ 07.00–22.00. Cold-weather clothing & Nepalese knock-off North Face rucksacks (more suitable for casual travellers than serious trekkers).

BOOKS

Leh is the only place in Ladakh where you'll find a good selection of bookshops selling English-language titles, maps & postcards. The shops below are particularly well stocked.

THE LADAKH MARATHON *Keith Mackintosh*

For those visitors to Leh wishing to do more than walk, there's the Ladakh Marathon (w ladakhmarathon.com), held in September each year. Beginning at dawn with a wild stampede from the Shanti Stupa to the Indus, the 42km route heads up the south bank, passing through deserts and villages beneath the snows of Stok Kangri. And then, after skirting the Holy Fish Pond of Shey, the last 10km is a tough climb back up to the finish in Leh – hard work in the thin air.

It's just one element in a day packed with music, speeches, celebrations and traditional dance – a wonderful event that brings together fast and slow, young and old, local and tourist. There's also a 10km race around Leh itself, a more manageable and popular option full of eager schoolchildren. And for superhumans, there's even a 70km ultramarathon, up and over Khardung La.

Whatever the distance, they're all quite challenging routes, and not to be done unless you've acclimatised. So forget about your personal best, and take the opportunity to enjoy a slow run through this vast and beautiful landscape.

Himalayan Book Shop [78 B3] Raku Complex, Fort Rd; ⊕ 08.00–20.30. Carefully chosen selection of books on Buddhism, trekking maps & Ladakhi language guides. Closes early if there's a power cut.

Ladakh Book Shop [78 D2] Next to SBI, Main Bazaar; ☏ 256 464; m 986 811 1112; ⊕ 08.30–21.30. Very large collection of coffee-table books, maps, guides & non-fiction titles, with a small number of novels in English, too. Agents for the Delhi-based publisher Hanish & Co. Shop is on the 1st floor of the building.

Lehling Book Shop [78 D3] Main Bazaar; ☏ 244 192; m 962 298 000; ⊕ 08.00–20.30. Friendly shop packed floor to ceiling with English-language books, postcards & stationery. Prices are theoretically fixed, but the owners are happy to negotiate a discount if you are buying several items.

FOOD

Leh has no supermarkets as such, but there are a number of small dried & packaged goods stores where you can pick up snacks & other supplies for trekking. They tend to be fixed price & have a limited range of items. Check the 'best before' dates before buying, as tins in particular may have been sitting around for rather a long time.

Chospa Supermarket [78 D3] Main Bazaar; ⊕ 08.30–21.00 Mon–Sat, 08.30–18.00 Sun. Basic store selling packaged foods, spices by weight, cosmetics & hair products & a freezer of ice cream that may or may not have defrosted in the most recent power cut.

Modern Bazaar [78 C3] Fort Rd; ⊕ 06.00–23.00. Tucked into a corner & more reminiscent of a garage than a food store, this shop nevertheless sells dried & tinned goods, snacks & soft drinks. You can buy bottled water in bulk.

OTHER PRACTICALITIES

COMMUNICATIONS
Internet

Leh's internet providers give an erratic service, with the central system often down for hours at a time, especially if the cable from Srinagar has been damaged by flooding or rockfalls. Almost all the hotels & many tourist restaurants have password-protected Wi-Fi for customers.

Potala Cyber Café [78 E4] Main Bazaar; ☏ 252 111; ⊕ 09.00–17.00. The best of Srinagar's internet cafés, which has reasonable connections but also loads of kids playing computer games.

Post

Tourist Post Office [78 D3] Cnr Main Bazaar & Fort Rd; ⊕ 10.00–18.00 Mon–Sat. The most useful of Leh's 2 central post offices, although note that many of the services listed on the wall (including STD phone calls) are not actually available here & some of the staff don't speak English.

Telephone

Getting a **SIM card** anywhere in J&K has always been a bit of a hassle (page 65), but in the last couple of years things have improved marginally. **Aircel** [78 E4] (Main Bazaar; ☏ 251 132;

⊕ 10.00–18.00 Mon–Sat) & **Airtel** (off Main Bazaar; ⊕ 10.00–17.30 Mon–Sat) both now offer pay-as-you-go SIM cards, but the catch is that they work only up to around 30km from Leh (depending on general reception). You will need to submit 4 passport photos, photocopies of your passport & that of your local sponsor, & getting a connection frequently takes up to 4 working days. Most of the more traveller-savvy hotels are happy to act as a 'sponsor' &, if possible, you should go to the office with your sponsor. **Top-ups** are available from numerous stands around Main Bazaar & Changspa; look out for the logo of your service provider.

If you need to make a call but do not have your own handset or SIM, STD & VoIP lines are widely available in all parts of the town, including at all internet cafés (see left). Almost all international calls are routed via the web, so bear this in mind if the internet goes down. Expect to pay Rs10 per minute. Public telephones are all marked as STD (local calls) or ISD (international calls).

HAIR AND BEAUTY

The dust & heat of India inevitably take their toll, even before you go trekking, so now & then a bit of pampering is in order, if only to keep you looking vaguely presentable.

Aaina Beauty Parlour [78 B3] Library Rd; m 849 293 2231; ⏰ noon–19.00. Run by English-speaking Rajni & her husband, this outfit offers manicures & pedicures, haircutting, facials, threading, head massage & a variety of other treatments for both men & women. They also sell a small range of cosmetics inc lipsalves.

LAUNDRY
Most hotels & guesthouses will wash your clothes, albeit for an inflated fee. Otherwise, try the following:

Highland Dry Cleaning [78 C2] Zangsti Rd. Situated in the centre of town, but with inflated prices to match. As well as washing it also, as one might expect, does dry cleaning.
Wonder Wash Behind Namgyal Shunu Complex, opp FCI bldg, Airport Rd, Skalzang Ling. Laundry using borehole water, so your clothes will end up cleaner than if the *dhobi* (washerman) dunks them in the river.

MEDICAL
Leh is the only place in Ladakh with reasonably well-developed medical services. Staff typically speak English, standard medications are readily available & you can get treatment for most illnesses and injuries.

✚ **Het Ram Vinay Kumar Chemists** [78 D2] Main Bazaar; ☎ 252 160; ⏰ 10.00–21.00 Mon–Sat, closed 14.00–16.00 for lunch. Near the Jama Masjid, this is Leh's best-stocked chemist. The pharmacist is helpful & speaks good English. Antibiotics & altitude-sickness medication are sold over the counter without need for a prescription. Stocks cosmetics, baby products & food supplements.

✚ **Ladakh Physiotherapy & Rehabilitation Centre** [78 C3] Behind Splash, Gompa Complex, Old Fort Rd; m 962 227 0829; e rigzindolkar@ gmail.com; ⏰ 16.00–20.00. Friendly clinic with 2 qualified physiotherapists. Treatments for neck, shoulder & back pain & sports & trekking injuries. Rs250/hr.
✚ **Potala Medicos** [78 D3] 1st Flr, Batta Complex, Main Bazaar; m 990 699 8525; ⏰ 09.00–10.00 & 17.00–19.00 Mon–Sat, 17.00–19.00 Sun. Dr Tashi Thinlas runs this daily polyclinic, akin to a GP surgery.
✚ **SNM Hospital** [74 C6] Nr main bus stand; ☎ 252 014. Large & well-run district hospital with competent staff in most specialisms. If you require treatment for altitude sickness, you'll likely be brought to the SNM. Doctors here, though sympathetic, are rightly weary of dealing with those who have ignored advice about acclimatisation & then got into trouble.

MONEY
Foreign exchange is widely available in Leh, with everyone from travel agents to shop owners cashing in on the business. The following banks have 24-hour ATMs, though there are frequently queues to use them & they often run out of cash before everyone has been served, in which case you'll need to get a cash advance on a Visa or MasterCard.

$ **HDFC Bank** [78 D2] Main Bazaar; ⏰ 10.00–16.00 Mon–Fri, 10.00–13.00 Sat. 24hr ATM.
$ **J&K Bank** [78 C3] Cnr Fort Rd & Old Fort Rd. 24hr ATM.
$ **Paul Merchants Ltd** [78 D2] Khawaja Complex, Main Bazaar; ☎ 255 309; m 729

OXYGEN BAR

Many people flying into Leh suffer from the effects of the reduced oxygen at this altitude (you are, after all, at a breathless 3,520m above sea level). If you're lucky, the effects will be nothing worse than a light headache and a sense of breathlessness. However, there is always a risk of potentially fatal altitude sickness, so if you're feeling the effects then pop down to the Oxygen Bar [78 C3] (⏰ 10.30–19.00 Mon–Sat, 10.30–16.00 Sun), located above the tourist office. Staff here will give you an examination (Rs20) and, if needed, stick you on a bottle of near-pure oxygen. Note, though, that this is no replacement for good acclimatisation.

For those travelling from Leh to the Nubra Valley, Dha Hanu or the Southern Lakes, it is necessary to get an Inner Line Permit (see box, page 101). You can either try to obtain this yourself once on the ground in Leh or you can apply online (though the system can be a bit temperamental!) at w lahdclehpermit. in. If you decide to apply for the relevant permit yourself, you will need to find at least two other people to apply with you.

If doing it in person, take your passport, photocopies of your passport, a print-out of your intended itinerary and a covering letter addressed to the **Deputy Commissioner's Office** [78 D4] (\ 252 010; ⊕ 09.00–15.00). The permit itself costs Rs20 per day, with an additional one-off environmental fee of Rs300 plus a Rs100 compulsory contribution to the Red Cross. The permit will usually be issued on the same day. If you are short of time or need additional people to apply with, give your paperwork to a local travel agent (page 76) as they seem to be able to rustle up the requisite additional people and can get the permits at great speed, sometimes even at the weekend.

If you plan to climb one of Ladakh's many peaks, you'll need to buy a permit from the **Indian Mountaineering Foundation** [80 D5] (\ 253 437; w indmount.org). Peak fees are calculated according to height and start from US$50. You can apply through a local travel agent (page 76) but it's easy enough to do it yourself and, providing the peak is under 7,000m (above which requires special permission from Delhi and hence months of paperwork and hassle) then formalities can be completed in under an hour. Take with you half a dozen photocopies of your passport and visa, and also the name and contact details of your guide, as he/she will be responsible for you on the mountain.

854 0340; e pmlleh@paulmerchants.net; w paulmerchants.net; ⊕ 10.00–20.00 daily. Part of a nationwide chain of Forex offices. Also processes Western Union transfers.
$ PNB [78 D3] Main Bazaar. 24hr ATM.
$ SBI [78 D2] Main Bazaar; ⊕ 10.00–16.00 Mon–Fri, 10.00–13.00 Sat. Forex during branch hours only; 24hr ATM. Note that in the winter months the branch opens & closes 30mins later.

REGISTRATION

Visitors arriving in Leh by air are expected to fill in the foreigners' registration form, which contains virtually the same set of information you'll have provided on arrival in India. Fill in approximate dates if you don't yet know when you'll depart: like with so much of India's bureaucracy, you're obliged to submit the form at the airport desk but the chances are it'll then disappear into a storage room, never to be seen again.

ACTIVITIES

Whatever your interests, there are plenty of things to keep you occupied in Leh. The majority of options are, inevitably, on offer during only the summer months, though you're welcome to meditate year-round.

CLIMBING

Gravit [78 A3] Raku Complex, Fort Rd; m 999 931 6648; e elevateyogaclasses@gmail.com. Indoor climbing wall & bouldering. Can organise frequent rock-climbing trips in the surrounding countryside.

MEDITATION

Mahabodhi International Meditation Centre \ 264 372; e infomimc@gmail.com; w mahabodhi-ladakh.org. The best place in Ladakh to do a meditation course is at this complex just outside Leh in Choglamsar (page 96). The centre can accommodate as many as 50 people on retreat at any one time & regular 3-day meditation courses are scheduled throughout the summer, both for beginners and for more advanced students. The centre also has a smaller but very convenient **Leh branch** [80 B4] (m 962 295 7460; ⏰ 09.00–19.30 Mon–Sat) on Changspa Rd, which hosts daily meditation classes with yoga & also public talks.

MOUNTAIN BIKING AND MOTORCYCLING
Bike hire is big business in Leh & there are numerous companies offering everything from pushbikes to 500cc Royal Enfields. See page 76 for more details.

PAINTBALLING
Paintball Yard m 990 634 3834/959 698 1936. One of Leh's more unexpected options is nonetheless popular with gap-year students (& most other people after a few beers). Just past the bridge on Changspa Rd, at 3,524m, it is apparently the highest paintballing site in the world. Prices start from Rs450 for safety gear, markers & 20 balls; Rs350 gets you an additional 30 balls. Call to arrange a game as there are no fixed opening times.

RAFTING
White-water rafting on one of Ladakh's many rivers is a popular attraction & easily arranged from Leh. Although many of the regular travel agents (page 76) do offer rafting packages, you'll have a better experience if you arrange it through a specialist operator.

Splash Ladakh [78 C2] Gompa Complex, Old Fort Rd; m 962 296 5941/ 941 988 8787; w splashladakh.com. A river-rafting specialist with highly trained staff & well-maintained equipment. They offer regular expeditions on the Indus & Zanskar rivers, as well as kayak trips; safety is improved by the presence of outriders in kayaks.

YOGA
Though there are not as many opportunities to study yoga in Leh as in other parts of India, a few companies have spied a gap in the market & are offering classes for tourists. Daily yoga classes combined with meditation are also available from the Leh branch of the **Mahabodhi International Meditation Centre** on Changspa Rd (page 89)

Shiva Yoga Centre [80 B3] Nr Wonderland, Changspa Rd; m 849 281 4196. 5- & 7-day classes starting every Mon & daily drop-in sessions of Ashtanga (07.30) & Hatha yoga (09.00 & 16.00) offers Reiki treatments, meditation sessions & month-long yoga teaching courses.

WHAT TO SEE AND DO

OLD TOWN Much of your time in Leh will be spent in and around the Old Town, where the majority of sights, hotels and restaurants are located. The mix of old Tibetan-flavoured architecture and blatant commercialism makes for a colourful and endlessly absorbing experience.

Leh's Old Town appears on the World Monuments Fund's list of Watch Sites. Natural erosion of the mud-brick buildings in the wind and rain is the principal threat, though the pressures of modern urban life – unregulated building, motor vehicles, the need for proper sanitation, etc – are all taking their toll. Despite these threats, however, restoration and preservation work is taking place throughout.

Leh Palace ✳ [78 E1] (Namgyal Hill; ✆ 252 297; ⏰ dawn–dusk; admission Rs5/100 local/foreigner, video camera Rs25) Towering across Leh and viewable from almost any street corner in the town, Leh Palace seems to feature on every postcard, and quite rightly so. Purportedly modelled on the Potala Palace in Lhasa (though at just nine storeys considerably shorter), the mud-brick and wood structure is undoubtedly impressive, albeit in places in a poor state of repair.

Leh Palace was built by Sengge Namgyal in 1600 and took three years to complete. It has more than 100 rooms (though many of them are no longer accessible) and when inhabited was divided into two distinct areas: animals were stabled and fodder, dried meat and vegetables were stored on the lower levels, while the upper floors housed the royal apartments, reception halls, throne room and private prayer hall.

Inside the palace there is sadly now little to see: none of the rooms are furnished, with the exception of the colourful **prayer room**, one wall of which is lined with carefully wrapped sacred manuscripts. Enlargements of early 20th-century photographs of Ladakh and Tibet line some of the corridors, and temporary exhibitions are displayed in what was once the **audience hall**. From some of the lower terraces you can survey the carved **wooden balconies** and window frames that are a local speciality.

The highlight of a visit to the palace is the view from the roof. The rooftops of storeys eight and nine (the latter of which is accessed via a ladder) have **panoramic views** across to Stok Kangri and the Shanti Stupa, and further up the cliff to the Tsemo Fort and Gompa. The skies seem to be clearest in the morning, and if you come at this time you'll not only avoid the midday heat but also have the palace virtually to yourself.

There are no signs to indicate the function of different areas, which makes a local guide an essential addition if you want to properly understand the palace's layout and history. Wear proper footwear, as many of the floors and staircases are uneven, and be sure to carry a torch as many of the interior corridors are unlit.

Note that photography inside the palace is banned.

From the town centre you can reach the palace either by taxi (Rs202–234 one-way; Rs263–305 return), which will drop you right by the entrance, or by walking the clearly signposted 10-minute route through the Old Town. Take the path from Main Bazaar that leads away from the Jama Masjid, and follow it to the left just past Lala's Art Café. A short way further on the palace is confusingly signposted both to the left and the right: the path to the left is a somewhat steeper short cut that brings you past LAMO (see below) and up through the courtyard of the Chokhang Vihara Gompa (page 92).

Ladakh Arts and Media Organisation (LAMO) [78 F1] (Below Leh Palace; 📞251 554; e info@lamo.org.in; w lamo.org.in; ⊕ 11.00–17.00 Mon–Sat; admission Rs 50/100 local/foreigner) Opened in 2010 in two sensitively restored buildings dating from the 17th century, the LAMO centre comprises multiple exhibition spaces, a study centre and library. A charitable trust, it exists to conduct outreach programmes, research, workshops and exhibitions into Ladakh's visual culture, performing arts and literature. LAMO lies immediately below the palace complex, and you'll pass right by if you approach the palace via the short cut (see above).

The main focus of the centre from a visitor's perspective is the **temporary exhibition**, which changes each summer. Previous exhibitions have examined the cultural heritage of Leh's Old Town, the production and craftsmanship of pashminas and the early mapping of Leh by foreign travellers. Images and maps are drawn from the centre's extensive visual archives and supplemented by related artefacts. All the displays are accompanied by well-written captions and information boards (all of which are in English), and the knowledgeable staff are happy to chatter about the various projects they're undertaking with the local community.

Tsemo complex [74 D3] Looking down on Leh Palace, the Tsemo complex is the small collection of white-and-red buildings perched like a bird's nest at the

high point of the mountain and encircled by streaks of primary-coloured prayer flags. It is possible to drive up (15mins; Rs247–286 from the taxi stand) but rather more popular is the 15-minute steep climb along the zigzag footpath from Leh Palace. Do not attempt this climb if you are already suffering from the effects of the altitude. The complex consists of three buildings, the uppermost of which is a former fortress, parts of which date back nearly 1,500 years. On the whole though, most of what you see today dates from the 16th century.

The solid, dark-red structure at the base of the complex is **Tsemo Gompa** (⊕ 07.30–19.00; admission Rs30), where a monk sits in the shade selling tickets and reminding visitors to circumnavigate the site in a clockwise direction. The gompa houses the two-storey **Maitreya Buddha**, whose serene expression is visible only when you are standing at its feet, and surrounding prayer rooms decorated with slightly nightmarish **murals** of demons.

Climbing past the gompa brings you to the **Tsemo Fort** (⊕ 08.00–18.30; admission Rs20), a simple, whitewashed building bedecked in coloured prayer flags that flutter in the wind. Inside the dark, wooden prayer room is a miniature stupa flanked by two multi-faced female statues. Devotees prostrate themselves here in prayer, so be careful not to stand in their way.

Make sure you take a walk around the rickety-looking (but fortunately perfectly stable) covered walkway around the outside of the prayer hall. The views down across Leh are quite simply breathtaking, especially when the mountains are clearly visible too, and the prayer flags add an elegant and wholly appropriate frame to any photos you take.

Central Asia Museum [78 D1] (⊕ 10.00–13.00 & 14.00–18.00 daily; admission Rs100) A remarkable modern structure on the edge of the Old Town, this museum briefly showcases the ancient Silk Road across China and central Asia and includes displays in English relating to Ladakh's important role on this trade route. The building has been inspired by traditional Ladakhi architecture and is made from stone and wood carved by local craftsmen. There's also a small photo gallery and a café, and the complex also includes an ancient mosque within the courtyard.

Guru Lhakhang Shrine [78 E1] (Free admission but donations welcome) This Buddhist shrine dates from the early 17th century and is situated southwest of the palace in the lower part of the Old Town. Constructed on a rectangular plan and with walls up to 70cm thick, the original timber frame and paintings were damaged by water but then restored in 2004–05 with the help of the Tibet Heritage Fund, which has a detailed report on the conservation work on its website (w tibetheritagefund.org). There are some modern murals and also a **statue of Guru Rinpoche**. Unfortunately, the building is closed more often than it's open.

MAIN BAZAAR The Main Bazaar has long been the centre of life in Leh. It would once have dealt in food stuffs and exotic products brought in on Silk Road caravans from central Asia and China, but today it trades mainly in trekking gear and tourist souvenirs, and there are many more Wi-Fi-enabled coffee shops than in days past. Even so, it remains a fun place to hang out and has a number of interesting sights.

Chokhang Vihara Gompa [78 D2] (Opp SBI, Main Bazaar; free admission but donations welcome; ⊕ 24hrs daily) If you spend any time around Main Bazaar, or indeed have ventured up to the palace, the chances are that you'll have caught a

glimpse of the golden, pagoda-like roof of the Chokhang Vihara Gompa poking out above the surrounding flat-roofed buildings: it is by far the most attractive piece of architecture in the vicinity.

Entering through the gate brings you into the large, shady courtyard that surrounds the gompa itself. Take a look at the small **library** and, if it's of interest, go in, take tea and have a chat at the office of **Ladakh Buddhist Association**: it's straight across the square. From the open area to your left you'll have an unobstructed view up to Leh Palace and Tsemo Fort, and it's a peaceful place to sit and reflect. You can fill up your water bottle for a few rupees at the clearly marked **drinking-water tap**.

The gompa itself (confusingly also known as Tsug Lhakhang and the Choskhang, Jokhang or Soma Gompa) was built in 1956 to celebrate Buddha's 2,500th birthday. Inside, the temple contains an important image of the **Sakyamuni Buddha** (the historic Buddha) made in Tibet in 1959, the same year that the Dalai Lama fled into exile.

Jama Masjid [78 E2] Leh's Jama Masjid, or Friday Mosque, stands in the corner of Main Bazaar. Non-Muslims are welcome to come inside providing they are appropriately attired and behave in a respectful manner (page 66), though it is best if you do not visit on a Friday afternoon when prayers are in progress.

The mosque was built in 1666–67 by the Mughal emperor Aurangzeb, a religious zealot in comparison with his predecessors, who was nonetheless responsible for some fine sacred architecture, including the wonderful Badshahi Mosque in Lahore. The construction of this mosque accompanied the signing of a treaty between the Ladakhi king Deldan Namgyal and Aurangzeb to jointly oust Mongol forces from Ladakhi soil.

Much of what you can see today is sadly not original. The mosque was largely rebuilt (and expanded) from 2002–05, so it is in essence a modern building, albeit with a few historical features.

The Jama Masjid serves Leh's Sunni community. A second mosque for Shiite Muslims, the **Inumbra Mosque** [78 D4], is further south along Main Bazaar.

CHANGSPA AND KARZOO Changspa and Karzoo are the centre of Leh's – indeed Ladakh's – tourism scene, and the whole area is crammed full of hotels, guesthouses and traveller cafés offering what are generally fairly similar menus. Tourism sights are fairly thin on the ground, but there are a couple of stupas worth exploring.

Gomang Stupa [80 B2] (Changspa Rd; free admission) This whitewashed complex is thought to date back more than 1,000 years and there are some fine Mani stone carvings dotted around the place. The complex also contains a small library showcasing numerous Buddhist texts. Given its proximity to the town centre, it is surprising how few people come here; those who do tend to be praying or meditating.

Shanti Stupa ✳ [74 B2] (Shanti Stupa Rd; ☉ dawn–21.00 daily; free admission but donations welcome) One of Leh's most iconic images is the view west across the town to Shanti Stupa. The snow-white dome shines out against its dusty, mountain backdrop, drawing your eye. Despite this, it's a relatively recent addition to Leh's skyline and its shape and decoration are somewhat different from others in the area, no doubt due to the era of its construction (the early 1990s) and the fact that it was Japanese Buddhists rather than locals who paid for its construction. Relics of the Buddha are contained within the stupa's base, making it an important pilgrimage site as well as a tourist attraction, and there are some brightly painted relief carvings visible from the terraces that encircle the structure.

Shanti Stupa is one of Leh's most popular tourist sites, so if you want to appreciate it without hordes of other people, you need to get there early. Come at dawn and you might just get half an hour's peace in which to relish the sunrise and absorb the spirituality of the place.

OTHER AREAS

Sankar Gompa [74 C2] (Free admission but donations welcome) Just 2km north of Leh in the hamlet of Sankar is this monastery, which belongs to the Gelug-pa sect. A dozen or so monks attached to the main monastery at Spituk (see opposite) live and worship here.

Built in the 19th century during the lifetime of the previous Bakula Rinpoche, the three-storey gompa houses a richly painted *dukhang* dedicated to the White Tara and also to Kangyur Lhakhang. The **murals** depict scenes from monastic life and there are also fine images of Avalokiteshvara (an earthly manifestation of the self-born eternal Buddha Amitabha), Tsongkhapa and Vajrabhairava.

A taxi to the gompa from Main Bazaar will cost you from Rs174 one-way or from Rs226 return.

Tisseru Stupa [74 C1] (Gyamsa Rd; free admission but donations welcome) In the northwest of Leh and easily combined with a visit to Shanti Stupa is the far older Tisseru Stupa, a crumbling brick-built structure reminiscent of a fairly squat ziggurat. It dates from approximately the 11th century (though some archaeologists have dated it as late as the 1400s) and was once part of a complex of more than 100 temple buildings.

The name Tisseru (also written as Tisuru) comes from Tibetan and means 'yellow rock'. Legend has it that an evil spirit used to occupy the site, causing death and disease among the local population and their livestock, but that the king wisely constructed the stupa on top of the spirit's lair and thus protected the community.

The stupa is built on a metre-high foundation block; the upper structure is tiered. It is thought that there were once nine terraced levels (making it similar in appearance to the tiered stupa in Paro, Bhutan), but only the lowest ones survive. It is possible to make out some of the floor plan, specifically the positions of shrine rooms and corridors, but the mud-brick construction has largely crumbled, leaving us to speculate on its former glory. A taxi from central Leh costs from Rs247 one-way.

Zorawar Fort [74 A5] (Skara Rd) This is the fort that gives Fort Road its name and yet sadly few visitors ever come down into Skara to check it out. It was built by Thanedar Magna in 1836 on the orders of Wazir Zorawar Singh (1786–1841), whose statues and pair of cannon mark the entranceway. The fort itself is built of mud bricks and is still in use by the Indian armed forces: you may well be invited to join the officer on duty for lunch or tea.

Inside the fort is the small **Army Museum** (⊕ Apr–Oct 10.00–13.00 & 16.00–19.00; Nov–Mar 10.00–13.00 & 15.00–17.00 daily; admission Rs20) dedicated to the Dogra warriors. Cross the bridge over the dry moat, go through the arched gateway and then turn immediately right along the red path; the museum is on your left. If it is locked, continue along the path to the barracks and ask someone to open it for you. The museum's **lobby** is decorated with regimental flags, shields and well-written information boards about three prominent military figures: Mehta Basti Ram, Raja Gulab Singh, and General Zorawar after whom the fort is named.

There's an interesting black-and-white photograph of Zorawar's final resting place in To-Yo, Tibet.

The room on the right is the **information room**, where you will find boards, again clearly written, detailing the 1st Ladakh Campaign (1834–36), the region's subsequent consolidation, the Baltistan Campaign (1839–40) and the Tibet Campaign (1841). A small number of artefacts, including leather and metal shields and a steel and brass breastplate, the design of which seems hardly to have changed since the Classical period, add visual interest to the display.

The **artefacts room**, on the opposite side of the lobby, has rather more to see, though without so much background detail. Of particular interest here are the cabinet of metal wine and tea pots; the **collection of musical instruments** (including the oboe-like *shahnai* and several pairs of *bhugjal* or cymbals); and the set of rather intimidating gladiator-like masks. There are also a few dusty items of traditional costume, and a case of finely worked silver jewellery and other small items. You can walk to the fort in about half an hour or hop in a taxi.

Mani Ringmo
[74 C6] (Nr the main bus stand) Mani stones are oversized pebbles inscribed with the Avalokiteshvara mantra: 'Om mani padme hum'. Often stacked into cairns or, in this case, a long wall, they're typically found by roads and rivers. Travellers passing by add their own stone to the pile as an act of devotion. You should circumnavigate the wall in a clockwise direction and think of the stones as a collection of prayers slowly added to over hundreds of years.

Nezer Latho
[74 C4] (Nr the main bus stand; free admission but donations welcome) The Nezer Latho shrine is south of Main Bazaar but still well within the limits of the town. The shrine itself, which is linked to the gompa at Spituk, is an unprepossessing whitewashed cube a steep climb atop a barren, rocky hill, but its raised position offers superb views across the town to Leh Palace and Tsemo Gompa or, in the other direction, towards Stok Kangri. Nobody really seems to know much about when and by whom it was established.

Nezer Latho is accessible only on foot: if you're coming by taxi or minibus you should ask the driver to drop you at Leh Main Gate and follow the footpath up the hill.

AROUND LEH

Leh is a convenient starting point from which to explore neighbouring towns and villages, many of which are easily accessible by public transport.

HALL OF FAME (Airport Rd; ⊕ Apr–Oct 09.00–13.00 & 14.00–19.00 daily; admission Rs100/200 local/foreigner; camera Rs20) This army-run venue on the opposite side of the road to the cantonment has exhibits that commemorate the events and heroes of the 1962 Sino-Indian War (page 16), the 1999 Kargil War (see box, page 156) and the role the army has played in development and disaster relief in the area. Unless you have a particular interest in these subjects, however, it's probably not worth coming here especially.

SPITUK GOMPA (⊕ 07.00–18.30 daily; admission fee Rs30) Almost overlooking Leh airport, this 11th-century (but much-restored) Buddhist monastery is perched in a superb position atop a hill, overlooking the Indus. Climb right to the top of the site where a monk sits outside a small temple, ringing his bell and directing visitors into the inner sanctum. Standing outside, you are rewarded with impressive views in every direction, and especially across the airport towards Leh. Inside, the temple's interior is dark and slightly eerie, decorated with grotesque masks, flickering bulbs and shrouded statues. The military clock looks somewhat out of place here. The antechamber is filled with oil lamps, flames dancing above a floor sticky with oil.

A taxi from Leh costs Rs323/423 one-way/return.

CHOGLAMSAR To the south of Leh, just past Spituk, is the sprawling settlement of Choglamsar, a village inhabited almost entirely by Tibetan refugees that is an important regional centre for Buddhism. Here you can visit the **Tibetan Children's Village and School** (TCV; w sos-childrensvillages.org/where-we-help/asia/india/ leh-ladakh), which has around 600 boarders and 400 day students; and also the only **Bon Temple** in Ladakh. The ancient Bon religion (see box, below) predates Buddhism's arrival on the Tibetan plateau, but practitioners follow aspects of both ancient Hindu and Buddhist rituals. The temple itself was inaugurated in 1994.

Those interested in learning more about Buddhist philosophy and in serving the local community should plan to spend some time at the **Mahabodhi International Meditation Centre** (MIMC, Dewachan Choglamsar; \ 264 372; e infomimc@ gmail.com; w mahabodhi-ladakh.org). Founded by the Venerable Bhikkhu Sanghasena in 1986, the centre not only offers meditation teaching and inter-faith programmes but also plays a vital, practical role in the local community with schools and hostels for 500 underprivileged children, a monastery and nunnery, a care home that caters to the elderly, poor and those with disabilities, a hostel for the blind, a public health-care centre offering Western, Chinese and Tibetan treatments, an adult literacy programme, and environmental projects such as solar energy and organic food production. MIMC actively encourages foreign volunteers to come, stay and work on its projects, in particular to teach English in its schools (see page 67 for more details). The centre also has a small branch in the centre of Leh (page 89), where meditation and yoga classes are taught.

Most importantly, however, when the **Dalai Lama** (see box, opposite) comes to Leh (which he has done a number of times over the years, though with his increasing age these appearances are becoming less frequent), he lives in Choglamsar and delivers his *puja* or teaching sessions at the Ladakh Buddhist Association's Showground.

BON

Bon is not a distinct religion in its own right but an offshoot of Tibetan Vajrayana, or Tantric, Buddhism. Legend has it that Guru Shenrab, a Tibetan prince, began his journey looking for a horse that had been stolen by a demon, but ended up on the path to enlightenment.

Bon was originally a shamanistic and animistic faith. Shamans were thought to be possessed by either demons or spirits, sometimes those of ancestors, and to receive divine visions, especially when they retreated into the wilderness. It then developed into Yungdrung Bon, at which stage there are clear parallels with other forms of Tibetan Buddhism.

Today Bon has relatively few followers. It was estimated that there were 300 Bon monasteries in Tibet immediately prior to the Chinese invasion, but it is unclear how many of these survive. Elsewhere in the world there are Bon monasteries in Nepal and in India, the most significant of which is at Dolanji in Himachal Pradesh.

The Dalai Lama is a high lama of the Gelug school of Tibetan Buddhism. The position is primarily as a spiritual leader, though the current Dalai Lama also served as the head of state for the Tibetan Government in Exile until his retirement from that post in 2011. When one Dalai Lama dies he is reincarnated, and it can take two to three years to identify the next reincarnation. Visions and omens guide the lamas to the child, who must then pass various tests to confirm he is indeed the Dalai Lama.

The current, 14th Dalai Lama was born in eastern Tibet in 1935, the son of a farming family. He was one of seven children to survive into adulthood, and his eldest brother had already been identified as a reincarnation of the Lama Taktser Rinpoche. His home was seen in a vision and then sought out, and when presented with an array of objects, the young boy was correctly able to identify those that had belonged to the 13th Dalai Lama. He was then formally recognised as the Dalai Lama and given the title Jetsun Jamphel Ngawang Lobsang Yeshe Tenzin Gyatso (Holy Lord, Gentle Glory, Compassionate, Defender of the Faith, Ocean of Wisdom).

The Dalai Lama's childhood was split between the Potala Palace and his summer residence at Norbulingka. He had both monastic and secular tutors, and was eventually awarded a Lharampa degree, the equivalent of a doctorate in Buddhist philosophy, at the age of 23. He was by this time already the temporal ruler of Tibet, having been enthroned in November 1950 at the age of 15. In this early period of his rule, the Dalai Lama worked alongside the Chinese government, ratifying the Seventeen Point Agreement for the Peaceful Liberation of Tibet, attending the National People's Congress and meeting with Chairman Mao. By 1959 the relationship had deteriorated significantly, however, and the Dalai Lama was forced to flee for his life at the outset of the Tibet Uprising. He sought asylum in India and formed the Tibetan Government in Exile in Dharamsala. Around 80,000 refugees followed him into exile, and he has spent much of the following decades appealing at the United Nations for the rights of Tibetans.

The Dalai Lama has not returned to Tibet in more than 50 years. He continues teaching Tibetan exiles and travelling extensively within India and abroad, engaging in inter-faith dialogue with the Pope, Archbishop of Canterbury and other senior religious figures. He was awarded the Nobel Peace Prize in 1989 and is vocal on peace, human rights and environmental issues. His Twitter handle is 🐦 @DalaiLama; he announces some appearances through tweets.

Leh AROUND LEH

3

Advertised well in advance and typically starting at 08.00, the Dalai Lama draws crowds of well over 100,000 people. His sermons are delivered in Ladakhi and Tibetan but also translated into English. The sight of thousands of people crossing the dusty fields on foot and then sitting entranced before the teacher is something to behold. You'll need to stand close to the front to hear the English version, so arrive early. It is highly advisable to bring a mat to sit on as the ground becomes swampy if it has rained, an umbrella or hat to protect you from the sun, and to wear plenty of sunscreen. A bottle of water and a few snacks wouldn't go amiss if you plan to stay for the whole session. Note that you will be gently frisked by security on the way into the ground. You are not allowed to carry cigarettes.

Getting there and away Getting to and from Choglamsar is relatively straightforward, except on *puja* days when every man and his yak is on the move and you'll need to get as far as you can by taxi or bus and then complete the journey on foot. Minibuses leave Leh every 15 minutes between 07.00 and 20.00; tickets cost Rs15. Alternatively, if you prefer to travel by taxi, you will pay Rs341–396 one-way or Rs443–515 return.

4

Northeast Ladakh

Hidden in the northeastern corner of Ladakh towards the border with China, the Nubra Valley is probably the most popular destination with both foreign and domestic visitors in Ladakh after Leh itself. The road from Leh (the imaginatively named Khardung La Road) is a stunning journey that's an attraction in its own right, mainly due to the dramatic Khardung La mountain pass. The road winds its way initially along a vibrant green valley where streams cascade over rocks and each irrigated field is lined with shade-giving trees, substantial houses and large white stupas. The road then begins to climb, gently at first but then becoming steeper, the hairpin bends contorting across the hillside. The loose scree slopes are barren and dry, and only the red, iron-rich rocks break up the dusty, brownish-grey landscape.

KHARDUNG LA

Khardung La is the top of the world, at least if you believe the signposts. Locally touted as the highest motorable road on earth (in reality it's more like the 10th or 11th highest – but we can forgive some calculation errors at this altitude!), it climbs to 5,602m, so it's not only the views that will leave you breathless. It's a hugely popular destination for domestic tourists, the majority of whom come here on a day trip from Leh in order to snap innumerable selfies, but it's also the principal route via which people access the Nubra Valley.

GETTING THERE AND AWAY By far and away the easiest way to reach Khardung La (and get back again) is by **taxi** (Rs2,773–3,179 return) from Leh, 40km to the south. There are always plenty of other tourists willing to make the trip if you want to share a ride. The journey takes anywhere from 1 to 3 hours each way depending on the weather, road conditions and whether or not you have to wait for rocks to be cleared.

Almost as popular is getting to Khardung La by bike. **Motorbike hire** in Leh costs from Rs800 per day, including helmet (page 76), but given the combination of rough road surface and altitude the journey wouldn't be advisable for complete novices. Those with thighs of steel and strong nerves may also consider getting a lift to the top of the path and then **mountain biking** back down to Leh: rates start from Rs800 per person (page 76).

If you do plan to travel by motorbike or mountain bike, leave early in the day to ensure you are off the pass by nightfall. Travel slowly, make sure you have acclimatised well in Leh beforehand, and be aware of the impact that the altitude will have on your physical and mental capacity. Don't forget to wear a helmet and take a scarf and sunglasses to keep the dust out of your eyes and mouth.

The rough-surfaced road is open daily, albeit with delays, from 1 June to 31 October. In the winter months it is often closed without prior notice, both due to

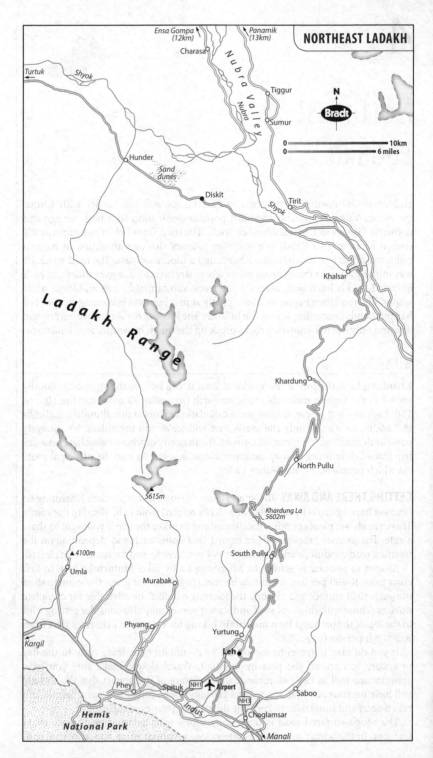

NORTHEAST LADAKH

Turtuk

Shyok

Ensa Gompa (12km)

Panamik (13km)

Charasa

Tiggur

Sumur

Nubra Valley

Nubra

N

Brandt

0   10km
0   6 miles

Hunder

Sand dunes

Diskit

Shyok

Tirit

Khalsar

Ladakh Range

Khardung

North Pullu

5615m

Khardung La
5602m

4100m

South Pullu

Umla

Murabak

Phyang

Yurtung

Leh

Kargil

Phey

Spituk

NH1

Airport

NH3

Saboo

Choglamsar

Hemis
National Park

Indus

Manali

The Inner Line Permit is the government-issued travel document that enables non-Ladakhis (both Indian and foreign nationals) to travel to parts of Ladakh that are close to the Chinese border. It is compulsory to have the permit if you wish to travel to Khardung La, the Nubra Valley, the Southern Lakes or Dha Hanu, and the permit will be checked at numerous police posts and army checkpoints along the road. Make sure you have plenty of photocopies (four to six should be fine) that you can leave at the checkpoints if required.

The only place to get the permit is in Leh. You can apply yourself at the District Commissioner's office or, with far less hassle, ask a local travel agent to do it for you (page 76). In order to make an application there must be more than two people in the group submitting paperwork. However, once you have the permit there are no restrictions on you travelling alone. Travel agents will usually be able to find additional people also in need of permits if you're travelling on your own.

At the time of going to print, the government had established an online permit application form (see w lahdclehpermit.in). There were reports of a few teething issues, but these will hopefully be ironed out in due course. Applications cost Rs400 as an environmental fee or Rs20 per day if travelling in restricted areas. In most cases, you still need to be a part of a group of at least two people.

snowfall and for essential maintenance. Some 14km before you reach the top of Khardung La is the smattering of prefab buildings known as South Pullu. There is a military checkpoint here and you are required to show both your passport and your Inner Line Permit (see box, above). There is also a basic first-aid post. After South Pullu, the road surface deteriorates substantially: expect bone-shaking pot-holes and regular delays as road crews with bulldozers work to clear the latest rockfall and widen the road sufficiently so that two cars can pass. There's nothing to do but sit back and admire the view.

✗ WHERE TO EAT AND DRINK The **Rinchen Cafeteria** claims to be the highest in the world and yet somehow still manages to boil water for tea. The plastic cups are tiny and the tea sickly sweet, but it's Rs15 well spent, especially if you have an unexpected stop here while they blast the road below. There are a few basic snacks on sale, but a quick chat with the soldiers who make up the bulk of the clientele is definitely more rewarding than the catering.

WHAT TO SEE AND DO The principal attraction of Khardung La is the pass itself and the views from either side, either looking back towards Leh or down into the Nubra Valley. **Glaciers** are currently visible in two places (though given the rate at which they are melting they might not be here for too much longer) and on a clear day you have a fine view of the peak of Stok Kangri too.

If there's still air in your lungs you can scramble up to the small prayer-flag-strewn **shrine** overlooking the road, or browse the **souvenir stand**. Music and chanting blares out of the loudspeakers, creating a party atmosphere, and of course you need to stop and pose for a picture in front of one of the two road signs declaring the height of the pass.

AROUND KHARDUNG LA

North Pullu Coming down off the pass into the valley, the first settlement you reach is North Pullu, which is about 16km from Khardung La. This small army encampment belongs to the Ladakh Scouts, who seem to spend much of the day sitting lazily by the stream and dangling their feet in the water. The tarmac, which is noticeably absent as you cross Khardung La, restarts just before you reach North Pullu.

The other sign of development here is the presence of a few cafés catering to passing tourists. They are all in the second part of the village, past the whitewashed buildings with their camouflage-painted roofs. Two of the **cafés**, identifiable only by their collections of aged patio chairs, serve hot tea and soft drinks; the third proclaims itself a **Garden Restaurant** and also has rooms to rent (**$**).

Khardung The first civilian settlement after the pass, Khardung village, 17km from North Pullu along an adequate road, is a fairly miserable ribbon development. If you're on foot or cycling you might be tempted to stop at the **Maitreya Mid-way Café** (**$**) or the even more grimy **Skitchan Restaurant and Guesthouse** (**$**) next door, but otherwise just give it a miss.

THE NUBRA VALLEY *Telephone code: 01980*

Easily accessible from Leh and yet far enough to feel like you're getting out into the wilderness, the Nubra Valley is one of the most popular destinations for trekkers and adventure seekers, and quite rightly so: the views are splendid, there's an endless array of interesting gompas, mosques and other sights, the trekking routes are varied and the tourist infrastructure is reasonably well developed.

Although the valley takes its name from the Nubra River, there are actually two rivers here: the Shyok River originates in the Rimo Glacier and winds its way from Pakistan, across the Line of Control (LoC) and through the villages of Turtuk, Hunder and Diskit. Its tributary, the Nubra, flows south out of the Siachen Glacier through Panamik and Sumur. The confluence of the two rivers is just to the east of Diskit, and they continue in a southeasterly direction, ultimately joining the Indus.

Historically, the Nubra Valley was of great importance as a trading route: it was only after independence in 1947 that the trade routes were severed. Camel caravans travelled the length of the Karakoram range to China and into central Asia as a part of the Silk Road: the descendants of these pack animals are the Bactrian camels now used to give rides to tourists on the sand dunes outside Hunder.

DISKIT The largest settlement in the valley, Diskit has grown up around the gompa of the same name. Tucked between the cliffs and the river, it's an attractive place to base yourself if you want to explore Nubra's cultural sites, though you'll also find it a convenient break in your journey when trekking or continuing by road to Turtuk. The tree-lined lanes are pleasantly dappled with shade, and it's an easy stroll to the river and back. The vast Maitreya Buddha (page 105) surveys his domain munificently: everywhere you go you'll be under his watchful gaze.

History Diskit's written history begins in the 1400s, though it was undoubtedly inhabited long before this and travellers and traders would also have passed through. The local ruler, Nyingma Gragspa, supported Sharap Zangpo in the building of the gompa (page 105). In the century that followed, the combined palace and monastery was heavily fortified in order to withstand invaders, including the Mongol general Mirza Muhammad Haidar Dughlat, who invaded Ladakh in both 1533 and 1540. Although Mirza Haidar was defeated, it was as a result of intervention by the King of Leh, and so Diskit came under the king's influence. Trade flourished and local chieftains grew rich on the trade with Yarkand and made territorial gains in Baltistan, as well as fighting against the Mughals.

Getting there and away It's a 118km **drive from Leh** to Diskit, a journey that takes around 5 hours but is inevitably longer if snow or rocks have blocked the road. Unless you have entered the valley **on foot from Phyang** (page 139), you will most likely have reached Diskit by road having come across Khardung La (although there is another minor route over the wild Wari La (5,308m) that also connects the valley to Leh). If you hire a car you could make an interesting loop by travelling to Nubra over the Khardung La and back over the Wari La. Shortly after the village of Khalsar (where there are various roadside places offering archery and quad bike rides, both of which are popular with passing tourists), the main road splits in two: the right fork crosses the river to Sumur and Panamik; the left fork continues on to Diskit and Hunder.

In the summer months **minibuses** make the journey from Leh three times a week (06.00 Tue, Thu & Sat; Rs197 one-way, departing from Leh's main bus stand. Going the other way, buses leave Diskit at 07.00 (Wed, Fri & Sun).

Due to the greater flexibility and comfort, most visitors choose to travel to Diskit **by car**, either hiring a taxi themselves or riding in a shared jeep. The Ladakh Taxi Operator Co-operative Ltd (LTOCL) offers a number of options for getting to the valley: a basic day return from Leh to Diskit starts from Rs7,159 and if you want to travel from Leh to Diskit, on to Turtuk and back again (over two days), rates start from Rs11,626. Adding an extra day to any of these routes (recommended) costs an additional Rs2,668 per day for the cheapest vehicles. Fare information about any of the above-mentioned routes can be found at w ladakhtaxiunion.com.

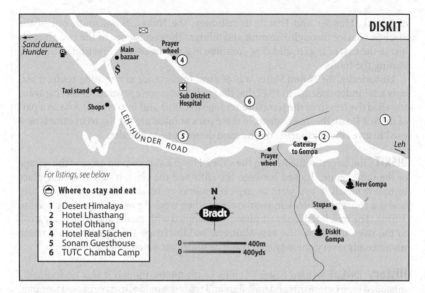

DISKIT

Getting around Travelling within the valley, there are **minibuses** twice a day from Diskit to Sumur (2hrs; 08.00 & 15.00, exc Sun; Rs59) and more frequent services shuttling the short distance between Diskit and Hunder (30mins; Rs15). From the bus stand at Diskit, **jeeps** can be hired to Hunder (Rs465 one-way), Sumur (Rs1,543 one-way) and Panamik (Rs2,641 one-way).

 Where to stay and eat *Map, above*

Diskit has the greatest variety of accommodation options in Nubra, rivalled only by Hunder. Hotels and camps here predominantly target Indian domestic tourists and so offer combined packages of rooms and meals.

Desert Himalaya (25 tents) m 989 196 0222; e deserthimalayaresort@gmail.com; w deserthimalayaresort.com; ☉ May–Sep. Upmarket camp offering luxury tents erected on hard-standing floors with views up towards the Maitreya Buddha & mountains. Every tent has its own immaculate bathroom with hot shower. You can fish for rainbow trout in the pond & come nightfall there is a bonfire & option to BBQ. The onsite restaurant seats 80. **$$$$$**

✳ TUTC Chamba Camp (15 rooms) ☎220 192; w tutc.com; ☉ May–mid-Oct. Plush top-end camp situated a short way below Diskit Gompa, with luxurious, colonial safari-style tents with big dbl beds, work desks, beautiful bathrooms & stunning desert views. The communal meals are an absolute highlight. If you can afford it then it's one of the best places to stay in Ladakh. **$$$$$**

Hotel Lhasthang (10 rooms) Beneath Diskit Gompa; m 982 050

1211; e info@hotellhasthangnubra.com; w hotellhasthangnubra.com. The sister property to Hotel Olthang (see below), this slightly more expensive hotel has large, light & fairly comfortable rooms. The dining hall has impressive views across the valley & a generator ensures constant power. All rooms have en-suite bathrooms. **$$$**

Hotel Olthang (21 rooms) m 982 050 1211; e info@hotelolthangnubra.com; w hotelolthangnubra.com. Probably the longest-established hotel in Diskit & the sister hotel to the Lhasthang (see left), Olthang has a central location on the main road through the village & small courtyard garden. All rooms have attached showers but there's hot water in the morning only. A backup generator guarantees the electricity. Meals are available on request. **$$$**

Hotel Real Siachen (4 rooms) Behind prayer wheel; ☎887 900 1171; m 982 050 1211; e info@hotelrealsiachennubra.com;

w hotelrealsiachennubra.com. Basic hotel in the centre of the village, hidden behind a tall wall. The welcome is less warm than at Sonam (see right), but it is perfectly serviceable if all you want to do is sleep. **$$**

🏠 **Sonam Guesthouse** (4 rooms) Nr Sub District Hospital; 📞 220 109. Welcoming family-run homestay with large, clean rooms & lots of helpful advice. Delicious meals are freshly prepared to order, often with vegetables from the garden. **$$**

Shopping Diskit has a small **bazaar** selling basic consumer goods and packaged foods, the centre of which is just south of the main road. There is also a short run of **shops** selling sweets and soft drinks as you leave the village on the road towards Hunder.

Other practicalities The **Sub District Hospital** is located in Diskit, on the lower road. It is somewhere between a GP's surgery and a polyclinic, but does have its own ambulance, x-ray machine and the capacity to handle (at least at a very basic level) emergencies. If you need medical care but it is not an emergency, you can attend the daily outpatient clinic (🕐 10.00–16.00), where several of the doctors speak English.

What to see and do The **Diskit Gompa** clings to the rugged cliffside and has somehow defied gravity for centuries. Built originally as a royal palace in the 15th century, the buildings were heavily guarded with huge watchtowers and two heavy wooden gateways, one of which survives. Close to the location of the lower gate (now removed) is a chessboard etched into the stone: this is how the guards would entertain themselves in their downtime.

The palace's defences were clearly effective: only once were they penetrated by a Mongol chieftain in the early 1500s, and even then his victory was short-lived. The unlucky chap was caught in the palace temple and decapitated. His head and one hand were then offered up to the temple guardian: this grisly gift was clearly accepted, as since then the fortifications have not been breached. The body parts remain in the temple to this day.

The monastery was founded by Lama Sharap Zangpo, a disciple of Tsongkhapa, and its 120 or so monks follow the Gelugpa school of Tibetan Buddhism. Like Thiksey Monastery (page 121), Diskit is also under the direction of successive reincarnations of Skyabsje Khanpo Rinpoche.

Diskit's **New Gompa** is slightly below the main monastery, away from the cliff face and closer to the river. The gompa itself is of little architectural or historical interest, but there are two things here worth seeking out. The first is the **photang of the 14th Dalai Lama**, which houses an exhibition of antique *thangka* paintings. The second is almost unmissable, standing at some 30m tall and painted in gold and garish colours: the vast **Maitreya Buddha** (also known as the Gyalwa Chamba), which not only tops the site but also dominates the surrounding landscape, clearly visible from both directions along the valley. It was inaugurated by the Dalai Lama only in 2010. Standing at the Buddha's feet you feel both dwarfed and humbled, but at the same time thrilled by the panoramic views.

If you have the time and inclination, you can also step inside the first-floor **temple** built into the Buddha's plinth. Though far less ornate than many of Ladakh's other temples, it nonetheless houses three interesting statues: of the Buddha himself; of the Tantric Buddhist master Guru Padmasambhava (commonly known as Guru Rinpoche) (AD717–762); and of Tsongkhapa (1357–1419), founder of the Gelugpa, or Yellow Hat, sect of Tibetan Buddhism (see box, page 22). There are also a number of smaller, gilded statues and sacred manuscripts wrapped in colourful fabric and protected behind glass cabinets.

Northeast Ladakh **THE NUBRA VALLEY**

4

You can visit both gompas on a single ticket (Rs30) that has to be purchased from the elderly monk in the shed at the fork where the road to the two sites divides. Don't worry about missing him: he'll have watched you all the way up the hill and be ready to spring out as soon as you draw near. The money is used for the restoration and maintenance of the monastery buildings and so falls somewhere between an entry fee and a donation.

Leaving Diskit on the road towards Hunder brings you to Nubra's **sand dunes**. It's possible to go **camel riding** here on Bactrian camels, the legacy of Ladakh's historic Silk Road ties. Renting your own camel (moderately trained) costs Rs350 for half an hour. It's hardly the stuff of high adventure but it's a nice way to see the dunes and the masses of domestic tourists lend a surreal and colourful edge to the experience.

HUNDER

Hunder is a strange place: you get the sense that it wouldn't exist if it weren't for the military and the tourists. The army camp and tented camps lie side by side (though thankfully each unaware of the other) and there's nothing to see in the village itself, though the nearby sand dunes and Chamba Buddha are intriguing, and the village has a decent array of accommodation, which makes it a useful base for exploring the area.

History

Although today's settlement at Hunder is relatively new, there has been continual habitation in the local area since at least the 7th century AD. It is likely that rock carvings such as the Chamba Buddha (see opposite) were created beside the river as markers to guide traders and pilgrims as they travelled through the valley: think of it as a kind of early signpost.

Getting there and away

By road Hunder is set back to the right of the main road as you travel northwest from Diskit but it is clearly signposted so you won't miss it. When you reach the army base, turn left and this brings you into the centre of the village.

If you are hiring a **taxi** to reach Hunder, the LTOCL's rates apply: one-way rides from Leh in the cheapest taxis cost Rs5,628, but you'll have no trouble finding people to car-share with.

Far cheaper is the thrice-weekly **minibus** (7hrs; Rs197) from Leh to Diskit (page 75). Some of these buses do continue on to Hunder (charging Rs224 from Leh) but if not you can take the more regular local bus (Rs15 one-way) between the two villages, or hire a jeep from Diskit bus stand (Rs465 one-way).

THE NUBRA VALLEY TREK

This wonderful four- to six-day (depending on your route) trek from Phyang to Hunder is of moderate difficulty. Starting at Phyang village, you climb first to Phyang Phu (4,621m) and then on to Lasermo La, which at 5,438m is the physical high point of the hike and offers superb views down along the Shyok Valley. The trek continues through fragrant meadows where nomads graze their flocks to the Hunder Dok villages before descending through the Hunder Gorge to Hunder itself.

Tashi and Cristina of Hidden North Adventures (w hiddennorth.com) live in Phyang itself and so are well placed to arrange the trek for you and to guide you through these passes. Their immaculate guesthouse (page 141) also makes the perfect start or end point for your trek.

On foot It is also possible to walk the fairly flat 7km route from Diskit to Hunder in a little over an hour. Additionally, providing you have the time, stamina and inclination, it is possible to reach Hunder on foot by trekking from Phyang (see box, opposite), thus eliminating the need to come across Khardung La.

Where to stay and eat
Hunder features on the tourist trail solely because of its accommodation options: there is really little else here. The upside of this is that you have numerous options to choose from, some of which are quite luxurious, although when things are quiet you can haggle for a substantial discount. Despite this, an increasing number of foreign travellers are eschewing Hunder altogether and basing themselves in either Diskit or Turtuk.

In general, there's electricity only in the evening and occasionally first thing in the morning, and although most places have Wi-Fi, expect it to be erratic at best.

Nubra Organic Retreat (20 tents) m 979 734 7647; e organicvillageretreat@gmail. com; w nubraorganicretreat.com. One of Hunder's luxury accommodation options is this friendly & very comfortable tented camp set among apple & apricot orchards. The exterior of the tents is hardly eye-catching, but inside you'll discover solid beds with thick blankets & en-suite bathrooms. There's an organic vegetable garden to supply the kitchen, hammocks by the stream, bonfires each evening &, if you're feeling more energetic, a badminton court. STD phone calls can be made here. $$$$$

Karma Inn (21 rooms) \ 221 042; m 941 961 2342; e karmaleh@yahoo.co.in; w hotelkarmainn.com. Manicured lawns surround this large, well-run hotel. Rooms are large & those on the top floor have superb views. Most have balconies. There's 24hr hot water. Extra beds in the family rooms cost Rs1,551; rates can be discounted by up to 20% so make sure you ask. $$$$

Nubra Ethnic Camp (20 tents) m 941 951 8129; e nubraethenic@gmail.com; w nubraethniccamp.com. Reasonable tents with distinctive wall patterning, en-suite bathrooms, electricity & locally made easy chairs on the deck. The camp is in a shady garden setting & staff are attentive. Meals available. $$$$

Himalayan Guesthouse (7 rooms) \ 221 131; m 946 917 7470; f himalayanhunder. A long-standing backpacker favourite, the Himalayan Guesthouse continues to charm with its whitewashed bungalow set in a delightful garden where only the crowing cockerel might disturb you. Meals are made with homegrown vegetables & herbs. Rooms are clean & there is hot water in the bathrooms. $–$$

Goba Guesthouse (15 rooms) m 982 050 1211/887 900 1171; e info@gobaguesthouse. com; w gobaguesthouse.com. This smart, cheap guesthouse with wood-panelled rooms is proving to be a big hit with budget travellers. Friendly, helpful & cleaner than many budget options. $

Café 125 By the main gate of the army base. Serves tea, soft drinks & biscuits. If you're caught short, there's a public toilet next door, though only the brave should enter. $

Around Hunder Returning to the main road and continuing 4km towards Turtuk brings you to the **Chamba Gompa**, which is on the right-hand side of the road just before the bridge. The gompa is, at least by Ladakhi standards, unremarkable from the outside but it is thought to date from the 15th century and there is a large, if rather severe-looking, golden Buddha inside, as well as some attractive frescoes. As rather fewer tourists venture here than, say, to Alchi (page 146), you'll have plenty of time to look at the wall paintings without being chivvied on by the crowds.

On the opposite side of the road, a short scramble down from the track leading away up into the hills, is the **Chamba Buddha**. Look for the small shrine on the patch of grass: the Buddha is immediately to its left. Only the head and torso of the statue remain, and even they are rather weathered, but you can still make out its erstwhile size and glory, and the skilled craftsmanship that went into its creation.

Dating of the Buddha is sketchy, but it is thought to have been made sometime between the 7th and 10th centuries and to have originally stood in excess of 2m tall.

TURTUK

TURTUK At the northwestern end of the valley, Turtuk is the furthest point in Nubra that foreigners are allowed to visit, even with an Inner Line Permit. The severing of historic overland trading routes by the LoC has turned it into a quiet backwater, a place to sit back and relax beneath hundreds of apricot trees in terraced gardens. The apricots are ripe in August, adding colour to the scene and also giving you the opportunity to gorge yourself on handfuls of fruit. Travelling between Hunder and Turtuk you will pass the tiny village of Changmar, which marks something of a dividing line between the Ladakhi-Buddhist culture of the east and the Muslim Balti people of the west.

Turtuk itself is only a small place but it is divided into three distinct areas: Turtuk Farul is inhabited by Noorbakshi (Nurbakshi) Muslims; it is segregated from Turtuk Yul, home of the Sunni Muslims, by a small tributary to the Shyok; and there is a third area, Turtuk Chuthang, on the banks of the Shyok River. Turtuk is increasingly used as an alternative – and far more attractive – base than Hunder.

History It is likely that Turtuk was once a trading post for merchants travelling across the Karakoram range, although little of that period of its history is visible in the town today. Instead, its more modern history shapes what you see today: until the India-Pakistan War in 1971 Turtuk was part of Pakistan. Unlike other parts of Nubra that are predominantly Buddhist, almost all of Turtuk's population is Muslim, with 70% of them following the Noorbakshi (Nurbakshi) school of Sufi Islam. This religious difference means that instead of colourful fluttering Buddhist prayer flags and temples, you will instead be greeted by the melodious call to prayer from the village mosques. Due to its proximity to the LoC, foreigners were prevented from travelling to Turtuk until as late as 2010, but the area is relatively safe now.

Getting there and around Turtuk is at the end of the line: it is only about 12km from the LoC and so foreigners can get there only by travelling along the road running parallel to the river from Hunder. As yet, it is not possible to cross the LoC from Pakistan to Turtuk.

A weekly **bus** (06.00 Sat; Rs315 one-way) travels the 212km from Leh, but it may be more convenient to take the minibus from Leh to Diskit (page 103) and then change for the local minibus from Diskit to Turtuk (3hrs 30mins; 14.30 daily, exc Sun; Rs80 one-way). The bus makes the return journey the following morning at 06.00.

However, the majority of people come by **taxi**: the LTOCL's fares start from Rs9,106 for a one-way trip from Leh to Turtuk with an overnight stop. It is also possible to get a taxi from Diskit (Rs3,821/4,969 one-way/return). You can expect to pass through a couple of police checkpoints, where you will have to show your passport.

Local travel agents There is no formal travel agency in Turtuk but Ataullah at Turtuk Holiday Camp is able to make transport and accommodation bookings and also to arrange cultural tours and trekking guides.

Where to stay

 Turtuk Holiday Camp (14 tents)
Turtuk Chuthang; ☎ 248 103; m 990 699 3123;
e turtukholiday@gmail.com; w turtuk.com;
⊕ Jul–Sep. Situated in a quiet spot with basic but

clean facilities. The hospitable staff will set up your dinner in a gazebo by the river & can also arrange for you to enjoy a traditional Balti meal with a family in the village. **$$$**

🏠 **Maha Guesthouse** (11 rooms) Turtuk Farul; 📞 248 040; m 962 298 2145; 🅵 Maha-Guest-HouseTurtukNubra-261390667392175. Clean & comfortable guesthouse set in an organic garden. Shared bathrooms have hot & cold running water. Multi-cuisine restaurant uses ingredients from the

garden. Also pitches tents (**$$$**) in the summer months. **$$–$$$**

🏠 **Ashoor Guesthouse** (6 rooms) Turtuk Farul; m 946 928 6300; e ashoor.turtuk@yahoo.com; w turtukashoorguesthouse.com. Of the really cheap options, you can't beat Ashoor's, which has simple but inspired rooms with polished tiled bathrooms. The highlight of a stay, though, is the superb home-crafted meals & entertaining banter with the owner. **$**

✖ **Where to eat and drink** Turtuk is a Balti village, so grasp the opportunity to eat traditional Balti food with both hands. The walnut and buckwheat breads served with herby yoghurt, mulberries and sun-dried tomato chutney are especially delicious. The guesthouses and tented camp serve both Balti and Indian dishes; check whether or not meals are included in your rate. There are a couple of cafés in town, including the **Selmo Restaurant** (**$**), which sounds rather grander than it is. It serves instant noodles and a few other basic snacks.

If you come during Ramadan, note that the local people will be fasting from dawn until dusk, so meals may not be served during daylight hours.

Shopping Small stalls in the **market** sell attractive stone figurines, while the local blacksmiths produce finely worked brass bangles inlaid with red and green enamel. This kind of jewellery is unique to Baltistan and therefore makes a memorable souvenir or gift.

What to see and do Turtuk has a number of sites that, though not marketed at tourists, are nonetheless of interest. There are no formal opening times or entry tickets: just turn up and ask politely to see inside. If you're fortunate, someone will give you a guided tour, in which case it is appropriate to give them a tip and, in the case of the mosques or gompa, leave a small donation.

Situated on the site of a 16th-century mosque, **Turtuk Yul Mosque** is shared by both of Turtuk's Muslim communities and is therefore particularly busy during Friday prayers. Unusually, the mosque's interior is particularly decorative. Turtuk's second mosque, the **Tsangzer Mosque**, was built only in 2011 and is in a prominent position on the hillside: climb up here for superb views of the valley.

The 300-year-old **Khan's Palace** is an attractive wooden structure that is to this day the home of Mohammad Khan Kacho, the latest member of the Yagbo dynasty of Chhorbat Khapulu. The family can trace its lineage back more than 1,000 years and the khan is a gracious and well-informed host. There is also a small, one-room museum with displays relating to the family and the valley's history. Admission is free and the khan himself might show you around.

Turtuk does have a small **gompa** but it is not an old one: as there are no longer any Buddhists in the village, this one was built in 1972 to serve the needs of Buddhist soldiers in the Indian army who had been posted on the LoC. Inside is a simple fresco showing the Buddha flanked by two Padmasambhava figures.

If you happen to be in Turtuk on Navruz (Persian New Year, 21 March), check out the annual **polo match** and related celebrations that last for a period of ten days. The feats of horsemanship on show will make you want to cover your eyes, while still peeking through the cracks in your fingers so that you don't miss a move.

SUMUR Sumur is a pleasant, green place that sits at the confluence of the Nubra and Shyok rivers. It's the home of the impressive Samstanling Gompa (see below) and also a few sand dunes, which although less dramatic than those between Diskit and Hunder still offer the opportunity for camel riding. The town itself is unremarkable, but it is a convenient and pleasant spot to break your onward journey.

Getting there and around There is a **minibus** departing from Leh's main bus stand to Sumur two days a week (6–7hrs; 06.00; Thu & Sat; Rs287 one-way). The price is actually for Panamik further up the valley, but bus drivers will likely make you pay a full fare even if you get off in Sumur. It is also possible to take the minibus from Leh to Diskit (page 103) and then take the local minibus (2hrs; 08.00 & 15.00 daily; Rs75 one-way) from Diskit back along the road you've just come in on to the crossroads and then turn north to Sumur.

Taking a **car** and driver from Leh will cost you from Rs7,157 for a return journey (Rs5,506 one-way). Alternatively, you can go via the wild Wari La pass for Rs10,123 return.

🏠 **Where to stay**

🏠 **Mystique Meadows** (23 tents, 4 rooms) m 941 917 8254; e mystiquemeadows.ladakh@ gmail.com; w mystiquemeadowscamp.com. Choose between conventional tents & Mongolian yurts in this well-run camp located close to the monastery. All tents have attached toilets & are pretty spacious. A backup generator ensures electricity supply after dark. Multi-cuisine meals & cultural shows available on request. **$$$$**

✳ 🏠 **Nubra Ecolodge** (9 rooms) m 979 798 3088/948 408 2433; e enubraecolodge@gmail. com; w nubraecolodge.com. Almost overlooking the confluence of the rivers, this wonderful lodge has a mixture of stylish rooms & safari tents that blend bright linens & locally made furnishings with modern designs. Good meals using largely homegrown, organic produce are available & service is top-notch. **$$$$**

🏠 **Valley Flower Camp** (15 tents) ✆223 516; m 941 917 8844; e valleyflowercamp@gmail. com; w valleyflowercamp.com. Slightly uninspired tent camp in a quiet setting. The tents are well-maintained with king-size beds, clean linens & a backup generator for power, but they're a bit too close to each other. Dining tent seats 50 people. **$$$$**

🏠 **AO Guesthouse** (6 rooms) Next to J&K Bank; m 946 973 1976. In a shady garden in the centre of the village lie several buildings given over to paying-guest accommodation. It's a quiet spot, back from the main road, & you're welcome to camp if you have your own tent. Ground-floor rooms are cheaper than those upstairs. Staying here is warmer, cheaper & offers more of a local experience than the tented camps. **$–$$**

✗ **Where to eat and drink** There are two simple restaurants in the centre of Sumur, by the junction with the bank: **Gyal Restaurant ($–$$)** and **Larjey Restaurant ($–$$)**. They're both cheap and not terribly cheery and could do with a good clean.

Other practicalities There is a branch of **J&K Bank** (⊕ 10.00–14.00 & 14.30–16.00 Mon–Fri, 10.00–13.30 Sat) in the centre of Sumur, located at the junction by the colourful prayer wheel.

What to see and do Clinging to the cliff face between Sumur and the neighbouring village of Tiggur is the **Samstanling Gompa** (⊕ 08.00–noon & 13.00–18.00 daily) and, in its immediate surroundings, a smattering of even more gravity-defying shrines. Founded in the early 1840s by Lama Tsultim Nyima, the Samstanling Gompa is still directed today by his incarnations. Some 50 or 60 monks, plus neophytes, live a life of strict asceticism: unlike monks in other monasteries they do not dance, make offerings or have any personal possessions, including books or clothes.

The gompa is set into the hillside and best approached on foot alongside the Mani wall. There are three principal dukhangs or temples: in the **Men Dukhang** you'll find elaborate murals depicting the 35 Buddhas; in the **Mandala Dukhang**, which, ironically, does not contain a single mandala, are two vast statues of the Buddha, wall paintings and numerous smaller statues; and in the **Old Dukhang** are yet more murals, again showing the 35 Buddhas as well as scenes from the life of the Buddha, his disciples and the various protective guardians. If you continue up the hill behind the gompa you come to a large **bas-relief** depicting two bodhisattvas and stupas.

Much hyped by Indian visitors and their tour companies, the **sand dunes** surrounding the village have lost much of their meditative charm under a swarm of quad bikes, camel rides and piles of litter discarded by domestic tourists. Camel men and quad-bike owners will find you as soon as you arrive in the village and do all they can to get you on to one of their steeds.

PANAMIK Famed for the curative properties of its hot springs, Panamik is a tiny, scruffy place that probably won't be one of your Ladakhi highlights. However, it is the access point for the interesting holy lake of Yarab Tso and also the Ensa Gompa.

Getting there and around Most visitors to Panamik hire a **car** and driver from Leh and thus pay for a package from LTOCL. A **taxi** ride currently costs from Rs5,780 one-way, or Rs9,880 for a two-day return journey. If you are reliant on public transport, it is easiest to take the **minibus** from Leh to Diskit (page 75) or Sumur (see opposite). The same local minibuses that go from Diskit to Sumur continue north to Panamik and the journey takes 3 hours. On the return journey to Diskit, the minibus leaves Panamik at 15.00. Alternatively, take the Saturday bus to Charasa or the Tuesday bus to Khimee, both of which depart from Leh at 06.00 and stop in Panamik en route. Tickets cost Rs282 one-way.

Panamik itself is a small enough village to explore on foot. If you plan to go to Yarab Tso, you will need to trek as there is no road access, and the same applies to the last part of the journey to Ensa Gompa, as there is only a footpath from the road up to the gompa itself.

Where to stay and eat There are a couple of homestay-style guesthouses in Panamik. Both are inexpensive but very basic, and there's really very little to recommend one over the other. It's better to come here on a day trip from Sumur. All guesthouses serve very simple meals of the instant noodle variety and there's an equally unimpressive café at the hot springs.

Other practicalities There is a **primary health-care centre** on the right-hand side of the road as you enter Panamik from Sumur. Staff do not speak English and facilities are basic, but in an emergency and when you have no independent transport, it would be the best place to wait while doctors are called out from the hospital in Diskit (page 105).

What to see and do Panamik is famed for its **hot spring** (⊕ dawn–dusk; admission Rs30), a naturally occurring sulphur bath that is said to have medicinal properties, particularly for the treatment of rheumatism, but is sadly rather underwhelming to look at. Panamik's Women's Alliance has taken over management of the site and has overseen the construction of a modern, segregated bathhouse. There is also a small café onsite. However, everything is tatty and run-down, making it a bit of a sub-par attraction compared to what else the Nubra Valley has to offer.

In the centre of the village itself are an exquisitely painted **wooden gateway** and **prayer wheel**, both in vivid colours. Continuing past them along the main road brings you to the **Memorial of BSF Mountaineers** on the edge of the village, a well-cared-for site inscribed with the names of those who have died while climbing locally.

AROUND PANAMIK There are two significant sites around Panamik, neither of which can be reached by road: even if you start your journey in a 4x4, you'll have to finish it on foot.

Yarab Tso is a sacred lake 90 minutes' walk from Panamik village. No river flows into the lake, so the source of the water is unclear. Yarab Tso's holiness comes from the belief that a person born in auspicious circumstances will be able to look into its waters and see clearly the gompa at Lhasa. We did have a look, but sadly our stars are not properly aligned.

On the opposite side of the river from Panamik is the **Ensa Gompa** where some elderly monks live out their days, most of them in silent solitude. If you have a vehicle, pass through Panamik and continue along the main road for 3km until you reach the police checkpoint. Turn left on to the Kobed Bridge Approach Road and then cross over the river. Once on the far bank, turn left. Beware that the road condition here deteriorates significantly.

From here you must continue on foot. Follow the track between the cliff and the riverbank until you reach a large field surrounded by a wall. Cut across the field, and then take the steep trail up the track on the left. The narrow valley takes you straight up to the gompa. In total the walk should not take more than 3 hours from Panamik and substantially less, of course, if you drive the first part of the way.

Only five monks still live at Ensa, though the monastic community was once far larger. The buildings are partially renovated and include a **lhakhang** with two statues of the Buddha, one wearing a crown; a slightly depressing **dukhang** with murals and statuary; and a **second dukhang** that is on the verge of collapse and has some badly decayed murals featuring the White Tara, Red Amitabha, the Buddha and his disciples.

CHARASA Once the capital of the ancient kings of Nubra, Charasa is nowadays scarcely visited by tourists as it has no bridge and thus takes a long time to reach. However, with its palace ruins and two monasteries, it is a place worth the effort.

Getting there and away Every Tuesday there's a **bus** to Charasa from Leh (around 7–8hrs; Rs282 one-way). Otherwise, take the daily minibus that leaves Diskit at 15.00 for Sumur and Panamik and ends its journey in Charasa around 20.00. **Walking** from Panamik to Charasa is possible with an optional detour to Ensa, but as it takes around 8 hours, you'll need to allow a full day. In winter it is possible (and far quicker) to go on foot directly from Sumur to Charasa across the frozen river in just half an hour, but since roads are officially closed during the winter months, and are only accessed by hardy locals and the occasional intrepid tourist when conditions allow, Charasa cannot seriously be considered as a tourism destination in winter. The minibus has to go past Panamik to the bridge and then double back on the other side of the river, necessitating a drive of around 5 hours.

THE CURIOUS LIFE (AND DEATH) OF PANCHEN LHACHUN

Born in the Nubra Valley, Panchen Lhachun was a Buddhist monk who returned home from his studies in Lhasa and began to teach. Consequently, he came into conflict with a Muslim cleric who attacked him by cutting him in two with a sword and then threw the pieces in the river. Half of the body floated ashore here and was encased in the stupa; the rest was found and placed in the gompa at Tiggur.

In the 1960s, the state of the stupa at Charasa had deteriorated considerably and it was decided to reinter the body in a new structure. Much to the surprise of the monks and other spectators, the body (specifically the torso and one arm) was perfectly preserved. A photo of the mutilated corpse was taken by a local man and is kept for posterity in the monastery.

Where to stay and eat There is not currently an official place to stay or eat. You may be able to arrange bed and board with a local family, but you'll have to turn up and ask.

What to see and do The first of Charasa's gompas is the **Serdun Gompa**: its monks belong to the Gelugpa school and it's related to the monastery at Diskit. The main temple is dedicated to Panchen Lhachun, a Buddhist scholar from the 15th century (see box, above), and the remains of his body are said to be encased in the golden stupa alongside his statue.

Charasa's second gompa, **Singkhar Gompa**, houses just one monk and some small statues. It is attached to the gompa at Hemis. Alongside it are the ruins of the Winter Palace, which belonged to the ancient kings of Nubra. The remains you see here date from the 17th century but were built on the foundations of much older buildings, supposedly by the Ladakhi King Nyima Namgyal who stayed here occasionally to pay his respects at Panchen Lhachun's stupa.

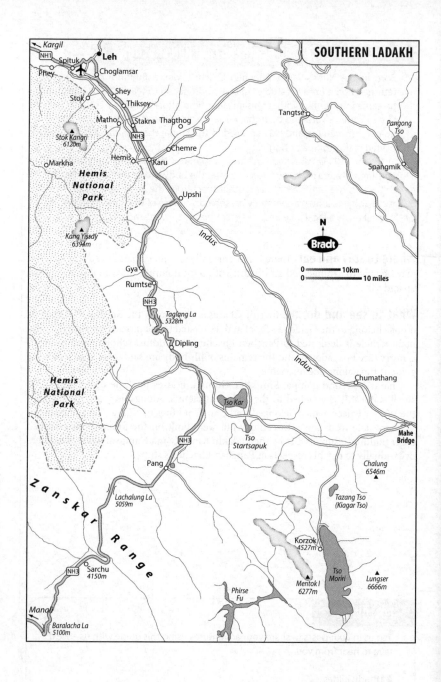

5

Southern Ladakh

Some of J&K's wildest, remotest and most beautiful scenery is to be found in the south of Ladakh. Here the human population is scant, especially as you move away from the monasteries, but in the parts where people fear to tread, the mountains and lakes roar across the landscape, ripping up the land into jagged peaks through which mighty rivers flow.

It is among such geological anger that you will find some of Ladakh's most famous monasteries: striking Thiksey Gompa with its vast Maitreya Buddha; perennially popular (if overly commercialised) Hemis; and dark Thagthog, the only Nyingmapa monastery in Ladakh. They lie almost side by side with holy fish ponds, carved stone Buddhas and two royal palaces, offering a rich cultural experience for visitors.

Despite this, it is the natural sights that act as the area's real draw: the southern lakes of Pangong Tso, Tso Moriri and Tso Kar may be far from habitation and along pretty awful roads, but their turquoise waters and unspoiled surroundings more than justify the bumpy journeys out to reach them. Likewise, some of the most popular treks are to be found in the Markha Valley, which is more easily accessible from Leh.

Destinations in this chapter are explored in the following order: sites south of Leh on or close to the Leh–Keylong Rd (NH1); Chemde and Thagthog, which can be visited as day trips from Leh; the Markha Valley, which is Ladakh's number-one trekking region; and lastly the three southern lakes of Pangong Tso, Tso Kar and Tso Moriri, all of which require at least an overnight stay. Most journeys within southern Ladakh will start in Leh, and you will have to pass through the towns along NH1 to reach either Markha or the lakes.

STOK   *Telephone code: 01982*

Just 15km to the south of Leh is the beautiful village of Stok, a settlement on the banks of the Indus River that is watched over not only by the towering peak of Stok Kangri but also the imposing Stok Palace. It's easy to see the sites and return to Leh in a day, but the village also serves as the starting point for ascents of the mountain.

HISTORY In the early part of its history, Stok was simply the site of a monastery: there has been a gompa here since at least the 14th century, and houses and smallholdings grew up around it to provide goods and services for the monks. Stok came to prominence in 1834, however, when General Zorawar Singh annexed Ladakh. King Tsepal Tondup Namgyal was forced to abandon his palace in Shey (page 119) and consequently relocated the royal family to Stok: his descendants still live in a wing of Stok Palace today.

Stok Kangri (6,120m) has India's highest trekkable summit, so it should come as no surprise that it's a firm favourite with tourists during the summer months and base camp can get quite crowded. It is possible to climb the peak any time from July to November, though due to the deteriorating weather conditions, July to September is the optimum period. Even then, temperatures at base camp fall to below freezing at night, so you'll need to have suitable clothing and equipment.

The trek takes six or seven days and starts from the village of **Shang** (3,657m), which is reached by taxi from Leh (from Rs2,027 one-way), and where enterprising locals sell biscuits and other small snacks to the trekkers. The first day's climb leads you first along a jeep track and then trails to the flat plateau at **Shang Phu** (4,343m). It's only a little over 11km, but trekking guides typically allow 6 hours.

On day two you cross **Shang Phu La** (5,115m), the first high-altitude pass on the trek. The next 8km of trekking takes you through a narrow valley lined with juniper bushes at first, then into open grasslands with snow-capped peaks on the horizon and superb views down to Matho Gompa. You camp for the night at **Matho Doksa**.

Day three is a short day of no more than 4 hours' walking, beginning with an ascent of **Matho La** (4,850m), from where you have an uninterrupted view of both Stok Kangri and Matho Kangri (6,100m). From here, you also look down on **Gangpoche** (4,435m), the grassy plateau criss-crossed with streams where you'll spend the night.

On day four you'll ascend to **Stok Kangri Base Camp** (4,968m). Visually this is probably the most spectacular day of the trek, as when the weather is clear you can see right across to Khardung La (page 99), as well as into the Mankarmo Gorge. For much of the day Stok Kangri itself is hidden from view, but as soon as you see the prayer flags you know you're getting close.

Depending on how well you've acclimatised, you may want to insert a **buffer day** here. This will also give you greater flexibility if there is bad weather as, having got this far, you don't want thick cloud cover spoiling your view from the top.

Not everyone attempts the **summit**, but if you do you'll need to get to bed early as the ascent begins at midnight. The air is thin and there are two stretches of snow to traverse, for which you'll need to use crampons. Though not strictly necessary, some trekkers choose to use ropes too. On the summit day you can expect to spend at least 14 hours walking, and 16 hours is not uncommon, especially if you're having trouble with the altitude.

GETTING THERE AND AWAY The road from Leh to Stok is in good condition and covered with tarmac for the entire route. It narrows to the width of a single vehicle once you reach the outskirts of the village, but there are plenty of places to pass.

Minibuses shuttle back and forth from Leh to Stok twice a day, departing from Leh's main bus stand at 08.00 and 17.00 and returning at 10.00 and 18.00 (30mins; Rs25). If you prefer to take a **taxi**, a drop-off at Stok Palace from Leh starts from Rs603/781 one-way/return. If you choose to combine Stok with other destinations, you can visit Stok, Stakna and Matho from Rs1,988; and Stok, Hemis, Thiksey and Shey in a very long day from Rs2,530. Numerous other alternatives are available as well.

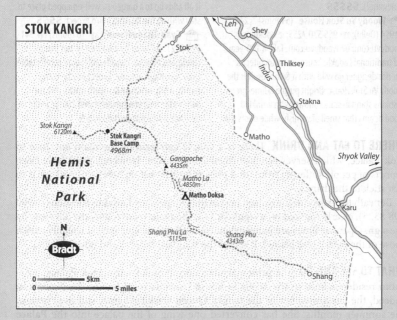

STOK KANGRI

Leh
Shey
Stok
Indus
Thiksey
Stakna
Stok Kangri 6120m ▲
Stok Kangri Base Camp 4968m
Gangpoche 4435m
Matho
Shyok Valley
Hemis National Park
Matho La 4850m
▲ Matho Doksa
Karu
Shang Phu La 5115m
Shang Phu 4343m
N
Bradt
Shang
0 ━━━━━ 5km
0 ━━━━━ 5 miles

On the final day of the trek you'll descend from base camp to **Stok** (3,615m). The descent is fairly rapid, usually taking around 5 hours, and it's best started early in the day as it includes crossing back and forth across the river on a number of occasions (the volume of water increases as the day progresses). Highlights include passing through the gorge at Mankarmo, which you'll have seen in the distance earlier in the trek, and returning from the barren mountainsides into the lush green fields that are irrigated on the valley floor.

Note that the timings given here are those suggested by local trekking guides who are used to guiding domestic tourists with little mountain experience. If you are moderately fit and have trekked in similar conditions before, you could feasibly complete the trek in five days or fewer, though doing so would increase the risk of altitude sickness – we'd recommended budgeting for the maximum amount of time. Any of the recommended Leh tour companies can organise this trek for you. Do not attempt it without a guide.

WHERE TO STAY Given the proximity of Stok to Leh, most people choose to come here on a day trip rather than stay the night. There are, however, some quite stunning places to bed down if you want to break away from the Leh circus. All listed hotels have Wi-Fi.

Stok Palace Heritage Hotel (12 rooms) 242 010; e reservations.stokpalace@gmail. com; w stokpalaceheritage.com. It's not every day that you get an opportunity to go & stay with a royal family, but this is what you get at this simply divine hotel set within the royal palace. If they're around, it's likely that you'll get to eat dinner with blue-blooded types as well. The rooms are everything you would expect of such a place & are loaded with period charm with genuine antiques & quality materials throughout. They also have some modern villas out in the gardens that are slick, modern & very comfortable (underfloor heating is a blessing!). $$$$$

🏠 **Woody Vu Stok House** (5 rooms) 📞 246 22 954 (Delhi); m 955 570 7255; e bookings@ woodyvu.com; w woodyvu.com. Take a 100-year-old traditional Ladakhi house, let an architect & interior designer go wild with it & the result is the Woody Vu Stok House. Bright purple & lime-green cushions stand in stark contrast with wrinkled wood beams that smell of varnish, while doors the deep, dark red of monks' robes add flashes of colour. It all adds up to a gorgeous, well-equipped place to stay with all the facilities you'd expect. $$$$

🏠 **Gyab-Thago Homestay** (6 rooms) m 941 921 8421. This may be a homestay, but living conditions here are considerably more comfortable than you might assume. Expect toasty, warm rooms, a big welcome & superb meals. Ask the owners to show you their restored 200-year-old heritage home just next door. $$

✖ **WHERE TO EAT AND DRINK** There is a simple **cafeteria** by the main entrance to Stok Palace, which serves tea, soft drinks and snacks. However, there have been reports of people suffering from food poisoning after eating here so our advice is to just stick to the drinks.

Beneath the palace in the central part of the village is the **Ladakhi Kitchen** (m 990 698 8325), clearly marked on a signboard on the main road: follow the alleyway by the sign. Opening times are inconsistent but during summer should roughly match those of the palace (see below). It serves the standard momos and noodle dishes.

WHAT TO SEE AND DO The principal attraction in Stok itself is **Stok Palace**, a 77-room residence built in the 1830s to house Ladakh's royal family, the Namgyals; indeed, the latest member of the family, Queen Deskit Angmo, still lives here in the summer months. She has converted one wing of the palace into the **Palace Museum** (⊕ May–Oct 08.00–13.00 & 14.00–19.00 daily; admission Rs80), the only part that is open to the public, which showcases royal artefacts and items of anthropological interest.

The museum is arranged around an **internal courtyard** decorated with pots of geraniums and the rather musty heads of an ibex and a sheep. Climbing the staircase to the first floor brings you to the temple and exhibition galleries, the first of which is a light room where daylight streams through the windows and a skylight in the roof. The roof is supported on wooden pillars and the woodwork is finely painted, though it needs some restoration work to remove the decades of dust and reveal the colours in their former glory. Exhibited here are gilded statues and a large number of silken banners.

Next door is a room of **armour and weaponry**, both of which look quite Mongol in style. In addition to the chain mail you can closely examine the quivers, slingshots and shield. Two garishly coloured dreamcoats that Joseph would have been proud of are displayed here too.

The **royal kitchen** is stuffed full of copper and brass cooking and serving vessels. The kettles are particularly finely worked. Take a look at item 32: it's a copper steamer for cooking momos. On the shelves are also small quantities of silver and porcelain.

Elsewhere, you'll find many displays of high-quality *thangka* paintings, some of which are 300 years old; printing blocks for producing holy books; gruesome ceremonial items, including part of a skull and a trumpet made from a human thigh bone; a collection of hats; and some beautiful murals painted on plaster and wood.

Although you can take photos of the outside of the building, photography inside is prohibited.

Situated above the palace is **Stok Gompa**, a 14th-century Gelugpa monastery founded by Lama Lhawang Lotus. In addition to several temples (one of which is claimed to be the oldest in Ladakh) and stupas is the **library**, which contains 108 volumes of the Buddha's teachings, as well as other sacred manuscripts. The monastery has some ancient wall paintings that include depictions of the Sakyamuni Buddha, White Tara and a 1,000-handed and 11-headed Avalokiteshvara to whom the monastery is dedicated. It becomes particularly busy during the **Stok Guru Tsechu Festival** (see box, page 127 for dates).

A large and fairly new **Maitreya Buddha** sits calmly contemplating the world not far past the gompa. You can get there on foot or by road.

SHEY *Telephone code: 01982*

Famed for its palace and holy fish pond, Shey is only 15km from Leh and makes for an interesting excursion either on its own or en route to Thiksey and Hemis.

HISTORY Shey was the first capital of Ladakh and its earliest ruins date from the 10th century. The fort was built by Ladakh's first king, Lhachen Spalgigon, and its successor, Shey Palace, remained a royal residence of the Namgyal dynasty until they relocated to Stok following the Dogra invasion in the 1830s.

GETTING THERE AND AWAY Around seven **minibuses** leave Leh throughout the day for Shey, and it's a drive of no more than half an hour as the road surface is very good (Rs30). If you prefer to hire a **taxi** from Leh, fares start from Rs443/575 one-way/return.

WHERE TO STAY Being so close to Leh, most people just come to Shey on a day trip, but if you want to stay overnight then there are a couple of nice options.

The Indus River Camp (8 rooms) m 705 137 9442; e theindusrivercamp@gmail.com; w indusrivercamp.com. Fantastic, riverside community-run camp with luxury safari tents that are tastefully furnished & kitted out with hot water, an electricity supply & big dbl beds. Staff welcome you with a broad smile & there's a decent on-site restaurant. **$$$$**

Besthang Guesthouse (3 rooms) 267 556. This authentic homestay-style guesthouse is set in a traditional Ladakhi house among gardens facing the gompa. Rooms are large (1 with attached bathroom & kitchen) & groups can make use of the comfortable dorm. **$**

Dokpa Guesthouse (7 rooms) m 979 748 5435; w dokpaguesthouse.in. Yangdol, Phuntsog, their family & pet dog welcome long- & short-stay visitors to their friendly guesthouse set in a potage garden shaded beneath apricot & apple trees. B/fast, dinner & occasionally lunch included for guests only. **$**

WHERE TO EAT AND DRINK On the opposite side of the road to the palace is **Shilkar**, a very basic café serving tea, soft drinks and snacks. It seems to have very irregular opening times, so don't count on being able to get anything to eat here.

WHAT TO SEE AND DO

Shey Palace (⊕ 07.00–dusk; admission Rs30) Once the royal residence of the Namgyal dynasty, Shey Palace inhabits an imposing position almost overhanging NH1. There is no designated parking so taxis stop by the roadside, from where it's a steep climb past a line of small prayer wheels to the palace's main entrance. While catching your breath at the top, be sure to turn around and look back at the idyllic surroundings provided by the artificially irrigated fields and the **holy fish ponds**. At certain times of day the palace is reflected in the water.

The façade of the palace rises dramatically into the sky and is punctuated by numerous wooden balconies, prominent features in traditional Ladakhi architecture. Built during the reign of Deldan Namgyal (1620–40), the palace sits atop the ruins of a far older fortified structure, parts of which are still visible. Climbing to the top of the site not only enables you to see these ruins close up but also allows you to survey the 108 **stupas** below, among which you'll also find the **Sakyamuni Temple** with its historic statuary.

The highlight for many visitors to Shey is the **Sakyamuni Buddha** (see box, below) inside the **Dresthang Gompa** at the top of the hill. Made from a mixture of copper and brass covered with gold plate, this 7.5m-tall statue is the largest metal statue in Ladakh and includes more than 5kg of gold, studded with precious and semi-precious stones. It was made in 1633 by a Nepalese sculptor and legend has it that the artist who painted the eyes did so with his back turned to the idol so that he did not show disrespect by staring into the eyes (and therefore the soul) of the Buddha.

Other sites   Right on the road, almost beneath the palace, is a vast rock with an **early Buddha carving**. The images have been weathered by time and the elements, but if you look at them in the late afternoon, the shadows make the carving appear more prominent. Due to the angle of the rock face, you'll see the carvings best if you are passing through Shey to Leh: coming the other direction it's easy to drive straight past.

THE SAKYAMUNI BUDDHA

The Sakyamuni (or Shakyamuni) Buddha is the historical Buddha, the primary figure of Buddhism who is believed by followers to have been enlightened. Although there are many accounts of his life, it is thought he was an Indian prince named Siddhartha Gautama who was born sometime in the early 5th century BC. The oldest surviving biographical manuscripts are not from until at least 400 hundred years after his birth, but tradition has it that he was born into the Ksatriya family. His father was an elected chieftain from the Shakya clan, and his mother was a princess. The night he was conceived, Siddhartha's mother dreamed of a white elephant with six tusks, a sign that the child within her would be something very special indeed.

Siddhartha's mother died during or immediately after childbirth and so he was raised by his aunt. During his childhood and young adulthood he was sheltered from all suffering and given everything he could possibly want, including a wife and son, but at the age of 29 he left his palace to find out what went on in the world beyond its walls. For the first time, he encountered the elderly, the sick and the dead, an experience that shocked him so much he gave up everything to become a mendicant.

Siddhartha took up yoga, fasted and tried to find enlightenment. These traditional paths gave him nothing, however: he had to find a new way. He developed instead the Middle Way, the so-called Noble Eightfold Path, which espouses the importance of having the right view, intention, speech, livelihood, action, effort, mindfulness and concentration. Siddhartha sat beneath a pipal tree and meditated for 49 days until, at the age of 35, he finally attained enlightenment.

For the remaining 45 years of his life, Siddhartha travelled and taught. His followers called him Buddha, the enlightened or awakened one.

On the far side of Shey as you leave towards Thiksey is the hard-to-miss **Naropa Photang** on the left-hand side of the road, a vast field of white stupas surrounding a **nunnery** of the same name. The nuns welcome visitors, and it makes for a fascinating contrast to the monks and monasteries you'll visit elsewhere in Ladakh. The entrance to the *photang* is next door to the **Druk Padma Karpo School** (w dwls.org), which shot to fame in the 2010 Bollywood film *3 Idiots* and counts both Richard Gere and Joanna Lumley as honorary patrons.

THIKSEY *Telephone code: 01982*

It's easy to overdose on gompas in Ladakh, but if you only visit one, make sure that it is Thiksey. Not only does it have a striking position and staggering views, but you get the sense that you are visiting a living, working monastery, and although there are other tourists here, you'll feel part of the monastic community.

HISTORY Thiksey's inspiring monastery was founded in the 15th century by two followers of Tsong Khapa (founder of the Gelug school of Tibetan Buddhism). In the following years the small village grew up around the monastery. Today it's one of the biggest cultural tourism landmarks in Ladakh.

GETTING THERE AND AWAY Just 18km from Leh and a stone's throw past Shey, Thiksey is easily combined with Shey for a single day trip. There are at least seven **minibuses** from Leh every day and the journey takes under an hour (Rs35).

Taking a **taxi** from Leh, LTOCL rates start from Rs696/910 one-way/return. Hiring a **taxi** for a combined sightseeing tour of Shey and Thiksey starts from Rs1,030, and if you want to visit Hemis and Stakna too, then prices begin at Rs2,530.

 WHERE TO STAY Thiksey is a simple day trip from Leh, and few people bother to stay the night. However, there are a couple of options – including one magnificent tented camp – if you want an early start at the monastery.

✳ 🏠 **Chamba Camp** (14 tents) m 901 090 2222. A short walk from Thiksey Monastery, this stupendous tented camp is one of the finest places to stay in all of Ladakh. Highly exclusive (it doesn't even have a dedicated website & must be booked through upmarket partner websites such as w mrandmrssmith.com), the large safari tents are impeccably decorated in an old colonial style & feature raised wooden decks & the best bathrooms you've ever likely seen in a tent. Service is second to none & guests can enjoy an array of expertly guided excursions, activities & delicious meals. **$$$$$**

🏠 **Chamba Hotel** (30 rooms) Thiksey; ✆ 267 385; e kthiksey@gmail.com. Run for the benefit of the monastery, this hotel has a black, white & red colour scheme that mirrors that of the gompa up the hill. The majority of rooms are considered deluxe & demand a high price tag, but there are also 8 standard rooms that are a more backpacker-friendly price. FB & room-only available. **$$$$**

🏠 **Chattnyanling Nunnery** (6 rooms) Nyerma; m 990 698 5911; e tarahomestaybooking@gmail. com; w ladakhnuns.com. Only 5mins' drive from Thiksey Gompa, this small, quiet guesthouse is run by nuns & set in attractive surroundings. Rooms have attached toilets; b/fast & veg dinner inc. Men & women welcome. Proceeds go towards education & upkeep of the nunnery. **$$**

✖ **WHERE TO EAT AND DRINK** There is a medium-sized and apparently well-run **restaurant** ($) at the foot of the gompa serving breakfast, light lunches and dinners, as well as various snacks and soft drinks. Profits go to the monastery. Elsewhere, the unexpectedly sophisticated Café Cloud (Nr Government High School, Leh–Manali

Highway, ☏267 100; $$) serves pizzas, good Indian dishes, pastas and a good range of coffees and teas.

SHOPPING There is a well-stocked **souvenir shop** at the gompa. In addition to postcards, books and calendars you can also buy T-shirts, garish clothing and various trinkets, and profits go towards the upkeep of the monastery.

OTHER PRACTICALITIES There is a small branch of **J&K Bank** on the road south from Thiksey. It is also possible to buy **Aircel** and **Airtel** talk-time from the roadside kiosks.

If you fall sick or need to buy medication, **Chamba Health Services** has its premises at the main entrance to the gompa. The doctors here practise both Western and Tibetan medicine and they have a small pharmacy.

WHAT TO SEE AND DO Thiksey Gompa (☏267 005; ⊕ 06.00–13.00 & 14.00–18.00 daily; admission Rs30) is certainly one of the most architecturally impressive buildings in Ladakh. If you are approaching by road, it suddenly rises up out of the high desert plateau and looks for all the world like a miniature version of the famed Potala Palace in Lhasa (Tibet). Having left the main road to drive through Thiksey village, the road doubles back on itself and climbs to the foot of the gompa where there is a large and well-ordered parking area, from where you must proceed on foot. You enter the site through a **red gateway** painted with colourful mandalas (see box, opposite). Looking left you have unobstructed views across to **Stakna Gompa** (page 125), then a line of buildings that include public toilets, and the gompa's restaurant and souvenir shop.

Your first stop should be Thiksey's **museum** (☏ generally 06.00–18.00, closed 13.00–13.30 & 16.00–16.15; admission included with gompa ticket), although note that this is below ground level and the steps down to it are somewhat precarious, so proceed with caution and keep hold of small children. Although it initially appears to be a single room, the museum is in fact divided into three areas: the main room, a room of scrolls and books, and a third space containing assorted ceremonial tea vessels. In all areas the choice of exhibits is eclectic, with many of the items relating in some way to worship or spirit invocation. Look out for the trumpet made from a human thigh bone, the sound of which is supposed to drive away evil forces; portable altars; bows, swords and shields seized from Muslim invaders; and some fearsome ritual dance costumes.

From the museum you should continue up the steps to the gompa's **main courtyard**, around which the most important temples are located. The courtyard is cloistered and the walls are painted with some attractive **modern murals**. Two small **Foo dogs** guard the space and a long, thin prayer flag flutters in the wind.

Go first into the **Temple of the Maitreya Buddha**, the Buddha of the future, the icon of Thiksey that adorns an infinite number of postcards. One of the finest Maitreya Buddha statues in Ladakh, the Buddha wears an expression of absolute serenity and the workmanship on the statue's crown in particular is quite exceptional. The smell of freshly cut wood mingles with the slow-burning incense, and the space is well lit with daylight streaming through large windows on three sides of the building.

Up the stairs to the left-hand side of the courtyard is a second **temple**. Murals here depict the guardians of the four cardinal directions: the white Yulkhor Sung (east); blue Phah Skespo (south); red Chanme Zang (west); and the yellow Natos Ses (north), whose accompanying mongoose spits out gemstones. Far more

top left	Eurasian golden oriole (*Oriolus oriolus*) (MP/S) page 8
top right	Black-necked crane (*Grus nigricollis*) (OP/S) page 8
above right	Eurasian hobby (*Falco subbuteo*) (AE/S) page 8
left	The elusive snow leopard is the creature everyone wants to see when hiking in Ladakh (SS) page 7
below	The Bactrian camels seen in the Nubra Valley are the descendants of the pack animals that once travelled the length of the Silk Road (DR/S) page 106

above The 12-terraced Nishat Bagh in Srinagar is one of the famous Mughal Gardens, built in accordance with traditional Persian landscape design inspired by the Islamic view of heaven (s/S) page 196

left Shey Palace sits atop a rocky outcrop surrounded by artificially irrigated fields and holy fish ponds (FD/S) page 119

below Originally a trading post on the Silk Road, today Leh is the capital of Ladakh, home to a bustling bazaar and remarkable historical sites such as Tsemo Fort and Leh Palace (T/S) page 71

top   Padum is the main base for treks in the remote Zanskar Valley (ND/S) page 169

right   Jammu's Mubarak Mandi complex was once the royal seat of the region's rulers, and its architecture is a riot of European Baroque, Mughal and Mewari styles (s/S) page 223

top   Built in memory of Indira Gandhi, Srinagar's stunning Tulip Garden is ablaze with colour in the springtime (J&KT) page 194

above left   Gulmarg is India's winter sports capital; its gondola transports skiers and snowboarders up to a height of 4,267m (I/S) page 199

above right   Trekking on horse to the Thajiwas Glacier is a truly memorable experience (NN/S) page 183

below   Translating as 'the meadows of gold', Sonamarg couldn't be more appropriately named (k/S) page 182

above   The mighty Indus River snakes through Ladakh; its rapids are ideal for white-water rafting (sz/S) page 150

right   Easily accessible from Leh, the Nubra Valley is one of Ladakh's most popular destinations for trekkers (PH/AWL) page 102

below   The ever-changing colours of Pangong Tso entrance visitors, and its beautiful scenery has provided the backdrop to many a Bollywood movie (cp/S) page 132

above   J&K's most popular sport is undoubtedly polo, and games draw vast crowds of spectators (KD/S) page 27

below   Artistic traditions from carpet making to woodcarving are still practised in the backstreet workshops of Srinagar, while the city's floating vegetable market is a photographer's dream (MEP and PL/S) pages 192 and 194

top Inhabiting the northern Indus Valley, the Brokpa people are descendants from Alexander the Great and their festivals are a riot of colour (SS) page 155

above Traditional Ladakhi dress features jewellery and headdresses inlaid with turquoise, coral and lapis lazuli (MT/S) page 26

below The Ladakh Festival is a major celebration of regional culture and a good opportunity to see traditional costumes, archery competitions and masked dances (AJP/S and J&KT) page 85

above Tso Moriri is arguably the most beautiful of southern Ladakh's trio of lakes (DR/S) page 135

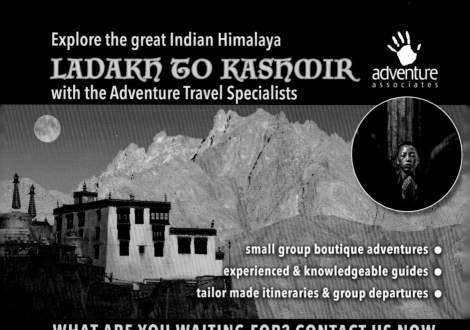

so than the other areas of the gompa, this temple feels particularly old, and this feeling is only emphasised by the darkness. Many of the wall paintings here are in their original, unrestored condition, as is attested to by the occasional cracks and unfortunate water damage. On display here are two jade-green **ceremonial drums**, the monks' **yellow hats** (worn only on special occasions) and, on the back wall, a tantric *chakrasamvara* **statue** depicting a man and woman in a particularly intimate embrace. Given the proximity to Leh, many visitors choose to come to Thiksey early in the morning to join the monks in this temple for prayers. You'll need to arrive before 07.00 and sit still and in silence for the duration of the meeting.

Behind the main temple room is a small **antechamber** with a collection of larger statues and a finely worked painting of a *begtse* or protector. There are two further small temples here, less dramatic than those mentioned above but still worth visiting. The **gonkhang**, or Temple of the Protectors, is crowded and the air is thick with incense. The giant statues of the guardians are shrouded so you cannot see their faces. Also step inside the tiny **Tara Temple**, which is arranged like a Chinese curiosity cabinet with every little statue placed in its own cupboard space.

Before leaving the gompa make sure you see the picturesque row of **nine stupas** garlanded with prayer flags: on a clear day with a bright blue sky there are few sights that better epitomise Ladakh.

MATHO AND STAKNA   *Telephone code: 01982*

MATHO Taking its name from the Tibetan for 'much happiness', Matho receives far fewer visitors than many other monasteries due to its location off the main highway. The exception to this is at festival time when Buddhist pilgrims and tourists alike flock here in their hundreds to see the oracles and hear their predictions for the coming year. The village is worth a visit simply because it receives far fewer tourists than some of the better-known monasteries around Leh.

Getting there and away Situated 26km from Leh, the approach road to Matho is long and straight towards the mountains; the gompa comes into view on the right-hand side above your usual line of sight. It's an arid, featureless landscape save for the old irrigation ditch that now lies dry.

MANDALA PAINTINGS

The mandala, or wheel of life, depicts the Buddhist universe and is comprised of three concentric circles. In the **innermost circle** are depicted man's three greatest vices: the snake, which is symbolic of anger; desire, shown in the form of a cockerel; and the pig, representing ignorance. Moving outward, the **middle circle** depicts six realms: the worlds of the gods, demi-gods, ghosts, men, animals and, lastly, hell. The **outermost circle** is made up of 12 symbols that collectively represent the chain of cause and effect. Look in particular for the blind man who symbolises lack of knowledge; the house with six windows, one for each of our senses; the pain of an arrow to the eye; and the fate that awaits us all: a corpse being carried.

Mahayana Buddhists believe that the mandala, or *bhavacakra*, was developed by the Buddha himself as a teaching aid. You will find them either painted directly onto the walls of Tibetan Buddhist temples, or painted on canvas or paper and then hung up where everyone can see.

Matho Gompa has two oracles who predict the future, collectively known as Lha Rong-btsan. In the middle of the first Tibetan month (based on the lunar calendar; check exact dates locally), Matho celebrates their festival and people visit from all over Ladakh to witness the oracles in a trance.

The second day of the festival begins with a masked dance performed by the monks of Matho, which lasts for more than an hour before the oracles emerge. Each year, the monastery chooses two monks to perform the oracle: these monks have to go through a month-long retreat in a dark room filled with barley grain offered by local villagers. On the day of the festival, the monks paint their bodies black from head to toe and wear thick, black wigs on their heads. Then their eyes are covered with nine black blindfolds.

Before they go into their trance, monastery artists paint a fearful face of a deity on their stomachs, making sure to paint the deity's eyes at the very end. It is said that as soon as the eyeballs are painted in, the oracles begin to shake their bodies vigorously and jump up to run around the roof edge of the five-storey building of the monastery, their eyes still blindfolded. In their left hands they hold *drilu* (the Tibetan bell) and in their right the *daru* (a ritual drum), all the while performing acrobatic feats. Then they stand on the roof edge facing the main courtyard of the monastery where all the people wait for their blessing and prophesies for the whole valley, and listen for the method to remove any potential obstacles. After hearing these, all the people shout 'Ki-Ki-So-So-Lhar-Gyalo' ('Victory to the Gods') three times. Then both oracles go around the monastery building and come down to the main court, standing on a platform, again giving their blessings and prophesies for the village. Once again all the people shout 'Ki-Ki-So-So-Lhar-Gyalo'.

Historians say that originally the two oracles were brothers who came from the Kham province of Tibet. When the Sakya Lama, Drungpa Dorje, came to Ladakh from Tibet, the two oracles accompanied him and the lama appointed them as protector deities of the Matho gompa.

For forthcoming festival dates at Matho Gompa, see the box on page 127.

Unlike Thiksey and Hemis, Matho is not on the main highway and there are only two **buses** a day directly from Leh. They turn around immediately on arrival, so aren't terribly helpful if you actually want to look around. If you are dependent on public transport, it's better to take the far more regular bus to Thiksey instead (page 121) and then walk via Stakna (see opposite). It's a pleasant stroll and will take you no more than 90 minutes.

Taking a **taxi** from Leh will cost you from Rs1,053/1,369 one-way/return, or you can combine it with a trip to Stakna and Stok from Rs1,988.

What to see and do Matho Gompa (m 962 295 5999; ⊕ 08.30–18.00, closed 13.00–14.00; admission Rs30) is the only Sakya monastery in Ladakh. Sixty monks and 30 novices live in this gompa, which was founded in the early 15th century by the great Sakya Pandita Drungpa Dorje during his visit to Ladakh. The buildings are generally in a poor state of repair, save for the modern **dukhang** built in 2005. A museum was under construction here at the time of our visit. The planned collection will showcase the art of Ladakh and reveal something of monastic life. The gompa festival (see box, page 127), during which the gompa oracles make predictions for the coming year, is one of the most interesting in Ladakh.

STAKNA Perched like a crow's nest atop a hill by a bend in the Indus River, Stakna has one of the most photogenic locations of any monastery in Ladakh. The shape of the hill is said to resemble a tiger's nose, from where the gompa takes its name.

Getting there and away Stakna Gompa is clearly visible from Thiksey, and the village lies just off the main highway between Thiksey and Hemis, half an hour's drive from the latter. The climb to the gompa itself is along a succession of switchback bends.

A single **bus** leaves Leh for Stakna, 25km away, each day at 16.30 and returns to Leh the next morning at 08.45, which isn't very useful if you want to just do a day trip. It is better, however, to take the bus to Thiksey (page 121), as it has to turn around by the bridge crossing the Indus on the road to Stakna, from where you can **walk** to the gompa in 15 minutes.

By **taxi** from Leh you'll pay Rs1,090/1,416 one-way/return, but given that there is a limited amount to see here, you'll probably want to combine your visit with Matho and/or Thiksey.

Where to stay and eat There's nowhere to stay in Stakna but there is an exceptionally basic **tea stall** by the roadside, which is a pleasant enough place to wait for the bus or to refresh yourself before the walk.

What to see and do Founded in the 1500s by a Bhutanese monk and scholar, Chosje Jamyang Palkar, **Stakna Gompa** (✆ 267 577; ⏲ 06.30–19.00, closed around 13.00–14.00; admission Rs30) is home to 30 or so monks who follow the Drugpa, or Red Hat, school of Buddhism, which originated in Bhutan. The monks are welcoming of visitors and, though there is an admisson fee, it feels far less commercialised than neighbouring Hemis.

Don't be fooled by the plain exterior of the gompa, as this belies what you'll find inside: bright and exquisitely painted **murals**. The centrepiece of the gompa is the **16th-century prayer hall**, where paintings have been sensitively restored and the colours are vibrant.

HEMIS *Telephone code: 01982*

Probably the most famous, and certainly the richest, of all Ladakh's monasteries is Hemis, the religious heart of the region for Ladakh's Drukpa Buddhist community and a stand-out Ladakhi sight. It has one of the most elaborate Buddhist festivals, the Tsechu Festival, and it is claimed that a lost Gospel relating to the life of Christ is also secretly preserved inside.

HISTORY It's thought that a monastery has existed in Hemis for over a 1,000 years. Today's structure dates from the 16th century, although it's been significantly altered in the years since.

GETTING THERE AND AWAY Hemis is on the main highway 43km south of Leh. The **bus** ride takes under 2 hours and the road surface is, at least by Ladakh's standards, good all the way. There are two direct **buses** that depart from Leh at 09.45 and 16.00 and return at 07.00 and 12.30.

Coming by **taxi** is slightly faster: allow 90 minutes. If you just want the car to drop you from Leh to Hemis then prices start from Rs1,347/1,857 one-way/return.

🏠 WHERE TO STAY AND EAT

🏠 **Hemis Monastery Guesthouse** (12 rooms) ✆924 3544. If you wish to stay at Hemis, the most atmospheric option is this little guesthouse. Facilities are basic & there are mattresses on the floor rather than proper beds, but at least you feel you are getting the authentic monastery experience (which includes being cold at night!). Rooms are reasonably clean & prices are charged per person rather than per room, making it cost effective if you're on your own. The downside is that you can't book in advance. **$$**

✕ **Hemis Gompa Restaurant** m 962 237 2915; ⊕ 07.30–20.00 daily. To the left of the gompa, a little down the hill, is this little restaurant; it may be rudimentary, but the setting among the trees is pleasant & you can hear the sound of the river. Dishes are either Tibetan or Indian & you can fill up on noodles for very little. A cup of black tea, much needed once you've been around the gompa, is Rs15. **$$**

JESUS IN KASHMIR

During the late 19th century, a Russian aristocrat, writer, military officer and Great Game spy by the name of Nicolas Notovitch travelled to Ladakh and spent a prolonged period at Hemis Gompa in 1887. While there, he claimed to have been shown a manuscript, written in Pali and brought to Hemis from Tibet, entitled *Life of Saint Issa, Best of the Sons of Men*. Notovitch translated the text into French and published it in 1894 with the title *La vie inconnue de Jesus Christ*, Issa or Isa being the Arabic form of Jesus.

The book caused outrage. It claimed that Issa came to India from Israel at the age of 14 and studied Pali and the Buddhist texts. He returned to Israel aged 29 to preach, his study of Buddhism heavily influencing his teachings. Though Notovitch was declared both a heretic and a fraud, and the noted German historian Max Mueller went as far as writing to the head lama at Hemis to question what Notovitch had written, two others followed in his footsteps and went to see the manuscripts for themselves. Swami Abhendananda, a disciple of the Indian mystic Ramakrishna, confirmed Notovitch's assertions and published his own book, *Kashmir O Tibeti*, in Bengali in 1922; and the Russian Nicolas Roerich visited Hemis in 1925, mentioning in his work the manuscript's existence.

If the manuscript is still here, the monks of Hemis are tight-lipped about it. Local people claim that there is a sealed room inside the monastery where only the most senior lama may enter. As he resides in Lhasa, the room and its contents cannot be reached.

On the other side of J&K, in the Kashmir Valley, a complementary tradition exists: that of Yus Asaf, the healer or shepherd. Here some Muslims believe that Yus Asaf was a preacher and prophet, the same Issa (or Jesus) mentioned in the Koran. An inscription once carved in what is locally known as the Temple of Solomon supports this view.

Yus Asaf lived in Kashmir in the 1st century and was buried in Srinagar in AD88. The first structure covering his tomb was built in 112 and the grave is aligned to point to the east and west as per the Jewish tradition: Muslim bodies are buried on the north–south axis. Alongside the tomb, carved into the stone are two footprints, each with marks above the toes that are said to be the scars of crucifixion. No other such footprints have been identified in Kashmir.

Hemis is famed for its spectacular Tsechu Festival. Held over two days starting from the tenth day of the fifth lunar month (normally around June), the festival celebrates the birth of Guru Padmasambhava (Guru Rinpoche) and features two days of masked dances depicting how Padmasambhava and his eight manifestations defeated the enemies of Buddhism. Every 12 years, a huge *thangka* (a Tibetan Buddhist painting on cotton or silk) depicting Padmasambhava is unveiled during the festival. The next unveiling is due to occur in 2028.

WHAT TO SEE AND DO When you arrive at **Hemis Gompa** (☏ 249 011; ⊕ year round 08.00–18.00 daily, closed 13.00–14.00; admission Rs100) your transport will most probably drop you in the car park, from where there's the inevitable climb up steep steps to the ticket desk and an advertising board proclaiming that Hemis is the largest monastic institution in Ladakh.

Passing the gift shop (where you can buy all manner of (probably) Chinese-made souvenirs you don't really want or need) and lockers brings you into the **central courtyard** where the famous masked dances take place on festival days: you'll most likely recognise it from the postcards. A long, vertical prayer flag flutters on its pole, and to the right a line of **prayer wheels** are spun by absent-minded tourists and an occasional devotee or monk.

The **main prayer hall**, which was renovated in 2014, is a swirl of Buddhist murals and statues, while the outside of the hall has some attractive paintings. If you look up to the roof, you'll see a line of skulls. Note that you are not permitted to take photographs inside the gompa: cameras must be left in the lockers by the gift shop.

Perhaps the most intriguing items at Hemis are within the **museum** (⊕ Apr–Oct 08.00–18.00 daily, closed 13.00–14.00; included in admission to the monastery), which is downstairs from the courtyard. The collection is somewhat eclectic, but pieces include some fine statuary, turquoise masks, beautiful scroll cases decorated with gold filigree work, a cylinder for making butter tea, and a magnificent 14th-century conch shell with a silver and copper mouthpiece, the surface of which is embossed with a dragon and inlaid with pieces of turquoise, coral and lapis lazuli.

CHEMDE AND THAGTHOG   *Telephone code: 01982*

CHEMDE Spread across the hillside and surrounded by a sprinkling of stupas, Chemdey Gompa (or Chemde for short) is by no means the most striking of Ladakh's monasteries, but a charming diversion nonetheless. Like all languages, Ladakhi has changed faster in its spoken than written form, and so Chemde is actually found in the village known as Chemre.

Getting there and away Chemre is 40km from Leh in the Sakti Valley, and there are several daily **buses** from Leh that stop in Chemre before continuing to Thagthog (2hrs; Rs50). By **taxi**, prices start from Rs1,919 for the return trip from Leh, though it is advisable to combine Chemre, Thagthog and Hemis, for which the fare starts at Rs2,620.

Where to stay There is no formal accommodation at Chemre but there is space at the monastery where you can pitch a tent. As a matter of politeness you should ask the monks for permission and leave a donation: Rs250 per person is appropriate.

What to see and do Chemde Gompa was founded in the latter part of the 17th century by Lama Tagsang Raschen and is dedicated to Sengge Namgyal, king of Ladakh from 1616 until his death in 1642. It is home to 120 monks from the Drugpa school, and the chief lama here is also in charge at Hemis.

The principal part of the monastery is set across three floors. On the ground floor is the **dukhang**, where the walls are brightly painted with seven rows of Buddha figures. A library of ancient manuscripts partially covers one section, and three large, antique mandalas are on display. Above this is the **lhakhang** (in fact there are two lhakhangs here), home to statues with noticeably Mongolian features. On the top floor is a light room, recently painted with murals, in which you'll find an impressive **Padmasambhava statue** on its throne.

THAGTHOG (*Telephone code: 01982*) Thagthog (also known as Tak Thok or Traktok) takes its name from the cave where Guru Rinpoche meditated and around which the gompa is built. The only Nyingmapa monastery in Ladakh, it has a very different atmosphere from the other gompas and some visitors have reported feeling a sensation of exceptional unease with physical symptoms, though the monks are friendly enough.

THE ORDERS OF BUDDHISM

In Ladakh there are four principal orders (schools or sects) of Buddhism represented. They are all variations of the Vajrayana path, a form of esoteric Buddhism that incorporates aspects of tantric Hinduism.

NYINGMAPA The oldest of Ladakh's four orders is the Nyingmapa, founded in the 8th century by Guru Padmasambhava, who is credited with bringing Buddhism from India to Tibet. Legend has it that he meditated in a cave at Thagthog (page 128) and a monastery consequently grew up around the holy site. Thagthog is the only Nyingmapa monastery in Ladakh.

KARGYUD The Kargyud, or Order of Oral Transmission, dates from the 11th century but 100 years later split further into the Drigungpa and Drugpa sects. The order is based on the teachings of a lineage of four scholars: Tilopa, Naropa, Marpa and Milarepa. Lamayuru and Phyang are both Drigungpa monasteries.

SAKYAPA The White Earth, or Sakyapa, order was founded at Sakya (in what is now Tibet) in 1073, and is based on the teachings of Indian yogis.

GELUGPA The Gelugpa, or Yellow Hat, is the most visible of Ladakh's Buddhist orders. It evolved out of the 11th-century Kadampa sect when the scholar Tsongkhapa (1357–1419) demanded reforms to restore what he saw as the purity of older ideas. His disciple Lama Lhawang Lhotos founded the Gelugpa sect at Likir.

Getting there and away It's 45km from Leh to Thagthog and the public **bus** runs to Sakti (passing through Thagthog) every day except Sunday (2hrs; Rs60). By **taxi**, fares start from Rs2,201 return, though you may wish to combine your visit with a trip to Chemde (page 127) and Hemis (page 125).

Where to stay and eat There is a **guesthouse ($)** run by the monks at the foot of the gompa. Theoretically it is always staffed, but in reality you'll have to ask around to find someone to open the gate for you. Rooms are simple but clean and have attached bathrooms; breakfast and dinner are available on request. A better option is the smart **Sakti Villa** (11 rooms; \ 251 063; e sales@saktivilla.com; w saktivilla. com; **$$$$**), a boutique guesthouse with seven guestrooms with subtle décor and four luxury tents kitted out with everything you don't normally expect to find in a tent, such as proper beds with thick mattresses and good linens, and decent bathrooms. Good meals are available for guests.

What to see and do Thagthog Gompa has grown literally out of the rock: Padmasambhava (Guru Rinpoche) is believed to have meditated in the cave, the cave became a shrine, and, eight centuries after his visit in the mid-1700s, much of the monastery you see today was built. The new temple, just below the main complex, was consecrated by the Dalai Lama only in 1980, however, and so is not an original structure.

The **cave** is the physical and spiritual heart of the monastery, although it's often occupied by meditating monks and is frequently closed to visitors. If you can get in, then you'll discover that it's a small but not claustrophobic space and the walls are black and sticky with the oily soot of butter lamps. If you look closely you can make out eight painted circles, each one depicting a different manifestation of the Padmasambhava, but you'll almost need to press your nose to the wall to see them. Elsewhere in the gompa are some **historic frescoes**, a four-armed **statue of Avalokiteshvara** and an important collection of **ancient manuscripts** brought here by refugees from Tibet.

THE MARKHA VALLEY

The Markha River, a tributary to the Zanskar, has created one of the most scenic valleys in Ladakh, and it is quite rightly one of the region's most popular trekking destinations. Accessible via either Ganda La near Spituk, or from Kongmaru La (5,260m, also called Gongmaru La) near Hemis, much of the valley falls within the borders of the Hemis National Park. Most of the trekking routes are best attempted between July and September, though some are accessible until mid-October.

GETTING THERE AND AWAY Given that most people come to Markha to trek, it makes sense to travel to Spituk (page 95) or Hemis (page 125) and then cross the passes **on foot**. If you are short of time, however, or simply wish to visit the valley on a day trip, you can take a **taxi** from Leh. Driving to Rumbak-Zingchen via the bridge at Spituk will cost from Rs1,719 one-way; to get there via the bridge at Choglamsar will cost from Rs2,219 one-way.

WHERE TO STAY AND EAT An offshoot of the Snow Leopard Conservancy India Trust (see box, page 7), **Himalayan Homestays** (w himalayan-homestays.com) has organised a series of excellent homestays throughout the Hemis National Park, many of which are in the Markha Valley. Visitors are rotated around different homes

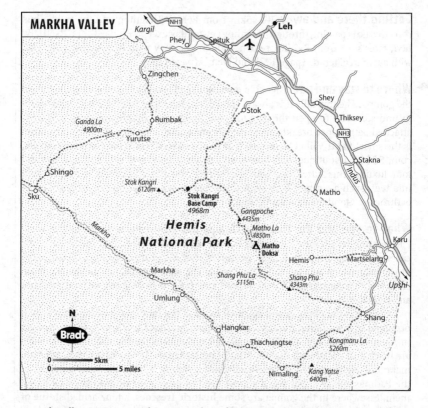

MARKHA VALLEY

in each village to ensure the money benefits as many local families as possible. You'll pay Rs1,000 per person for a warm bed and delicious, home-cooked meals, and it's the best way to get to know local people and their way of life. There are currently homestays in Rumbak, Yurutse, Shingo, Kaya, Sku and Chilling.

If you have lightweight equipment and/or porters to carry it, **camping** is also a viable option. There are a number of designated camping spots (local guides know where they are), and you can sometimes arrange to camp in someone's field or on the outskirts of their village. Always ask permission if you do this, and be prepared to make a small payment (Rs200 or thereabouts).

WHAT TO SEE AND DO You come to the Markha Valley to see the scenery and the wildlife, and to trek. The trekking options are numerous and varied: local tour operators in Leh will be able to make recommendations based on your level of fitness, interests and the amount of time you have available. The following trek is our particular favourite.

Ganda La and the Markha Valley trek Ladakh's classic trek, the Markha Valley offers an intoxicating mix of trans-Himalayan scenery and authentic Tibetan culture. It's the most popular trek in Ladakh, though it's still far from commercialised. There are any number of variations on the route, depending on exactly where you start and end the trek, and how long or short you wish to make the average walking day (the route can be covered in as little as four days, and as many as nine). We would highly recommend devoting more rather than less time to the trek.

Although it is possible to do the standard trek alone, due to climate conditions and the high altitude we would strongly advise you to take a guide. Every trekking company in Leh can quickly organise this (page 76), and you'll be able to choose between a teahouse (homestay) or camping trek.

The standard trek starts at **Spituk** (3,307m), just outside Leh, on the bridge across the Indus River. It's a dusty 3-hour tramp along the old jeep road up into the Zingchen Valley, then a further 2 hours along the Zingchen (Jingchen) River (by which time the landscape is fresh and green) to the hamlet of **Zingchen** (4,560m), where there is a campsite and, helpfully, a tea shop.

Zingchen is on the edge of the Hemis National Park and so, as you penetrate the reserve on day two, you can hope to catch a glimpse of mountain hares, marmots, wild dogs and foxes, as well as, if you're lucky, Great Tibetan sheep and Ladakhi urial. Climbing through the gorge brings you to a series of golden barley fields around **Rumbak** (4,050m), where blue sheep are occasionally visible on the slopes. A short distance on is tiny **Yurutse**, where there is a homestay, or you can continue on to the **campsite** (4,545m) at the base of Ganda La, which has majestic views of Stok Kangri.

On day three there's around 6 hours of walking, starting with a 2-hour, zigzagging ascent of **Ganda La** (4,900m). Marmots and hares lark on the slopes, and stupas and prayer flags mark the top of the pass. Look to the west for the most impressive views, be sure to take some photos, and then begin making your way down the trail to **Shingo** (4,200m), where there's a homestay if you need it, and thence through the gorge and back and forth across the stream to **Sku** (3,300m). There are some fortified ruins here, supposedly part of what was once a royal residence, that are worth having a look at too. There are homestays here, and more in the neighbouring hamlet of Kaya.

You need to allow for 7 hours of walking on day four. The trail follows the Markha River for much of the way and passes through several seasonal settlements used by the nomads. In each of these places there are small Buddhist shrines and many Mani stones. The valley is hot and exposed, which makes for a tiring day, but it ends in **Markha** (3,810m), the largest village in the valley, where you'll hopefully get a good night's sleep. If you've still got energy for sightseeing, there is a ruined fort and a small gompa.

Day five is culturally rich as you pass by both a ruined castle and the Techa Gompa, poised high on the cliff above Markha itself. The trekking trail weaves its way back and forth across the river to **Umlung**, from where you'll first see towering **Kang Yatse** (6,400m), then on through the meadows to **Hangkar** and finally the campsite at **Thachungtse** (4,250m). Allow 6 hours to reach the camp.

On the sixth day, from Thachungtse to the Nimaling Plateau where nomads graze their sheep and goats, it's only a 4-hour walk but the path is steep and, at 4,700m, **Nimaling** is the highest campsite on the trek. Sweeping views take in not only the Markha Valley but large parts of the Zanskar Range too, so if you're at all artistically inclined, this is the time to get out your camera or sketchpad.

The penultimate day of the trek starts with a crossing of **Kongmaru La** (5,260m; also called Gongmaru La), the physical high point of the journey. You descend from here into the **Shang Gorge** and proceed to **Chuskurmo**, a natural spring that is thought to have medicinal properties. The night is spent in the village of **Shang Sumdo** (3,660m).

Day eight brings you from the village along the jeep road to **Martselang** (3,450m), which connects to the main road. It's a pleasant stroll of just 2 hours, leaving plenty of time to head back to Leh or elsewhere by vehicle (best pre-arranged in advance).

Running up towards the Chinese border, the vast open plateau of southeastern Ladakh is sprayed with lakes that glint in multi-hued blues. This is a landscape guaranteed to make you feel small, where wolves streak over the horizon and nomads set up yak-hair tents among barren plains. If you've had your fill of monasteries, retreating into this grand wilderness and dipping your toes in icy waters or staring up into a seemingly endless star-filled sky is the perfect remedy.

Unless you have a lot of time available, you'll probably need to choose either to visit Pangong Tso or to go to Tso Moriri and Tso Kar lakes. Both require a long and uncomfortable car journey, and as getting there and back from Leh is expensive, your decision may well be shaped by whom you can share a car with.

The road south from Leh to the lakes is the main Leh–Manali road, National Highway 3 (NH3). It splits at Upshi, an army base that also hosts a small line of **shops** and **cafés**. From here it is 110km to Pangong Tso, 115km to Tso Kar and 175km to Tso Moriri.

Due to the proximity of the lakes to the Indo-Chinese border, you are required to have an Inner Line Permit (see box, page 101) to travel there. If you do not have a permit (and the requisite number of photocopies), you will not be allowed to travel past the police checkpoints.

PANGONG TSO Straddling the border of India and China, Pangong Tso is a 604km^2 endorheic lake: a closed basin with no river flowing out from it. A natural dam has shut off the stream leading into the Shyok; the only water leaving the lake does so through seepage and evaporation.

People frequently come to Pangong Tso and say that it leaves them spellbound. The backdrop to many a Bollywood movie, including parts of *3 Idiots* with Aamir Khan and *Dil Se* starring Shah Rukh Khan, it has waters that change colour constantly, mesmerising the viewer. A visit during the full moon is unforgettable due to the silver-white reflection on the surface of the lake. However, it's by far the most popular of the lakes and in season the shores can get busy and rubbish left by thoughtless tourists is becoming an increasing problem.

Getting there and away From May to September there is a bi-weekly JKSRTC **bus** from Leh to Spangmik, a village on the northwest shore of Pangong Tso, which departs from Leh on Saturday and Sunday at 06.00, returning to Leh the following morning at 07.00. It costs around Rs270 each way and the journey takes at least 8 hours, and more if you have a flat tyre, which is much more likely here than in Europe due to the general poor maintenance of vehicles, or some other delay. On Sundays and Wednesdays there is also a bus at 06.30 to the village of Chushul (Rs394), just south of the lake, which travels via the shore-side villages of Man and Merak and takes roughly 8 hours if not longer as well.

If you need more flexibility in your timing, a seat in a **shared taxi** will cost Rs1,500 each way, and hiring a **taxi** for yourself will cost from Rs8,201 if you go there and back to Leh in a day, or Rs9,762 if you go one day and return the next.

Where to stay and eat Most of the accommodation is in Spangmik, although it's not the most attractive of villages and can become quite over-run with tourists in summer. At the time of research, there was talk of relocating all the summer tented camps elsewhere, and if this happens then the only options in the village itself will be a number of basic but adequate homestays. All of these currently charge Rs550 per person including breakfast and dinner.

Tented camps

Pangong has a growing range of tented camps. Most are comfortable enough though hardly the height of luxury, and from afar they're something of a blot on the landscape.

🏠 **Pangong Sarai** (10 tents) m 198 3251 363; e bookings@ladakhsarai.com; w ladakhsarai. com. Located in the village of Man, this relative newcomer to Pangong isn't quite as upmarket as it likes to think, but it's still a surprisingly comfortable & very well-run spot considering the remote location. The round, yurt-like tents are a little plain but have attached bathrooms & the food on offer is definitely in a class above the other camps. **$$$$**

🏠 **Camp Redstart** (10 tents) m 941 9233 499/941 9177 245; e contact@campredstart.com; w campredstart.com. One of the newest camps on the lake & with the largest tents, all of which overlook the lake. All have attached hot-water bathrooms & staff are obliging. The camp is even kitted out with oxygen supplies for those suffering from the altitude. **$$$$**

🏠 **Camp Water Mark** (15 tents) ☏011 405 803 34 (Delhi); w campsofladakh.com/ water-mark.html. Also at Spangmik, this camp's cleanliness & comfort require particular mention, as does the standard of the food. Hot water is available in the mornings on request. **$$$$**

🏠 **Camp Whispering Waves** (15 tents) ☏011 405 803 34 (Delhi); w campsofladakh.com/ whisperingwaves.html. This is on the southern shore of the lake at Spangmik, the furthest point where foreigners are permitted to go. All tents are carpeted & have en-suite bathrooms & multi-cuisine meals are served in the communal dining tent. **$$$$**

Homestays

Of the homestays there's the friendly **Gomgma Homestay** (m 946 953 4270; **$**) and the **Diskit Khangcher Guest House** (m 941 968 2755; **$**), which is a step up in quality from most of the other options. Some of the rooms even have attached bathrooms. In the village of Merak, the **Peaceful Homestay** (m 094 6928 0274; e rdolker1983@ gmail.com; w peacefulhomestaymerak.in; **$**) also gets good feedback.

❌ **Where to eat and drink** You should eat your meals in your accommodation or bring food with you from Leh, as there is little to buy locally. The exception is the traditional *chang* (homemade barley beer), which will set you back about Rs15.

What to see and do Most visitors come here to soak up the ever-changing waters of the lake; the colour depends markedly on the time of day and the season. In the midday sun you might see it in vibrant turquoise, while looking back from a distance in the afternoon it might be royal blue, and up close, staring into the water when it's overcast, it's a brackish brown. In spite of its salinity, the lake freezes completely in winter.

There are few, if any, fish in the lake but this doesn't stop large numbers of migratory birds resting here in the summer months: they feed on crustaceans and the herbs and scrub growing in the marshy patches at the water's edge. Bar-headed geese and Brahmi ducks are both common sights, and it is hoped that the lake will soon be recognised as a Ramsar wetland of international importance.

TSO KAR The smallest of the three main lakes is Tso Kar, an attractive salt lake whose tourist potential is – thankfully – yet to be fully realised: the development of hotel and restaurant infrastructure is far behind that at Tso Moriri, for example, and the lake is all the more spectacular for it.

Getting there and away There is no public transport here, so you will need to hire a taxi from Leh. The 155km drive is almost entirely along NH3 and takes around 7 hours. The road is in generally good condition, but snow and ice can be a problem at any time of year. When the road forks at **Upshi**, continue along the road, heading right towards Manali. You will also pass through **Gya** (26km from Upshi), where there is a small gompa across the river (use the rickety footbridge) from the village, and **Rumtse** (29km from Upshi), from where it is a demanding seven-day trek to Tso Moriri if you feel so inclined (see box, page 136).

South of Rumtse you must cross the **Taglang La** pass (5,328m; 31km from Upshi). The views are probably best when driving north, but in either direction you should pause to soak up the panoramas as the mountainside and twisted shoelace of a road simply seem to fall away beneath you. Don't try to do anything here too quickly as the altitude takes its toll, even if you've already acclimatised in Leh.

The last settlement before you reach the turn-off for Tso Kar is **Dipling**. It's far from impressive, composed as it is of just a row of temporary-looking buildings and tents serving basic meals. Some 2km further on is the grandly named **Dipling Restaurant**, a solitary tent serving tea and momos, and it is here that you leave NH3 and turn left on to the track for Tso Kar.

If you are driving between Tso Moriri and Tso Kar, there is a largely unmade road between the two lakes. Providing it is dry, it's not an uncomfortable ride and the views are superb. The distance is only around 50km but it takes a full 3 hours. You may well be asked to pick up hitchhikers in one of the villages en route and to take them as far as the NH3 as there is no public transport locally and few other vehicles pass this way.

Taxis from Leh offer trips to Tso Kar only as part of a longer five-day package, which includes stops in a choice of monastery towns on the way down as well as Pangong Tso. Prices start from Rs33,068.

Where to stay and eat Tso Kar village is less developed than the settlements at Pangong Tso and Tso Moriri, and probably wouldn't exist at all if it weren't for the passing tourist trade. Despite a small number of mud-brick buildings, your options for eating and sleeping are all under canvas. **Pastureland Camp** (30 tents; $$$$) has a superb location and it is particularly popular with birdwatchers, but it's overpriced. The **Lotus Camp** (10 tents; m 941 981 9078; w lotuscamptsokar. com; $$$$) is a newer and, in our opinion, slightly more desirable camp with a smaller and more intimate feel. Also along the lakeshore are a couple of very basic 'parachute-style' camps made from old military parachutes, all charging Rs550 including breakfast and dinner.

Rice and dal lunches, instant noodles, tea and inflated-price snacks are available from **Tso Kar Restaurant** ($), a round, white tent on the edge of the village with a few tables inside. There's a slightly gruesome (but still impressive) skull and horns of a long-dead sheep immediately outside the entrance.

What to see and do The smallest of the three principal southern lakes, **Tso Kar** is a 9km² saline lake conjoined with its smaller sister, Tso Startsapuk. Though the lakes' inlets contain fresh water, the lakeshore is covered with a thick, white crust of salt that gives the lake its name (*kar* means white). Changspa nomads used to collect this salt, process it and export it to Tibet.

Tso Kar is far less visited than Tso Moriri and Pangong, but birdwatchers flock here (if you'll excuse the pun) in order to scope out Brahmi ducks, great crested grebes and rare black-necked cranes, which congregate here to lay their eggs between late October and March.

A short scramble above the village, away from the lake, brings you to **Tso Kar Gompa**. The building itself is neither particularly old nor particularly interesting but it offers a fine vantage point from which to survey the lake and its mountainous backdrop, and this is what justifies the climb.

TSO MORIRI In our opinion, Tso Moriri is the most beautiful of the three lakes, though inevitably there will be plenty of people to argue otherwise. It's best seen early in the morning or late in the day, when the shadows are long and the romance of the place is at large. However, you'll need to walk a short way from Korzok, the village on the northwest shore, to be able to really appreciate the pristine environment and peace. Some 34 species of bird, including 14 waterbirds, are found in the Tso Moriri Wetland Conservation Reserve (page 138), as are rarely seen snow leopards, Tibetan wolves, Great Tibetan sheep and marmots.

Getting there and away
The 215km **drive** south from Leh can take as long as 8 hours, as extensive sections of the journey are on unmade roads. Leaving by 10.00 at the latest and not stopping en route will ensure you reach Tso Moriri when the lake and surrounding mountains are at their most photogenic, swathed in a warm afternoon light.

Significant (though by no means substantial) settlements en route include **Upshi** where the road forks: you can stop here for steamed momos or an omelette at **Padma Restaurant** ($) and pick up snacks for the road in the small **shops** before heading out of the village to the left (the right fork takes you to Tso Kar and then on to Manali and, eventually, Chandigarh). You can also do a loop from Leh taking in Tso Moriri and Tso Kar by following the dirt track between the two.

At riverside **Chumathang** there is a decidedly dusty-looking hot spring, a bar serving Kingfisher beers and various noxious local spirits, and two cafés: **Skit Tsau Restaurant** ($) and the marginally more presentable **Paradise Restaurant** ($–$$), both of which are fine for a quick snack. Look right as you leave Chumathang and you'll see one of the flimsier-looking footbridges in the area: it's probably only held together by the prayer flags.

Past Chumathang is the **Mahe Bridge**. Although the main road continues along the left bank, the road to Tso Moriri crosses the bridge and sweeps around to the right, with dry, gorse-like bushes on the valley floor and purple and yellow flowers scattered across the slopes. From Chumathang to the lakeshore it's 74km, but allow a couple of hours to make the journey.

Travelling to Tso Moriri by road, you will need at least three copies of your Inner Line Permit (see box, page 101), which you will be required to present at the police checkpoints at Upshi and Mahe Bridge, and to the Indo–Tibetan Border Police at Korzok, regardless of your method of transport. The latter will also require you to sign a form stating the number of cameras and GPS units in your vehicle, and confirming that you are not carrying a satellite phone.

If you do not have your own vehicle, there are three buses a month from Leh (Rs370), departing on the 10th, 20th and 30th at 06.30. You would, however, need to wait a full ten days for the return bus, or arrange for a car to bring you back. It would better suit those planning to drive in and trek out. Taxi drivers in Leh offer Tso Moriri only as a part of a longer multi-day trek stopping in a choice of monastery towns on the way down as well as Pangong Tso (page 132).

Where to stay and eat
All of Tso Moriri's accommodation and eating options are in the small village of Korzok, the only permanent settlement on the lakeside. Business here is seasonal and the variety of places to stay limited, but you'll have no difficulty finding a warm(ish) bed and hot meal, even if you turn up unannounced.

The best **budget accommodation** is at one of nearly a dozen **homestays** in the village, each of which has two to three rooms and will provide all your meals.

The trek from Rumtse to Tso Moriri traverses spectacular, wild scenery where a smattering of nomadic settlements will be your sole human encounter. In our opinion, it's easily one of the best treks in Ladakh, though you should note that it's more about wide-open Tibetan-style vistas than close-up views of soaring mountain giants. Best completed between June and mid-October, it's a challenging trek that climbs to a maximum elevation of 5,435m and takes seven days.

Starting at **Rumtse** (4,095m) on the Leh–Manali Highway, 2 hours' drive south of Leh, the first day of the trek follows the road as far as the Government Bungalow, then cuts up the trail on the right-hand side of the valley, past some old army buildings, and then to the river. It's necessary to cross both the river and the stream to its left before continuing along the valley to the campsite at **Kyamar** (4,383m). In total it will take you no more than 4 hours.

Day two starts with a slow ascent of **Kyamar La** (4,870m). Take time to look out for the mighty Indus River snaking by below. When you finally catch your breath at the top, the track splits in two: you need to follow the path to the right that crosses a small stream and then climbs **Mandalchan La** (4,996m). It's a steep descent from the top of the pass to the campsite at **Tisaling** (4,800m). Allow 5 hours for this section of the trek.

The third day starts gently enough but the climb is steady and ultimately brings you out on top of **Shingbuk La** (5,016m), one of the physical high points of the trek, from where it is possible to see across to Tso Kar. By evening you will be at **Pangunagu** (4,398m) in the sparsely populated Tso Kar basin. Again you should allow 5 hours for the day's walking.

Tearing yourself away from the campsite may be tough, but you can console yourself with the fact that the first 2 hours of day four are around the rim of the lake on the dusty but little-used jeep track. A sandy trail then takes you away from Tso Kar, winding through irrigated fields to the campsite at **Nuruchan** (4,500m). You should have plenty of time to picnic, birdwatch and generally idle along the way, as it will take you no more than four hours.

Day five is the shortest day, with just 3 hours of walking. There's a straightforward river crossing first thing, followed by a gentle climb up **Horlam Kongka La** (4,712m). Coming down the other side you have to cross several small streams to reach the campsite at **Rjungkaru** (4,668m), where it is likely you'll meet Tibetan nomads grazing their flocks.

The penultimate day is the longest: allow 6 hours. It begins with a strenuous ascent of **Kyamayur La** (5,125m), and once you've crossed that pass the trail continues to another slightly smaller one, **Gyama La** (5,100m). The rest of the day is spent making your way downhill, across a few small streams, to **Gyama Lhoma** (4,895m), which is the base camp for the Korzok Pass.

On the final day of the trek, start out early and follow the stream through the wild-flower meadows to the top of **Yalung Nyaulung La** (5,450m). By

Homestays are marked with white signs: simply knock and see if they have space. You can also pitch your own tent at the **campsite ($)** on the far side of the village. There is a temporary toilet block and water seems to come from the stream.

If you are not staying in Korzok but need to stop here for a meal, your best option is **Lhasa Restaurant ($)** in the centre of the village. The fare is unimaginative but portions are hot and filling and prices are reasonable.

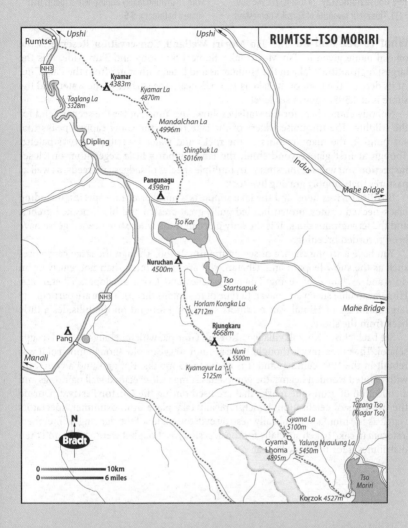

Bradt

0 — 10km
0 — 6 miles

mid-morning you'll be standing at the top of the pass surveying the panoramic views not only of Tso Moriri but of the surrounding mountains as well. This is the reward for your effort. The trek ends with a steep descent along the Korzok Phu River into **Korzok**, where the creature comforts of Tso Moriri Camp (see below) await.

🏠 **Tso Moriri Camp** (15 tents, 5 huts) m 982 050 1211; e info@tsomoriricampandresort.com; w tsomoriricampandresort.com. Owned by Camps of Ladakh, this is the first of the tented camps you see on the right as you enter Korzok & it's the pick of the bunch with simple but comfortable tents &

plenty of blankets for the cold nights. Every tent has an attached bathroom with proper toilet & running water. Meals are served buffet-style in a large maharaja's tent. If you haven't packed for inclement weather, they also sell colourful, hand-knitted socks. **$$$$**

🏠 **Goose Homestay** (4 rooms) m 946 959 1231. This is our favourite of Korzak's homestays, with an inviting family atmosphere & rooms that share a bathroom. **$$**

What to see and do The Tso Moriri Wetland Conservation Reserve is the official name given to Tso Moriri lake. Some 19km long and 3km wide, it is the largest high-altitude lake in the Himalayas and is fed with water from the Pare Chu. At its deepest the floor of the lake is 105m beneath the surface of the water, and the shore is at 4,595m above sea level.

Nobody comes here for the statistics, however. You visit for the scenery and for the wildlife. The turquoise waters of the lake reflect the snow-capped peaks that surround it, the many colours of the rocks and water a veritable artist's palette. Though at first glance you'd think the land supports little vegetation, on closer inspection you will see marshes with multiple species of sedges and reeds, as well as pastures that support grazing livestock.

Birdlife thrives here, and the lake supports a number of rare species, including black-necked cranes, brown-headed gulls, great crested and black-necked grebes, and the ferruginous duck. It is the only place in India where bar-headed geese have been recorded breeding.

You have a strong chance of seeing **mammals** too. Though the large carnivores such as the snow leopard and Tibetan wolf are, more often than not, elusive, you do stand a chance of seeing Tibetan gazelles and Goan antelopes, Tibetan ass, Himalayan blue sheep and nayan (a type of mountain sheep). There are particularly large numbers of Himalayan marmots sauntering around on the hillsides a little back from the shore.

Set back above Korzok village is **Korzok Gompa**, which belongs to the Drugpa school. The monastery is thought to be around 300 years old, though much of it was rebuilt in the 19th century, and it is home to 35 monks. Built around a courtyard with painted wooden beams, the gompa has some well-executed wall paintings and a collection of grotesque masks that are used during the **Gustor Festival.** During the two days of celebration, which typically take place in midsummer, spectators watch as the monks symbolically destroy evil: the leader of the dancing dismembers a *storma* (a cake baked specially for the occasion) as though it were a body, and then distributes it for the crowd to eat.

6

Northwest Ladakh

Far too often tourists race along the highway from Leh to Srinagar without pausing to see what's en route. Though the sights here may be lacking in publicity, scarcely mentioned in general tourist literature, this is an unfortunate oversight, as the area is home to a rich blend of Muslim and Buddhist cultures, fascinating historical sites and some stunning natural landscapes. Indeed, this northern part of Ladakh is a natural adventure playground: visiting adrenaline junkies can pit their strength and skills against the rivers while white-water rafting and kayaking, or explore yet more of the trekking routes linking the Ladakh and Zanskar ranges. Driving on the main roads is straightforward enough, but get away from NH1 and you'll be testing your off-road skills, fording rivers and traversing rocky ground.

Some of Ladakh's richest cultural sites are found here, too: Likir is a lively monastery where novice monks giggle and play beneath the watchful eye of a vast, golden Buddha; the beautifully carved and painted shrines at Alchi date back to at least the 12th century and are remarkable for both their age and state of preservation; and the settings of Basgo and Lamayuru, each among rugged, rocky landscapes, are truly sights to behold, not to mention masterpieces of architecture and engineering. Continuing north into Kargil district, you'll find some of the largest and most impressive standing Buddhas in the world, reminiscent of those destroyed by the Taliban at Bamiyan in Afghanistan. There's also the opportunity to visit the fascinating villages of Dha and Hanu, as well as those around Bartalik, home to the Brokpa people who claim descent from the troops of Alexander the Great.

THE LEH–KARGIL HIGHWAY   *Telephone code: 01982*

Northwest of Leh, National Highway 1 (NH1) runs parallel to the Indus, sharing the valley that the mighty river has carved out for itself. Sadly rushed through by many travellers, it's a region of soaring rocky bluffs and timeless gompas filled with the sound of chanting monks, so it's worth trying to set aside a few days to explore the area in greater depth.

PHYANG Set in a picturesque side valley a short distance north of the NH1, Phyang's gompa rises dramatically out of the earth, dominating its surroundings. Look past the gompa, however, and you'll find a higgledy-piggledy patchwork of yellow and green, the irregular layout of fields interspersed with thin, willowy trees, single-storey houses topped with drying fodder, and contentedly grazing *dzo* (a cross between a yak and a cow).

Although most people visit on a half-day trip from Leh, there are a couple of superb places to stay that make Phyang an enticing – and much more tranquil – base for exploring this part of Ladakh, and even Leh itself.

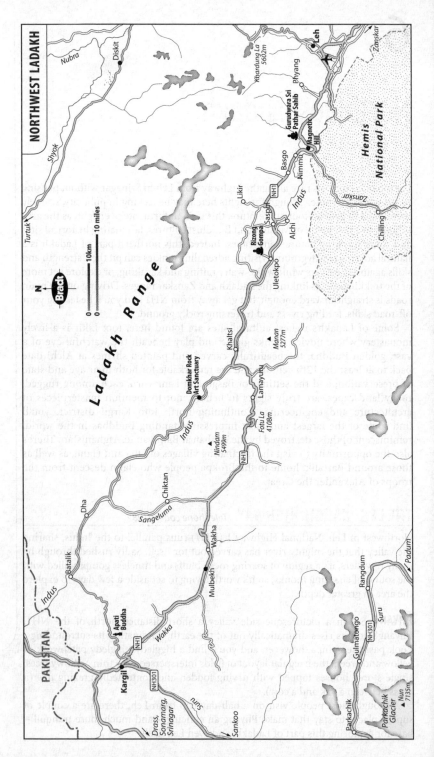

Getting there and around There are three **buses** a day between Leh and Phyang, departing Leh at 09.00, 14.30 and 16.30. The 17km journey takes approximately 30 minutes (depending on the number of request stops) as the road is in fairly decent shape, and the fare is Rs25 to the gompa or Rs30 to the top of the village. If the altitude is getting to you, the same buses can be used to get from the gompa to the guesthouse; otherwise it is half an hour's walk.

If you prefer to take a **taxi** from Leh, prices start from Rs812 for a drop-off at the gompa (it's a little cheaper to the town itself) and Rs1,054 to go there and back. There is also a rewarding **trek** from Hunder in the Nubra Valley to Phyang (see box, page 106).

Where to stay and eat Phyang is blessed with two superb places to stay.

Hidden North Guesthouse (8 rooms) m 990 699 9950; e office@hiddennorth. com; w hiddennorth.com. Perched at the top of the village with what have to be among the best views in Ladakh, this guesthouse is run by a charming Ladakhi-Italian family who have been in the tourism business since the 1990s but opened their home up to guests in 2010. Fast Wi-Fi & immaculate bathrooms, as well as camping facilities. If you're taking your meals here (which are delicious), expect lively conversation in your choice of English, French, German, Italian or Ladakhi. Husband Tashi is an experienced trekking guide & can arrange a variety of treks & tours, inc a 5-day trek from Phyang to the Nubra Valley, through his travel agency **Hidden North Adventures** (see box, page 106). **$$–$$$**

Nyanjan Guest House (8 rooms) m 979 733 7910; w nyanjenfamilyguesthouse.blogspot. com. This gorgeous family-run guesthouse is set in pretty flower gardens & has tastefully decorated rooms with a floral theme & smart, modern bathrooms. You can even help out on the farm with milking the cattle & tending the crops. Decent home-cooked meals are available. All in all, it's a fantastic cultural experience. **$$**

What to see and do

Phyang Gompa (✆ 226 005; ⊕ 08.00–20.00; admission Rs50) Today the home of 70 monks, this gompa was founded in 1515 during the reign of King Jamyang Namgyal, but there may well have been a settlement here prior to this. The bulk of the buildings were constructed two decades later.

Parking is at the rear of the gompa, and from here you climb a steep slope that passes beneath a yellow **gateway** topped with two golden (but anatomically questionable) deer – these represent the deer at the Sonarth, the site of the Buddha's first sermon. On your left is the gompa's **carpentry workshop**, where everyday items such as new window frames and doors are made, and set against the wall are several slabs of stone etched with stupas and Tibetan script. At the top of the slope, where you may well have to stop to catch your breath (blame the altitude), the new parts of the monastery are to your right and the older, more interesting parts are to your left. It is traditional to circulate a Buddhist temple or gompa in a clockwise direction (page 66), so visit the old part first.

The **old section** of the gompa is a bit of a warren: expect to get lost. Wherever you walk, watch your head and your feet, as doors are low and the floors and stairs are very uneven.

Your first port of call should be the **main prayer hall**, which is accessed up a decidedly rickety wooden staircase from the internal courtyard. A single monk stands guard in the antechamber, collecting admission fees and ensuring no photos are taken inside. The prayer hall is a particularly dark space, the only light entering through the doorway and a single window beneath the roof. The ceiling is supported on a dozen red pillars, evenly spaced, and as your eyes adjust to the gloom, the fabulous

murals start coming into focus. Predominantly depicted in shades of red and green, the facial characteristics of these 200-year-old figures are in some cases decidedly Mongol. A trio of brocade silk banners further break up the room, and along the back wall devotees leave Rs10 offerings at the feet of ten statues of varying sizes, each one representing a significant figure in the development of Tibetan Buddhism.

Making your way carefully back down the staircase and out of the courtyard, turn left. Immediately on your right is a pair of short, red doors with brass knockers. These doors are kept locked, so if there's no monk present to let you in, you'll need to return to the prayer hall and ask. This lower room contains the much-advertised highlight of the gompa: finely preserved **16th-century wall paintings**. For us, however, the accompanying objects were also of great curiosity: look out for the grotesque, tiger-legged statue of four-armed Mahakala who converted four demons to Buddhism; a ceremonial drum and severed goat horns; and Mongolian spears and shields left as offerings by warriors who visited here.

Working your way around to the **modern part** of the gompa, you'll see more of the monks, as this is where they live and work. The western end of the building has some impressive **modern decoration**, with hundreds of garish colours and patterns competing for your attention, and also three newly painted **stupas** set alongside a fourth, red reliquary reminiscent of a Royal Mail post box.

AROUND PHYANG Leaving Phyang west on NH1, you pass a number of intriguing sites, starting with the small **Gurudwara Sri Pathar Sahib**, 15km west of Phyang. Although it attracts a small number of Sikh devotees and an occasional tourist, most visitors to the area drive straight on to the clearly marked **Magnetic Hill**. This optical illusion makes it appear that cars are rolling uphill, defying gravity, and it's a popular diversion for domestic tourists in particular. A short way further on is the dramatic **confluence of the Indus and Zanskar rivers**, around 25km west of Phyang, where a number of popular rafting trips begin (page 90).

NIMMU Though you would never plan your itinerary to incorporate Nimmu, a ribbon development that's grown up to service the local army base at the western edge of the village, it makes for a good rest stop if you're passing through. The central part of the village is composed of a run of largely unsigned shops on both sides of the road, where you'll find **Norling Restaurant** ($) serving cheap Tibetan dishes. Several shops along from here (facing away from Leh) is a pharmacy, the **Rafta Medical Hall** (⊕ 09.30–18.30), while on the opposite side of the street is the slightly larger and cleaner **Namgyal Restaurant** ($–$$), which also sells bottled water and fresh juices, and an **SBI ATM** (⊕ 24hrs).

As you're leaving the town westwards, take a quick look at the unusual **sky-blue stupa** and also the larger, crumbling **white stupa** that is gradually being engulfed by the army base. Refrain from taking photos of the latter.

⌂ **Where to stay and eat**

✱ ⌂ **Nimmu House** (11 rooms) ☎ 844 775 7517 (Delhi); e contact@nimmu-house.com; w ladakh.nimmu-house.com. One of the best hotels in Ladakh, this boutique property was once the home of the cousin of the King of Ladakh. Today the royal luxury continues with 4 beautiful heritage rooms incorporating natural products & locally sourced antiques & crafts. Out in the pretty orchard are 7 deluxe safari tents with solid wood furnishings & touches of local art. Superb meals are available & guests can also participate in yoga & cookery courses. **$$$$$**

⌂ **Hotel Takshos** (10 rooms) ☎ 225 064. Reasonably well-equipped & looked-after rooms as well as a fair-sized garden restaurant where tour buses occasionally stop. **$$**

BASGO Few places in the world can boast a landscape as dramatic as that at Basgo. The village takes its name from a rock the shape of a bull's head (*ba-mgo*) and it is situated at a point where the Indus Valley narrows, the fort and monastery temples clinging precariously to the cliffs above.

History The history of Basgo can be traced back to the 15th century with the construction of the Rab-brtan Lhartse Khar (Divine Peak of Great Stability), the rock-top citadel whose ruins are still visible today. It is possible that sections of an older, 11th-century, structure are underneath, but it is not known for sure. The citadel was the residence of Gragspa Bum, ruler of Lower Ladakh, who alternated his capital between Basgo and Tingmosgang.

The gompa's Chamba Lhakhang dates from this early period of construction, and later buildings were added to the complex during the reigns of Tsewang and Sengge Namgyal in the 16th and early 17th centuries. The first European visitor, a Portuguese named Diego d'Almeida, visited Basgo in 1603, appreciating it in all its glory.

Basgo was besieged by Mongol forces for three years in the late 1600s and thanks to its natural water supplies and carefully stored food reserves survived the ordeal. When Basgo was attacked by the Dogras in 1834 it was not so lucky, however: the buildings were ransacked and many of the treasures they contained carted off by the soldiers.

Getting there and away Basgo is situated 42km from Leh and the road is decent enough to travel along, unless of course you get stuck behind a military convoy. If you're coming by **bus**, you'll be dropped on the main road about 20 minutes' walk from the monastery. The side road leading up to the monastery winds past small houses to a river, which is crossed on a small bridge and then the road continues into the village. **Taxis** can be hired from Leh from Rs1,301/1,691 one-way/return.

Where to stay and eat There are several unassuming but convenient places to stay in Basgo. The small but reasonably well-kept **Chamba Guesthouse and Restaurant ($)** is on the main road, quite a trek from the gompa. Other options include the **Lagang Guesthouse** (✆225 102; **$**) and **Tsering Khangsar Guesthouse** (✆225 108; **$**), both of which are in the village itself. For a greater variety of options, including mid-range hotels, you'll need to continue to Likir or go back to Leh.

If you want a quick snack, try the basic but easily accessible **National Highway Restaurant** (✆225 648; **$$**), which is on the main road.

What to see and do Basgo Gompa was founded in 1515 but much of what you see dates from a century later. Perched on top of a rocky crag above a jade-green oasis, this crow's nest of a gompa seems to be pushing organically up out of the ground. In fact, sadly, the movement is the other way round: as our guide told us emphatically, 'it is melting'. With every passing year the elements take their toll, the rains dissolving the baked mud bricks, until one day in the not so distant future the gompa and surrounding buildings will return to the earth whence they came.

There are four main parts to the complex, the most impressive of which is the **Chamba Lhakhang** (admission Rs30). The oldest of the three temples, it is built mostly from mud brick and mud mortar, with some additional sections of compressed earth, which is why it is so fragile. The incredible **wall paintings** inside were commissioned by King Tsewang Namgyal in the 16th century and so are a little newer than the building. It is thought that this is the only temple from the period to survive with its murals intact. Look out for the Buddhas of the past, present and future; a depiction of the Drugpa scholar Padma Karpo; and panels showing the king and his courtiers. The temple's central hall has an exquisitely **painted ceiling**, supported on colourful **wooden columns**, beneath which is a three-storey **Maitreya Buddha**, made from clay but covered with gilt.

The **Serzang Khakhang** (admission Rs30) houses the copper-gilded **Maitreya Buddha** it houses. Though the idol was actually built earlier, it was gilded on the orders of Sengge Namgyal in 1622 and Queen Khatun, his mother, donated the precious stones used in its ornamental crown and bracelet. Beautiful brocade silk covers the lower part of the statue.

The third of the temples is the rather squat-looking (but recently restored) **Chamchung Lhakhang**, a small structure dedicated to protector deities. Given its similarity in design to a Balti mosque, some academics have suggested that this may have been its original purpose, though it was certainly used as a Buddhist temple soon after. Surrounding the temples are the ruins of the **palace**. Unlike the gompa buildings, no maintenance work was ever done here, and indeed the wooden beams that supported the roofs were likely repurposed for other buildings. It is still possible to appreciate, however, the scale of the site and what an impression it must have made on early visitors.

LIKIR Overlooked by a grand gompa, the small and traditional village of Likir is utterly charming. Most people just stop off and have a quick poke around, but staying the night here gives you the chance to explore the gompa in the early morning or late evening without the presence of other tourists. Note, however, that the village of Likir is around 3km away from the gompa itself.

Getting there and around There is a daily **bus** direct from Leh to Likir, which departs around 16.00 (3hrs; Rs100) and returns from Likir at 07.00. Far more frequent are the buses to Saspol and other locations further along the highway: you can take one of these and get off at the crossroads to Likir. It's a total distance of 52km along a well-maintained road (excluding the last bumpy 6km side road if you continue from the crossroads to Likir itself) and the journey takes 2 hours 30 minutes. Tickets cost Rs90. Heading south, if you stand on the main road you can hail one of the buses going to/from Lamayuru. This journey also takes 2 hours 30 minutes and costs Rs90 per person.

Likir village and gompa are a 10-minute drive from the main road along a largely unmade track. You can **walk** this route but it's hot, dusty and takes well over an hour. Consequently, hitchhiking here is common. If you're in a car, it's likely you will be asked for a lift.

🏠 Where to stay Accommodation options in Likir are limited.

🏠 **No Mind Homestay** (20 rooms) 📞941 921 8358; **e** choszang.namgial@gmail.com; **w** nomindladakh.com. A guesthouse rather than a homestay, this is an attractive option with comfortable, traditionally decorated rooms. It offers yoga & meditation courses for serious students. Good meals are available. **$$$$**

🏠 **Norboo Spon Guesthouse** (11 rooms) **m** 941 984 0149. Long-running basic but comfortable guesthouse that's been given a bit of a facelift thanks to the addition of Tibetan-style motifs & festival masks on the walls. Some rooms have great mountain views. Meals are available. **$$**

🏠 **Gompa School** (4 rooms) Above the teachers' quarters are several clean guest rooms offered 1st to volunteers at the school & then to other visitors. Water is from a tap in the yard & the toilets (1 Western, 1 squat) are round the back, but this is more than compensated for by the fun & games of the young monks. You can also join them for dinner. No charge is made for accommodation or meals but a donation is appreciated: Rs500pp for a room & evening meal is appropriate.

✗ Where to eat and drink The small, outdoor **Namglal Restaurant** (**$–$$**) next to the gompa's parking area has an unremarkable selection of Indian and Chinese dishes, and more often than not only noodles are available, but the redeeming feature is undoubtedly the filter coffee. Free black tea is served to all visitors at the **Gompa School**.

There is one small shop in Likir, also located by the gompa's parking area, which sells sweets, crisps, biscuits and bottled soft drinks in lurid colours, but that's about it.

What to see and do One of the oldest monasteries in Ladakh, **Likir Gompa** (⊕ May–Oct 08.00–13.00 & 14.00–18.00, Nov–Apr 10.00–13.00 & 14.00–16.00; admission Rs20) was founded in the mid-10th century (although the exact date varies depending on who you're asking!) during the reign of King Lhachen Gyalpo, and then rebuilt 700 years later. There are around 70 adult monks living here as well as two-dozen or so boys who are studying. Today the monks follow the Gelugpa school of Buddhism, but prior to the 15th century the monastery was connected to the Tibetan Kadampa order. The head lama is the brother of the Dalai Lama, though he's permanently absent from Likir.

The most striking thing at the gompa is the 23m **Maitreya Buddha**. This golden statue stands out above the monastery buildings, surveying the land around, and was completed in 1999. The best place to photograph it from is the roof of the monastery school: there's a ladder from the first floor.

The entrance to the **Main Dukhang** is beneath a covered veranda painted with the guardians of the four directions. Inside you'll fine a throne for the head lama, stupas containing statues of Avalokiteshvara and Aitabha, and three very large statues: two of the Sakyamuni Buddha and a third of the Maitreya Buddha. The ancient *thangkas* attached to the walls are unrolled during only the winter festival. One shows the Sakyamuni Buddha and the other Likir's guardian deity.

The **New Dukhang**, diagonally across the courtyard, is around 200 years old. It too has a painted veranda but, unusually, the figures here are not the four guardians but instructional scenes showing lamas how to behave and how to wear their robes. Inside the walls are richly painted with more modern murals including the 1,000-armed Avalokiteshvara, the 35 Buddhas and the 16 *arhats* (those who have achieved nirvana).

Outside the New Dukhang is a ladder leading to the **zinchen** above. This is the head lama's room and it is where the Dalai Lama stays when he visits. It's an

Aladdin's cave of *thangkas*, statues and other curios, and particularly fine are the 21 variations of the White Tara.

ALCHI Alchi is one of Ladakh's foremost cultural attractions on account of its superbly preserved frescoes, many of which date from the early medieval period. However, as the monks are no longer in residence, and it's a key stop on package tours in the summer months, it can feel overly touristy: try to get here early or late in the day when it is not crowded, and appreciate it as you would a museum rather than as a living monastic community.

History Alchi's position, tucked back from the historic caravan route that winds through Ladakh, has been its saving grace. After the monastery was founded in the 11th century it was a relatively wealthy place (as attested to by the superb murals) but attracted little attention from outside. In around the 15th century, the centre of monastic activities was moved from here to Likir, and ever since then there have never been more than a few monks present in Alchi. This is probably why, when the Dogra invasion came in the 1830s, many of Ladakh's monasteries were sacked but Alchi passed beneath their radar, and consequently the frescoes survived.

Getting there and away Two **buses** a day make the 70km journey along a decent road from Leh to Alchi (2½hrs; Rs110), but it's also possible to take any bus heading between Leh and Kargil on the highway (for example, the bus from Leh to Lamayuru; page 144) and to get off at the turn-off to Alchi, walking the last 4km. **Taxis** from Leh to Alchi cost from Rs2,114/2,747 one-way/return. You can combine Likir, Alchi and Lamayuru in a long return day trip from Rs5,064, or add Phyang and Basgo to that itinerary (split over two days) from Rs11,485.

Where to stay *Map, opposite*
Accommodation in Alchi is considerably more expensive than in the surrounding villages, on account of the popularity of the gompa as a tourist attraction. You might, therefore, consider staying elsewhere (eg: 19km away in Likir; page 144) and visiting Alchi for the day, especially if your budget is tight.

Alchi Resort (22 rooms) m 941 921 8636; e alchiresort@gmail.com; w alchiresort.com. Close to the taxi stand, Alchi Resort comprises a large house behind which are a number of bungalows set a little too close together. It seems rather chaotic & is in desperate need of updating but is nonetheless popular with domestic tourists who have bought their room & all meals as a package. Our advice, however, is to look elsewhere. **$$$$**

Zimskhang Holiday Home (16 rooms) 227 086; m 941 917 9715; e zimskhang@ yahoo.com; w zimskhang.com. Norboo Gaitsan & his team run this pleasant guesthouse midway between the taxi stand & the gompa: it's on the pedestrian street so you'll need to carry your bags. Rooms are clean & in season you can relax with

a freshly squeezed apricot juice in the garden. **$$$$**

Heritage Home Alchi (11 rooms) 227 125; m 941 981 1535; e heritagehomealchi@ rediff.com. Heritage Home is situated right on the doorstep of the gompa but hence accessible only on foot. It's an attractively carved building with substantially more character than most of the other accommodation options. **$$$**

Potala Hotel (11 rooms) m 941 988 0182. The Potala may have seen better days, but carpets & linens are clean despite being worn. The bathrooms are reasonable & have running hot water; the bedrooms are large & light. If you're not bothered about living at the height of luxury, then this place, which offers homemade meals eaten sitting among the fruit trees in the garden,

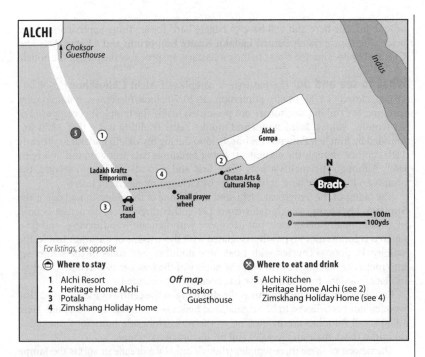

ALCHI

↑ Choskor Guesthouse

Ladakh Kraftz Emporium ●

Alchi Gompa

⑤ ①
④
③ 🚕 Taxi stand

Chetan Arts & Cultural Shop ②

● Small prayer wheel

N

Bradt

0 ————— 100m
0 ————— 100yds

For listings, see opposite

🏠 **Where to stay**

1 Alchi Resort
2 Heritage Home Alchi
3 Potala
4 Zimskhang Holiday Home

Off map
Choskor Guesthouse

❌ **Where to eat and drink**

5 Alchi Kitchen
Heritage Home Alchi (see 2)
Zimskhang Holiday Home (see 4)

---

is a friendly option. The owner is an expert in traditional Tibetan medicine & is happy to share his knowledge. **$$–$$$**

🏠 **Choskor Guesthouse** (12 rooms) m 941 982 6363. Situated 1km from the gompa back towards the main road, Choskor is nevertheless one of the more pleasant places to stay, with mature gardens & a roof terrace. Meals are available on request. The guesthouse is set back from the road: stop at the prayer wheel & look for the turquoise building with stained-wood window frames. **$$**

❌ Where to eat and drink *Map, above*

☀ ❌ **Alchi Kitchen** m 941 943 8642; �Ⓕ @Alchi.Kitchen; ⊕ 08.00–22.00 daily. The best meals in Alchi – & perhaps in all of Ladakh – are to be had at the wonderful Alchi Kitchen, which is on the road leading towards the monastery. With vivid imagination, the chefs at this classy place stir traditional Ladakhi dishes into modern masterpieces such as saffron paneer momos. If you want to learn more, join one of their short cookery classes held with advance reservations at 18.00 (Rs1,000). **$$$$**

❌ **Heritage Home Alchi** A shady spot in the Heritage Home Alchi garden; the red-&-white gingham tablecloths give it a cutesy feel. **$$**

❌ **Zimskhang Holiday Home** The large garden restaurant of Zimskhang Holiday Home popular with tour groups; there are plenty of tables, most of them in the shade, & the menu is wide, if unimaginative. **$$**

🍺 **Golden Oriole** (aka the German Bakery) If all you want is a coffee or a quick snack, this is a reasonable alternative to those above. Situated on the main pedestrian street, they serve a variety of fresh juices, milkshakes & *lassis* as well as homemade cookies (Rs30) & croissants (Rs40). Everything looks as though it could do with a good scrub, but the free Wi-Fi might tempt you in regardless. **$**

Shopping The pedestrian street between Alchi's taxi stand and the monastery is lined with shops and stalls selling all manner of naff and rather pricey souvenirs, including the usual selection of turquoise beads, bundles of prayer flags, bangles, incense, grotesque masks and occasional wooden puppets. You won't find anything unique for sale here and will have to haggle hard for anything approaching a fair price. The appropriately named **Ladakh Kraftz Emporium** and **Chetan Arts and Cultural Shop**, situated closer to the monastery, are probably the pick of the bunch.

What to see and do The monastery complex of **Alchi Chhoskhor** (⊕ 08.00–18.00, closed 13.00–14.00; admission Rs20/50 local/foreigner; photography, smoking & drinking alcohol are not permitted inside the temples) is composed of six temples, stupas, Mani stones and monks' cells. Tradition has it that Alchi was founded by Rinchen Zangpo (see box, below) during his visit to Ladakh in the early 11th century, though the earliest surviving buildings date from around 200 years later. Although it remains a holy place first and a tourist attraction second, the monks no longer live here: it is cared for by Gelugpa monks from Likir.

The oldest of the temples at Alchi, and indeed one of the oldest in Ladakh, is the **Sumtsek Lhakhang**, which dates from 1217. This three-storey structure is built in a traditional Tibetan style but decorated with delicate woodcarvings and fine, tapered columns more typically associated with the artisans of Kashmir. Inside, the wall by the door is covered with 1,028 blue Buddhas, and some of the statues set into niches are as much as 5m tall. The quality of the frescoes is unrivalled, though in places modern restoration work has been poorly executed.

Roughly contemporary to this is the **dukhang** at the centre of the complex. The wooden door is believed to be original, and hence is more than 800 years old. Here 1,000 small Buddhas are painted on to the walls alongside numerous mandalas, divinities (both male and female) and protectors of the temple.

The newest of these three temples (though only by a decade or so!) is the **Jampe Lhakhang**, which experts have inferred dates from around 1225. The interior here is less well preserved (probably due to its proximity to the river), but there are still some striking items: the four images of the bodhisattva Manjushri (from which the lhakhang takes its alternative name, the Manjushri Temple) sitting back to back atop a vast platform; further images of Manjushri seated on a lion throne, flanked by lions, wearing a crown of flowers, and bedecked in jewels; and a painted wooden ceiling.

Southwest of Alchi, away from the Chhoskhor, is the **Shangrong Lhakhang**, part of a complex of stupas and other small structures dating from the 1400s.

RINCHEN ZANGPO

Visiting Alchi, Mangyu or Lamayuru, you cannot help but come across the name of Rinchen Zangpo, the Lotsawa or 'Great Translator'. Born in Guge in 958, Rinchen Zangpo was ordained at the age of 13 and travelled across India numerous times in search of ancient Buddhist scriptures. He studied at the leading centres of Buddhist learning, returning later to Kashmir and Tibet with the texts that he would then translate. During his lifetime, Rinchen Zangpo is credited with building 108 monasteries and temples, and in doing so reviving Buddhism in Tibet and Ladakh. He engaged the services of 32 Kashmiri artists to decorate the monasteries he founded, and so we have him to thank for the oldest artworks at Alchi, Basgo, Lamayuru, Nyarma and Sumda, among others.

En route to Tibet once again in 1042, Rinchen Zangpo met St Atisa and the two entered into a lengthy debate as to the nuances of the sacred texts. Rinchen Zangpo realised that his earlier translations had missed certain subtleties of meaning, and so at the ripe old age of 84 he became a student once again. He died aged 98 in 1055.

One of the best short treks in Ladakh is the five-day hike between Alchi and Lamayuru via the cloud-scraping Stakspi La pass (5,153m). The route takes the lucky walker through picturesque farmland and over barren mountain slopes via remote monasteries and interesting villages, as well as over Kongskil La (4,948m). The panorama from the two passes is exceptional, with close-up mountain views. Perhaps the most rewarding aspect of the trek, however, is the village homestays dotted along the route, which adds a fascinating cultural dimension to an already fantastic trek. A guide is required and can be organised through most of the better accommodation options in Alchi (page 146) or through agencies in Leh (page 76).

On the verge of collapse in 2007, it has since been repaired by the Achi Association (w achiassociation.org). The interior frescoes, which include an illustration of the 84 Mahasiddhas and several important inscriptions, are among the few surviving examples linked to the Drigung school of art.

AROUND ALCHI Two hours' walk west of Alchi is tiny **Mangyu**, home to an interesting gompa. Founded by Rinchen Zangpo at roughly the same time as Alchi, it is a much smaller complex and there are four principal temples, each housing interesting statues, as well as a number of murals, though less well executed than those in Alchi. To get here you must cross the small bridge across the Indus and follow the track past the village of Gera into a gorge. The track ascends from the right bank of the stream, and although the path is not signposted, it is fairly clear due to the number of feet that have walked this route before. You chance upon the gompa quite suddenly as it is low-lying and pretty well camouflaged behind the rocks.

ULETOKPO Boasting an attractive location by the river, Uletokpo is a resort town with some excellent places to stay for those travelling between Leh and Kargil. It is also the closest settlement to the 19th-century Rizong Gompa and its sister nunnery, Chulichan.

Getting there and away The road from Alchi to Uletokpo is in good condition. Unlike Alchi, Uletokpo is on the NH1, so any of the **buses** running between Leh and Kargil (or villages along the route) have to pass by: you can ask any of them to stop here and, if they have space, have them pick you up.

By **taxi**, LTOCL offers a two-day trip to Basgo, Likir, Alchi, Rizong, Uletokpo and Lamayuru from Rs8,023. Alternatively, you can get there from Leh from Rs2,373/3,086 one-way/return.

🏠 **Where to stay and eat** Visitors are advised to book a meal plan at their camp if staying in Uletokpo as the food in all places listed below is superb.

🏠 **Uley Eco Resort** (26 rooms) m 941 997 0214; e uleyadv@gmail.com; w uleyecoresorts. com. Similarly luxurious to sister property Uley Ethnic Resort & home to some very funky huts, but really there's nothing to choose between the 2 in terms of levels of service or eco-friendly credentials. There's bike hire & the camp offers white-water rafting trips on the Indus, which is virtually on your doorstep. $$$$–$$$$$

✳ 🏠 **Ule Ethnic Resort** (31 tents, 15 cottages) \ 253 640; m 941 988 7000; e ulecamp@gmail.com; w uleresort.com.

Laid out across a large area of apple & apricot groves overlooking the river, this has to be one of the most photogenic holiday camps in Ladakh. The wooden cottages, which resemble alpine chalets, have hot water thanks to solar panels on the roof. Meals are homemade, organic & delicious. Highly recommended. **$$$$–$$$$$**

🏠 **West Ladakh Camp & Resort** (17 tents) m 983 388 3881; w campsinladakh.in. Run by Camps in Ladakh, set amid a 20-acre ranch on the bank of the Indus, West Ladakh offers en-suite tents & bathrooms have hot water. Multi-cuisine meals are served in a communal tent or out in the garden. **$$$$**

What to see and do Uletokpo offers easy access to the Indus and is a popular starting point for **white-water rafting** trips. Although you can arrange these through the local resorts/camps, you will probably be charged a premium for doing so: it is better to contact Splash Ladakh in Leh (page 90).

Other than to have a relaxing break amid stunning scenery, the reason for staying in Uletokpo is that it is just 5km from the **Rizong Gompa** (☉ dawn–dusk daily), also known as the Yuma Changchubling. This is a relatively new monastery, established by the Lama Tsultim Nima in 1831, although there was a hermitage here before. Some 40 monks from the Gelugpa order reside here and they follow the strict Vinaya rules: they are not allowed to leave the monastery unless seriously ill; in the hours of darkness they are forbidden to leave their cell, which has neither bedding nor a fire; they may not touch anything handled by women (including family members); and they may have no personal possessions. The gompa comprises a number of attractive whitewashed buildings, and among the items preserved here are a **statue of the Mahakala** (a protector deity prominent in both the Buddhist and Hindu pantheons); **relics** of the gompa's founder; and, in the Thin-Chen shrine, **frescoes**.

A further 2km on from the gompa is the **Chulichan Nunnery** (☉ dawn–dusk daily), where younger nuns follow a curriculum of Tibetan language classes and meditation, and older nuns work in the fields, spin yarn and press apricot kernels to make apricot oil. About 20 nuns live here, and the nunnery is subordinate to the monastery.

KHALTSI Khaltsi is a lively place, a market town situated at the point where the road from Kashmir first enters the Indus Valley and where the majority of people you see are locals. It is the point, historically and now, where there has been a bridge across the Indus River. It's not necessarily a place you'd want to visit in its own right (though there is a gompa and the ruins of a fortress here) but if you have your own transport and want somewhere to stretch your legs and have a cup of tea, it's a conveniently located option.

History The area around Khaltsi has been occupied for at least 2,000 years, and a fragmentary rock inscription discovered locally has been attributed to the Kushan king Vima Kadphises (rAD90–100). Roughly contemporary with this, other carvings thought to have been made by the Dards (page 20) depict a man hunting antelope, and a woman carrying a basket on her back.

The first major bridge on the site was constructed by the Dardic king Lha Chen Naglug in the mid-12th century. It must have revolutionised local transport and certainly would have been responsible for Khaltsi becoming a prominent local settlement. It was a shrewd move by the ruler, not only for the local economy, as he could charge customs duties on every shipment crossing the river to Khaltsi.

Getting there and away Khaltsi lies 99km from Leh along the reasonably well-maintained NH1. There is a direct daily **bus** (departs 15.30 in summer & 13.00 in winter; Rs115; 4½–5hrs), or you can take one of the buses heading to Lamayuru or Kargil. By **taxi** the fare from Leh starts from Rs3,253/4,428 one-way/return. If you are approaching Khaltsi from the Kargil side (or indeed carrying on through the village towards Mulbekh), you will need to stop at the **police checkpoint** and show your passport. Formalities take a matter of minutes, though you may be asked to stay for tea and a chat.

Note that Khaltsi is also written as Khalsi or Khalatse on some maps.

🏠 **Where to stay and eat** Khaltsi is the kind of place you drive through rather than stop and spend an extended period of time. However, if you've missed breakfast and are ravenous, you might try the large and fairly clean **Punjabi Dhaba ($$)**. Immediately across the street is the enchantingly named (though less enchanting-looking) **NH1 Garden Café ($–$$)**, but the Dhaba is probably a better bet. Unless you suffer some kind of transport breakdown you probably wouldn't spend the night here, but if you do there are a couple of very basic guesthouses.

What to see and do As you enter Khaltsi from the direction of Leh, **Khaltsi Gompa** is up a signposted side road to the right. It's a higgledy-piggledy structure that looks both to have grown out of the surrounding rock and to be collapsing once again into it.

There was once a **fortress** at Khaltsi, guarding the strategically important river crossing, though today scarcely anything is visible of the original structure. Some significant **petroglyphs** have been identified in the grounds, however, including an image of a yak charging at a snow leopard.

AROUND KHALTSI Immediately after Khaltsi's police checkpoint, the road forks: the left branch (the NH1) continues to Kargil and ultimately Srinagar, while the right fork is signposted for Batalik and Dha-Hanu. Taking the latter brings you to the **Domkhar Rock Art Sanctuary** after 62km. This outdoor museum encompasses some superb petroglyphs of human figures, stupas, animals and religious symbols and shows the artistic mastery of Ladakh's early people. They are akin in style to rock carvings further north on the Silk Road in Tajikistan and Kyrgyzstan.

LAMAYURU Set in a lunar landscape befitting a science-fiction movie, Lamayuru has one of the most striking locations in Ladakh. The gompa is one of the oldest and largest in the region, and it is a convenient place to spend the night en route from Kargil to Leh. The town is also the start or end point for a number of spectacular trekking routes.

History Legend has it that Lamayuru was formed following the visit of the 10th-century Buddhist scholar and sage, Naropa. He drained the lake that filled the valley and then founded the gompa, which he built with Rinchen Zangpo (see box, page 148).

Getting there and away Lamayuru is situated 115km from Leh and 103km from Kargil. It's on NH1, just to the east of Fotu La, which is, at 4,108m, the highest point on the highway. The road surface in both directions is reasonable and so the going is good: Kargil to Lamayuru takes under 5 hours and you should be able to get from Lamayuru to Leh in no more than 6 hours.

If you are coming from Leh by **bus**, you need to take the service towards Kargil or Chiktan (departing at 09.00 on Tuesday, Friday and Sunday, returning

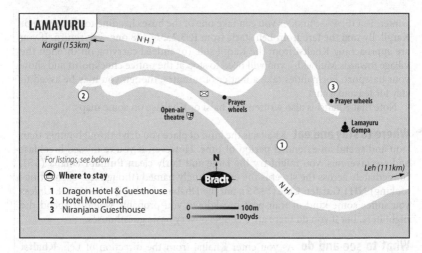

For listings, see below

LAMAYURU

Kargil (153km)

NH 1

Open-air theatre

Prayer wheels

Prayer wheels

Lamayuru Gompa

Leh (111km)

NH 1

N

Bradt

0 ——— 100m
0 ——— 100yds

Where to stay
1 Dragon Hotel & Guesthouse
2 Hotel Moonland
3 Niranjana Guesthouse

the following morning; Rs195). From Kargil, the bus leaves around 05.30 on Wednesday, Saturday and Monday, but it is worth checking at the bus stand the night before for confirmation as times can shift about an hour in either direction.

Whether you are starting from Kargil or Leh, the cost of reaching Lamayuru by **taxi** is the same, starting from Rs4,098/5,299 one-way/return.

If you plan to come to Lamayuru from Zanskar, it's almost as quick to **trek** as it is to drive: east of Rangdum there is a track across Kanjil La (5,255m), which links up with NH1 close to Lamayuru. A person of moderate fitness can complete this trek in two days.

Where to stay and eat *Map, above*

Hotel Moonland (26 rooms) m 941 988 8508; e hotelmoonland@gmail.com; w hotelmoonland.in. Large, comfortable if rather impersonal hotel with a range of rooms & prices. Upstairs rooms have views of the mountains & monastery; those downstairs overlook the garden. There is a restaurant on site that serves reasonable meals & woollen handicrafts made by the Women's Self-Help Group at Mundki (\ 252 944) are on sale. Some staff speak English. Ask for discounts in low season. There are 4 cheaper rooms with shared b/rooms. **$$$**

Niranjana Guesthouse (20 rooms) Next to the gompa; \ 224 555; m 941 987 0872; e hotelniranjanalamayuru@yahoo.com. The super location at the foot of the gompa is Niranjana's

key selling point, as the rooms are fairly bland & don't represent great value. Buffet-style meals are served in a large dining hall with an attractively painted ceiling. It's convenient, but don't expect much service. **$$$**

✳ **Dragon Hotel & Guesthouse** (8 rooms) m 965 094 9347; e dragonskyabu@gmail.com; w dragonhotellamayuru.wordpress.com. The choice is an easy one when it comes to choosing a Lamayuru base; the family-run Dragon Hotel & Guesthouse has super helpful staff & the well-maintained rooms are pristine with lots of warm blankets, decent bathrooms & unusually fast Wi-Fi. The garden restaurant is also a great place to eat. The owners can help organise multi-day treks & other activities in the area. **$**

What to see and do The earliest parts of **Lamayuru Gompa** (w lamayuru.com; ⏱ 07.00–19.00 daily; admission Rs50) date to the 10th century, making it one of the oldest monasteries in Ladakh. It is also one of the largest, and at its peak it housed some 400 monks, though there are only around 150 still in residence today.

You can drive right up to the gompa and, once inside, there are far fewer steps than normal, making Lamayuru relatively accessible for those with trouble walking (though it is still not really wheelchair-friendly). Inside the main building is a small **cloistered courtyard** with bright modern murals, off which is a tiny room lit solely with butter lamps, and also a fair-sized **temple** with a lingering smell of incense. Large windows in the roof let in natural light, enabling you to properly appreciate the large Buddha statues with crowns made of silk, and the cabinets containing the 108-volume Tri-Pitaka scriptures, each one wrapped in orange cloth. Between the cabinets look out for the entrance to the **cave of Naropa**, where he is said to have sat and meditated. The dark **antechamber** contains more fine statues, two large silver horns and, unusually, a set of plastic toy animals.

A staircase off the courtyard leads you to a smaller **prayer room** with much older wall paintings, two ceremonial drums (one with dragon finials), seven painted clay statues, three small stupas and a collection of carved wax offerings. Outside the main gompa building you will find a large number of **prayer wheels** and also larger **stupas** decorated with lions and phoenix.

Note that women are not permitted to remain on the monastery premises after dark and are also asked to take any used sanitary products with them when they leave.

Beneath the gompa on the main road is an **open-air theatre**, a showground where festival performances take place. Look out for the ornate gateway and colourful, pagoda-like building.

A few kilometres to the east of Lamayuru is the **moon landscape**, a naturally occurring geological formation that resembles the peaks of whipped meringue or, indeed, how one might imagine the surface of the moon to be.

MULBEKH (*Telephone code: 01985*) The last predominantly Buddhist settlement on the NH1, Mulbekh is a small town that would be unremarkable if it weren't for the presence of the enormous Maitreya Buddha carved into the rock face. Even if you are just driving through, you should stop off to appreciate this mighty work of art.

Getting there and away Mulbekh lies 180km from Leh and 45km from Kargil on the NH1. By **bus**, there is a daily service between Leh and Kargil. Coming from Leh, the bus leaves at 05.00 and takes 10 hours, while from Kargil, allow 2 hours for the journey (it also leaves at 05.00). From Leh you might be asked to pay the cost of a journey all the way to Kargil (Rs400).

If you prefer to travel by **taxi**, you have two options from Kargil. **Shared taxis** depart from the bus stand at 07.00 and should ideally be booked the night before. You'll pay around Rs1,000 for a seat. If you prefer to have a taxi to yourself, a ride from Kargil to Mulbekh costs Rs1,650/1,980 one-way/return and Rs6,011/7,814 one-way/return from Leh. If you are driving all of the way between Leh and Kargil, drivers will happily stop for a cup of tea or a bite to eat while you look at the Buddha. If you are driving yourself, there is a rare **petrol station** 1.5km outside Mulbekh on the road towards Leh.

 Where to stay and eat *Map, page 154*
Don't expect too much of the accommodation within Mulbekh itself – it is of a pretty low standard, although fine for the night. For a very quick bite to eat you can get hot snacks and cold drinks at the **Lobzang Hotel Restaurant** (m 946 973 7773; $) and the **Sharma Dabha** (m 946 924 0125; $), both of which have excellent views of the Maitreya Buddha but leave something to be desired on the hygiene front. There is a **general store** opposite the Maitreya Buddha where you can buy bottled water and chocolate.

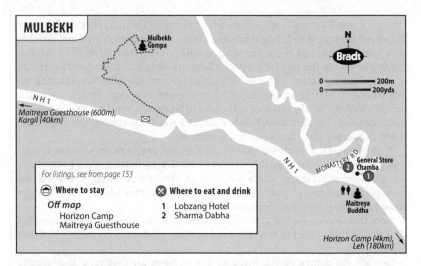

For listings, see from page 153

MULBEKH

Mulbekh Gompa

N

Bradt

0 ——— 200m
0 ——— 200yds

NH 1

Maitreya Guesthouse (600m),
Kargil (40km)

NH 1

MONASTERY RD

General Store
Chamba

2

1

Maitreya
Buddha

Horizon Camp (4km),
Leh (180km)

For listings, see from page 153

🏠 **Where to stay**
Off map
 Horizon Camp
 Maitreya Guesthouse

❌ **Where to eat and drink**
1 Lobzang Hotel
2 Sharma Dabha

🏠 **Horizon Camp** (12 tents) m 941 988
8788; e horizonladakhcamp@gmail.com;
w horizonladakhcamp.com. By far the best
option around Mulbekh, the Horizon Camp is
situated in the village of Wakha a few kilometres
to the east. The tents are fairly small & closely
packed together but thanks to the proper beds,
thick blankets & a garden setting, they make for

a pleasant stay. Staff are friendly & full of local
travel advice. **$$$$**

🏠 **Maitreya Guesthouse** (5 rooms) ☎ 270
035. Situated at the far western end of town, the
family-run Maitreya is the best of a fairly bad lot
of cheap guesthouses. It has solar-heated water &
brightly painted rooms. **$$**

What to see and do The **Maitreya Buddha**, also known as the Chamba Buddha,
is a 9m-tall deep-relief carving cut into a large rock at the eastern end of Mulbekh,
right on the main road. The combination of Shaivite symbolism and Kashmiri
artistic influences (in particular the pronounced kneecaps) suggest that it was
constructed by Kashmiri Buddhist missionaries, possibly in the 8th century AD.
Though the statue is referred to as the Buddha, some art historians have argued that
this is in fact a depiction of Avalokiteshvara, as the figure has four arms and other
symbols associated with him: a lotus flower, a vase of water, a string of rosary beads
and a jewel held in one hand.

The modern **Chamba Lhakhang** (admission Rs20) was built in 1975 immediately
in front of the Buddha, with the frustrating consequence that you now either have
to look at the statue cut off below the waist, or stand at its feet and get a distorted
view of the body. It is guarded by a monk from Hemis.

Mulbekh Gompa is high up on the cliff, towering 200m above the western end
of Mulbekh, but the access track to reach it is at the opposite end of town, just
after the Maitreya Buddha as you're entering Mulbekh but on the opposite side of
the road. There are, in fact, two gompas on the site, one belonging to the Gelugpa
order and the other to the Drukpa order. Historically this location was important
as it enabled local rulers to guard the caravan route below: potential attackers were
visible well in advance of their arrival. The principal gompa is a stocky structure,
and certainly would have been easy to defend, but it is far less ornate than the
monasteries elsewhere in Ladakh and so in reality you're unlikely to want to make
the climb up here.

THE NORTHERN INDUS VALLEY

At Khaltsi, the road forks: the left arm follows the NH1 west to Kargil and Srinagar, while the right arm heads north through the Indus Valley. This rather bumpy road passes through a smattering of settlements inhabited by the Brokpa, an isolated tribal people of Dardic origin who claim descent from the forces of Alexander the Great. Ethnically, linguistically and culturally distinct from other groups in Ladakh, they are, in fact, more closely linked to the Kailash of Afghanistan. Interestingly, unlike other tribal groups in the area, the Brokpa have not domesticated the cow, considering both her milk and dung to be taboo. Though the area is undoubtedly beautiful and the culture unique, it can feel like a bit of a tourist trap.

The Brokpa have two important festivals, and if you are able to watch (or even participate in) them, they will be a high point of your trip. The dates are fixed to neither the solar nor lunar calendar, but do happen at roughly the same time of year. The Brokpa's **New Year** festival, which sees most of the community dressing in colourful traditional dress and partaking in dance and songs, takes place at the start of January, and every third year at the start of October they celebrate **Bono Nah** with costumed dances and songs that describe the history of their people. The next Bono Nah celebration will be in 2022.

DHA-HANU The twin settlements of Dha and Hanu are the first villages of note you will pass through from Khaltsi, simple places where you come to appreciate the landscape and meet the people. There is a small **monastery** in Dha, built in 2009 on the site of an older building. It is notable not for its architectural features but because the Brokpa maintain many of their early beliefs, including respect for the Bon pantheon of gods (see box, page 96), alongside Buddhism. Behind the monastery is a wild apricot orchard beneath which appear to be simply piles of rubble and stones: this is, in fact, what remains of the **fort** or palace at the centre of the first Brokpa settlement, founded in the 1st century AD.

Getting there and around A daily **bus** (except Sunday) leaves Leh at 09.00 and arrives in Dha around 17.00 (Rs235), although note it drops you on the main road rather than in the centre of the village, so you have to continue the last section on foot (about 15 minutes). It returns to Leh the following morning, departing from Dha at 08.30. There is also a bus from Leh to Hanu on Friday only, departing at 09.00 and arriving at around 17.00 (Rs183), as well as a daily bus between Khaltsi and Dha (2½hrs; Rs95). There is currently no bus between Kargil and Dha.

By **taxi**, fares from Leh to Dha start from Rs5,661/7,359 one-way/return journey, and to Hanu from Rs5,103/6,636. If you are planning to come here on a day trip, however, it is much faster and cheaper to come from Kargil: you'll pay around Rs2,800/3,400 one-way/return.

If you wish to visit both Dha and Hanu, note that there is no public transport available between them: you would have to find a private vehicle to take you or, alternatively, walk the 8km.

Where to stay and eat Note that there is no mains electricity in Dha or Hanu: what power there is has to come from a generator, so be particularly sparing with what you use.

Hotel Aryan Residency m 941 917 9631; w hotelaryanresidency.com. The best hotel in the area offers large, well-kept rooms with private bathrooms & a warm welcome. There's a reasonable restaurant serving north Indian & Tibetan dishes. **$$$**

🏠 **Skyabapa Guesthouse** (4 rooms) Dha. Simple rooms in a comfortable Tibetan house. Meals are taken on the terrace. **$**

OTHER SIGHTS South from Dha, on the road that leads to the NH1, you'll come to the next villages of **Chiktan** and **Shakar**, both home to people of Tibeto-Balti and Tibeto-Dardic origin who are principally Muslim. Many local people still wear traditional dress and ornate accessories, especially at festival time, and at Chiktan you can also see the ruins of **Chiktan Khar**, the castle.

Heading west from Dha, rather than heading straight on to Kargil, take a detour at the village of Garpung to the **Apati Buddha**. As impressive as the Buddha at Mulbekh (page 154), it is at least 1,300 years old and also carved in relief from the rock.

KARGIL *Telephone code: 01985*

For most Indians, Kargil's name will forever be associated with the Kargil War, and for foreign tourists it is known as little more than an overnight way-station on the Srinagar–Leh road. This is a deeply sad state of affairs, however, as Kargil and its surrounding area has so much to offer. Kargil town lies in an attractive setting at the confluence of the Suru and Nallah Wakha rivers, and it has been at the crossroads of overland trading routes for centuries. The Munshi Aziz Bhat Caravanserai attests to Kargil's important position on the Silk Road, and the Munshi Aziz Bhat Museum has quite probably the most interesting collection of artefacts of any museum in the state. Just outside the town, you'll discover both ruined fortresses and rock-carved Buddhas.

Plan your visit to Kargil carefully and factor in the weather: the town experiences an extreme shift in temperatures between summer and winter. In July and August temperatures are very pleasant, usually in the mid-20°s C, but in the winter months it is not uncommon for it to be as cold as −20°C, which is quite a lot less pleasant. Not all hotels provide heating.

HISTORY Located almost equidistant between Srinagar, Padum, Skardu (now in Pakistan) and Leh, Kargil has been a trading post for centuries: goods passed through

THE KARGIL WAR

The Kargil War was an armed conflict that took place along the LoC between Indian and Pakistani forces between May and July 1999. The previous winter, Pakistani troops had been sent covertly to the Indian side of the line: it was initially claimed that these were rogue elements, or mujahideen, though senior Pakistani officers later confirmed they were regular troops.

The war itself, though short, had three distinct phases: the crossing of the LoC by Pakistani forces; the discovery of the incursion by Indian patrols, and India's subsequent mobilisation of troops; and finally direct conflict between the two sides. It was this final phase that was most serious and resulted in international pressure being brought to bear, as it is to date the only international conflict in which both sides were nuclear powers.

The exact number of casualties resulting from the war will probably never be known due to the covert nature of its early phase. Pakistan confirmed it lost 453 troops and India gave its official casualty figures as 527 dead, though non-military estimates from both sides can be twice as high.

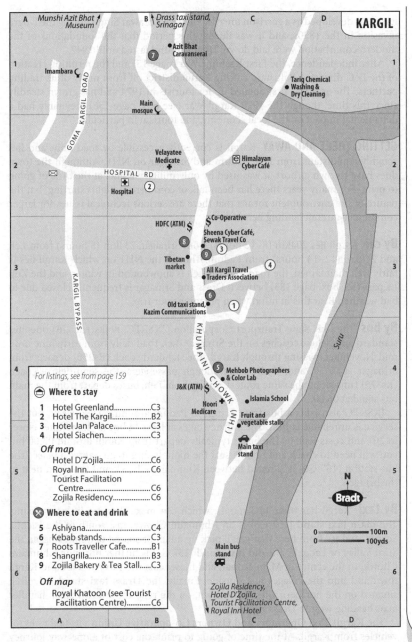

A · Munshi Azit Bhat Museum   B ⬆ Drass taxi stand, Srinagar   C   D   **KARGIL**

1

⬤**7**   ● Azit Bhat Caravanserai

Imambara ☾

● Tariq Chemical Washing & Dry Cleaning

GOMA KARGIL ROAD

Main mosque ☾

2

Velayatee Medicate ✚

☒ HOSPITAL RD

ⓔ Himalayan Cyber Café

✉

Hospital ✚ ②

3

HDFC (ATM) $ $ Co-Operative

⑧   Sheena Cyber Café, Sewak Travel Co

⑨   ③

Tibetan market ●   ● All Kargil Travel Traders Association ④

KARGIL BYPASS

⑥ ●

Old taxi stand, Kazim Communications ①

KHUMAINI CHOWK

4

For listings, see from page 159

⑤ ● Mehbob Photographers & Color Lab

J&K (ATM) $

Noori ✚ Medicare

● Islamia School

● Fruit and vegetable stalls

🅿 **Where to stay**
1 Hotel Greenland..................C3
2 Hotel The Kargil.................B2
3 Hotel Jan Palace.................C3
4 Hotel Siachen.....................C3

Off map
Hotel D'Zojila......................C6
Royal Inn.............................C6
Tourist Facilitation Centre.............................C6
Zojila Residency..................C6

🍴 **Where to eat and drink**
5 Ashiyana............................C4
6 Kebab stands.....................C3
7 Roots Traveller Cafe...........B1
8 Shangrilla...........................B3
9 Zojila Bakery & Tea Stall.....C3

Off map
Royal Khatoon (see Tourist Facilitation Centre).............C6

Main taxi stand

Suru

N

Bradt

0 ———— 100m
0 ———— 100yds

Main bus stand
🚌

Zojila Residency, Hotel D'Zojila, Tourist Facilitation Centre, ⬇ Royal Inn Hotel

Northwest Ladakh   KARGIL

6

here from as far away as Turkey, Afghanistan and China, and Kargil's merchants profited from the sale of luxury goods such as silk, ivory and precious stones, as well as more mundane items. The surrounding territories were amalgamated into a single kingdom for the first time by Gasho Tatha Khan in the 9th century.

Kargil district came under Balti influence in the 16th century, during the reign of Ali Sher Khan Anchan, the Maqpon king whose capital was at Skardu. Kargil

157

itself was developed as a garrison town by General Zorawar Singh during the Dogra invasion in the 1830s, and it was during this period that the foundations of the modern conurbation were laid down. Dogra control lasted until 1947.

After independence, the First Kashmir War (page 15) and the resulting creation of the LoC dissected Baltistan, cutting Kargil district off from many of its trading partners. The area was first opened up for tourists in 1974 and has grown steadily since this time, though the 1999 Kargil War (see box, page 156) inevitably had a detrimental impact on the local economy, and tourism in particular.

GETTING THERE AND AWAY Kargil is currently accessible by road only, and lies roughly equidistant from Leh, Padum and Srinagar on NH1. Although the town does have its own airport, it was used by only military flights at the time of going to print. For many years there has been talk of commercial flights starting, but the nature of the environment means that there are serious technical issues for larger commercial aircraft landing here.

By car Kargil lies 204km (8–12 hours) from Srinagar, 234km (8 hours) from Leh and 240km (12–14 hours) from Padum. Though the NH1 on which Kargil lies is fairly well maintained, the road towards Leh is snowbound in winter, and the Zoji La pass (see box, page 183) between Drass and Srinagar is frequently closed due to bad weather. Bear this in mind when planning your trip.

By bus The J&K State Transport Corporation (JKSRTC; w jksrtc.co.in) operates standard and deluxe coaches on the Srinagar–Leh road daily from early June until mid-November, passing through Kargil. The standard coach (Rs250) departs from Srinagar at 07.30, and, if there are enough passengers, the semi-deluxe coach (Rs375) runs along the same route. Coming from Leh, buses depart from the main bus stand at 06.00.

JKSRTC also runs a bus from Kargil to Padum around once a week, but the service is unreliable at best. The journey takes at least 14 hours (sometimes closer to 20) and costs Rs850. The buses typically depart from Kargil around 03.00 but you will need to check and book a seat the night before to guarantee a place. The bus station [157 C6] is situated between Khumaini Chowk and the river, next to the bridge.

By taxi Kargil has three taxi stands, which can make things a little confusing. The **main taxi stand** [157 C5] is on Khumaini Chowk, just south of the Islamia School, and it's from here that you'll pick up a taxi or shared taxi for Zanskar, the Suru Valley or Ladakh. The **old taxi stand** [157 C3] is further north on Khumaini Chowk, in the centre of Main Bazaar, and these taxis will ferry you around Kargil town and into the villages just outside. Finally, the **Drass taxi stand** [157 B1], situated on the northern side of the town, on the road towards Srinagar, handles taxis heading west to Drass and Srinagar.

The **Kargil Taxi Operators and Owners Co-operative Union** sets taxi rates for vehicles from Kargil. At the time of going to print, the cost of a one-way journey to major destinations is as follows: Drass Rs1,670; Lamayuru Rs4,325; Leh from Rs7,126; Mulbekh Rs1,140; Padum Rs14,000; Pahalgam Rs8,910; Parkachik Rs2,960; Rangdum Rs5,720; Sonamarg Rs6,000; and Srinagar Rs6,400.

Note that there are sometimes disputes between the Kargil and Leh taxi unions, and when this happens you might have to swap from a Kargil taxi to a Leh taxi somewhere along the route. Drivers will organise this.

GETTING AROUND The town's **minivans** ply its two main streets, running up and down to the bazaar. A single seat will cost you Rs10; taking the whole vehicle costs Rs100. Note that later in the evening, especially if you are travelling away from the bazaar, you may be obliged to pay for the whole vehicle if there are no other passengers going in your direction.

Most of Kargil is accessible **on foot**. Walking from Bimathang to Main Bazaar will take no more than 20 minutes, and another 10 minutes will get you to the museum.

TOURIST INFORMATION AND TOUR OPERATORS A Tourist Facilitation Centre [157 C6] (☏ 232 721; w jktourism.org; ⊕ 10.00–16.00 daily) is operated by **J&K Tourism** in Bimathang, signposted from the bridge and not far from Hotel D'Zojila. The English-speaking staff can offer maps and vague information, and the centre also contains a restaurant (page 160) and has rooms and a conference centre.

A better source of information, assistance and bookings is the **All Kargil Travel Traders Association** [157 C3] (Hotel PC Palace, nr Old Taxi Stand; ☏ 233 736; m 946 922 1111; e allkargiltraveltrade2013@gmail.com). Spearheaded by local travel agent Mohammad Hamza, it publishes tourist brochures and provides contact details for hotels, guesthouses and travel agencies in and around Kargil.

Near the Co-operative Bank on Khumaini Chowk, Sewak Travel Company [157 B3] (☏ 233 736; e yasoobs9@gmail.com) offers sightseeing, trekking and rafting packages as well as flight, train and hotel bookings. Manager Mohammad Ali speaks excellent English and has a detailed knowledge of local tourism options.

WHERE TO STAY Kargil doesn't have the huge range of accommodation options that you'll find in Srinagar or Leh, but even so standards are improving and there are already a number of options that are comfortable and well run, whether you're staying for one night or much longer.

Main Bazaar

✳ 🏠 **Hotel The Kargil** [157 B2] (30 rooms) Hospital Rd; m 981 199 5752; w hotelthekargil. com. Bringing big changes to the Kargil hotel scene, this new place has super smart, business-class rooms with impressive modern art above the beds. The bathrooms are a delight to splash about in & the service is good. The in-house restaurant is one of the better places to eat in town. **$$$$$**

🏠 **Hotel Jan Palace** [157 C3] (20 rooms) Nr SBI, Public Pk Rd; ☏ 050 1211; m 887 900 1171; e info@janpalacekargil.com; w hoteljanpalacekargil.com. Decent & well-run hotel in the town centre. Rooms are plain but well looked after & the owners are keen to help. Rooftop restaurant serves Kashmiri & international cuisine. Wi-Fi. **$$$$**

🏠 **Hotel Siachen** [157 C3] (27 rooms) Off Main Bazaar; ☏ 232 221; m 941 917 6032; e sales@hotelsiachen.com; w hotelsiachen.com. Centrally located & very comfortable. Staff are polite & helpful; meals in the on-site restaurant are tasty & affordable. Rooms are quiet & come with thick blankets. Heating is available in winter for an additional Rs750/day. **$$$$**

🏠 **Hotel Greenland** [157 C3] (33 rooms) Main Bazaar; ☏ 232 324; m 962 219 2431, 818 560 5523; e greenlandkargil@gmail.com. Small (sometimes uncomfortably so) rooms that aren't bad, but they're also hardly the stuff of hotel fantasies. It's clean & warm though & staff try their best to help. **$$$**

Other areas

🏠 **Hotel D'Zojila** [157 C6] (53 rooms) Bimathang; ☏ 232 360; m 941 917 6212. Somewhat removed from the centre of town, D'Zojila is used predominantly by tour groups passing through. All rooms have attached bathrooms, 24hr hot water & fans but could do with a thorough scrub. There's a restaurant on site & the local muezzin gives a tuneful wake-up call. **$$$$**

🏠 **Royal Inn Hotel** [157 C6] (15 rooms) Zamstiang; 📞 232 114; e info@royalinnkargil.com; w royalinnkargil.com. Around 4km south of the town centre, the Royal Inn has a fab riverside location & the rooms take full advantage with giant windows from which to take in the views. Thick rugs & blankets help to keep you cosy on even the coldest nights. Riverside garden & terrace with a restaurant overlooking it. **$$$$**

☀️🏠 **Zojila Residency** [157 C6] (18 rooms) Nr Brigade Bagh, Bimathang; m 941 917 6249. A short way south of town, this excellent hotel has pleasingly decorated rooms with colourful bedspreads, pictures on the wall & wooden desks & wardrobes. As good as the rooms are, however, the best thing about the hotel is the epic view over the river & mountains. There's a small in-house restaurant where you can get north Indian meals. **$$$$**

🏠 **Tourist Facilitation Centre** [157 C6] (10 rooms) Bimathang; m 946 946 4964. Very good value budget digs can be found at this hotel. Rooms have frilly bedspreads & are kept clean. The suites are positively gigantic & have sofas & comfy imitation leather chairs. **$$**

🍴 **WHERE TO EAT AND DRINK** Kargil has a relatively limited number of places to eat, and indeed the best food may well be had in your hotel. Still, the below options are fine for a quick bite and if you fancy a change of scene. Another option is the kebab stands (**$**) set up next to the taxi stand [157 C3] on Khumaini Chowk each evening, which send a divine smell wafting down the street, while the Zojila Bakery & Tea Stall [157 C3] (**$**) has a selection of sweet and savoury pastries that you can eat in or take out.

🍴 **Ashiyana Restaurant** [157 C4] Opp J&K Bank, Khumaini Chowk; m 946 973 8002. Friendly 1st-floor restaurant inside the (not very impressive) hotel of the same name. There's a solid line-up of Indian & Chinese dishes & helpings are large. **$$**

☀️🍴 **Roots Traveller Café** [157 B1] Jamia Masjid Rd, Main Bazaar; m 949 128 9275; 📘 @RootsLadakh. If we're being brutally honest the multi-cuisine food isn't that great here, but for most people stopping by this travel-centric hub that hardly matters. It's all about the social scene, drinking tea, the cool décor & the staff who can offer tips on things to see & do around Kargil. Books & board games are also available. They offer tours to the abandoned Hundarman village, too (page 162). **$$**

🍴 **Royal Khatoon Restaurant** [157 C6] Tourist Facilitation Centre, Bimathang; 📞 946 946 4964. Large, clean restaurant serving multi-cuisine meals but frequently closed due to lack of business. **$$**

🍴 **Shangrilla Restaurant** [157 B3] Nr Co-operative Bank, Khumaini Chowk; m 946 944 8836. Visually underwhelming 1st-floor restaurant with a wide menu of vegetarian & non-vegetarian dishes that aren't actually available. The vegetable fried rice was passable & other diners were tucking in happily to chicken legs. Service with a smile is very much dependent on who is serving. **$$**

SHOPPING AND OTHER PRACTICALITIES
Communications
📧 **Himalayan Cyber Café** [157 C2] Hospital Rd; 📞 234 017; ⏰ 10.00–20.00. Photocopying, printing, scanning & passport photos as well as internet access. Rs40/hr.

📧 **Sheena Cyber Café** [157 C3] Nr Co-operative Bank, Khumaini Chowk; m 946 973 6736; ⏰ 09.00–midnight daily. Well-run internet café with a dozen or so terminals & a reasonable broadband connection speed. Rs40/hr.

Laundry
Tariq Chemical Washing & Dry Cleaning [157 C1] If you've run out of clean clothes or have something that is dry-clean only, try this place next to the bridge in the northern end of the town.

Medical
➕ **Hospital** [157 B2] Hospital Rd; 📞 232 382. Kargil has a large hospital that is, by local standards, well equipped. Doctors generally speak English & most specialities are covered. The hospital is capable of handling A&E cases.

➕ **Noori Medicare** [157 C4] Khumaini Chowk; m 941 927 1694. Well-stocked pharmacy with a daily doctor's clinic (⏰ 09.00–10.00 & 16.00–18.00).

✚ **Velayatee Medicate** [157 B2] Hospital Rd; m 941 934 2982; ⊕ 09.00–10.30 & 16.30–18.00 Mon–Sat. Small clinic equivalent to a GP's surgery.

Money
Some of the merchants in the **Tibetan market** [157 B3] next to HDFC Bank will also exchange foreign notes for rupees. Ask around to get the best rate.

$ **HDFC Bank** [157 B3] Khumaini Chowk. 24hr ATM. Branch will unofficially change sums up to US$500 for foreigners.

$ **J&K Bank** [157 C4] Khumaini Chowk. Small branch & 24hr ATM.

Photography
Mehbob Photographers & Color Lab [157 C4] ✆ 232 535; m 941 917 6167; ⊕ 10.00–21.00 daily. Sells rechargeable batteries, memory cards, mobile phones & accessories.

Post office
✉ **India Post** [157 A2] Kargil's large post office lies at the junction of Hospital Rd & Dak Bungalow Rd.

WHAT TO SEE AND DO
Munshi Aziz Bhat Museum [157 A1] (Munshi Grong, Lankore; m 941 917 6061; w kargilmuseum.org; ⊕ summer 09.00–18.00 daily, winter closed; admission Rs30/50 child/adult) Prior to the solidification of India's borders following independence in 1947, Ladakh's merchants traded goods the length and breadth of the Silk Road, from Turkey in the west to Mongolia in the east. This museum (also known as the Central Asian Museum) houses a gem of a collection and is the undisputed highlight of Kargil town, passionately curated by Aziz Hussain Munshi and Muzammil Hussain, descendants of the late 19th-century merchant Munshi Aziz Bhat (page 162).

The first room of the museum displays **carpets and kilims**, many of which were made to be placed beneath a horse's saddle. The finest examples belonged to aristocrats and wealthy merchants and have come from as far afield as Kokand and Tajikistan. Of particular historical importance is the central Asian woven carpet decorated with eight tigers that belonged to Mohan Lal, assistant to Alexander 'Bukhara' Burnes. The room also contains **stone carvings** found at Kharcher Khar near Rangdum and dating from the 6th to 8th centuries.

The balance of the collection is in the main hall: items are grouped by type and clearly labelled in English with their approximate date and place of origin. Items of **costume** include British breeches, the name of their original owner still visible in ink on the waistband, and gowns and coats from Kashmir and Gilgit, Russia and central Asia. There are numerous **hats**, the earliest made in Mongolia in the 16th century, and also well-preserved examples of **shoes and boots**, including locally made *kratpa*, winter shoes sufficiently large that you could pack your feet around with straw to keep them warm.

Some of the most intriguing displays show local products and their foreign counterparts: **locks and keys**, European and Tibetan **medicines** (the latter with their original prescriptions) and **weaponry**. Central Asian **embroidered textiles** are exhibited alongside the British-made **embroidery threads** used to produce them.

The museum's **manuscript collection** is shown in an antechamber to the main hall. Highlights include Tibetan and Ladakhi texts on handmade paper and cloth that date back to the 14th century; what is quite possibly the earliest surviving Koran made in Ladakh; and various newspaper and magazine cuttings from the 1950s that offer insight into a bygone age.

The museum is only a few minutes' walk northwest from town, and has an elevated position, which gives a great view over the surrounding countryside.

Aziz Bhat Caravanserai [157 B1] (Between Khumaini Chowk and the river) Very little of Kargil's architectural heritage survives, but this three-storey caravanserai – the only known remaining caravanserai in Ladakh – is a notable exception, built by prominent local businessman Munshi Aziz Bhat (1866–1948) in 1920. Horses and fodder were kept on the ground floor; goods were traded on the first floor; and visiting merchants were lodged on the upper floor. Having been locked up for half a century, the artefacts and documents discovered here have formed the basis of the collection at the Munshi Aziz Bhat Museum (page 161). The building itself is in a perilous condition, threatened not only by its own physical decay but also by financial pressure to demolish it and redevelop the site.

Kargil's mosques The majority of Kargil's population is Muslim and two places of worship are particularly attractive. The **main mosque** [157 B1] is towards the northern end of Khumaini Chowk, after the crossroads on the left, and it is also possible to visit the **Imambara** [157 A1] (Nr the Munshi Aziz Bhat Museum), which is used for special celebrations at Eid.

Around Kargil Some 15km southeast of Kargil on the road towards Leh is the village of Pashkum, where there are two ruined fortresses. The **Chuli Khar For**t, set above the hamlet of Khardung, was built by the King of Pashkum, Habib Khan, in the late 17th century. Rather older, and even more tumble-down, is the neighbouring **Broq Khar**, the fortress of the Dard chieftain Kheva Khi Lde.

The traditional stone-walled village of **Hundarman** lies huddled in a tight knot of houses on a hillside around 11km northeast of Kargil. Up until 1971 the village used to be a part of Pakistan, but during the India-Pakistan War of that year it fell under Indian control. When the Indian army bore down on the village, the locals locked up their houses and hurriedly fled westward into Pakistan, taking with them only what they could carry. The settlement was then largely forgotten and, until recently, only a few shepherds ever visited the old village (though a new village was established nearby by those who didn't flee).

In recent years, however, Hundarman has been 'rediscovered' by the crew behind the excellent Roots Traveller Café (page 160) in Kargil, who have started offering fascinating tours (Rs250 per person, Rs800 taxi return trip). When the village houses were first re-entered, people were shocked to discover that many of the original inhabitants' possessions had been left exactly as they were when they'd had to flee, with personal mementoes, cooking utensils and even half-finished embroidery left untouched. The tours include a visit to the old village as well as to a nearby museum that now showcases some of these items.

The route to the village brushes very closely along the boundary with the LoC. At a small tea shack en route, binoculars (Rs30) are available through which you can peer across this much fought-over border at the closest Pakistani villages.

DRASS *Telephone code: 01985*

The town of Drass is a glorified army camp, where sunlight glints off the corrugated-iron roofs and soldiers sit around twiddling their thumbs. It is a fair-sized settlement and still expanding, but though there are interesting things to do in the environs, it's not a place where you'd want to stay any great length of time.

GETTING THERE AND AWAY Drass is situated on the NH1, 56km from Kargil and 157km from Srinagar. There is a police checkpoint at Mina Marg, to the west of Drass, where you have to show your passport and complete a Foreigners' Registration Form.

If you are travelling through Drass en route to Sonamarg and Srinagar, be sure to stop outside the police station (✆ 274 003) to check the Zojila Pass noticeboard: this is updated daily and tells you the current status of the pass (whether it is open or closed); and if it is closed, why it is closed and when it is expected to open again. The same information can be gained by calling the police station.

Shared taxis run to Drass from Kargil (2hrs; Rs1,670 one-way). If you are coming from Srinagar (Rs6,400 one-way), you'll need to allow at least 6 hours to reach Drass, although it can take as long as 10 hours if there are delays at Zoji La (see box, page 183). Really, though, it makes much more sense to take the taxi all the way from Srinagar to Kargil, just stopping briefly in Drass.

Travelling by **bus**, there is a daily JKSRTC service from Srinagar to Kargil that passes through Drass en route. It departs from Srinagar at 07.30 and costs Rs240 for the normal bus and, if demand allows, Rs375 for the semi-deluxe bus.

 WHERE TO STAY AND EAT Drass's accommodation options are very limited: unless you absolutely have to stay the night here, you'd be better off continuing to Kargil or Sonamarg. For a quick snack, try **Mehfooz Bakery and Sweets** ($) on the main road.

🏠 **White Mountain Hotel & Restaurant** (10 rooms) Drass market; ✆556 924. The town's best hotel (though that's not saying much) offers a warm welcome & bright pink rooms. There's a restaurant serving simple meals. **$**

OTHER PRACTICALITIES There is a branch of **SBI** (🕐 10.00–16.00 Mon–Fri, 10.00–13.00 Sat) with ATM opposite the police station on the main road, although it's not possible to change money here. There is a second ATM belonging to **J&K Bank** next to the mosque. Also along the main road are a number of small shops selling mobile phone credit and offering STD phone lines, as well as a small **hospital** (✆ 274 016) where you would be able to get basic medical attention in an emergency. For more minor incidents, and to buy medication, try **Zahoor Medicate** on the main road.

WHAT TO SEE AND DO Drass is famed for its polo matches, and there is a large **polo ground** in the centre of the town. The polo season is in summer and games are reasonably regular, so ask around for forthcoming fixtures. In winter, sports fans can also watch **ice hockey**, usually played by teams from the Indian army.

On the outskirts of Drass (Kargil side), situated at the bend in the road where the old NH1 road runs parallel to the new one, is a shrine with Buddhist prayer flags, an unusual sight in this predominantly Muslim area. Here you'll find an attractive **stone Buddha** around 1.5m tall, as well as four other statues too badly weathered to identify. You'll need to pull back some of the prayer flags to see the statue properly, so be sure to put them back afterwards. We were told that the damage to the Buddha's face was caused some 15 or so years ago by a local man who objected to the presence of the idol and had it removed. When he and members of his family fell sick, they were concerned they were being punished for the act, and so returned the statue to its original location.

AROUND DRASS On the eastern side of Drass, 7km from the town, is the **Bhimbut Stone**. Legend has it that this is the petrified body of Bhim, the Pandava warrior whose exploits are central stories in the *Mahabharata* epic. The second of the Pandava brothers, Bhim is credited with slaying all 100 of the Kaurava brothers in the probably mythical Kurukshetra War. The stone is becoming a fairly popular place of pilgrimage for Hindus.

'War tourism' is a growing attraction in the area for the domestic tourists who take tours to **Tiger Hill**, **Mushkoo** and **Tololing** (all of which were battle sites during the Kargil War). Those with a more general interest in the Kargil War, however, should stop only at the **Kargil War Memorial**, 5km east of Drass. It's an attractive monument constructed from red sandstone, and is inscribed with the names of Indian soldiers who lost their lives during the conflict. The giant Indian flag fluttering above is said to weigh 15kg, and there is also a small **museum** on site.

LADAKH, JAMMU & THE KASHMIR VALLEY ONLINE

For additional online content, articles, photos and more on Ladakh, Jammu & the Kashmir Valley, why not visit w bradtguides.com/ladakh?

7

Zanskar and the Suru Valley

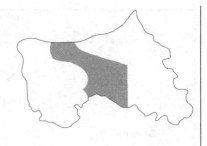

The region of Zanskar is a little slice of heaven, a place where the mountains reach up to kiss the sky. We were once told that only the pure of heart can reach here, and certainly the human population is thin on the ground. Largely cut off from the outside world (and even now with limited road access in winter), Zanskar is reached by only a few tourists each year, but those who do make the effort are won over by the sheer scale of the scenery, the charm of the local people and the absolute sense of peace.

Motives for visiting Zanskar are varied. Some will come for the art found in the many monasteries and temples – some of which are perched in improbable cliff-top locations – while others relish the chance to interact with locals in the small and remote villages where time is marked by changing seasons rather than ticking clocks. Arguably, though, the best reason for visiting the region is the bountiful trekking opportunities through unsurpassed Himalayan mountain scenery – indeed, Zanskar is home to some of the best routes in the Indian Himalayas and the beauty of walking here is that any trek will combine fabulous scenery with village stays and pauses to visit temples. What more could you ask for?

Those approaching Zanskar from Kargil will also discover the Suru Valley, a softer environment where the road winds through well-tended fields. A couple of sights here are worth your time: the impressive Buddha at Kartse Khar can be visited on a day trip from Kargil or en route to Zanskar, and the twin peaks of Nun and Kun make both a stunning backdrop to travels in this area and a formidable challenge for determined mountaineers.

THE SURU VALLEY *Telephone code: 01985*

The photogenic Suru Valley stretches south from Kargil as far as Penzi La, the source of the Suru River. For the most part, the road south follows the river's path along the valley bottom, passing through simple villages where people make their livings from the land. The valley is particularly colourful in late spring, when the slopes are filled with flowers, and at harvest time when the fields are full of men and women cutting and threshing their grain, and carrying it home to store for the winter.

Unlike Buddhist Zanskar, the population here is a mixture of Tibetans and Dards, the majority of whom are Muslim. Evidence of the area's historic Buddhist population does, however, survive.

For hardy cyclists the villages of Zanskar make a good goal. The roads into the valley are much quieter than the main Leh–Srinagar road and the scenery is such

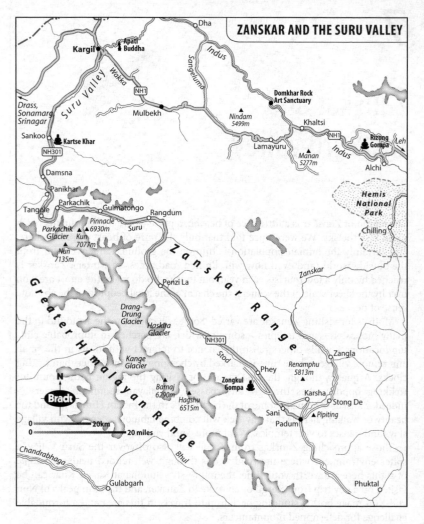

that you'll barely notice the cycling aches and pains. Come prepared to camp and self-cater though.

GETTING THERE AND AWAY Most travellers hire a jeep and driver from Kargil, Leh or Srinagar – be sure to fill up with fuel before setting out. This main road is generally in good condition, though winter ice does leave its scars so expect some rough patches and pot-holes. Check in advance with police, transport operators and hotels if the road is open, as it is frequently blocked by snow.

Public transport into the valley is limited, but if you're patient you'll get there in the end. All of the places along the main road are accessible by bus and taxi from Kargil: see individual entries for details.

KARTSE KHAR Once a fortified town, Kartse Khar (White Castle) is no more than a village today. The sole surviving feature that tells us of Kartse's former glory is the 7th- to 8th-century **Chamba Buddha**, a 7m-tall rock-cut Buddha similar in style and quality to the one in Mulbekh but far less well known. It is thought to have been carved by visiting Buddhist missionaries, and academics believe it was inspired by similar standing Buddha carvings in the Swat Valley (now in Pakistan) and Afghanistan, including the Bamiyan Buddha destroyed by the Taliban.

Kartse Khar is a little off the main road: travel along the main Suru Valley road to Sankoo, a lively village 42km south of Kargil, then cross the river and continue east for around 8km along a smaller side valley to Kartse. The journey from Kargil normally takes around 2 hours. On public transport, a bus leaves every morning at 11.00 (Rs100), while a taxi from Kargil will cost Rs2,000 (one-way).

PANIKHAR AND DAMSNA A further 20km from Sankoo is **Damsna**, a pretty place with stone-built houses where you'll get your first sighting of Mount Nun (see box, below). You will need to show your passport at at least one police checkpoint along this stretch of the road to be allowed to continue.

Some 4km further south, **Panikhar** is a tiny place but there is a **J&K Tourist Bungalow ($)** here if you are cycling (or otherwise travelling slowly) and need to spend the night.

To get here from Kargil, a daily bus leaves at 07.00 (Rs80), or you can hop in a taxi for Rs2,285 (one-way).

PARKACHIK Most people will only ever pass through the village of Parkachik en route to Zanskar. Set to one side of a particularly rough stretch of road that is rocky and often too narrow for two vehicles to pass, this unremarkable village is situated up the hill: follow the left-hand fork in the road as you are approaching from Kargil.

If you plan to climb Nun or Kun (see box, below), however, you'll want to stop here as the closest base camp is just 6km away. There is also one budget accommodation option in the village, the **Parkachik Alpine Hut ($)**, though there is also a flat area of grass by the river where you could ask to pitch a tent. The Alpine Hut is a J&K

CLIMBING NUN AND KUN

The Nun-Kun Massif encompasses a number of peaks, the three highest of which are **Nun** (7,135m), **Kun** (7,077m) and **Pinnacle** (6,930m). British and Dutch mountaineers first explored the area at the turn of the 20th century. The first ascent of Pinnacle was accomplished by husband-and-wife team Fanny and William Hunter Workman in 1906; Kun was climbed by the Italian mountaineer Mario Piacenza in 1913; and Nun was finally summited in 1953 by Bernard Pierre and Pierre Vittoz.

The Indian Mountaineering Foundation (see box, page 89) allots climbers with ascent routes, and all mountaineers must obtain a permit from them.

Base camp can be reached in a day's trekking from Tangole (midway between Panikhar and Parkachik), Gulmatongo (midway between Parkachik and Rangdum) or via the Parkachik Glacier. Climbing is possible from June to October, though July and August are most popular. You will need to allow a minimum of 14 days to acclimatise at each level and complete an ascent.

Make no mistake about it, though: this is no Stok Kangri (see box, page 116). It is a challenging Himalayan mountain-climbing expedition that should only be attempted with a guide and by those with lots of Himalayan mountaineering experience.

Tourism-run property with a local caretaker, where you can expect a simple bed for the night and that's about all. Meals are available on request.

The bus to Parkachik leaves Kargil daily at 11.00 (Rs112), while a taxi will cost Rs3,308 (one-way).

ZANSKAR *Telephone code: 01958*

If you want an easy-to-organise trek in the Indian Himalayas, but are frustrated by the overly popular routes in Ladakh, then Zanskar is the perfect antidote. A subdistrict of Kargil, right in the heart of J&K, it is sufficiently inaccessible that first-time visitors to the region rarely make the effort to get here, preferring the quicker routes into and out of the Markha and Nubra valleys, but providing you are not in a rush, it is well worth the challenging journey.

Treks in the valley vary from easy day hikes, such as the route across the valley floor from Zanskar's administrative centre, Padum, to Karsha, to numerous opportunities to blaze out along remote routes that see no more than a handful of trekkers each year. There are still places where even the trekking guides haven't been, and a single monk may be the only source of information that can supplement your map. In winter when the road is often closed due to snow, the only way in and out of Zanskar is by doing the arduous Chadar Winter Trek (see box, page 178) along the frozen Zanskar River, providing insight not only into the challenges of living in this landscape but the lengths that local people will go to in order to ensure that the local children receive an education.

RANGDUM Rangdum is a tiny settlement in a stunning location, surrounded by strange but beautifully striped geological formations. Though probably not a planned destination in its own right, it is the key transit point in and out of Zanskar, and you can see its reddish gompa from miles away as it contrasts starkly with its sandy surroundings.

Getting there and away Rangdum is approximately midway between Kargil and Padum, about 110km south of Kargil. Getting there takes a full day, mostly through the Suru Valley and then into Zanskar itself. Though paved in parts, much of the road is little more than a sand and gravel track and, depending on the time of year, you may well find that there are small streams to ford. There is a **police checkpoint** in Rangdum village where you have to present your passport, and another at the base of the gompa.

The **bus** from Kargil to Padum (page 158) passes through Rangdum and you are welcome to get off there, though you may be asked to pay the full fare (Rs400). Remember, though, that the next bus will not come for a week and even then may not have space to pick you up, so factor this in to your onward journey. It is more comfortable and flexible to take a **taxi** from Kargil, splitting the cost between several people if you need to reduce the bill (Rs6,000 one-way).

If you are travelling to Rangdum or into Zanskar proper from anywhere along the Kargil–Leh Highway, you might be surprised to learn that it is almost as fast to get there **on foot** as it is to drive, and the trek is perfectly feasible for someone of moderate fitness and agility. East of Rangdum there is a track across Kanjil La (5,255m), which links up with the NH1 close to Lamayuru. The walk is easily completed in two days (or one and a half if you are really fast). Along the way you will pass through several valleys famed for their medicinal herbs: the Dalai Lama's personal *amchi* (see box, opposite) is said to come here to collect plants.

Tanzin Norbu (w mountaintribalvision.com)

Amchi means the 'medicine man', and is a person greatly respected in Tibetan, Ladakhi and Zanskari communities. The remote valleys of Zanskar and Ladakh were beyond the reach of Western medicine for centuries, and thus relied heavily on the *amchi* of their villages to cure a wide range of diseases. *Amchi* practise Tibetan herbal medicine. They are not only expert in diagnosing and curing disease, but also skilled in identifying Himalayan medicinal plants and medicinal preparation. *Amchi* use various methods to diagnose diseases, such as pulse, iridology, analysis of the tongue, and urine sampling. It is a long process to become an *amchi*, only becoming qualified after five years of intense training. During the summer, *amchi* go high into the mountains to collect various medicinal plants, flowers, roots and shoots, from which they prepare medicines after drying them in the sunlight.

Where to stay and eat There are two simple **cafés** in Rangdum village where you can buy tea and small snacks. They also offer very basic accommodation (**$**), but there is no electricity and water is in buckets. Typically only the truck drivers stop here.

Nun Kun Deluxe Camp (20 tents) By Rangdum Gompa; **m** 941 997 9372; **e** info@zanskartrek.com; **w** zanskartrek.com. Two things make Nun Kun a worthwhile place to stay: the spectacular views across the valley to the mountains with their colourful strata & the excellent home-cooked food. The tents themselves are comfortable enough but hardly the 'deluxe' their name suggests. **$$$$**

What to see and do Rangdum Gompa (⊕ 08.00–19.00; donation around Rs100) is a 5km drive past Rangdum village: there is a road that skirts the edge of the valley, but most drivers prefer to continue along the rough track straight across the (mostly dry) riverbed. The gompa is perched atop a rocky outcrop and clearly visible for quite some distance. The monastery dates from the 17th century so it is relatively recent by Zanskari standards. Around 40 monks belonging to the Gelugpa order live here, and though some people might tell you the donkeys sleep inside with them at night, this sadly seems to be a fallacy. If you go into the small and very dark **temple**, look out for the ceremonial cup made from a human skull. Providing you ask, the monks are happy for you to climb up on the roof, which gives an interesting perspective not only on the gompa but also of the surrounding scenery.

PADUM *(Telephone code: 01983)* The largest settlement in Zanskar, Padum is still only home to a little over 1,000 people (the overall population of the valley is around 25,000). It is a pleasant place laid out either side of one main street, Mani Ringmo, and in the summer months it is fairly lively and a good place to meet other travellers: almost everyone trekking in Zanskar starts or finishes their trip here.

The local population is a mixture of both Tibetan Buddhists and Muslims, and this is reflected in the local culture. There is both a gompa and a mosque in town, and the food in the restaurants is quite varied. There are some superbly executed and well-preserved rock carvings of Buddhas and stupas down by the river, which are well worth a few hours of your time, and Padum is within easy striking distance of Karsha, Zangla and Zongkul if you are looking for a day trip or three.

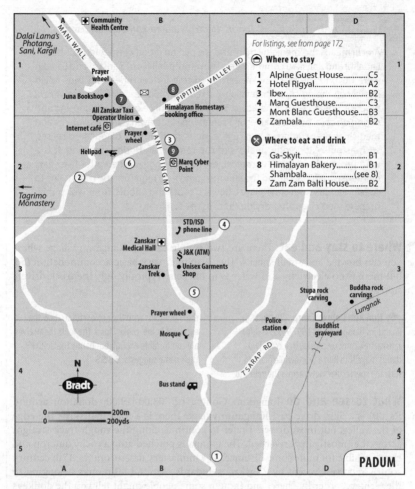

For listings, see from page 172

Where to stay

1	Alpine Guest House	C5
2	Hotel Rigyal	A2
3	Ibex	B2
4	Marq Guesthouse	C3
5	Mont Blanc Guesthouse	B3
6	Zambala	B2

Where to eat and drink

7	Ga-Skyit	B1
8	Himalayan Bakery	B1
	Shambala	(see 8)
9	Zam Zam Balti House	B2

PADUM

History Padum is an ancient settlement in the Zanskar Valley and it was once the seat of the kings of Zanskar. The royal palace was sadly destroyed in 1823 by an army from Lahaul, and nothing of it now remains. Most of the town you see today – the new town – post-dates this destruction.

Getting there and around It is a long and uncomfortable 240km **drive** from Kargil to Padum, and the road is normally only open from mid-July until early November. At other times of year the only way in and out of the valley is on foot (see box, page 178). Around 90km of the route is covered with tarmac; the rest is compressed gravel and dirt. Fortunately the ever-changing scenery, and some superb views of both mountains and glaciers, takes your mind off the bouncing and jolting.

Buses between Kargil and Padum are very unreliable. There is a weekly service (when the roads are open!) from Leh to Padum that stops for the night in Kargil, but there's no guarantee of a seat if you're intending to board in Kargil. The journey from Kargil takes at least 14 hours (sometimes closer to 20) and costs Rs400.

ZANSKAR TAXI RATES

As in Leh and Kargil, the taxi union (All Zanskar Taxi Union), which is based in Padum, sets the official taxi fares. A copy of the latest rate list is posted inside its office on the corner of Mani Ringmo and Pibiting Road. The prices below for 2019 were correct at the time of going to print but will be revised at least on an annual basis.

All journeys listed here originate in Padum, and prices are given in rupees (Rs). You can book a taxi by going into the office, or by calling the office manager, Norboo, on his mobile (m 946 969 1683).

Destination	One-way	Return
Kargil	13,400	N/A
Karsha	800	1,200
Karsha Gompa	900	1,300
Leh	17,000	20,000
Pibiting	150	225
Rangdum	7,000	9,000
Srinagar	17,500	22,500
Stong De	800	1,200
Stong De Gompa	1,100	1,700
Zangla	2,000	3,000
Zongkul Gompa	2,200	3,000

Due to the unreliability of bus travel into and around Zanskar, almost all visitors end up travelling by **taxi** from Kargil (Rs13,400 one-way). It is often possible to find someone to share with you, reducing the price by splitting the cost. For prices starting in Padum, see the box above.

Returning from Padum, **shared jeeps** and the occasional lorry with a space in the back depart for Kargil from the crossroads by the office of the All Zanskar Taxi Union (see box, above). Drivers are frequently hanging around in the vicinity of their vehicle on the day before departure, but if not often leave a note affixed to the windscreen with their mobile number and planned departure time. If the vehicle is already full they may depart early, so do keep checking.

Helpful, patient and with a good command of English is Padum-based taxi driver **Tsering Mutup** (m 946 945 8059), who has a comfortable 4x4 and can be hired both for the drive from Padum to Kargil and for more local trips.

Local travel agencies/guides There are a small number of competent local travel agencies in Padum, all of which focus on trekking. If you want to do a combination of trekking and sightseeing with a knowledgeable English-speaking guide, it is advisable to contact Tanzin Norbu at **Mountain Tribal Vision** (see box, page 33) before you go.

Zanskar Trek [170 B3] Mani Ringmo; (01982) 245 136; m 946 936 9581; e info@zanskartrek. com; w zanskartrek.com. Leh-based trekking agency with local office in Padum. Organises treks & wildlife tours around Zanskar. Has own 4x4 vehicle for transfers.

Trekking guides The following trekking guides all come highly recommended and can be hired independently as well as through travel agents in Leh (page 76).

Himal Singh Magar m 979 764 1131;
e himalallungeli@yahoo.co.in. Nepali trekking
guide who spends the summer months in Zanskar.
Good English.
Phunchok Mutup Kalyan m 962 295 8019;
e kalyanmutup@gmail.com. Reliable trekking
guide with good knowledge of Zanskar's cultural
sites too.

Raju Khan e rajukhan.in34@yahoo.com. Warm,
knowledgeable & with a fair command of English,
Raju can usually be found at Ibex Hotel or the
neighbouring Zam Zam Balti House when not in
the mountains with clients.

Where to stay
The accommodation options in Padum are the best in Zanskar,
though that's not saying much. If you plan to be here in August, try to book ahead
as it can get very busy. Most accommodation options close between October
and May or June (though some will open up if pre-booked). Homestays around
Zanskar can be booked through the **Himalayan Homestays booking office**
[170 B1] (Pibiting Rd; m 946 936 9406; w himalayan-homestays.com), and they
invariably fit into the shoestring bracket and typically include dinner.

Unlike in most of Ladakh and Kashmir, none of the places to stay in Zanskar
offer Wi-Fi. Enjoy the opportunity to switch off and enjoy the here and now!

Marq Guesthouse [170 C3] (10 rooms)
Off Mani Ringmo; \245 223; m 941 800 2171.
Probably the best option in Padum though service
can be hit & miss. Rooms are clean & all have
immaculate attached bathrooms. 24hr power is
provided by a backup generator & water is solar
heated. **$$$$**

Alpine Guest House [170 C5] (4 rooms)
Behind Padum Khar, Mani Ringmo; m 946 973
0700; e alpineguesthousepadum@gmail.com. Run
by the ever-smiling Abdul Salam, the Alpine Guest
House has rooms split across 2 floors of the family
house. Those on the upper floor are definitely
much more inviting than the darker ground-floor
rooms. **$$$**

Hotel Rigyal [170 A2] (10 rooms) Nr
helipad; m 946 922 4500; e hotel-rigyal@yahoo.
com; w hotelrigyal.com. Run by monks, this small
hotel is kept exceptionally clean & has good hot
showers. Camping is possible in the garden. No
English is spoken but you should still be able to
make yourself understood. **$$$**

Ibex Hotel [170 B2] (15 rooms) Mani
Ringmo; \245 214; e ibexpadumzanskar@
gmail.com. For many years Padum's most popular
spot for backpackers benefited from its central
location, but today it has been surpassed in
quality by some of the town's other options.
Rooms are built around a pleasant courtyard. The
manager speaks good English. Meals are available
on request but tend to take a while, as the hotel is
short-staffed. **$$$**

Zambala Hotel [170 B2] (12 rooms) Mani
Ringmo; m 946 962 9336. A short walk from
the town centre, this attractive budget hotel has
bright rooms with thick blankets on the beds &
bathrooms with hot bucket showers. **$$$**

Mont Blanc Guesthouse [170 B3] (4
rooms) Mani Ringmo; m 946 923 9376. Simple
but cosy & welcoming guesthouse in the centre of
town, set back from the main drag in a pleasant
garden. Rooms are carpeted, with several sgl beds
in each. **$**

Where to eat and drink
All the restaurants in Padum are open for lunch and
dinner unless otherwise stated: for breakfast it is easiest to eat in your guesthouse
or hotel.

Ga-Skyit Restaurant [170 B1] Mani
Ringmo; m 946 936 9828. 1st-floor restaurant
close to the crossroads. Dishes are mostly
Tibetan, with a few Chinese & Indian options.
$$

Zam Zam Balti House [170 B2] Mani
Ringmo. Lively diner next door to the Ibex
Hotel. There are good meat dishes on the
menu as well as simple, often deep-fried snacks.
$$

✗ Shambala Restaurant [170 B1] Pibiting Rd; m 946 909 6716. 1st-floor restaurant serving Tibetan & Chinese staples such as *thukpa* & chow mein. If you're looking for something simple, they also do reasonable omelettes. **$–$$**

✗ Himalayan Bakery [170 B1] Pibiting Rd. Downstairs from Shambala Restaurant, this is the best of several bakeries in Padum. Though nothing exciting, the loaves of bread, savoury pastries & biscuits are helpful additions to your trekking provisions. Take-out only. **$**

Shopping
Several general stores along Mani Ringmo sell basic dried and packeted food items.

Juma Bookshop [170 A1] Behind prayer wheel, Mani Ringmo; ☉ 10.30–19.00. Friendly store selling stationery & a small selection of games, books & trekking maps.

Unisex Garments Shop [170 B3] Next to J&K Bank; ☉ 09.30–19.30. General clothing store selling waterproof jackets, gilets, fleeces, duffel bags, torches, multi-tools, padlocks & sunglasses.

Other practicalities

Communications
Padum's internet connection is erratic at best. There are 2 **internet cafés** on Mani Ringmo (both of them close to the crossroads) but they are rarely open & connection speeds are such that it might be faster to send your message via carrier pigeon.

STD & **ISD** phone calls can be made from the shop on Mani Ringmo, just before the driveway leading to Marq Guesthouse [170 B3].

✉ **Post office** [170 B1] Mani Ringmo, opposite the Ga-Skyit Restaurant; ☉ 10.00–16.00 Mon–Sat. The red metal shutters are always down, even when the post office is open, so go in through the door on the right.

Medical
In the event of a medical emergency or other requirement for immediate evacuation, Padum has its own **helipad** [170 A2], set just back from Mani Ringmo in the centre of the town.

✚ **Community Health Centre** [170 A1] ✆ 245 015. Zanskar's largest hospital is composed of 2 buildings: an outpatients clinic & a newer building (opened in 2012) containing male & female wards,

the casualty department & operating theatres. The hospital is well equipped for the region, with facilities including an X-ray machine & laboratory. In addition to several English-speaking surgeons & general medical staff, there are also a pharmacist & a dentist.

✚ **Zanskar Medical Hall** [170 B3] m 946 909 2711; ☉ 09.00–19.30. Almost opposite J&K Bank is this small pharmacy with an English-speaking pharmacist. It stocks most generic drugs as well as disposable syringes & scalpels contained in sealed packets.

Money
There's a **J&K Bank ATM** on Mani Ringmo [170 B3], but it's often out of action so bring all the cash with you that you might need. If you get stuck then individual merchants may agree to change dollars for you, but the rate is poor.

Police
Should you need police assistance, the **police station** [170 C4] (✆ 245 003) is in the Old Town, close to the Buddhist graveyard & petroglyphs. The regular police force is generally friendly & some of them speak English.

What to see and do If you've had your fill of gompas, Padum has a wonderful surprise: hidden in the north of the town by the river are two sets of **ancient petroglyphs** [170 D3]. Turning left off Tsarap Road, continue past the police station until the road bends round to the left. Continue straight along the footpath running parallel with the stone wall, and follow it round to the right: in front of you is an orange-coloured rock carved with **images of stupas**.

Behind the rock is a red-tiled pathway: follow it to the left and then downhill towards the river. This brings you to the **Five Buddhas Rock** [170 D3], so named because of the line of five Buddha carvings, each one sitting meditating in the lotus position. At some point in the relatively recent past the faces have been partly repaired with concrete, as have some of the limbs, but they are magnificent nonetheless.

Immediately to their right is a **standing Buddha** [170 D3] around 3m tall, and at the base of the rock are various smaller human figures. The top section of the rock features several tiered stupas. Unlike the Chamba Buddha at Mulbekh (page 154), you have an unobstructed view of the carvings and can even climb on top of the rock for impressive views in both directions along the valley.

Continuing down the steps, the rock face pointing towards the river has yet more petroglyphs, including a **meditating Buddha**, but these are substantially more weathered than the other carvings, and a large bush partially obscures several of the images. Stop for a while to sit on the rocks by the river and soak up the peaceful atmosphere: you're unlikely to be disturbed by anything other than a cow, and maybe the rushing of the water.

Padum does have a gompa too: the **Tagrimo Monastery** [170 A2]. Dating from the 17th century, it belongs to the Drukpa school. Its frescoes are in good condition thanks to sensitive renovation works in 2005, and there is also a small library. The gompa is about 30 minutes' walk from Mani Ringmo and overlooks the town.

Padum is also home to the only **mosque** [170 B4] in Zanskar: it's the attractive green-roofed building in the centre of town. Unlike the Shiite Muslims of the Suru Valley further north, Zanskar's small Muslim population are Sunni. Finally, don't forget to spend a bit of time wandering around the **Padum Khar** (Old Town) quarter at the southern end of town. It's an interesting little area of tumble-down buildings built among the debris of huge boulders.

Excursions from Padum

Pipiting Visible from much of Padum is Pipiting, the hill in the middle of the plain atop which sits a large **stupa** and small gompa, cared for by two monks from Karsha. The oldest part of this monastery dates back around 600 years. There are some fine wall paintings, and also three impressive statues of the Chamba Buddha, Padmasambhava and the 11-headed Chenrezi.

Sani It takes around 2 hours to walk the 8km (5 miles) back along the main road north from Padum to Sani, which is a small but attractive settlement with three sites that are well worth visiting.

On the opposite side of the road from the town is the **Sani Lake**. The lake itself would not be remarkable if it weren't for the large, modern Buddha statue rising from its centre. You can reach the island on which the Buddha stands by hopping from one stepping stone to the next. On the right-hand side of the Buddha's crown are three turquoise stones, and the one at the bottom left (you'll need a telephoto lens or binoculars to see if from the ground – and some imagination...) appears to have the face of the Dalai Lama naturally occurring in the pattern of the stone.

Sani Gompa is the only gompa in Zanskar to be built on the plain: all the others are set into the mountain slopes. Though the current gompa dates from only the 17th century, there has been a religious community on this site far longer, as attested to by the Kanishka Stupa, which is thought to date from the 2nd century AD. Also of note here is a beautiful bronze statue of Naropa, housed in a small building behind the main gompa.

Sani is also home to **Kachod Ling**, a Buddhist nunnery belonging to the Drukpa order. It's a relatively small nunnery with only 14 or 15 nuns, the majority of whom work in the village during the day. Their historic lhakhang has been sensitively restored and has some attractive wall paintings; and there is also a new dukhang.

Zongkul Gompa (donation around Rs100) Up a side valley, some 6km southwest of the main road, is the quiet cave monastery of Zongkul, founded on the site where Naropa once meditated. It is rarely visited by tourists, but worth a half-day's excursion from Padum. Situated up a narrow track of crushed rock, not far from the village of Tangkar, and belonging to the Drukpa lineage, the monastery has grown up around a cave where Naropa is thought to have meditated.

The **cave** itself is at the centre of the monastery: it is a dark, claustrophobic place. The cave's roof is plastered with small coins, stuck with the oil from the butter lamps, and the footprints of Naropa are cut into the rock. There are six finely worked statues, five depicting the Buddha and one of Naropa. Elsewhere in the monastery there is an attractive **prayer room** with brightly painted wooden beams and columns, ceremonial instruments (specifically drums and trumpets), a collection of large paintings on cloth, and a line of statues. The statue of Lama Kunga Churlak (third from the left) is particularly unusual as he is shown with a beard and moustache. Monks are normally clean-shaven.

In the **smaller prayer room**, a square space in which the rock forms part of the roof, there is more natural light, showing off the painted statuary. The decorative cabinets in which the statues are displayed caught our eye: they are works of art in their own right.

The **library** contains hundreds of printing blocks that would once have been used for making religious manuscripts. Today all the Buddhist texts are printed on modern machines in Dharamsala, but the blocks are preserved nonetheless. The room also contains painted display cases decorated with silken banners in numerous colours and patterns, silver plates and a few other decorative items.

Check out the **glass swastika** embedded in the floor of the entrance hall when you leave. As in Hinduism, the swastika has been a sacred symbol in Buddhism for thousands of years.

Zongkul is quite a dark monastery and the floors and doorways are very uneven. It is highly recommended that you bring your own torch and that you are careful of both your head and shins when making your way along the corridors, upstairs and through doorways.

Getting there and away Zongkul is best reached by **taxi** from Padum (Rs3,000 return). By road you travel past Sani, staying on the west bank of the river as far as Tangkar, from where there is a signposted track, rough underfoot, into the side valley leading up to the gompa. Due to the twists, turns and poor surface, it's a 15-minute drive from this crossroads.

If you are coming **on foot**, you'll need to allow 2 hours for the walk from Phey, 4 hours from Sani, and 6 hours from Padum. Carry plenty of water as it is dry and dusty and for much of the way there isn't any shade.

Where to stay If not day tripping from Padum, the closest accommodation to Zongkul is at Phey on the main road, 2 hours' walk from the Zongkul Gompa. Here it is possible to stay at either the **Darang Durung Guesthouse** (on the river side of the road) or the **ZDA Tourist Guesthouse** (behind the prayer wheel). Both have very basic facilities and fall into the shoestring (**$**) price bracket. They would also be convenient if you are hiking or coming by bike and won't make Padum before nightfall.

Karsha Visible right across the plain from Padum, Karsha has an impressive location, set into the soaring cliff face as though its buildings were a succession of whitewashed crows' nests. The **Chamspaling Phagspa Shesrab Gompa** is one of the friendliest we visited anywhere in Ladakh or Zanskar, and the views back down from it are second to none. The largest monastery in Zanskar, it is a steep site, with the numerous storeys built higgledy-piggledy into the cliff, so if you come by car, ask the driver to take you the long way round and drop you at the top.

There are three important figures in the history of Karsha's monastery: Phagspa Shesrab, the founder after whom it is named; Dorje Shesrab, who constructed the buildings you see today; and Shesrab Zangpo, who converted the monastery to follow the Gelugpa school. There are around 150 monks at Karsha, as well as a number of novices who race around the monastery's courtyards, causing good-natured mayhem. It seems that relatively few foreign visitors come here, but we were made exceptionally welcome: the monks invited us to attend their afternoon prayers in their beautifully decorated temple and were happy for us to take photographs of them providing we sat still and were quiet. They also shared their lunch with us afterwards in the courtyard, which was a highlight of our trip.

Due to its raised position, the views from the gompa are superb: not only do the plain and river stretch out before you, but you can easily see Padum, Stong De and Pipiting, and in the background stretch out peak after snow-capped peak.

Getting there and away There is just one **bus** a day between Padum and Karsha: it leaves Karsha at 08.00 and returns the same day around 16.00 (30mins; Rs25). A **shared taxi** also runs the same route with approximately the same departure times and price, but a shorter journey time (about 15 minutes).

If you want a private **taxi**, you need to take the car from Padum and get it to wait for you in Karsha, as there is no taxi stand there to pick up a different vehicle for the return journey. The return trip costs Rs1,200 (Rs1,300 to the gompa above the main village) and includes 90 minutes of waiting time while you explore.

You can also **walk** from Padum to Karsha via Pipiting in a little over 2 hours. Though it is flat, and hence easy walking, the plain is very exposed so make sure you wear a hat and carry plenty of water.

Stong De Stong De, or Tongde, is midway between Padum and Zangla, on the opposite side of the river to Karsha. The principal reason for coming here is to visit the **Marpaling Gompa**, one of the holiest sites in the Zanskar Valley. One of the oldest monasteries in the region, it is said to have been founded by Marpa himself (see box, page 23) in 1052, hence its name. The current buildings date from the 13th century, and the three dozen monks who live here follow the Gelugpa school. There are also around 20 novices.

The oldest part of the gompa is the **dukhang**, where the murals are in poor condition due to their age, but still visible. More visually impressive are the paintings in the **main temple**, which show a large Sakyamuni Buddha surrounded by smaller

Buddhas, and an **antechamber** in which the Buddhas are painted unusually as white silhouettes on a black background.

A 20-minute walk from Stong De village, the monastery has a fabulous location perched high on a hillside with views down to the fields below and barren mountains beyond. A colourful monastery festival takes place here on the last day of the fifth Lunar month and first day of the sixth (normally this would be around July), which is much less touristed than some of the better-known monastery festivals in Ladakh.

Getting there and away It's a pleasant 12km **walk** from Padum to Stong De, and it'll take you around 3 hours. The daily **bus** from Padum to Zangla passes this way (Padum to Stong De takes an hour), or you can hire a **taxi** from Padum. The ride from Padum to Stong De costs Rs800 one-way or Rs1,000 if you're going up to the gompa rather than just to the village. Plan on Rs1,500 for a return journey.

Where to stay There are no formal accommodation options in Stong De. However, it is sometimes possible for individuals and small groups to stay at the gompa or with a local family. If you have a local guide, they will arrange this for you, otherwise you'll need to ask around when you arrive.

ZANGLA Historically there were two kings in Zanskar: one had his capital at Padum, and the other ruled from Zangla. The latter's **palace**, now partially restored, is the village's obvious attraction, a fortified structure that is the only indication we have of how Zanskari royals would have lived, their other palace in Padum having been completely destroyed. Some restoration work has been undertaken by a Hungarian organisation, but you'll still need to use your imagination. Twelve remarkable statues do survive in one of the ruined structures: make sure you hunt them down.

On the opposite side of the village is the **Chanchub Choling Nunnery**, a welcoming place with around two dozen nuns and another dozen trainees. Here you will find an attractive **lhakhang** filled to the brim with religious books, as well as colourful murals depicting a range of divinities and also an unusual painting of grotesque Mahakalas set against a black background.

Close to the nunnery is another curious site, the **Philaphug Hermitage**. It looks like a pile of ruins but is in fact a succession of small rooms, some of which are painted with frescoes.

In the summer months you may also see nomadic families camping here with their flocks: they stop on the opposite side of the river when moving from pasture to pasture.

Getting there and away It's about 90 minutes' **drive** from Padum to Zangla along a reasonable (though unsurfaced) road. There is one **bus** in each direction (departing from Padum at 16.00 and from Zangla at 08.00) every day except Sunday, though it is more convenient to take a **taxi** from Padum (Rs3,000 return) if you need to get there and back in a day.

If you want to **walk** one or both ways, there are two possible routes, each of around 35km. Following the right bank, the walk takes 7–8 hours via Stong De; on the left bank via Karsha you can reach Zangla in 7 hours.

Where to stay and eat The **Dragon Guesthouse** (3 rooms; m 946 945 1481; **$**) is more of a homestay than a guesthouse. Rooms are very basic but the rate includes both breakfast and dinner. Several families will host visitors in their homes: ask in

If you think you're tough and want a challenge to pit yourself against, look no further than the Chadar Winter Trek, a six-day hike in sub-zero temperatures along the frozen Zanskar River from appropriately named Chilling to Zangla. Night-time temperatures frequently fall to –35°C and rarely climb above –15°C even in the daytime, which is probably a reassuring thing given that you'll be walking on the ice. The trek is possible only in January and February, and started out as a practical means for schoolteachers to get back to Zanskar after their Christmas break, the road from Kargil being closed in winter. *Chadar* means 'blanket', referring to the blanket of ice.

Chilling lies 64km southwest of Leh and is really no more than a small collection of army huts near the end of the road. From the very start of the trek you are out on the ice, waddling like a penguin at first and then slowly gaining confidence and learning how to get your boots to grip. Day one requires just an hour of walking to reach the campsite at **Tilat Sumdo** (3,100m), which lies at – and takes its name from – the confluence of the Zanskar and one of its smaller tributaries.

On day two you'll cover less than 10km, but it takes a full 6 hours. In places where the ice is thin (your guide will know how to spot this, and you will swiftly become adept at recognising it too), you will have to keep to the edges of the river where the ice is thickest, sometimes clambering beneath the overhanging rocks, scrabbling on your hands and knees. Your day's destination is the campsite at **Shingra Koma** (3,170m), which lies directly beneath a steep and imposing rock wall.

The trek from Shingra Koma to **Tibb** (3,225m) is 15km and will take you around 7 hours. It is probably the most tiring day of the route but also the most beautiful, with the landscape a winter wonderland of frozen waterfalls and solid walls of ice. In the afternoon you pass through narrow gorges that, at this time of year, scarcely see any direct sunlight: it's bitterly cold and gloomy, but when you reach this point you know that you are only 2 hours from camp. Rather than pitching on the flat, you'll spend the night sleeping in a natural cave, snug with as many as eight other people.

Day four starts early and begins with a walk amid cliffs and gorges. The highlight of the day is undoubtedly the **Nerak Waterfall**: prayer flags and juniper bushes signal that you are close, and there's a small wooden bridge nearby. The **Nerak campsite** (3,390m) is up a small trail from the river. In total today's trek is 12km and takes 7 hours.

From Nerak you trek for 7 hours to **Lingshed** (3,700m), a village that is only accessible when the river freezes. Here there is a Gelugpa monastery housing 60 monks; it's an important spiritual centre in the region. Camp here overnight.

On day six your destination is **Tsarak Do** (3,400m). It's a 2-hour trek on solid ground from Lingshed back to the river, then a further 5–6 hours along the ice. There is a homestay in the village, or you can camp.

particular for Tundup Tsering or Kalzang Chodak Namgyal. A bed and meals will cost no more than Rs1,000 per person.

PHUKTAL Breathtakingly beautiful Phuktal Gompa lies two days' trek south of Padum in a golden yellow gorge set back from the Tsarap River. It is well worth the effort of getting here, and indeed the journey itself is probably one of the best short

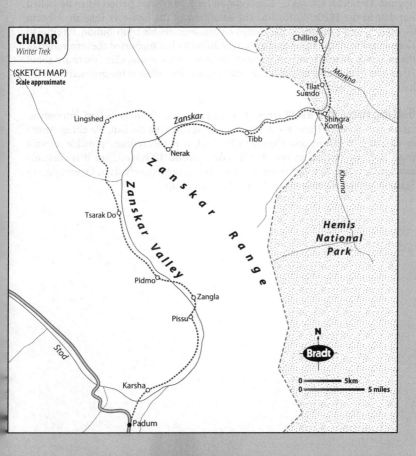

CHADAR
Winter Trek

(SKETCH MAP)
Scale approximate

Chilling

Markha

Tilat
Sumdo

Shingra
Koma

Lingshed

Zanskar

Tibb

Nerak

Khurna

Z a n s k a r   R a n g e

Zanskar Valley

Tsarak Do

*Hemis
National
Park*

Pidmo

Zangla

Pissu

N

Bradt

Stod

0 ——— 5km
0 ——— 5 miles

Karsha

Padum

It is possible to walk from Tsarak Do to **Zangla** (3,491m) via **Pidmo** (3,429m) in 10 hours providing you have the energy and leave very early in the morning, otherwise you will need to split this last part of the trek across two days. Highlights include passing through the gorge at Hanamur, and advancing on Zangla itself, the fort poised high and visible long in advance of your arrival.

If you wish to continue on foot all the way to **Padum** (3,657m), you will require one more day. The route goes via the village of **Pissu** (3,550m).

Note that at research time in 2018 there were rumours that tourists would be forbidden from doing the Chadar Winter Trek after the 2019 season. Ladakh- and Zanskar-based trekking agencies should be able to give you the latest.

treks in Zanskar. Clinging to the cliff around the mouth of a cave, it was founded by the famed translator Phagspa Shesrab in the 12th century and, a century or so later, Sharap Zangpo (a disciple of Tsongkhapa, founder of the Gelugpa school) travelled to Zanskar to convert the gompa to the Gelugpa lineage. While in Phuktal, Sharap Zangpo died, and his relics were interred in the **Sharap Zangpo Stupa**. The gompa continued to play an important part in history, as it was here that the Hungarian linguist Alexander Csoma de Koros stayed for a protracted period when he visited Zanskar in the 1820s. Koros was the co-author of the first-ever English–Tibetan dictionary, and a **plaque** at the gompa commemorates his contribution. It is due to Koros's link with the valley that a Hungarian NGO has supported the restoration of the palace at Zangla (page 177) and other important cultural sites. There are about 70 monks living at the gompa today, many of whom still wear the distinctive yellow hats of their order.

Getting there and away There is a road going south from Padum, but only as far as the village of Raru. From here you must continue on foot, via either Anmu or Chatang to Purne, and thence to Phuktal. It is theoretically possible to walk from Raru to Phuktal in one day (it takes around 12 hours), but it is certainly more pleasurable to split the journey over two more leisurely days. Overnight, try **Stanzin Samphel's Homestay ($)** in Anmu, or camp.

8

The Kashmir Valley

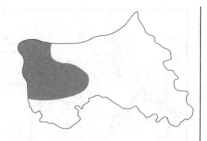

Stretching out along the Jhelum River between the Karakoram and Pir Panjal mountain ranges, the Kashmir Valley stands in stark contrast to the Buddhist desert lands of Ladakh, boasting a lush landscape that is truly alpine in feel and a population that is almost entirely Muslim. Its capital, Srinagar, is a sublimely beautiful lakeside city that should be an integral part of any itinerary (if the ever-fluctuating security situation allows for a safe visit). Whether you are drawn here by the houseboats and *shikaras*, the Mughal Gardens or the trekking or golfing opportunities, you'll quickly see why this was once India's premier tourist destination, and why there's now no reason it should not become so again. Elsewhere in the valley, you'll find the Himalayas' premier ski destination at Gulmarg, a charming hill resort in Pahalgam and one of Hinduism's most important pilgrimage sites at the Amarnath Cave.

It's a fascinating area to explore, with a lot of variety and few other tourists, but be warned: the Kashmir Valley was the point of rupture when India and Pakistan were torn violently into two at the time of partition in 1947. Sadly the wound has never quite healed, with both countries claiming the Kashmir Valley for themselves. Over decades of ongoing unrest, India and Pakistan have fought four wars over Kashmir and thousands of civilians and soldiers have died. After the third war (1971) a Line of Control (LoC) was established through the region that still holds today – indeed, it remains impossible to cross between the two nations anywhere in Kashmir. Unfortunately, no solution to the stalemate has been found and in recent years waves of civil unrest and terrorism have flowed back and forth over the valley. Violence reared its ugly head most recently in late 2019 – just as this book was going to print – with India and Pakistan again edging to the very brink of war and a communications blackout in force. The security situation remains unpredictable, so check before you travel for the current state of affairs (see box, below).

A NOTE ON SECURITY

At the time of going to print in late 2019, the security situation in the Kashmir Valley had become extremely tense thanks to increased militant violence, protests and rioting – not to mention a very strained stand-off with Pakistan. and the decision by the Indian government to revoke Article 370 (see box, page iii). As we're yet unsure how this will play out, we strongly advise that you check with your country's state department on the current situation before travelling.

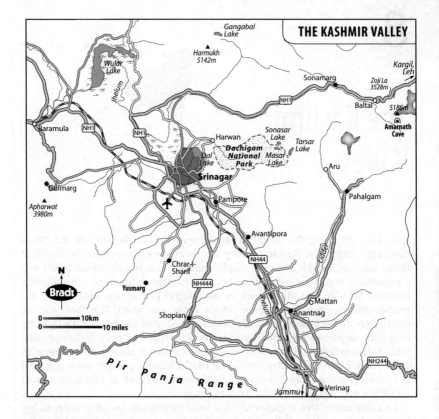

THE KASHMIR VALLEY

SONAMARG *Telephone code: 01942*

Translating as 'the meadows of gold', Sonamarg couldn't be more appropriately named. The valley along which the (admittedly not-too-attractive) town sprawls is a picture-perfect definition of alpine beauty: milky-white rivers crash over rocks, conifer forests and meadows stretch into the distance and, ahead, glaciers crunch and crash down the side of 5,000m+ mountains. The town thrives on domestic tourism, in particular business from pilgrims heading for the Amarnath Cave, but foreign visitors are only just starting to discover the exciting walking trails that wend up and down the surrounding valleys and peaks. There are also opportunities for white-water rafting, scenic picnic spots and places for trout fishing. You can choose from a selection of well-run resort hotels and campsites, and getting here is hassle-free as it is easily accessible from Srinagar.

GETTING THERE AND AWAY Sonamarg lies 87km northeast of Srinagar along the NH1 or, if you're approaching the town from the Kargil direction, 9km west of Zoji La.

In the summer months there is a daily tourist **bus** from Srinagar, which departs at 08.30 from the bus stand next to the tourist reception centre (3hrs; Rs380 return). Cheaper, but much less comfortable, is the regular JKSRTC bus (Rs240 one-way) between Srinagar and Kargil, which passes through Sonamarg. In winter, when the tourist bus is not running, this would be the only option.

By **taxi**, rates from Srinagar start from Rs2,000 one-way and are set by the local taxi union. Given the number of people travelling to Sonamarg each day in summer,

The Zoji La mountain pass lies between Drass and Sonamarg and, at 3,528m above sea level, is the second-highest point along the Srinagar–Leh Highway after Fotu La. A thrilling ride around hairpin bends and with numerous dramatic drops, it's no mean engineering feat and understandably shuts frequently in winter when ice and snow make it even more dangerous than usual. Several short cuts are possible on the way down only as their incline is too steep for vehicles to climb; the yellow bulldozers standing to attention, waiting for action, probably have to clear as many crumpled vehicles as piles of rock and snow.

A 14km tunnel beneath the pass is planned, and will enable the road to remain open year-round, but it is unlikely to be operational for some years to come.

it is likely that you'll be able to find other people willing to share a car. Travelling by taxi is slightly faster than by bus: allow a little over 2 hours.

WHERE TO STAY Sonamarg has a large number of accommodation options, some of them very good. Prices can be high, however, and in the height of summer you'll need to book ahead to be sure of getting a room. July and August are particularly busy.

Hotel Sonamarg Glacier (34 rooms) 241 7217; m 941 947 8432; e hotelsonamargglacier@ yahoo.com. Inspired by a Swiss chalet, the Sonamarg Glacier's rooms are wood panelled, warm & very comfortable. When the cloud lifts, there are chocolate-box views from the balconies. Bathrooms are immaculate & food in the restaurant is excellent. **$$$$**

Namrose Resorts (30 rooms) m 979 792 1087; e namrose-resorts@gmail.com; w namroseresorts.net. This modern hotel on the main road has large & reasonably comfortable rooms but with little character. The food served in the in-house restaurant is decent. Wi-Fi only reaches the rooms in Block A. Satellite TV & AC included. **$$$$**

Paradise Camping Resort m 941 907 4182; e paradisecamps@gmail.com; w paradisecampingresorts.com. On the eastern outskirts of the town, this offers reasonably low prices for expensive Sonamarg. It has large permanent tents with proper beds, little tables & attached bathrooms. There's a restaurant with a limited menu, electric blankets on the beds & evening camp fires. **$$**

WHERE TO EAT AND DRINK Eating out in Sonamarg is more a case of filling your stomach out of necessity rather than for sheer culinary pleasure. There are a few simple options in the town centre serving a mix of basic Punjabi, Tibetan and even Chinese dishes, but in general you're best off eating in one of the hotel restaurants.

OTHER PRACTICALITIES There is a branch of **J&K Bank** with an **ATM** on the main road in the centre of Sonamarg.

WHAT TO SEE AND DO The area around Sonamarg is picture-postcard perfect: even in summer the surrounding peaks are sprinkled with snow, and their lower slopes are covered with meadows and pine forest. Local companies offer **white-water rafting** on the Sindh River (ask your hotel for suggested companies), and it's also a popular spot for **anglers** as there are plenty of trout to catch.

The 4km climb to the **Thajiwas Glacier** takes around an hour on foot and is by far and away the most popular short trek from Sonamarg. Though most of the

The Kashmir Valley SONAMARG

8

The Amarnath *yatra*, or pilgrimage, is the principal draw for domestic tourists coming to this part of J&K: Baltal, not far from Sonamarg, is a popular starting point for the two-day trek (15km each way) through the mountains to the holy Amarnath Cave. The other possible departure point is Pahalgam (page 209), which is a longer three-day route (36–48km depending on exactly where you start and end).

According to the Hindu texts, the Himalayas are the home of Lord Shiva, and it was inside the Amarnath Cave that he recounted the story of creation to his wife, the goddess Parvati. Inside the cave is a large ice *lingam* – a phallic structure that is associated with Shiva – as well as two smaller *lingams* that are said to represent Parvati and Ganesh, the elephant-headed son of Shiva and Parvati. Without a doubt, this is one of the holiest shrines of Hinduism, and it is possible that the cave has been a place of worship since as early as 300BC.

Pilgrimage to Amarnath is only possible from late June until mid-August due to the inclement weather in the mountains. Even so, the route is frequently closed for several days during this period for safety reasons, and people do die each year on the way.

All would-be *yatris* (pilgrims) must register with the Shri Amarnathji Shrine Board (w shriamarnathjishrine.com) prior to starting their pilgrimage. Non-Hindus are welcome to complete the pilgrimage route too, but still have to register and provide a medical certificate confirming they are in good health. Huts and tents are erected along the route to provide shelter, and ponies and porters can be hired to carry your baggage. You must trek with a group, not alone, and due to the physical challenges, children under 13, adults over 75 and women who are more than six weeks pregnant are not permitted to participate.

Finally, even though the scenery is often spectacular, keep in mind that the huge majority of people are here for religious rather than scenic reasons and they can come in huge numbers. At especially auspicious times, there can be thousands of people on the trail and the trek becomes less of a walk and more of a queue. If you want to commune quietly with nature, then go elsewhere.

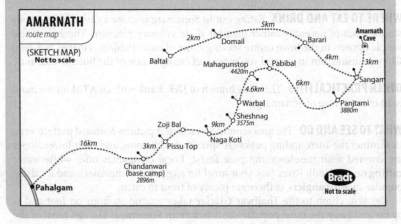

AMARNATH
route map
(SKETCH MAP)
Not to scale

Baltal — 2km — Domail — 5km — Barari — Amarnath Cave
Mahagunstop 4420m
Pabibal — 4km — 3km — Sangam
Warbal 4.6km — 6km — Panjtarni 3880m
Sheshnag 3575m
Naga Koti — 9km
Pissu Top — 3km
Zoji Bal — 16km
Chandanwari (base camp) 2896m
Pahalgam

Bradt
Not to scale

glacier has melted by summer, it is still a glorious place to walk or have a picnic. It is also possible to hire a pony and **horse trek** up here from the stand alongside the Hotel Sonamarg Glacier.

A much longer route is the magnificent **Great Lakes Trek**. Widely regarded as one of the best in Kashmir, this week-long trek, which begins (or ends) in Sonamarg and ends (or begins) in Naranag, takes in seven alpine lakes and three passes over 4,000m altitude. It's just starting to make an impression in international trekking circles, and trekking companies in Srinagar or local guides can help make arrangements.

SRINAGAR   *Telephone code: 0194*

If J&K is the crown of India, then Srinagar is the jewel in that crown. Breathtakingly beautiful as it rises from the mist that hovers in the early morning across the surface of the water in the lakes, the summer capital of J&K is a city rich in history, where the past is worn lightly on the sleeve. Artistic traditions, from carpet making to woodcarving, are still practised in backstreet workshops; architectural masterpieces displaying an array of influences dot the skyline; and the houseboats, where British memsahibs played games of bridge, hippies smoked and The Beatles strummed away the hours under the watchful eye of Ravi Shankar, still float timelessly on the water.

Srinagar is not trapped in the past, however: it is a city moving forward apace. A short tourist boom between 2012 and 2016 meant much new development had started to take place to cope with the expected rush of tourists. The last few years had seen the opening of a cable car to transport visitors to the Makhdoom Sahib Shrine, and the hill atop which the Hari Parbat fort is perched had been turned into an eco-reserve, a haven for local wildlife in an otherwise busy city. However, mid-2016 onwards saw a return to the old ways, with an increase in protests, violence and tit-for-tat killings causing tourism to plummet once again.

HISTORY Though the Kashmir Valley has been inhabited since prehistoric times, and some claim that Srinagar itself is more than 2,000 years old, the earliest major archaeological finds were unearthed at Harwan, 21km from the centre of modern Srinagar. Dating from the early centuries AD, when Kashmir was Buddhist, are the base of a stupa and a chapel. Tiles excavated from the site show the central Asian influence on local costume, and the fragmented terracotta statues of the Buddha are from the Gandharan school of art.

The arrival of the Huns in the 6th century ended this era of civilisation, but the city did eventually recover, and by the late 900s it was capital of the Kashmir Valley. A succession of Hindu rulers controlled the area until the mid-14th century, and many important religious sites, including the Shankacharya Temple, date from this period.

Shah Mir (r1339–42), a Muslim warrior probably from the Swat Valley (now in Pakistan), defeated the last Hindu ruler and formed a dynasty that ruled for the next 200 years. The Jamia Masjid was constructed, as were many of Srinagar's most important shrines, and, with the arrival of the Mughal emperors from the late 1400s onwards, the stunning Mughal Gardens were laid out.

The Mughal Empire disintegrated after 1707 and Srinagar was ruled first by the Durranis and then by the Sikhs. The 1846 Treaty of Lahore passed de facto control of the valley to the British, and their appointee, Gulab Singh, ruled the new princely state of Jammu and Kashmir from both Jammu and Srinagar.

As the summer capital of the state, Srinagar thrived economically and attracted huge numbers of tourists throughout the 20th century, including those travelling on the Hippie Trail. This period of wealth ended abruptly, however, when Srinagar

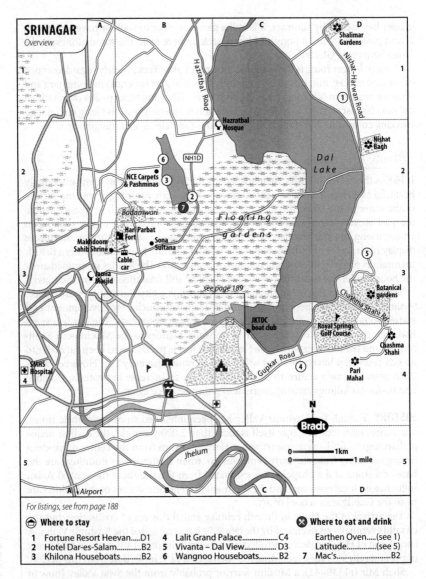

SRINAGAR
Overview

Hazratbal Road

Nishat-Harwan Road

Shalimar Gardens

Hazratbal Mosque

NH1D

6

NCE Carpets & Pashminas

3

2

7

Badamwari

Nishat Bagh

1

Dal Lake

Floating gardens

5

Hari Parbat Fort

Makhdoom Sahib Shrine

Sona Sultana

Cable car

Jamia Masjid

see page 189

Botanical gardens

Chashma Shahi Rd

JKTDC boat club

Royal Springs Golf Course

Chashma Shahi

SMHS Hospital

4

Gupkar Road

4

Pari Mahal

7

N

Bradt

0 ─────── 1km
0 ─────── 1 mile

Jhelum

Airport

For listings, see from page 188

⬣ **Where to stay**

1	Fortune Resort Heevan.....D1
2	Hotel Dar-es-Salam............B2
3	Khilona Houseboats...........B2
4	Lalit Grand Palace................C4
5	Vivanta – Dal View.................D3
6	Wangnoo Houseboats........B2

✖ **Where to eat and drink**

Earthen Oven......(see 1)
Latitude................(see 5)
Mac's............................B2
7

became the focus of separatist violence in 1989, and clashes between the Indian security forces and militants continued throughout the 1990s.

For a few blissful years in the noughties, things seemed to be on the up for Srinagar. The guns were largely laid to rest, a sense of calm started to return and development once again began to take place. All that changed in 2016, though, when Hizbul Mujahadeen commander Burhan Wani, a social media star who had become very popular with a disenchanted Kashmiri youth, was killed during an encounter with Indian security forces. Widespread protests erupted and over the next six months some 96 people were killed and over 15,000 injured. For the 53 days following Wani's death, Kashmir was placed under a curfew. Since 2016 there have been a number of attacks on Indian military and police forces, large street protests and strong crackdowns and curfews imposed by the security forces. Consequently, it is wise to check the latest travel advice before venturing to Srinagar.

GETTING THERE AND AWAY Srinagar is a regional transport hub and, although the railway does not yet reach the city, it is well served with flights, long-distance buses and taxis.

By road Although there are a number of **bus** stands in Srinagar, the principal one you will need is the Tourist Bus Stand [189 B3] (✆ 245 5107) next to the J&K Tourist Reception Centre. You should arrive at the bus stand at least half an hour before the scheduled departure to buy your ticket and get a seat. The following long-distance deluxe coach services depart from here: Delhi (24hrs; Rs1,400/1,650 seat/bunk), Jammu (10hrs; from Rs213), Kargil (7hrs; Rs650) and Leh (2 days with an overnight stop in Kargil; Rs1,300). From the same stand you can also take day trips to Gulmarg (2½hrs; Rs146–213 depending on bus size), Pahalgam (3½hrs; Rs153–224), Sonamarg (3hrs; Rs153–224) and Yusmarg (2hrs; Rs146–213).

Numerous **taxi** firms operate out of Srinagar, so you'll have both a choice of cars and, in low season, the ability to haggle somewhat on price.

By air Srinagar airport (SXR; ✆ 230 3000; w srinagarairport.com) is at the southern end of Aerodrome Road, on the southwestern outskirts of the city. Air Asia, Air India, GoAir, IndiGo, Spice Jet and Vistara all operate multiple daily flights to Srinagar from Delhi (90 minutes; prices from Rs2,800) and also daily flights from Jammu (45mins–1hr; prices from Rs1,200). For details of flights from Srinagar to Leh, see page 40.

Note that even if you have an e-ticket, you will still have to show a print-out of your flight confirmation in order to be allowed inside the terminal building. You may also be subject to additional restrictions on hand baggage at times of increased security concern: check on your flight operator's website for details prior to departure.

Taxis from the airport into the centre of Srinagar cost Rs500 and are available from the Taxi Union Stand.

GETTING AROUND Depending on where you're going, the quickest way from A to B in Srinagar may be across the water. The cost of a *shikara*, the gondola-like water taxis, vary depending on your bargaining ability (don't be surprised if boat owners start the bidding at Rs2,000 for an hour) but in general expect to pay around Rs500–600 per hour. For a short hop from Boulevard Road to your houseboat you'll pay around Rs70.

If you're staying on dry land, local **buses** criss-cross all areas of the city and tickets cost Rs5–6 depending on the route. You can hail a **taxi** or **auto-rickshaw** on the street with ease, and there are also a number of designated Tourist Taxi stands, including one opposite the tourist reception centre. A full day's sightseeing tour, including the Mughal Gardens, Shankacharya Temple and the Old City, will cost in the region of Rs1,850/2,050 for a non air-conditioned/air-conditioned car. For a **radio taxi** at any hour of the day or night, call Snowcabs (✆ 243 2432).

TOURIST INFORMATION The main source of tourist information in Srinagar is the large and modern **J&K Tourist Reception Centre** [189 B3] (TRC Rd; ✆ 959 609 8882; w jktourism.org), which offers a 24-hour information counter, a booking counter for JKTDC hotels and huts (🕘 10.00–16.00) and a wildlife information counter (🕘 10.00–16.00), and staff can provide assistance with houseboat and hotel bookings as well as transport arrangements. In winter (⊕ Nov–Mar 08.00–18.00) it also sells tickets for the gondola at Gulmarg.

Tourist permits If you need a **wildlife permit** to visit Dachigam National Park (page 198), you can get it from the counter in the tourist centre (page 187). **Angling permits** are currently only available directly from the Fisheries Department (Gogribagh; m 959 609 8882). If you do not have the time to arrange these permits yourself, or would like them ready when you arrive in Srinagar, local travel agents will be able to get them for you.

LOCAL TRAVEL AGENTS If you fancy exploring Srinagar and its highlights on foot and want a **local guide**, Renuka and Abeer of **Heritage Walks** (m 990 657 3224; e srinagar.walks@gmail.com) offer fascinating walking tours of the Old City that enable you to get under the skin of Srinagar. Focusing on either architecture or traditional arts and crafts, both guides are knowledgeable and passionate about preserving and promoting Srinagar's cultural heritage. Walks last several hours, are ideal for couples and small groups, and cost from Rs2,000.

Alhabib Travels \ 250 3034; e sales@ alhabibtravels.com; ⨍ @ALHABIBTRAVELS. Run by 2 wonderfully hospitable & knowledgeable brothers, Imtiyaz Bhatt & Hyder Ali, Alhabib is an exceptional outfit. In addition to local travel arrangements in J&K, they offer transfers from Delhi & other hubs & tours of the Golden Triangle.

Destination Paradise Tours & Travels [189 B2] Dal Gate; m 941 901 3256; e latif@destinationparadisetravels.com; w destinationparadise.in. Proprietor Latif spent a number of years studying & working in the US before returning home to Srinagar. He's an attentive guide, thoughtful in his suggestions & well informed about local history & politics. Winter sports & trekking packages are a particular speciality.

Fly Paradise [189 C2] Hotel Paradise, Boulevard Rd; \ 1800 123 2262; e flyparadisetravels@ gmail.com; ⨍ @flyparadisetravels. Young & enthusiastic, Sheikh Danish speaks excellent English & has imaginative ideas for excursions.

Johansen Travel Agency 7A, 1st Flr, Hotel Gulmarg Complex, Boulevard Rd; \ 213 3433; e rashid@johansentravels.com; w johansentravels.com. Established in 1943, Johansen is the oldest travel agency in J&K. Some 75 years on, it caters ably to both domestic & international tourists, has its own fleet of cars & can also provide expedition support.

RM Holidays [189 C3] Yatri Bawan Durganag Complex, Dal Gate; m 990 640 5254; e rmholidays@gmail.com; w rmholidays.com. Small, Srinagar-based operator providing packages to various parts of J&K & also car hire.

🏠 **WHERE TO STAY** Srinagar has a wealth of accommodation options, some of which are world class. In times of peace the city can become very busy in summer and around major holidays, however, so try to book as early as possible to ensure you get your first choice of houseboat or hotel. During more unstable periods prices can plummet as visitors dry up.

All hotels have Wi-Fi unless otherwise mentioned.

✳ 🏠 **Fortune Resort Heevan** [186 D1] (39 rooms) Nishat–Harwan Rd; \ 250 1323; e info@ahadhotelsandresorts.com; w ahadhotelsandresorts.com. Smart, modern & effortlessly stylish rooms with floor-to-ceiling windows, splashes of bold art & quality Kashmiri rugs on the floor. Staff are courteous & professional

& considering the quality the prices are low. **$$$$$**

🏠 **Hotel Dar-es-Salam** [186 B2] (14 rooms) Nagin Lake; \ 242 7803; e info@hoteldaressalam. com; w hoteldaressalam.com. A grand & charmingly faded hotel, Dar-es-Salam has superb views across Nagin Lake. Rooms are large, light &

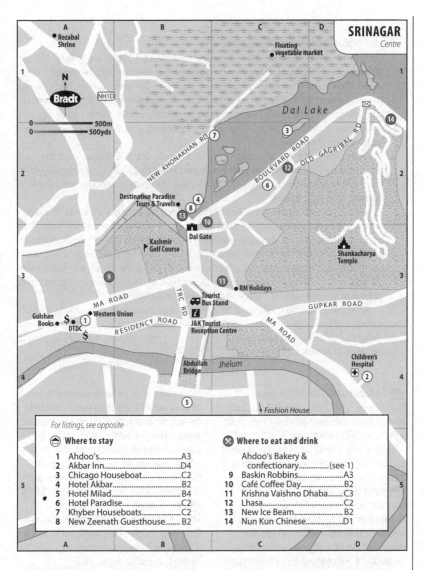

- Rozabal Shrine

N

Bradt

NH1D

0   500m
0   500yds

Floating vegetable market

Dal Lake

7

3

14

BOULEVARD ROAD

OLD GAGRIBAL RD

NEW KHONAKHAN RD

12

6

Destination Paradise Tours & Travels
8   4
13
10

Dal Gate

Kashmir Golf Course

Shankacharya Temple

9

11

RM Holidays

MA ROAD

TRC RD

Tourist Bus Stand

GUPKAR ROAD

Gulshan Books
DTDC
1   Western Union
RESIDENCY ROAD
J&K Tourist Reception Centre

MA ROAD

Children's Hospital
2

Abdullah Bridge   Jhelum

5

Fashion House

For listings, see opposite

Where to stay
1   Ahdoo's.................................A3
2   Akbar Inn..............................D4
3   Chicago Houseboat..............C2
4   Hotel Akbar...........................B2
5   Hotel Milad...........................B4
6   Hotel Paradise......................C2
7   Khyber Houseboats..............C2
8   New Zeenath Guesthouse........ B2

Where to eat and drink
Ahdoo's Bakery &
   confectionary................(see 1)
9   Baskin Robbins......................A3
10   Café Coffee Day.....................B2
11   Krishna Vaishno Dhaba........C3
12   Lhasa......................................C2
13   New Ice Beam........................ B2
14   Nun Kun Chinese...................D1

well maintained & the attractive gardens run down to the shore. Central heating is available in winter. Travel desk can arrange water skiing & motorboat hire. **$$$$$**

✳ 🏠 **Lalit Grand Palace** [186 C4] (113 rooms) Gupkar Rd; ☎ 250 1001; e srinagar@thelalit.com; w thelalit.com. The only heritage hotel in Srinagar, the extraordinarily opulent Lalit Grand is the former palace of Maharaja Pratap Singh, who built the main buildings in 1910. Notable guests include Gandhi & the Mountbattens & you can follow in their footsteps with a stroll through the gardens. Facilities

include indoor & outdoor swimming pools, a spa & several restaurants. Service is top-notch. If you can afford it, then you won't find a more beautiful bed in all of Kashmir. **$$$$$**

🏠 **Vivanta – Dal View** [186 D3] (84 rooms) Dal View, Kralsangi, Brein; ☎ 246 1111; e bookvivanta.srinagar@tajhotels. com; w vivantahotels.com. This rates as one of Srinagar's best hotels because of its position: the dreamy views down across the lakes & the city are quite simply breathtaking. The décor is elegant & understated, the service world class. **$$$$$**

SRINAGAR'S FLOATING PALACES

No trip to J&K could possibly be complete without a night (or, ideally, longer) aboard one of Srinagar's legendary houseboats, the beautifully carved cedar-wood structures that float romantically on lively Dal and quieter Nagin lakes. Originally built by the British to enable them to get around local restrictions on land ownership, the houseboats and the hospitality of the owners have become a Kashmiri institution, with many visitors returning year on year to spend their summers on the water.

There are quite literally thousands of houseboats in Srinagar, and they are regulated by the **Houseboat Owners Association** (250 2545; e khboa@yahoo. com; w houseboatowners.org), which also sets the prices for rooms and can make bookings on your behalf.

Having visited rather a lot of boats, those listed here are our absolute favourites and stand head and shoulders above the rest. That said, we couldn't visit all of them, so there will certainly be gems we've overlooked. Unless you're going on a reliable personal recommendation (and that hopefully includes ours), don't pre-book your houseboat, and especially not in Delhi. Packages are much more affordable if you arrange them directly in Srinagar, and you'll have the opportunity to look at several options before making your final choice.

All of the following boats have Wi-Fi. All of these houseboats are able to provide a variety of meal options, and as dishes are inevitably home-cooked and delicious, it's advisable to have your breakfast and evening meal aboard, even if you plan to be out and about during the day.

Ahdoo's Hotel [189 A3] (24 rooms) Residency Rd; 247 2593; e sales@ahdooshotel. com; w ahdooshotel.com. Between Residency Rd & the river, Ahdoo's boasts clean & subtly toned rooms that come with all the facilities you'd expect for such a hotel. Service is polished. There is a small amount of parking on site. **$$$$**

Hotel Akbar [189 B2] (37 rooms) Dal Gate; 250 0507; e sales@hotelakbar.com; w hotelakbar.com. You can expect a very warm welcome at Hotel Akbar, which is a large, clean property set around an attractive garden. Rooms are spacious & well equipped, beds are comfortable & the staff are helpful. Great location & an understandably popular choice. (Also consider Hotel Akbar's sister property, **Akbar Inn** [189 D4] (behind Children's Hospital, Indra Nagar; m 981 102 8205; **$$$$**), a short drive from the lake.) **$$$$**

Hotel Paradise [189 C2] (approx 100 rooms) Boulevard Rd; m 990 660 0995; e info@

hotelparadisesgr.in; w hotelparadisesgr.in. Smack on Boulevard Rd & with many rooms overlooking the lake, this huge hotel might not have the most appealing exterior, but the rooms are large & clean & you can negotiate good discounts from the rack rate out of season. We ate several tasty meals in the in-house restaurant & there is a rooftop pool. The hotel offers free airport pickup. **$$$–$$$$**

Hotel Milad [189 B4] (25 rooms) Nr Abdullah Bridge; 245 8509; w hotelmilad.com. Great-value if slightly bling rooms, but it's all tidy & welcoming & there's an in-house restaurant serving tasty Punjabi dishes. **$$$**

New Zeenath Guesthouse [189 B2] (15 rooms) Dal Gate; 247 4070. Probably the cheapest accommodation option on Dal Gate, New Zeenath has large, light rooms & is cleaner than you might expect from the price. Some rooms overlook the lake, but they can be a little noisy. The Wi-Fi is reliable. **$**

WHERE TO EAT AND DRINK Funnily enough, though Srinagar's hotel options are superb, the restaurants have some catching up to do. If you are staying on a houseboat, eat the wonderful, home-cooked meals on board; alternatively, opt for one of the tried-and-tested options here. Unless otherwise specified, restaurants are open all day.

✳ 🏠 **Chicago Houseboats** [189 C2] (6 rooms) Dal Lake; 📞 250 2558; m 941 906 1430; e bookings@chicagohouseboats.com; w chicagohouseboats.com. Houseboat owner Ajaz Khar lives with his family behind his 2 boats: he's the 4th generation of houseboatmen to welcome guests to Chicago. Hospitality is in his blood & you won't find a warmer welcome anywhere in the world. Stuffed with regal charm, his boats will float you away to a genteel, bygone age when there was always time for afternoon tea. However many nights you've booked to stay here, you'll wish it were more. The best houseboats on Dal Lake. **$$$$**

🏠 **Khilona Houseboats** [186 B2] (12 rooms) Nagin Lake; 📞 242 2398; m 990 656 6331; w cashmerehouseboats.com; see ad, page 212. Owned by the welcoming Wangnoo family, Khilona's boats are large, lavish & immaculately kept. Brightly coloured cushions complement the rich cedar-wood walls. Highly recommended. **$$$$**

🏠 **Wangnoo Houseboats** [186 B2] Nagin Lake; m 979 610 6666; info@kashmirboats. com; w wangnoohouseboats.com. Far quieter than the boats on Dal Lake, Wangnoo Houseboats, located on Nagin Lake, is a sublime place to relax, read a book & watch the sun set across the water. The Wangnoo family (who also own Khilona Houseboats above) are delightful hosts & the meals served on board are delicious. Though each of the boats is lovely in its own way, if it's available, request the one-bedroom boat: it's a little slice of heaven. **$$$$**

🏠 **Khyber Houseboats** [189 C2] (6 rooms) Dal Lake; 📞 213 3433; e info@ khyberhouseboats.com. Also highly recommended is Khyber Houseboats, whose comfortable boats have tastefully decorated interiors inc chandeliers & wood panelling. **$$$–$$$$**

✕ **Latitude** [186 D3] Dal View, Kralsangi, Brein; 📞 246 1111. Even if you can't afford to stay at the Vivanta (page 189), go here for dinner, soak up the atmosphere & enjoy the incredible views. Latitude has floor-to-ceiling windows overlooking the lake & hills, service is slick & the multi-cuisine meals delicious. Alternatively, the hotel's other restaurant, Jade Dragon (⊕ 12.30–14.30 & 19.30–22.30), serves authentic Sichuan dishes in decadent surroundings in the same price bracket. **$$$$$**

✕ **Earthen Oven Restaurant** [186 D1] Fortune Resort Heevan, Nishat–Harwan Rd; 📞 246 4100. For the best-quality Kashmiri & north Indian dishes you can't do better than this upmarket restaurant inside the Fortune Resort Heevan (page 188). The setting, service & tastes are all a level above most other restaurants in Kashmir. Try the biryanis and kebabs. **$$$$**

✕ **Nun Kun Chinese Restaurant** [189 D1] Reserve Forest Rd; m 979 969 9888. Set back from the road but still overlooking the lake, Nun Kun is run by the state tourist board but the Chinese-influenced food is tastier than you might expect. **$$$**

✳ ✕ **Krishna Vaishno Dhaba** [189 C3] Ram Munshi Bagh, off MA Rd; m 941 901 4707. With chipped Formica-topped tables & chairs & noisily rotating ceiling fans, this little place is far from extravagant. However, its superb traditional Indian vegetarian food & arm-length dosas draw people from across the city & you might even have to queue for a table. **$$**

✕ **Lhasa Restaurant** [189 C2] Lane 3, Boulevard Rd; 📞 250 0517; 📘 @Lhasa1976. Popular Tibetan-themed restaurant with indoor & outdoor tables. Both the Indian & Chinese menus are excellent & are written in English & the AC keeps it cool in the summer heat. **$$**

✕ **Mac's Restaurant** [186 B2] Nagin Lake; m 920 502 2555 Accessible only by shikara, Mac's Restaurant is tucked into edge of the floating gardens, just to the south of Nagin Lake. Though the food is nothing special, the location is fabulous & it's for this reason if nothing else that you should come. **$$**

SHOPPING Of all the destinations in J&K, Srinagar has undoubtedly the best options for shopping. Famed for **handicraft production**, many of its artisans

If you just want a quick snack at the end of the day, New Ice Beam [189 B2] (Dal Gate; ⊕ 09.00–13.00 & 14.30–22.00) has a good selection of ice cream and snacks, and owner Ishfaq is keen to chat. Baskin Robbins [189 A3] (MA Rd; ⊕ 09.00–18.00) also dishes out the cold stuff on a hot day. Coffee and various iced drinks are available at Café Coffee Day (Boulevard Rd; ⊕ 10.00–23.00) inside the Malik Palace Hotel. For tasty sweets and pastries, try Ahdoo's Bakery and Confectionery [189 A3] (Residency Rd; ⊕ 08.00–22.00).

still have their workshops in the winding streets of the Old Town, and Heritage Walks (page 188) can help you find them, to learn about the crafts and, of course, to recommend what to buy. Expect to go home with far more than you intended: thankfully both papier mâché and pashminas are light to carry. Carpets, however, will need to be shipped.

Fashion House [189 C4] The Bund; ☎ 247 4808; ⊕ 09.30–20.00 Mon–Sat. Over the years we've had a lot of tailoring done in India, but nowhere has done a better job than Fashion House. The master has an eye for detail & his cutting of a blazer or gentleman's suit is perfect. Expect to pay Rs1,200 for a made-to-measure shirt & around Rs8,000 for a three-piece suit. Highly recommended.

Gulshan Books [189 A3] Residency Rd; m 959 660 0055; ⊕ 09.30–20.30 Mon–Sat. Quiet, AC store with huge selection of English-language books & helpful staff. You could spend hours rummaging around & it's easily the best bookshop in the state for tomes on Kashmir.

Mr Marvellous Nagin Lake. Cruising around Nagin Lake each morning in his bright red shikara you'll find Mr Marvellous, the aptly named local flower seller. His father, the original Mr Marvellous, featured in a *National Geographic* photo shoot in 1958 & the son has carried on the family business, selling fragrant blooms to decorate the houseboats & charm the guests.

Mr Mehboob Nagin Lake. Yet another floating emporium, Mr Mehboob sells the fine papier mâché that Srinagar is famous for. Though his prices are slightly higher than elsewhere in the city, the quality is high & he'll lay out a carefully chosen selection of wares on the veranda of your boat. Prices start from Rs100 for papier mâché boxes & he also stocks baubles, trays & coaster sets.

NCE Carpets & Pashminas [186 B2] Behind WelcomHeritage Houseboats, Nagin Lake; ☎ 242 1001; e ncegroup@vsnl.com; w ncerugs.com. Genuine pashminas & Kashmiri carpets are expensive, even in Srinagar, so if you want to ensure you're getting the real deal, you have to go to the experts. Visiting the owner, Saboor, is an educational experience: he can arrange for you to watch the carpets being made & will explain painstakingly the manufacturing process, as well as how to identify the different materials & levels of quality. Carpets here start from US$500 & go up to more than US$40,000. Many are investment pieces & all of them are beautiful.

Sona Sultana [186 B3] Saidakadal Rd; ☎ 242 0797. Sona Sultana is primarily a woodcarving workshop rather than a shop, but it also sells finished pieces & it's wonderful to watch the artisans intricately carving everything from decorative boxes & elephant figurines to ornate screens & tables.

OTHER PRACTICALITIES
Communications
✉ **Post office** [189 D1] Boulevard Rd; ⊕ 11.00–20.00 Mon–Sat. Srinagar is home to what is probably the world's only floating **post office**, moored on Boulevard Rd. It is the only houseboat permanently docked on this side of the water & the bright red India Post gives it away in any case. The same boat also houses a small & uninspiring **Philately Museum** that is free to enter.

DTDC [186 A3] Residency Rd; ☎ 247 3242. To send anything of value, it is best to use a courier; DTDC is a reputable company.

Medical

There are pharmacies all over Srinagar, most of which are well stocked & have at least 1 English-speaking member of staff. Particularly convenient are the **Abi Zeenath Medical Hall** (Dal Gate; m 941 994 4559) and **Dhar Brothers Chemists** (Dal Gate; m 990 651 6949), which also benefits from having an attached polyclinic.

✚ **SMHS Hospital** [186 A4] Karan Nagar; ✆ 245 2013; w gmcs.edu.in/SMHS_Hospital. This is the most significant of Srinagar's medical facilities & is also part of the Government Medical College. The hospital has a 24-hour emergency department & well-qualified doctors.

Money

Most of India's banks have branches in Srinagar & there are plenty of 24-hour ATMs. The vast majority of these are on Residency Rd [189 A3] where you'll find **HDFC Bank** & **J&K Bank**, both of which have ATMs, & also **SBI** & **ICICI** ATMs.

If you need to send or receive money, there is a branch of **Western Union** [189 A3] in the Oriental Bank of Commerce on Polo View Rd.

ACTIVITIES

Angling Srinagar's rivers and lakes are rich in fish, in particular the fat brown trout introduced by the British in the 19th century. Fishing is permitted, but you need to get an angling permit from the **Department of Fisheries** (Gogribagh; m 959 609 8882; w jkfisheries.in). Permits can also be obtained at the tourist reception centre (page 187).

Golf Srinagar has a number of golf courses, the most exclusive of which is the 18-hole **Royal Springs Golf Course** [186 D4] Cheshma Shahi, Boulevard Rd; ✆ 250 1158; w rsgc.co.in. Set among 300 acres of rolling hills and, of course, the four springs that give the club its name, Royal Springs also has a pool, a gym and a restaurant. Green fees for non-members are Rs2,500/US$50 for Indians/foreigners.

An alternative option, much closer to the centre of town, is the 18-hole **Kashmir Golf Course** [189 B3] (✆ 247 6677; f @KashmirGolfClub) on MA Road, which is the oldest course in Srinagar. Non-members pay Rs3,000 on weekdays and Rs1,500 at weekends.

Watersports There's a JKTDC **boat club** [186 C4] on Nagin Lake, from where you can try your hand at sailing, kayaking and windsurfing. The clubhouse itself has natural pine interiors and large windows for spectators to enjoy the view. Local travel agents can also arrange white-water rafting on some of the rivers around the city.

If you prefer to explore the water in a more leisurely fashion, hire one of the colourful shikaras (Rs500–600/hr) and be paddled at your leisure among the floating gardens with their bright pink and white lotus flowers.

TREKKING EQUIPMENT HIRE

If you are planning to trek in the mountains around Srinagar and need to hire equipment locally, the most affordable and convenient option is JKTDC at the tourist reception centre (page 187). Authenticity and quality isn't assured, but it has a variety of trekking and camping items available, and sample prices per day/week are as follows:

Four-person tent	Rs300/1,500
Sleeping bag	Rs70/300
Crampons	Rs50/200
Ropes	Rs300/1,500

WHAT TO SEE AND DO Srinagar and its environs are packed with a bewildering array of incredible sites: you'd have to stay for months to be able to see them all and do them justice. Though your personal tastes (natural landscapes, formal gardens, religious buildings, archaeological sites, etc) will inevitably help shape your choice of itinerary, there are some places that no-one should miss: the floating vegetable market and lotus gardens; views across the city from the Hari Parbat fort; and an afternoon in one or more of the world-famous Mughal Gardens.

Badamwari [186 B2] (Nr Hari Parbat; ☉ 09.00–19.00) Historical but not technically a Mughal Garden, this lovely park at the foot of Hari Parbat takes its name from the almond trees (*badam* meaning almond) with which it was originally planted. The garden is especially attractive in the springtime when the almond trees are covered in fluffy white blossom: you can survey the site best from the Hari Parbat eco-reserve (see opposite).

Botanical gardens [186 D3] (Cheshma Shahi Rd; m 969 706 9964; ☉ 10.00–19.00; admission Rs10/5 adult/child) Srinagar's attractive botanical gardens, opened in 1969, complement the Mughal Gardens (see box, page 196) by providing both more informal areas of parkland and, importantly, nurseries for botanical research. In total the garden covers more than 80ha, and over 300 species of plant are represented. The gardens are family friendly and, in addition to picnicking in the grounds (which is especially popular at weekends), you can hire a pedalo on the manmade **boating lake** (Rs50/30mins).

The stunning **Tulip Garden** (☉ Apr only), built in memory of assassinated prime minister Indira Gandhi, is a riot of colour in the springtime, with different-coloured tulips carefully planted in stripes across the hillside to maximise their visual impact. The blooms don't last very long, however, so get there while you can.

Floating gardens [186 C2/3] Though Dal and Nagin lakes look on the map like two separate bodies of water, they are in fact joined with waterways through a labyrinth of floating islands, manmade areas reclaimed from the water where people live but also grow their crops. Like in Venice, water taxis are the only way to travel from A to B, and travelling the backwaters you'll see shikaras carrying children to school and people off to the market or on their way to visit friends.

Exploring any part of these waterways is a delight, but particular highlights are the **Lotus Gardens** where pink and white water lilies and lotus flowers float on the surface. Try to deter your shikara man from picking one for you: they look best in their natural setting.

Business at the floating **vegetable market** [189 C1] (☉ 04.00–06.30 daily) starts even before the sun comes up. Men in their open shikaras haggle enthusiastically for armfuls of knobbly green gourds, white radishes and bundles of spinach. Though large numbers of tourists do come to spectate, this is a real market, the place of choice for local people to buy their vegetables, fruit and fresh flowers.

Hari Parbat Fort [186 B2] (Hari Parbat Hill; ☉ 09.30–17.30 daily) Hari Parbat is actually the name of the hill, but it has come to be used for the fort on top of it too. Legend has it that the hill was once a lake and inhabited by the demon Jalobhava. The demon terrorised local people (as demons are wont to do), and so they called out to the goddess Parvati for protection. Taking the shape of a bird, Parvati flew into the sky and dropped a rock on the demon, crushing him to death. The rock continued to grow until eventually it was as large as a hill. There is a **Parvati Temple** on the western slope.

Many people will tell you that the fort is Mughal, built by Emperor Akbar in 1590, but this isn't actually true: the fortified outer wall was built by Akbar in anticipation of him building a new city inside, but this city never materialised. The present fort dates from 1808 and was built by the Afghan Shuja shah Durrani, though its red sandstone structure is certainly reminiscent of Mughal forts elsewhere.

Having been closed to the public for years, and partially occupied by the Indian army, the Hari Parbat fort finally reopened for tourists at the end of 2013. Relatively little conservation work has so far been done, and so you need to watch your feet as you explore the higgledy-piggledy courtyards, towers, tanks and terraced gardens. Though no longer roofed, the walls (and thus the layout) of internal rooms are still easily visible, and peering out through the archers' slits in the metre-thick walls gives an almost bird's-eye view of Srinagar.

Though you can drive straight up to the gates of the fort, it's far more pleasurable to walk up through the newly designated **eco-reserve**, which is stocked with fruit trees, aromatic plants and other indigenous species. A footpath winds its way from the road (close to Badamwari) up to the fort, with plenty of places along the way to stop and admire the view.

Hazratbal Mosque [186 C2] (Hazratbal Rd; ⊕ closed during prayers) On the western shore of Dal Lake is the pearl-like Hazratbal Mosque. 'Hazratbal' means 'holy place' and is earned by virtue of the fact that the shrine contains a holy relic, a hair of the Prophet Muhammad, referred to as Moi-e-Muqqadas (the sacred hair).

It is said that the hair was first brought to India by a descendant of the Prophet, Syed Abdullah, in the 1600s. The relic passed into the care of a wealthy Kashmiri merchant, Khwaja Nur-ud-Din Ishbari, but was then seized by the Mughal emperor Aurangzeb, who displayed it at the Chishti shrine in Ajmer, Rajasthan. Realising eventually that such a sacred item should not be taken by force, Aurangzeb repented and sent the hair to Srinagar, along with the body of Ishbari, who was recently deceased. Ishbari's daughter, Inayat Begum, became custodian of the relic and established the Hazratbal Shrine in which to preserve it in 1700. The hair was stolen again in 1963, but mysteriously recovered just eight days later. Nobody was ever charged with its theft.

The shrine building you see today, as magnificent in its reflection in the lake water as in reality, is the only domed mosque in the city: the others have distinct pagoda-like roofs. The mosque is relatively modern and was completed by the Muslim Auqaf Trust in 1979.

Jamia Masjid [186 A3] (Ganderbal Rd; ⊕ closed during prayers) Srinagar's main mosque was built in 1398 by Sultan Sikander, and later expanded by his son so that 33,333 worshippers could gather here to pray at any one time. During Friday prayers, the Jamia Masjid is almost full to capacity.

The architecture of the mosque is unique: the 370 pillars surrounding the magnificent courtyard are built from wood, as the area around the city was historically thickly forested. Each column is made from a single tree. Though the layout of the mosque is conventional, the pagoda-like design of the minarets shows the regional influence of Tibetan Buddhism. The building has been destroyed by fire three times, most recently during the reign of Maharaja Pratap Singh, but every time it has been rebuilt to the original design, just as elegantly as before.

The entire area around the Jamia Masjid is being renovated to improve its appearance: new façades on the shops mirror the mosque's own architecture, and there is a visitor centre over the top of the mosque's ablutions area.

It doesn't matter if horticulture isn't your thing: the Mughal Gardens are far more than collections of plants. Built in accordance with traditional Persian garden design, which in turn took its inspiration from the Islamic view of heaven, replete with flowing water, fruit trees and architectural follies, these were the pleasure gardens of the late medieval period. Sensitively restored and lovingly tended by teams of gardeners, they show a human desire and ability, now as when they were first made, to shape the wilderness, to tame aspects of nature to their will.

All of the following sites are open ⏰ 08.00–dusk and charge an admission fee of Rs20/10 adults/children.

CHASHMA SHAHI [186 D4] (Cheshma Shahi Rd) The 'Garden of the Royal Spring' was built in 1632 by Ali Mardan Khan, a noble at the court of Shah Jahan. Steep stone steps flanked with bright flowers lead visitors to the painted Mughal archway that marks the entrance to the garden. Laid out in the traditional Persian style across three terraces, replete with watercourses that delight the local pigeon population as well as small children, and immaculately maintained, the planting is carefully thought out and complements the fountains, watercourses and other architectural features. Though substantially smaller than some of the other Mughal Gardens, Chashma Shahi is a beautiful, calm place and well worth taking time to visit, especially in the early evening. You'll probably see people drinking the water from the springs that give the place its name; although most people seem to think its fine to do so, we've no idea how clean the water really is.

Though they speak little English, the gardeners are happy to chat about their work and will eagerly identify the different plants for you if you don't know quite what you're looking at. They'll also sell you a selection of ten different packets of seeds that they've collected from the garden (Rs100).

NISHAT BAGH ✳ [186 D2] (Nishat–Harwan Rd) On the eastern shore of Dal Lake, with views back across the water, the 'Garden of Joy' is thought to have been commissioned by Asaf Khan, brother-in-law of the Mughal emperor Jahangir, in the early 1600s. It is said that Jahangir's son, Shah Jahan, visited the garden in 1633 and, having repeatedly stated how beautiful he found it, he expected to be given it as a gift. When Asaf Khan demurred (he was, after all, rather fond of his garden himself), Shah Jahan ordered that the garden's water supply, which came from his own Shalimar Garden, be cut off. A servant disobeyed the order, and the garden and its plants were saved.

Nishat Bagh is divided into four equal parts, with a water channel separating each section and leading one's eye to the lake. Originally it had both public areas

In late December 2018, just as Friday prayers were coming to an end, a group of masked men carrying black ISIS flags burst into the mosque and clambered up onto the pulpit shouting slogans. The stunt was condemned by almost all major Islamic and political groups in Srinagar.

Makhdoom Sahib Shrine [186 A3] (Makhdoom Sahib Rd) Getting to the Makhdoom Sahib Shrine is half the fun; there is a cable car (⏰ 10.00–17.00 daily; Rs110 return) and the ride, though short, is very enjoyable. Various issues in the past have meant that the cable car is sometimes closed for long periods.

and a separate private section for the women of the *zenana* (harem), although this is no longer the case today.

The garden has a total of 12 terraces, and it is remarkable how the water flow is manipulated to pass from one to the next: there are successions of pools, chutes, channels and numerous fountains. Equally of note are the wooden *baradari* (pavilion), the octagonal towers flanking what was the *zenana* garden, and the *chadar*, the manmade waterfalls carved from slabs of marble and sometimes elaborately engraved.

PARI MAHAL [186 D4] (Chashma Shahi Rd) Above the Chashma Shahi is the Pari Mahal or 'Fairy Palace'. Founded by Dara Shikoh, the eldest son of Mughal emperor Shah Jahan, in 1635, the garden was originally watered by natural springs, though many of these have now run dry. The garden was built across seven terraces, five of which survive, and they lead up to the central building with its numerous archways. Perhaps originally built as a Buddhist monastery, it was converted by Dara Shikoh into an observatory, as he was a keen and able astronomer.

The Pari Mahal is floodlit at night, and indeed the early evening is the best time to come here. The soft light is flattering to both the buildings and the plants, and there can be no more romantic place from which to watch the sun set across the lake.

SHALIMAR GARDENS ✸ [186 D1] (Nishat–Harwan Rd) The largest and most famous of the Mughal Gardens is Shalimar, 'The Abode of Love'. There has been a structure on the site since the 6th century, but it was Jahangir who built the first garden here in 1619. It was then extended in 1630 on the orders of Shah Jahan, ultimately covering an area of 12.4ha.

The garden is made up of four terraces, the water for which is supplied by a nearby tank and a network of canals lined with chinar trees. The different terraces were originally for the use of the public, the emperor and his *zenana*.

Though the planting is as exquisite as in any of the other Mughal Gardens, it is the buildings that set Shalimar apart. Just above the entrance gate is the **Diwan-i Aam**, the public audience hall where the emperor would sit atop his black marble throne to attend to daily affairs of state. Little save the foundations of the **Diwan-i Khas** (private audience hall) remains, but there are a number of other attractive pavilions, including the **Black Pavilion**, a marble structure in the *zenana* garden, and smaller buildings that would have been used as guardhouses, preventing unwanted visitors from accessing the *zenana*.

Makhdoom Sahib, also known as Hazrat Sultan, was a Sufi saint who lived in Kashmir in the early 16th century. Highly educated, he was a mystic and several miracles are attributed to him: he grew a long, white beard in an instant, and having collected together in his hand the bones of a bird he had just eaten, the bones rejoined and the bird came back to life and flew away.

The shrine is Makhdoom Sahib's burial place, and it remains an important place of pilgrimage for Sufis, many of whom come here to pray. Men and women are welcome in the shrine (though only men are allowed into the inner sanctum). Shoes must be left at the entrance and women must cover their heads.

Rozabal Shrine [189 A1] (Ganderbal Rd) Small and unassuming, the Rozabal Shrine is also one of the most controversial sites in Kashmir: some people, including Muslims belonging to the Ahmeddiya sect, claim that Jesus did not die on the cross but in fact survived the crucifixion, moved to Kashmir to continue his teachings and was eventually buried here (see box, page 126).

Rozabal is, in any case, a holy place for Muslims: it is officially the tomb of Saint Yuz Asaf, and as such it is a place of prayer and quiet reflection. There has been some resistance to tourists coming here sightseeing (as opposed to visiting on pilgrimage) in recent years, so you should take advice locally as to whether or not you are welcome to go inside. In any case, you should behave, dress and speak respectfully here, as you would in any other holy place.

Shankacharya Temple [189 D3] (Shankacharya Hill; ◷ 06.00–18.00) Perched atop the hill, with superb (albeit frequently misty) 360° views down across Srinagar and the lakes, is the Shankacharya Temple. Thought to be the oldest Shiva temple in Kashmir, though previously dedicated to Jyeshthesvara, the current structure dates from the 9th century, though it is likely that it is on the site of an older building. This earlier building probably pre-dates the current temple by 200–300 years. The temple is set on an octagonal plinth (traditionally ascribed to King Gopaditya) and the inner sanctum contains a *lingam*, above which is a decorative ceiling built on the instruction of the Mughal emperor Shah Jahan in 1644.

Note that security around the temple is tight. There is a check at the bottom of the hill and all vehicle passengers must disembark, rejoining their car on the other side of the checkpoint. In the parking area at the top of the hill, 200 stone steps below the temple itself, there is another police checkpoint and you have to pass through a metal detector. Rules for those entering the temple are strict: you may not carry about your person any tobacco or meat products, mobile phones or other electronics.

AROUND SRINAGAR All of the following sites are accessible from Srinagar by taxi or rickshaw.

Harwan The village of **Harwan**, 3km north of the Shalimar Gardens (and so 21km from central Srinagar), looks unremarkable enough from the road. It is, however, the site at which the earliest archaeological discoveries around Srinagar were made, and hence is certainly worth a visit. A J&K Tourism board points you in the direction of the ancient **stupa**, evidence of the area's Buddhist past. The Kushan emperor Kanishka is said to have convened the Great Council nearby, so it is likely that the stupa dates from this period. Neighbouring the stupa site is **Harwan Garden** (◷ 08.00–dusk; admission Rs20/10 adult/child), another formal garden that appears to take its inspiration from the Mughal Gardens, with its lake, canals and chinar trees.

Harwan is also the preferred access point for **Dachigam National Park** (◷ 08.00–dusk), which covers some 141km². A protected area since 1910, the park takes its name from the ten villages that had to be relocated when it was made: Dachigam means '10 villages'. The park sprawls across the Zabarwan Hills and includes a substantial lake, the Sarband. Habitats in the park range from grassland and scrub to coniferous forest, and the mammal population includes otters, marmots and weasels, Himalayan black and brown bears, leopards and leopard cats, musk deer and jackals. The birdlife is similarly diverse, with regular sightings of black bulbuls, golden orioles, pygmy owlets, the Kashmir flycatcher, streaked laughingthrushes and bearded and Himalayan griffon vultures, among others.

Note that to gain access to the park you will need to get a **permit** from the chief wildlife warden (Wildlife Dept, nr Lalit Grand Hotel, Srinagar; ✆ 250 1069; Rs25) beforehand. It is issued while you wait, though allow two hours to be on the safe side.

Pandrethan Temple
Some 6km southeast of Srinagar, this temple dedicated to Lord Shiva was built between 913 and 921 and is situated at the centre of a pond or tank fed by a natural spring. It is the draining of this pool over the past millennium that has caused the structure to shift: it now tilts by approximately five degrees. The temple is relatively small, square and is built of stone. Its stone ceiling, carved with geometric patterns, is, remarkably, original and intact, and the temple attracted the attentions of numerous 19th-century visitors.

Pandrethan is situated inside an army cantonment, so you'll need to get permission from the officers on duty before going inside.

Naranag
Some 50km northeast of Srinagar is **Naranag**, a village set in a scenic valley. Though the flower-filled meadows have their own charm in springtime, the principal attraction here is the group of **Naranag Temples**, one of which is very similar in style and age to the Pandrethan Temple (see above). Dedicated to Shiva by King Laladitya in the 8th century, the temples are built of stone, and the main complex (which includes seven different temple structures) is really quite impressive indeed. Look out for the elaborate architectural details such as the trefoil arches, Graeco–Roman-style pediments and a vast gateway like the one at Avantipora (page 206).

From Naranag village it is a 9-hour trek to the high-altitude **Gangabal Lake**. This is a sacred site, considered by some Hindus to be as holy as Haridar, and in September each year a number of Kashmiri pandits still take a three-day *yatra* to the shore. Stunningly beautiful, unspoilt and a prime spot for camping, it is understandably popular with tourists too, many of whom trek up here and then spend a few days among the shepherds, fishing for the fat brown trout that thrive in the waters of the lake.

Wular Lake
Northwest of Srinagar, some 60km away, is this lake fed by the Jhelum River. Wular appears in a number of ancient texts, including the writings of the Persian traveller and writer Al Biruni (930–1031). You'll probably hear guides and local people tell you that it's Asia's largest lake, but this is true only if you discount the many other freshwater lakes that are in fact larger, such as Lake Baikal. More based on fact is that Wular is recognised as a wetland of international importance: it supports a large number of species of bird (including kites, sparrowhawks and eagles) and also vast numbers of fish. Fishing is a major local business, and more than 8,000 fishermen are thought to make their living from Wular's waters.

Since 2011, J&K Tourism has been developing various opportunities for **watersports** on the lake, including boat hire and waterskiing.

GULMARG *Telephone code: 01954*

In the 1500s, Gaurimarg ('the fair one') was renamed Gulmarg ('meadow of flowers') by Sultan Yusuf Shah. Both names are equally apt; set among rolling hills and thickly carpeted with flowers throughout spring and into summer, it's an idyllic place to walk and picnic when the weather is warm.

It's in winter, however, that Gulmarg comes into its own, as India's winter sports capital and the centre of the country's fledgling ski industry. The gondola is open year-round and from November to March transports skiers and snowboarders 5km

8

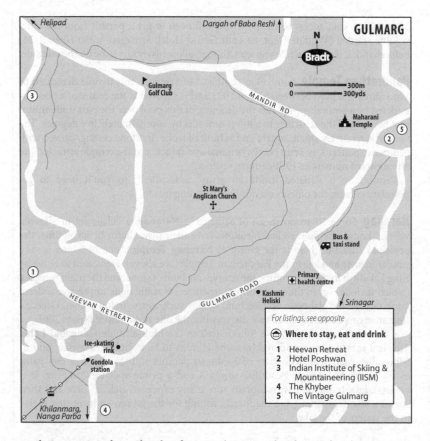

For listings, see opposite

🖐 **Where to stay, eat and drink**

1 Heevan Retreat
2 Hotel Poshwan
3 Indian Institute of Skiing &
   Mountaineering (IISM)
4 The Khyber
5 The Vintage Gulmarg

Map labels: Helipad · Dargah of Baba Reshi · N · Bradt · GULMARG · Gulmarg Golf Club · MANDIR RD · 0 ——— 300m · 0 ——— 300yds · Maharani Temple · St Mary's Anglican Church · Bus & taxi stand · Primary health centre · HEEVAN RETREAT RD · GULMARG ROAD · Kashmir Heliski · Srinagar · Ice-skating rink · Gondola station · Khilanmarg, Nanga Parba

up the mountainside to a height of 4,267m (so proceed with care if you've just come straight from the plains of India), and you can ski all the way down to Tangmarg. There are some excellent accommodation options (albeit all at the more expensive end of the spectrum) to choose from, and a lively crowd of youthful skiers (both Indians and foreigners) means you'll have plenty of playmates with whom you can enjoy the après ski.

HISTORY Easily accessible from Srinagar, Gulmarg has been a popular tourist spot ever since the medieval period. The Mughal emperor Jahangir came here to collect flowers for his garden, and the British found it a cool and pleasant playground where they could escape both the city and the heat of the plains. The British built the golf course and the Anglican church (page 203), and Gulmarg soon became a centre for golf competitions and general fun and frolics until its links with the outside world were severed by the militancy in 1989. Now on the road to recovery, its gondola was installed in two stages in 1998 and 2005, and the town hosted India's National Winter Games in 1998, 2004 and 2008. Sadly, these games seem to have faded away somewhat.

GETTING THERE AND AWAY Gulmarg lies 56km (2hrs) to the west of Srinagar, and is easily accessible by road. **Tourist buses** depart from the TRC Stand in Srinagar (2hrs; Rs146–213 one-way). **Taxis** will charge you Rs1,850 one-way for a non-air-conditioned car.

GETTING AROUND Gulmarg town is best explored **on foot**. If you plan to ski or otherwise go up into the hills, however, you'll need to take the **gondola**. From the base station you ascend the 400m to Kongdori (Rs400), then the second phase takes you up to Aparwath (Rs600). There is also a **chair lift** (Rs300) from Kongdori to Marry Shoulder. In winter, however, it is more cost-effective to get a ski pass (see box, page 202).

TOURIST INFORMATION Information about skiing in Gulmarg, and also use of the gondolas and chair lift, is available online from w skigulmarg.com.

Courses for all levels and information for advanced skiers are available from the **Indian Institute of Skiing and Mountaineering** (Nr Gulmarg Golf Course; 254 480; e skitigers@gmail.com; w iismgulmarg.in). For more general information about what to see and do in Gulmarg, you can try the Tourist Reception Centre in Srinagar (page 187), though don't expect a massive amount of solid information.

WHERE TO STAY AND EAT *Map, opposite*
Though Gulmarg does have some excellent accommodation options, they are quite expensive by local standards. If you are travelling on a budget, you will find it cheaper (though not as convenient) to stay in Srinagar and take the bus up here for the day. In terms of dining, most people choose to eat in their accommodation.

* **Heevan Retreat** (35 rooms) 0194 250 1323; e info@ahadhotelsandresorts.com; w ahadhotelsandresorts.com. Crisp white linens in cosy wood-panelled rooms welcome you to the restful Heevan Retreat. Staff are friendly, food in the restaurant is good & there's a games room with snooker tables to enjoy in the evenings. There's also a gorgeous lounge area with a big open fire – the perfect setting to recount the day's skiing & walking antics. **$$$$$**

The Khyber (80 rooms, 4 cottages) 254 666; e sales@khyberhotels.com; w khyberhotels. com. With a blissful location buried in the pine forests, this is Gulmarg's most upmarket resort. Built like an Alpine chalet, the large – & overly stately – rooms have teak floors & Kashmiri carpets. Meals are served in 1 of the 4 restaurants & cafés. There's a fabulous indoor pool & spa too. **$$$$$**

Hotel Poshwan (43 rooms) 254 506; e manager@hotelposhwan.com;

w hotelposhwan.com. Substantially cheaper than many of Gulmarg's hotels, Poshwan is centrally located & warm with wood-panelled walls & ever-so-frilly bedspreads, but it's a bit scruffy around the edges. **$$$$**

The Vintage Gulmarg 9796 100444; e info@thevintage.in; w thevintage.in. Externally the design of this hotel is a little abrupt, but internally you'll discover warm, comfortable rooms with attractively carved wooden bed heads, thick duvets, wardrobes & excellent bathrooms. There's a good restaurant & even a spa to ease away the aches from a day's skiing. **$$$$**

Indian Institute of Skiing and Mountaineering (IISM) Nr Gulmarg Golf Course; 254 480; e skitigers@gmail.com; w iismgulmarg.in. If you're a ski fanatic, the obvious place to stay is at the IISM. Rooms are large, comfortable & warm, bathrooms are clean & there's a restaurant on site. **$$$**

OTHER PRACTICALITIES There is a primary **health centre** on Gulmarg Road where you can get basic treatment. In the event of a serious accident, however, you'd need to go to the A&E department at the hospital in Srinagar (page 193). There's a J&K Bank **ATM** in the centre of Gulmarg.

ACTIVITIES
Golf If you fancy a putt on the greens, **Gulmarg Golf Course** (Outer Gulmarg Link; 254 507, 254 424; m 990 889 9111; ☉ Apr–Nov) lies at 2,650m above sea level, and hence is India's highest course. It was established by British colonel Neville

Chamberlain in 1890 (though at this early stage the course had just six holes) and was expanded in the 1920s. The first championship match was played here in 1922. Numerous competitions were held here throughout the 20th century, including the Northern India Cup, which was hosted at Gulmarg until it shifted to Delhi in 1989.

Today Gulmarg Golf Course is, at 7,505 yards, the longest golf course in India, and the 18 holes have a par of 72. The course was redesigned in 2011 and one of its greatest attractions (other than, of course, the golf) is the numerous species of wild flowers that are in full bloom on the fairways from June until September. The course is also renowned for its mischievous crows who take great delight in stealing golf balls!

Green fees are Rs800/1,200 for Indians/foreigners, regardless of which day of the week you play, and caddies can be hired for Rs300–500. Note that you need to bring your own golf balls, but you can hire clubs.

Winter sports If you're coming to Gulmarg in the winter, the chances are that you are coming to **ski**. Ski passes (see box, below) are a fraction of the price of those in Europe, the ski season lasts until April and the snow is very reliable, the slopes are gloriously uncrowded, and you can start from a dizzying height of 4,267m. Even if you're a pro, tuition by the **Indian Institute of Skiing and Mountaineering** (page 201) might prove tempting given the low prices. Its 14-day ski school, for example, will set you back the princely sum of Rs7,000 for those under 25 and Rs14,000 for anyone else. Do note, however, you'll need to book as far in advance as possible because demand generally exceeds supply.

There are three or four rental shops hiring out ski equipment and a (limited) range of snowboard gear. The equipment isn't always in the best of condition so

SKI PASSES

Ski passes in Gulmarg are issued by Gulmarg Gondola or, to give the company its official, rather more unwieldy name, the J&K State Cable Car Corporation. Prepaid ski passes can be purchased online (w gulmarggondola.com), and they're also available from the Tourist Reception Centre in Srinagar (page 187) and at the gondola base station. You pay separately for phases 1 and 2 of the gondola and for the chairlift, unless you buy a season pass.

The prices below are given in rupees.

Indians

	Phase 1	Phase 2	Chairlift	All lifts
One-time	370	480	270	
Day pass	740	1,210	700	
Week pass	3,150	7,130	3,000	
Season pass				36,680

Foreigners

	Phase 1	Phase 2	Chairlift	All lifts
One-time	370	480	270	
Day pass	1,210	1,900	1,200	
Week pass	6,050	9,490	5,000	
Season pass				36,680

check everything thoroughly first and don't expect to pay much less for rental than you would at a European ski resort.

Gulmarg isn't like most Western ski resorts in having set colour-graded runs. Instead, what you have is one main, patrolled and organised area directly above the village, which is called the Gondala Bowl. There are various route options here, but none are colour graded in a meaningful sense. The rest of the slopes, which is the great majority of the Gulmarg ski area, are unpatrolled and what would be termed as off-piste in a Western resort.

Take note that the ski lifts at Gulmarg can be like an uncooperative teenager and breakdowns are not unheard of. It's best to purchase only single-day tickets to avoid any wasted days, as you won't likely be refunded for days when the lift isn't working.

Heli-skiing is increasingly popular in the resort, and surprisingly affordable (though make sure you are adequately insured). **Kashmir Heliski** (c/o Hotel Global; m 959 625 1399; w kashmirheliski.in) arranges both heli-skiing and heli-boarding, as well as guided backcountry skiing. It offers a flexible helicopter charter package for Rs60,000 per day, which includes up to five runs.

There is also an **ice-skating rink** on the corner of Gulmarg Road and Heevan Retreat Road, and you can try **tobogganing** and **snow scooters**.

WHAT TO SEE AND DO If skiing is not your thing, or you fancy a few days off, Gulmarg has a number of interesting sites to keep you entertained. **St Mary's Anglican Church** stands proudly in the midst of the golf course. Dating from 1902, it certainly wouldn't look out of place in an English village. A little newer (1915) is the **Maharani Temple** (also known as the Mohineshwar Shivalaya), a curious, cone-shaped shrine that was used by the Dogra rulers. The temple shot to fame in the Bollywood film *Aap ki Kasam*, as one of the main songs was recorded here.

AROUND GULMARG A 6km trek east from Gulmarg (ask for directions) brings you to gorgeous **Khilanmarg**, by turns a snow- and flower-carpeted meadow from where it is possible to see the impressive mountain peak that is Nanga Parba (7,100m).

A similarly easy walk (8km) leads to the **Dargah of Baba Reshi**. The saint was a noble at the court of King Zain-ul-Abidin in the mid-15th century, but he renounced all worldly ties to follow the spiritual leader Sheikh Nur-ud-Din Noorani. When Baba Reshi died in 1480, he was buried here, and his tomb became a place of pilgrimage for Kashmiri Muslims. The tomb is east of Gulmarg and is best reached by following the very quiet country road leading off the main Gulmarg–Tangmarg road. Ask for the village of Ramboh, and the shrine is just on the edge.

THE SOUTHERN KASHMIR VALLEY

Although easy to access from Srinagar, the southern Kashmir Valley features rarely on the itineraries of tourists. If you have the time, though, it is a region well worth exploring, home to a heady mix of temples, religious legends and valuable spices.

PAMPORE AND AROUND (*Telephone code: 01933*) A small and unremarkable ribbon development along the main highway, Pampore lies just 14km to the south of Srinagar. It is famed for its saffron production (see box, page 204), and indeed this is the main reason for its existence, though inevitably the saffron crocuses are grown in the surrounding fields and not in the town itself.

Getting there and away All buses heading south from Srinagar's **Panthchowk bus station** pass through Pampore (30mins; no more than Rs10).

What to see and do The principal attractions of Pampore are the **fields of saffron** surrounding the town. Though there's little to see for much of the year, in the autumn it looks as though a carpet of violet and mauve has been thrown across the land. One of the largest local growers is **Kashmir Kissan Kasser** (Chandhar Pampora; m 990 687 5847), around 5km southeast of Pampore proper in the Chandhar neighbourhood, whose packaging is recognisable by the emblem of a man driving two oxen, and then a crocus bulb. The owner speaks some English and is happy to talk about his crocuses, his factory and the process of making saffron.

In Pampore itself you will find the **Khanqah-i-Khawaja Masood Wali**, the last surviving wooden *khanqah* (shrine) in Kashmir. Khawaja Masood was a prominent trader in the late 1500s, but he gave up his worldly wealth to move closer to God. His *khanqah* is built over two floors, and though many hideous additions have been made to the structure, its original beauty is still just about discernible.

On the northern edge of Pampore at Namblabal is the 15th-century **Shrine of Mir Syed Ali Hamdani**. A Persian Sufi and poet, Hamdani was influential in spreading Islam in Kashmir, and he is credited with shaping much of the unique

KASHMIRI SAFFRON

Saffron is the colour of Greek mythical passion, the scent of amorous queens and the taste of the finest Indian and Persian dishes. From the fabric dye of the early Buddhist monks to an anti-depressant tea of the modern era, saffron has been widely prized, traded, used and abused.

The humble *Crocus sativus* corm (not bulb) from which saffron is derived originated in Turkey and through the twists and turns of history found its way into the hands of an *arhat* (Buddhist missionary), Madhyantika, who is credited with introducing saffron to Kashmir in the 5th century BC. Where he got the corms from is unrecorded, but once in Kashmir they flourished in the light soils surrounding Pampore, and from there saffron spread to the rest of India. The Buddha loved the saffron dye so much that on his death those monks close to him decreed saffron to be the official colour for Buddhist mantles and robes, and so it has been since.

Each purple crocus blossom contains three stigmas, which are painstakingly hand-plucked from the flower in the early morning during harvesting. In October, the warm and gentle wind destined for the Himalayas makes the myriad mauve flower heads rock as though they are a violet sea. The scent is heavenly, as is the setting before a mountain backdrop. The harvest lasts for two to three weeks, ending in mid-November, after which the fields look quite bare.

Each one of the plucked stigmas forms a delicate, red saffron thread. It takes more than 85,000 stigmas to produce a kilo of raw saffron and, once dried and ready for packaging, this represents just 200g of marketable product. It is a labour of love indeed. Known locally as *kesar*, the stalls lining the road at Pampore sell tiny plastic boxes of the precious spice for a fraction of what you would pay at home, and it's an easily transportable souvenir that will bring pleasure for months to come.

Indo-central Asian culture that we associate with Kashmir today. Built by Hamdani's son between 1393 and 1405, this shrine too has been very badly damaged by vandals over recent years, but there is surviving woodwork beneath the roof that is of great architectural significance.

YUSMARG AND AROUND (*Telephone code: 01951*) Meaning 'the meadow of Jesus', Yusmarg is a glorious alpine valley that local people believe Christ once visited (see box, page 126). With grassy pastures that slowly give way to dense pine forest, all framed by a mountainous backdrop, it is exceptionally photogenic and a prime spot for short walks and picnics. It also has the advantage of being significantly quieter than the likes of Sonamarg and Gulmarg.

Getting there and away Yusmarg is 47km southwest of Srinagar, towards the end of a main road. The easiest and cheapest way to get here is by **bus**; you can hop on the ordinary J&K State Road Transport Corporation (JKSRTC) service (2hrs; from Rs146 each way), or in summer J&K Tourism Development Corporation (JKTDC) also runs its own daily service (Rs360 return). A **taxi** will cost about Rs2,500 return.

Note that in winter the road is only open as far as Chrar-i-Sharif, so after this point you would have to proceed on foot.

Where to stay and eat As relatively few visitors come to Yusmarg, the only accommodation option is the **JKTDC Tourist Bungalows and Huts ($$–$$$)**. Also known as Hotel Kongposh, it provides double rooms and whole huts but, if your budget won't stretch that far, dorm beds are also available for a very affordable Rs250. They also run a **restaurant ($$)** nearby serving basic Indian and continental dishes.

What to see and do It is a gorgeous, 10km **trek** from Yusmarg to the frozen lake at **Sang e safed**, and is easily doable in a day by someone of moderate fitness. The lake remains frozen for much of the year, and it is possible to camp on the shore, but note that the weather at this altitude can change unpredictably, so carry plenty of warm clothing with you. Rather less popular, but no less scenic, is the trek to **Tosa Maidan**, a vast meadow where Gujjar nomads graze their livestock. Used as an army firing ground since 1964, it re-opened to the public in 2015. Getting to the meadow requires you to cross the **Basmai Gali Pass** (3,962m), which was the traditional route from Kashmir into the Punjab.

AROUND YUSMARG Just before you reach Yusmarg you come to the bowl-shaped valley of **Dudhpathri**, a place poetically described as the merger point between the crystal-clear waters of Pahalgam and the mountains and meadows of Gulmarg. This is virgin territory, yet to be discovered by most tourists, so if you like your wilderness tranquil but still accessible by bus, this is the place to come. It is here that you will find the **shrine of Hazrat Sheikh Nur-ud-Din Wali**, which is surrounded by seven springs. A mystic and Sufi saint, he stayed and prayed at Dudhpathri for 12 years, teaching Islam to the local people. Legend has it that when he struck the ground, water and milk burst forth, and this could be the source of Dudhpathri's name, *dudh* being the word for milk.

Although you can get to Dudhpathri by bus, it's a mission that isn't without its complications. Firstly, you need to get a bus to Khan Sahib and then another – infrequent – on from there. Most people end up just renting a taxi.

The town of **Chrar-i-Sharif** is around 20km from Yusmarg, and in winter it's as close as you can get to Yusmarg by road. The settlement has grown up around the sacred, 600-year-old **shrine of Sheikh Noor-ud-din Noorani**, a poet who espoused the teachings of Islam through his verse. Also known as Alamdar-e-Kashmir (the flag bearer of Kashmir), Sheikh Noor-ud-din Noorani was a Sufi saint born in India in 1377. Legend has it that he refused to drink milk for the first three days of his life, at which point the Yogini Lal Arifa fed him from her own breast. While he was still in the cradle, she named him her spiritual heir. The sheikh's teachings spoke to both Hindus and Muslims in the valley: he preached non-violence, tolerance of other faiths, and vegetarianism. When he died, 900,000 people came to his shrine (already erected by a disciple on the site where he would come to pray). The shrine has twice been destroyed (most recently by fire in 1995), but each time it has been rebuilt, and people have lost none of their reverence for it. To this day, Chrar-i-Sharif is considered among the holiest shrines in India.

AVANTIPORA (*Telephone code: 01933*) Today a small and unassuming town spread out along the highway, Avantipora was once the capital of King Awanti Varman (855–83), from whose name Avantipora (Avanti's city) is derived. The main reason to come here is to see the two magnificent stone temples he built. The twin **Avanti Shovra** and **Avanti Sawami temples** (☉ 07.30–19.30; combined admission fee Rs200; camera fee Rs25) lie 500m apart in the centre of town, surrounded by modern development. Dedicated to Shiva and Vishnu respectively, they both date from the mid-9th century and, having been severely damaged by earthquakes at some time in their history, were only re-discovered during excavations by British archaeologists in the early 1900s.

The temples have been well restored, however, and you get a good sense of both the scale and the grandeur of the original structures. The majority of the pillars (or at least their bases) have been put back upright, enabling you to appreciate just how tall the inner sanctums would have been. Many of the stone construction blocks are richly carved, including with scenes of dancing girls and *afsaras* (angel-like figures).

Of the two temples, Avanti Shovra is generally quieter, and the curator may well spot you across the site and come over to show you things you'd otherwise be likely to miss. Avanti Sawami is, on balance, more impressive, but you might have to share it with a crowd. If you missed the opportunity to buy saffron in Pampore and are having regrets, there's a stall selling dried fruits and saffron immediately opposite Avanti Shovra.

While driving through the town, you will also see Avantipora's attractive **tiered mosque**, which is painted in white and green, the traditional colours of Islam.

Should you need to stop for cash, **J&K Bank** has an ATM on the main street in Avantipora, not far from the temples.

Getting there and away Avantipora lies roughly halfway between Srinagar and Anantnag, right on the national highway. All of the **buses** between these two cities drive through here, so taking one of them and jumping off early is the best way to reach the town. On the cheapest **bus**, expect to pay Rs25 (1½hrs).

The temples are both on the left-hand side of the road (as you are **driving** south) and are both easy to spot. For self-drivers, there is a **car park** opposite the Avanti Sawami Temple; outside the Avanti Shovra Temple you have to park on the road.

SHOPIAN (*Telephone code: 01933*) A district headquarters since the 1870s, Shopian marks the northern end of the historic Mughal Road (see box, opposite),

THE MUGHAL ROAD

The 84km Mughal Road stretches from Bafliaz in Poonch district to Shopian and was first used by the Mughal emperor Akbar during his conquest of Kashmir in 1586. The ties with the Mughals continued beyond this point, however, as it was while returning along this same road in 1627 that his son, the emperor Jahangir, died. His entrails were buried at Chingus Saria, and the rest of his body was carried on to Lahore.

For much of its history, the road would have been little more than a track, the high-altitude stretches in particular (it reaches a height of 3,500m) making it impassable by vehicles for much of the year. From the 1950s onwards the possibility of metalling the road was mooted, but though construction did begin in the late 1970s, it halted when the militancy began and the bridge at Bafliaz was targeted. When security improved in the mid-2000s, construction started again, and by 2013 the entire route was open with dual carriageways.

In addition to its Mughal links, the road is also home to numerous other historical sites, including several caravanserais, a Sufi shrine at Pir Ki Gali, and the Noori Chamb Waterfall, where Jahangir's favourite queen took her baths. The route is spectacularly beautiful, cutting through the meadows, valleys and passes of the Pir Panjal range, and also through a section of the remote Hirpora Wildlife Sanctuary where a variety of rare species, including the Markhoor goat, roam free.

which has recently been restored. History buffs will get a thrill out of just driving along this spectacular road, knowing that they are following in the footsteps (or, more likely, hoofprints) of the Mughal emperors as they wound their way north to Kashmir.

Getting there and away Shopian is almost due south of Srinagar, but lies to the west of the main highway. There are regular **buses** here from Srinagar (2hrs; Rs30 one-way).

ANANTNAG (*Telephone code: 01932*) A sprawling, ugly town, Anantnag has few redeeming qualities save its transport links to other destinations and its proximity to the remarkable **Martand Sun Temple** near Mattan, some 24km to the east. Built by King Lalitaditya (r724–60), this impressive temple comprises a central oblong sanctum, around which are arranged various small shrines. Substantial parts of the structure are still standing, many of the columns are still upright, and the carvings are well preserved. Attractive flower beds are laid out in the shape of a sun and rays, and the site looks particularly fine in the early evening light. Situated near the district jail in Kehrbal village, the temple is a twisty 4km from Mattan proper. In the centre of town you'll also find a more **modern temple** (⊕ 04.00–21.00) made of white marble.

Almost everything you'll need in Anantnag is situated on the main road through town, KP Road. This includes a **post office**, medical facilities (the **Al Raheem Polyclinic** and **Jan Medical Care** pharmacy), a branch of **HDFC Bank** and **ATMs** belonging to J&K Bank, SBI and PNB.

Getting there and away Anantnag is a major transport hub in the Kashmir Valley, so the chances are that you'll have to pass through here, and possibly stop a while to change vehicles. Minibuses and taxis all stop at the **taxi stand**, which is near to the Government Degree College. Intercity **buses** go from Anantnag across J&K and further afield: to or from Srinagar it's Rs30 (1½hrs); to Jammu it's Rs199 (6½hrs); and if you're going all the way to Amritsar it's Rs346 (10hrs). A seat in a **shared taxi** to/from Srinagar costs Rs80.

Though you might see signs in Anantnag for the **railway station**, this is, as yet, not actually connected to the Indian railway network.

VERINAG (Telephone code: 01932) Just off the Srinagar–Jammu Highway, the ancient spring at Verinag is the source of the Jhelum River. The central site in Verinag is the **natural spring** (admission Rs24), known locally as the Mughal Gardens, from which the Jhelum River flows. Legend has it that the goddess of the river, Vitasta, wanted to burst out from the rock here, but when she did so she found Shiva standing on the spot and was forced to choose another spring a short distance away. Dissatisfied with the way it looked, the Mughal emperor Jahangir constructed a vast **octagonal tank** around the spring in 1620, which he envisaged as the centrepiece of huge pleasure gardens and a palace. During his lifetime Jahangir expressed his desire to be buried by the spring when he died, but his wishes were never honoured and he was interred instead in Lahore.

The turquoise waters in the tank are striking, but it is the surrounding structure that we love. Each of the 24 surrounding arcade arches is perfectly proportioned and built from a creamy stone. In one of the arches you will find a **Shiva** *lingam*, and into the walls elsewhere are set two **stone slabs** inscribed with Persian prose, the most important of which reads:

> The king of seven kingdoms, the administrator
> of justice, the father of victory, Nur-ud-din, Jahangir
> son of Akbar, the martyr king, halted at this spring
> of God's grace in the 15th year of his reign. This
> construction was made by order of His Majesty.
> By Jahangir, son of King Akbar,
> This construction was raised to the skies.
> The architect of intelligence got its date –
> 'May the mansion last for ever together with the spring Vernag!'

Downstream from the tank lies the **garden**, with its crumbling pavilions and *hammams* (bathhouses). The traditional *char bagh* design has been altered slightly to accommodate the steep topography of the site, but the rectangular shape, the tank at the top and the division of the different garden areas with water channels is certainly in keeping with the style.

Immediately outside the Mughal complex is the **Nilanag shrine**, which is dedicated to Shiva. 'Naga' means 'deity of the spring', and Nilanag is the chief of spring deities, so this site is also known colloquially as Nilakunda, or the spring of Nila.

Getting there and away Verinag is 80km south of Srinagar, just east of the main highway. The main road either side of the town is prone to avalanches and is frequently blocked by rock falls, and though the authorities are efficient when it comes to clearing such blockages, you should factor in the possibility of delays nonetheless.

If you don't have your own vehicle, the cheapest way to get here is by **bus** from Srinagar (2½hrs; Rs45 one-way).

Where to stay and eat Cheap but fairly cheerless rooms are offered by **JKTDC** in Verinag for **$–$$** depending on the season.

PAHALGAM *Telephone code: 01936*

The most charming of the hill resorts in the valley, Pahalgam is home to some excellent accommodation options set among incredible natural beauty. It's a prime place to relax for a few days, reading a book in a pine forest grove or gazing into the rushing waters of the Lidder River. There are plenty of opportunities to lace up your hiking boots, too, and enjoy the beautiful and relatively undeveloped trails that fan out from the town.

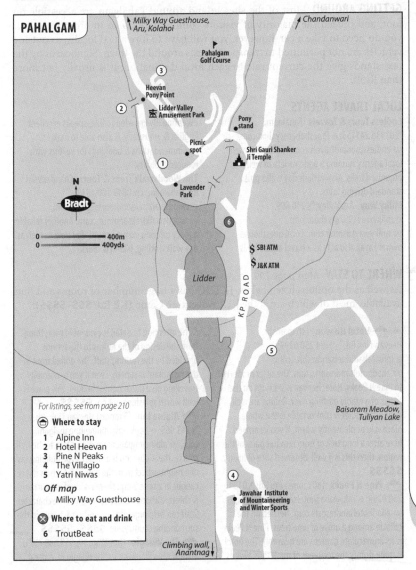

GETTING THERE AND AWAY Pahalgam is a popular tourist destination, and so transport links are reasonable. JKTDC operates a **tourist bus** from Srinagar to Pahalgam throughout the May to October summer season (2½hrs; Rs240 one-way), leaving Srinagar at 07.30 and returning between 16.00 and 17.00. Otherwise you will have to alight at Anantnag, from where you can pick up one of the frequent buses to Pahalgam (1½hrs; Rs80 one-way).

Taxis will charge from Rs2,100 from Srinagar to Pahalgam; the price is usually the same whether you go one-way or return.

If you are travelling in a private vehicle, note that there is a **tollbooth** 6km before Pahalgam. The toll for a car is Rs50.

GETTING AROUND Most of the sites in and around Pahalgam are accessible on foot, and indeed the majority of visitors coming here do so in order to trek. If you do need to take a car, however, you will have to hire a taxi locally, as outside vehicles are not permitted to transport guests around the town. Signboards by the taxi stands give the current rate to each local destination: it is usually not more than Rs50.

LOCAL TRAVEL AGENTS

Endless Tours & Travels Pahalgam; \01936 243153; e loneshaban@yahoo.com; w endlesstourandtravels.com. Highly regarded local agency running a wide variety of well-organised treks. Also various day walks plus standard driving tours.

Milky Way Aru Valley; \210 899; e milkyway1987@yahoo.com; w milkywaykashmir.com. Local guesthouse owner Fayaz also acts as a travel agent. He is exceptionally knowledgeable, speaks excellent English &, unusually, is also able to make recommendations & bookings for visitors with reduced mobility.

The Woodswalk Treks & Tours Chandanwari Rd, Pahalgam; m 0849 100 4833; e woodswalktreksandtours@gmail.com; w woodswalktreksandtours.com. Another reliable agency offering exciting multi-day treks as well as day walks, skiing, biking & tours.

WHERE TO STAY *Map, page 209*

As well as the options listed below, JKTDC has a large number of rooms and huts available, most of which are at the J&K Adventure Camp (KP Rd; $$$–$$$$).

❄ 🏠 **Hotel Heevan** (40 rooms) Heevan Link Rd; \0194 250 0299; e info@ahadhotelsandresorts.com; w ahadhotelsandresorts.com. The sister property to Pine N Peaks, Hotel Heevan is set right on the banks of a madly gushing river. Rooms are well appointed, quiet & comfortable & the whole place is kept pleasantly warm. If you've arrived here after a long trek or from remoter parts of the region, then this is a well-deserved slice of luxury. $$$$$

🏠 **Pine N Peaks** (80 rooms) Aru Rd; \0194 250 0299; e info@ahadhotelsandresorts.com; w ahadhotelsandresorts.com. Nestled on the hillside among a grove of pine trees, Pine N Peaks & its immaculate gardens are heavenly. The hotel is quite rightly the recipient of numerous awards & the attention to detail is evident in everything from the design of the rooms to the service provided by the waiting staff. The grilled trout in the restaurant is superb. Even if you're normally travelling on a much tighter budget, this place is well worth splashing out on. $$$$$

🏠 **Alpine Inn** (5 rooms) Heevan Link Rd; \243 065; e bookings@alpineinnpahalgam. com; w alpineinnpahalgam.com. Close to the golf course, the Alpine Inn is a chalet-type building (as one might expect from the name) & feels as if it is caught in a time warp: there's a lot of net curtain & chintz, although these only add to the character. Staff can help organise horseriding & hiking in the surrounding countryside. $$$$–$$$$$

🏠 **The Villagio** Nun-Wan; m 959 688 7571; e info@thevillagio.in; w thevillagio.in. A great compromise between the plush top-end options & the budget choices, the Villagio is a lovely big building set in spacious grounds. The exposed stone brick rooms are warm & cosy with plenty of wooden furnishings and service is top-notch. **$$$–$$$$**

✳ 🏠 **Milky Way Guesthouse** (12 rooms) Aru Valley; ☎ 210 899; e milkyway1987@yahoo. com; w milkywaykashmir.com. Set in a delightful garden in the Aru Valley, a short distance from Pahalgam town, the beds at Milky Way are as warm as the welcome. The owners can help organise fantastic treks & horseriding tours (see opposite). Highly recommended. **$$$**

🏠 **Yatri Niwas** Off KP Rd. A godsend for budget travellers, with dorm beds for just Rs250. In Jul & Aug your roommates will be pilgrims heading to the Amarnath Cave. **$**

✗ **WHERE TO EAT AND DRINK** *Map, page 209*
In Pahalgam the hotels invariably offer the best restaurants, but if you can drag yourself away from your window by the river, **TroutBeat** on the main thoroughfare is where you ought to go. Prices can be steep, but we didn't mind paying Rs550 for the buttery, lemony whole trout meunière.

SHOPPING The small boutique inside the Pine N Peaks hotel (see opposite) has a selection of high-quality handicrafts and textiles, including beautifully hand-painted papier mâché baubles and delicate papier mâché gift boxes. Staff are happy to help or to leave you to browse.

OTHER PRACTICALITIES **J&K Bank** and **SBI** have ATMs next door to each other on KP Road.

ACTIVITIES
Climbing There is a training wall for would-be climbers just to the south of Pahalgam town. You can turn up and climb if you know what you're doing and have your own equipment, or get in touch with the Jawahar Institute of Mountaineering and Winter Sports (page 212) for instruction and helmet and harness hire.

Fishing The Lidder River that runs through Pahalgam is replete with trout, as attested by the menus in the hotel restaurants and at TroutBeat (see above). The best season for angling runs from April to September.

Golf The 18-hole Pahalgam Golf Course (m 941 904 9402) is located in the centre of town and, as it both lies at an altitude of 2,740m and is built on a series of steep slopes, offers quite the challenge to golfers. Green fees are Rs1,200, hire of a golf cart is Rs500 (book ahead as only a small number are available) and hire of a caddy Rs250. Club rental fees are Rs1,200.

Trekking Almost all paths out of Pahalgam lead to a photogenic location, be it along the river or up into the hills. A superb overnight trek can be had by walking northwest to **Aru** (11km) and the Tarsar Lake and then onto the nearby Sonasar and Masar lakes. Basic homestay-style accommodation can be found in Aru. If you have several days available, you might want to consider trekking via **Lidderwat** to the hanging glacier of **Kolahoi** (35km), from where there are spectacular views across to **Kolahoi Peak** (5,370m). Shorter trails from Pahalgam lead to the lush **Baisaram Meadow** (6km), which is surrounded by pine forests, as well as southeast to the mostly frozen **Tuliyan Lake** (11km) with its ring of snow-capped mountains.

Hotel staff can suggest other routes and help arrange any equipment and guides you might need. Otherwise, all of these are available from the **Jawahar**

Institute of Mountaineering and Winter Sports (✆ 243 002; e principal@ jawaharinstitutepahalgam.com; w jawaharinstitutepahalgam.com) and **ponies** can be hired from either the Heevan Pony Point by Hotel Heevan or a second pony stand near Shri Gauri Shanker Ji Temple. With horseman, these cost around Rs1,000 for a day.

White-water rafting
Pahalgam has a growing reputation for white-water rafting on the Lidder River. Various routes are available from a short 2.5km to a moderate 5km and a more demanding 8km route. River runs cover grades II, III and IV respectively. While the two shorter routes shouldn't present any difficulties to most people, the longer 8km route takes in Grade IV rapids and is only suitable for more experienced rafters. The tour companies listed on page 210 can organise a rafting trip.

WHAT TO SEE AND DO Although Pahalgam's star attraction is its natural beauty, there are a few pleasant enough manmade sites to discover in the town itself. On the shore of the river, well-kept **Lavender Park** is a popular spot for picnics, and families with small children to entertain frequently find themselves dragged to the neighbouring **Lidder Valley Amusement Park**. Next door to the taxi stand is the **Shri Gauri Shanker Ji Temple**, which seems to be of interest for Hindu *yatris* passing through en route to Amarnath Cave, but is probably less of a draw for general visitors.

AROUND PAHALGAM For many domestic tourists, Pahalgam is just the starting point of their pilgrimage to the **Amarnath Cave** (see box, page 184), as it is only 16km along a motorable road to the trailhead at Chandanwari. Consequently, the town can become very busy during the pilgrimage, so bear this in mind and book your accommodation ahead if you're planning to come at the same time.

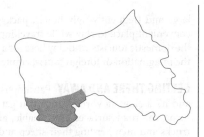

9

Jammu

Though it gives its name to J&K state, the region of Jammu is often overlooked by those rushing to see the remarkable sites of Kashmir and Ladakh. Situated in the southwestern corner of J&K, the lands around the holy Tawi River are, however, no less rich in history and culture than other parts of the state. Indeed, their Hindu identity gives an interesting cultural dimension to your visit that, though commonplace elsewhere in India, is less evident in this particular region.

Jammu city (often called Jammu Tawi to differentiate it from the surrounding areas) is a large, lively affair with good transport connections, some excellent hotels and such a wealth of religious sites that it has become known as the City of Temples. It is also the transit hub for pilgrims making their way to the Vaishno Devi and Shiv Khori shrines around Katra, and for the domestic tourism hotspot of Patnitop. Elsewhere in the area you'll find picturesque lakes, some attractive forts and palaces, and opportunities for adventure sports.

PATNITOP *Telephone code: 01992*

Patnitop has the potential to be a most charming hill resort: the natural environment with its majestic peaks, thick pine forests and springs is sublime. Its beauty is, unfortunately, also its downfall as mass tourism has brought with it

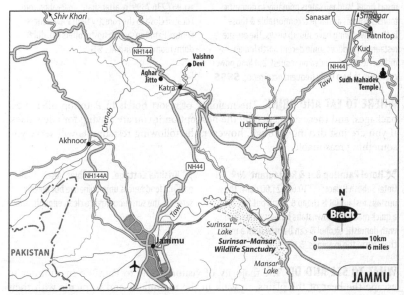

large and frequently ugly hotels, package tourists and their litter. It's certainly a convenient place to stay while travelling between Srinagar and Jammu but, unlike the domestic tourists who stay here for a week or more at a time, it's unlikely to grab the imagination of foreign tourists quite as much.

GETTING THERE AND AWAY Patnitop is 110km north of Jammu city along NH44, and it's a slow, slow road once you get into the mountains: the route twists and turns, the road surfaces are variable, and not infrequently you get stuck behind trucks and men herding their sheep and goats, especially at twilight. In winter the road is frequently closed due to snowfall.

The closest city to Patnitop is Jammu, and there are various transport options between the two. By **taxi** the journey takes just over 3 hours each way (Rs3,470 one-way), and while the **bus** takes significantly longer at around 5 hours, it can be cheaper (starting from Rs150 and going up to Rs1,000 for the deluxe coaches).

Coming from Srinagar, the best option is to take the **luxury bus** to Jammu, getting off en route at Patnitop, about 6 hours into the journey. The bus runs in summer only, departing from Srinagar's main bus station at 07.30. Arrive half an hour early to buy your ticket, which costs Rs599.

WHERE TO STAY

Hotel Natraj International (33 rooms) 287 520; e hotelnitrajinternational@gmail.com; w hotelnatrajinternational.com. This relatively new hotel has quickly claimed the title of the best place to stay in Patnitop. Smart service, competitive pricing & spacious though fairly ordinary rooms. **$$$$**

Vardaan Resort (44 rooms) 287 585; m 901 819 4040; e book@vardaanhotels.com; w patnitop.net. A sprawling & somewhat aging resort hotel, Vardaan caters primarily to domestic tourists. Rooms are large & comfortable & those in the newer wing have superb views. The on-site restaurant produces some decent north Indian dishes. Heating provided on request, but long power cuts seem to be a fairly frequent occurrence. **$$$$**

JKTDC Tourist Complex w jktdc.co.ln/PATNITOP.html. JKTDC operates a large tourist complex with a range of options inc bungalows (**$$$$**) & rooms at Hotel Alpine (**$$$**) & Hotel Maple (**$$**). The location of each is fantastic, but both options are a bit musty & aging. Full details & booking instructions are available online. Substantial discounts are available in low season (1 Aug–15 Dec & 16 Jan–31 Mar).

Youth Hostel (42 rooms) 287 540; m 962 236 7399; e aftabshah_16@yahoo.com. Located close to the Forestry Dept's Awareness Centre, Patnitop's youth hostel offers sgl, dbl & dorm rooms, all with AC. **$$**

WHERE TO EAT AND DRINK The majority of resort hotels in Patnitop offer meal packages, and these are generally the best option if you are staying for a few days. If you are just driving through, however, the following restaurants will serve you something reasonable.

Hotel Patnitop Bar & Restaurant Nr Hotel Subash Palace; 10.00–21.00 daily. The upstairs restaurant is cheap & bland but fine for a quick meal. The downstairs bar is well stocked with domestic alcohol & can be busy with a male clientele in the evenings. **$$**

Krishna Cottage Nr Jai Shree Hotel; all day. The food here is unimaginative but quickly served & the surroundings are clean enough. **$$**

WHAT TO SEE AND DO The majority of visitors come to Patnitop in summer to escape the heat of the plains, to walk in the mountains and to picnic with their families. There's a laidback feel to the place and plenty of pleasant paths to follow: the 8km route downhill to the apple orchards at **Batote** is particularly attractive and in places offers panoramic views of both the mountains and the Chenab River. If you come to Patnitop in January and February, it is possible to **ski**. Though the resort is far less developed than that at Gulmarg, there are several beginners' slopes around Madha Top (5km from Patnitop), classes are available, and the possibility of constructing a ski lift has long been under discussion (though so far nothing material has appeared).

Local devotees also visit the 600-year-old **Naag Temple** close to the centre of Patnitop. Dedicated to Naga (a semi-divine, part-human, part-snake race), this small and interesting temple is said to bring luck to visitors who make a wish and tie a red ribbon to the temple walls. Note that women aren't allowed inside the temple.

AROUND PATNITOP Situated 17km from Patnitop, **Sanasar** has been developed by J&K Tourism as a centre for adventure sports and, in particular, aerial sports.

Deriving its name from the two local lakes, Sana and Sar, it offers activities year-round: there's a nine-hole **golf course** with a lake at its centre, you can **paraglide** either across the lakes or all the way to the small town of Kud, and it is also possible to try **hot-air ballooning**. All equipment and instruction is available from the **JKTDC Tourist Complex** (w jktdc.co.in).

For those looking for something more cultural, the 400-year-old **Shank Pal Temple** overlooks Sanasar. Dedicated to Nag Shank Pal, it is about 3 hours' walk above the lakes and is notable for the fact that no mortar was used in its construction and yet the stones still stand solid.

A little further away, 42km to the southeast of Patnitop, is the **Sudh Mahadev Temple**. This holy site is believed by some to be as much as 2,800 years old (though the modern structure is far more recent); the inner sanctum contains a natural black marble *lingam* (representative of Shiva), Shiva's trident and a mace said to belong to Bhim (page 163). The temple is busiest during the Sudh Mahadev Festival (which takes place during the full moon in June–July), when pilgrims come to pray and also enjoy the song and dance.

Before entering the temple, devotees typically wash themselves in the **Pap Nashni Baoli**, a natural spring that has been developed into a step well. JKTDC provides a small amount of tented accommodation (**$**) here if you wish to stay the night, and devotees sometimes donate money for meals for travellers, served from various hot food and snack stalls. The easiest way of getting to any of these places is by hiring a car and driver or taxi.

UDHAMPUR *Telephone code: 01992*

The fourth-largest city in J&K, Udhampur is the Northern Command Headquarters of the Indian army. Though subtropical in climate and set among eucalyptus forest, it feels overwhelmingly like a garrison town as the army dominates all areas of life. There's no real reason for tourists to visit, although it might make sense to stop off as you pass through as it does have most amenities you could need.

GETTING THERE AND AWAY Udhampur lies 70km north of Jammu on NH44, and 47km from Patnitop. The road is wide and well maintained, and doesn't suffer from the rock falls and snow that plague it further north. By **bus** from Jammu, the standard single fare is Rs46; by **taxi** expect to pay Rs1,100.

The **railway** extension north of Jammu city, which will ultimately go as far as Srinagar once it is completed, already connects Udhampur to the rest of the Indian railway network. Though several trains do pass through the station each day, the most useful is the Jammu Mail (train number: 14034), which departs from Udhampur daily at 15.07, reaches Jammu at 16.15 and then continues through a variety of stops, finally reaching Delhi at 05.45. One-way prices on this train to or from Delhi and Jammu are sleeper/AC 3-tier/AC 2-tier/AC 1st class Rs325/885/1,270/2,130.

 WHERE TO STAY AND EAT

🏠 **Hotel Singh Axis** (32 rooms) NH1A, Raghunathpura; 🖂 273 598; e gm@hotelsinghaxis.com; w hotelsinghaxis.com. Udhampur's accommodation options are really nothing to write home about, but Hotel Singh Axis is the pleasant exception. Rooms are clean & many have mountain views. Staff are friendly & food in the on-site restaurant is tasty & affordable. Parking is free. B/fast inc. **$$$**

OTHER PRACTICALITIES If you need a **pharmacy**, Shiva Medical Store and several other chemists are situated near to Chibber Enclave. All the main **banks** are represented in the town: J&K Bank and Punjab National Bank have branches along NH1, and both they and SBI have **ATMs**.

WHAT TO SEE AND DO You wouldn't travel far out of your way to see it, but Udhampur's **rock garden** is a quirky sight. Rock-cut figurines of people represent different members of the community in miniature. The uniform-clad soldier clasping the hands of two schoolchildren is especially menacing. Elsewhere in the town, several **decommissioned tanks** and also a small **military aircraft** decorate public spaces.

KATRA *Telephone code: 01991*

The town of Katra lies in the foothills of the Trikuta range and is frequently known as Katra Vaishno Devi on account of it being the access point for treks to the Vaishno Devi Shrine. It is a thriving place that attracts around nine million Hindu pilgrims each year, as well as a number of non-Hindu tourists curious to see what all the fuss is about.

GETTING THERE AND AWAY You can get to Katra by either train or road. The fastest **train** service, the Shri Shakti AC Express (train number: 22461), departs from Delhi at 17.30 every day except Thursday. It stops in Jammu at 02.55 and then reaches its final destination, Katra, at 05.10 (3A/2A/1A Rs1,010/1,430/2,415). Standard **buses** leave from Jammu's railway station (1½hrs; Rs40 per person). If you prefer to travel to Katra from Jammu by **taxi**, expect to pay from Rs1,000 one-way, or Rs1,300 if you need a taxi with air conditioning.

🏠 **WHERE TO STAY AND EAT** Owing to the volume of pilgrims passing through, **JKTDC** has opened various options in Katra, all of which should be booked in advance at w jktdc.co.in or at the JKTDC Tourist Retiring Centre (nr bus stand; 🖂 232 309). The smartest of these options is **Hotel Saraswati** (off Ban Ganga Rd; 🖂 254 9065; **$$$**), with both AC and non-AC rooms, followed by **Hotel City Residency** near the shrine (**$$$**). The latter also has very cheap beds in vast dormitories, as does **Yatri Niwas** (both **$**).

🏠 **The Atrium on the Green** (61 rooms) Nr railway station; 🖂 232 027; e theatriumkatra@ gmail.com; w theatriumkatra.com. Head & shoulders above other hotels in Katra. Set among well-kept lawns & with a holistic spa on site, this is the place to relax. Staff are attentive & service is personal. Food in the restaurant is organic & the ice cream in the coffee shop is welcome. Be sure to book ahead in summer. **$$$$$**

🏠 **KC Residency** (57 rooms) Reasi Rd; m 979 759 0211; e kcresidency@kcresidencykatra.com; w kcresidencykatra.com. Large, modern & well-equipped hotel with AC rooms, many of which overlook the Trikuta Hills. Some of the furnishings

are a little garish (those gold-rimmed thrones are certainly something!), but it keeps it memorable. North Indian meals are served. **$$$$$**

🏠 **Hotel Maharaja** New Bus Stand; m 8881 690690; e maharajainn@shreeharihotels. com; w hotelmaharajainnkatra.com. Plain but comfortable rooms that are perfectly acceptable despite the overwhelmingly brown colour scheme. **$$$**

WHAT TO SEE AND DO

Vaishno Devi It is a 26km trek northwest from Katra to the Vaishno Devi Shrine and back, but each year nine million pilgrims still make the journey to what is one of Hinduism's holiest shrines. The site is accessible year-round, and while the majority of pilgrims travel on foot, it is also possible to travel by pony or take a seat in a helicopter.

The route to the shrine is paved, and along the way you'll spot stalls selling snacks and souvenirs. En route, devotees stop at **Ardhkunwari** to climb through a small cave where a goddess is thought to have meditated, and then again just short of the main shrine to bathe and offer prayers.

Inside the shrine, which is accessed via a long corridor, are three important idols, the goddesses Mahakali, Mahalakshmi and Mahasaraswati. Each one is represented by a natural rock structure, heavily decorated with gold jewellery and flowers. The final part of the *yatra* involves visiting the **Bhairav Temple**, 2km beyond the main shrine, which legend says was built '100 decades ago' – though how true this is remains uncertain.

If you wish to participate in the pilgrimage, you must register in advance with the **Mata Vaishno Devi Shrine Board** (w maavaishnodevi.org). Registration is free and can be done online, or in person at the Yatra Registration Counter near Katra's bus stand.

Other sights around Katra Katra is also the starting point for another pilgrimage route, that to **Shiv Khori**. Those who worship here believe it is the site where Shiva appeared to the demon Bhasmasura as a beautiful woman, tricking Bhasmasura

---

VAISHNO DEVI AND THE SHRINE

The origins of the Vaishno Devi Shrine are cloaked in legend. It is said that Bhairavnath, a famous Hindu Tantric, saw the young Vaishno Devi at an agricultural fair and fell madly in love with her. When she fled into the Trikuta Hills to escape his amorous advances, he followed in hot pursuit, and for nine months she hid and meditated in the Ardhkunwari Cave.

Bhairavnath eventually located Vaishno Devi and she fled once again, this time to the site of the main shrine. Here she assumed the form of the goddess Mahakali and struck out at Bhairavnath, cutting off his head with her sword. Bhairavnath's head hit the floor and bounced but still he was able to beg for forgiveness. Though she could not save his life, Vaishno Devi decided that a temple should be built in his honour, and that here too devotees would offer up prayers.

into turning himself to ash. Using his trident, Shiva was also able to cut a tunnel through the mountain, which is said to lead all the way to Amarnath.

Devotees must travel 78km from Katra northwest to the village of Ransoo, and thence proceed for 3.5km on foot to the holy cave, which is 150m long and has a 1.2m-tall tapered Shiva *lingam* inside it. Similar shapes in the cave are associated with Parvati, Ganesh and Nandi. Full information about the pilgrimage to Shiv Khori is available from the Shiv Khori Shrine Board (w shivkhori.org).

On the way from Katra to Ransoo, look out also for the **Aghar Jitto**, a cute, landscaped garden in which statues of the folk hero and saint Baba Jitto and his daughter are displayed. Baba Jitto gained renown 500 years ago as a revolutionary figure who stood up against feudal exploitation and was killed. A week-long festival, the Jhiri Mela, is held in his honour each year, normally in the first half of November.

JAMMU CITY Telephone code: 0191

The winter capital of J&K, Jammu city lies along the banks of the Tawi River – indeed, the name Jammu Tawi is often used for the city to differentiate it from the Jammu region as a whole. Colloquially, however, Jammu is known as the 'City of Temples', due to the vast number of Hindu temples and shrines that are found here, and, of course, the fact that the city is packed with Hindu pilgrims passing through on their way to the Vaishno Devi Shrine (page 217). All of this gives Jammu a very different feel to other places in J&K, and it is well worth planning to spend a few days here just to soak up the atmosphere.

HISTORY Archaeological evidence suggests that the area around Jammu has been inhabited for more than 4,000 years. There was certainly a town on the banks of the Tawi River in the early centuries AD, and the area was occupied in turn by the Hephthalites, Kushans, Guptas and Ghaznavids.

The history of modern Jammu begins, however, in the 17th century with Jamboo Lohan, the brother of the local chieftain credited with building Bahu Fort (page 223). It is said that Jamboo was out hunting one day when he saw a lion and a lamb standing side by side, both drinking from the Tawi River. Amazed, he decided to build a city on the site, and the foundation stones of Jamboo Nagar (literally Jamboo's place, and later corrupted to Jammu) were laid.

The Dogra dynasty ruled Jammu and Kashmir princely state from 1846 until 1947, and they made Jammu their capital. The Dogras introduced to Jammu many modern inventions, including the railway and the telegraph service, and patronised the construction of many of the city's temples.

GETTING THERE AND AWAY

By air Jammu airport (also known as Satwari airport; airport code IXJ) is in the southwest of the city on RS Pura Road. There is just one terminal, and it services domestic flights to Delhi (from 90mins; around Rs5,000 each way), Srinagar (around 45mins; from Rs1,870) and Leh (75mins; Rs5,000).

By train Jammu Tawi (station code JAT) is a vast, sprawling station on the imaginatively named Railway Road in the centre of Jammu, a few blocks south of the river. Large numbers of porters in red shirts are on hand to help with your luggage (information boards suggest appropriate rates of remuneration) and the staff at the information desk are helpful if you don't know where to go. Note that you will need a ticket to pass through security in order to get on to the platform.

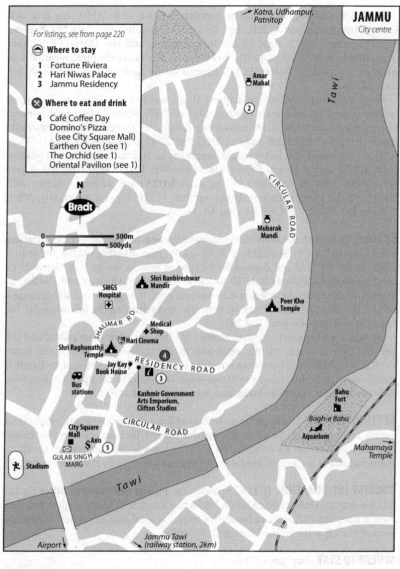

For listings, see from page 220

Where to stay

1. Fortune Riviera
2. Hari Niwas Palace
3. Jammu Residency

Where to eat and drink

4. Café Coffee Day
   Domino's Pizza
      (see City Square Mall)
   Earthen Oven (see 1)
   The Orchid (see 1)
   Oriental Pavilion (see 1)

JAMMU
City centre

Katra, Udhampur, Patnitop

Tawi

Amar Mahal

CIRCULAR ROAD

Mubarak Mandi

N

Bradt

0 ———— 500m
0 ———— 500yds

Shri Ranbireshwar Mandir

SMGS Hospital

Peer Kho Temple

Medical Shop

Hari Cinema

Shri Raghunathji Temple

Jay Kay Book House

RESIDENCY ROAD

Bus stations

Kashmir Government Arts Emporium, Clifton Studios

Bahu Fort

Bagh-e Bahu

CIRCULAR ROAD

Aquarium

City Square Mall

Axis

Mahamaya Temple

GULAB SINGH MARG

Stadium

Tawi

Airport

Jammu Tawi
(railway station, 2km)

The rail link from Delhi to Jammu was completed in 1897 and functioned well throughout the first half of the 20th century. However, when independence came in 1947 the line from Jammu to Sialkot was severed, and it would be more than 20 years before Jammu was reconnected to the Indian railway network.

Getting to Jammu by train is exceptionally easy and inexpensive. Six services run daily from Delhi to Jammu Tawi. The Malwa Express (train number: 12919) leaves New Delhi railway station (station code NDLS) at 05.20 and arrives in Jammu at 16.10 (Rs930/1,315 for class 3A/2A). If you prefer to travel overnight, the Jammu Mail (train number: 14033) leaves Delhi Junction (station code DLI) at 20.10 and arrives the following morning at 08.45 (Rs885/1,270/2,130 for class 3A/2A/1A).

There are also regular trains to Amritsar (station code ASR): the BTI JAT Express (train number: 19225; dept 01.25; 5hrs 10mins); the Tata JAT Express (train number: 18101; dept 08.20; 5hrs 50mins); and the Durg-JAT Express (train number: 18215; dept 16.00; 5hrs 40mins). Prices are the same regardless of whether you take the faster BTI JAT Express or the slow services: Rs495/700 for class 3A/2A.

From Rajasthan, the Aii Jat Express (train number: 12413) starts in Ajmer (station code AII) and stops in Jaipur (station code JP) before continuing to Jammu. The journey takes around 18 hours from Ajmer and 15 hours 40 minutes from Jaipur (Rs1,320/1,895/3,230 and Rs1,215/1,735/2,945 in classes 3A/2A/1A).

There are longer and less frequent departures to Jammu from Mumbai (station code BDTS) on the Swaraj Express (train number: 12471; Mon, Thu, Fri & Sun only; 30hrs 50mins; Rs1,935/2,830 for class 3A/2A) and Kolkata (station code HWH) on the Himgiri Express (train number: 12331; Tue, Fri & Sat only; 36hrs 35mins; Rs1,980/2,895/4,995 for class 3A/2A/1A).

By road Long-distance **taxis** are managed by the **Special Tourist Taxi Association** (Residency Rd; m 941 914 1213; ☺ 06.00–21.00) from its office outside the tourist office. Rates are fixed and depend on the type of vehicle. For an Indi Car with air conditioning you will pay Rs1,500 to Katra, Rs4,650 to Amritsar and Rs4,800 to Srinagar. Prices given here are for one-way journeys, though you can also arrange a return. Driving to Patnitop, staying overnight and returning the following day, for example, will cost you from Rs4,200.

By **bus**, travel is much cheaper. Jammu has two bus stands, the **public** and the **private**. They are, conveniently, next door to one another on Old Hospital Road. JKSRTC (w jksrtc.co.in) operates a regular bus service from Amritsar to Jammu's public bus stand (3hrs; from Rs400 one-way). Travelling in the opposite direction, buses to Srinagar take 8–10 hours and fares start from Rs400.

GETTING AROUND If you prefer to hire a car for a day or half a day, rather than simply hailing taxis on the street, the **Special Tourist Taxi Association** (see above) charges Rs900 for an air-conditioned Indi Car for 4 hours' hire and up to 40km. **Auto-rickshaws** are readily available and you can either go by the meter or haggle.

TOURIST INFORMATION JKTDC operates the **tourist information office** (❧ 252 0432; e jkdtourism@yahoo.co.in) on Residency Road. Staff speak English and they have a selection of maps and brochures featuring local sites of interest. There is a second branch at the railway station (❧ 247 6078).

🏠 **WHERE TO STAY** *Map, page 219*
Accommodation in Jammu is aimed more at Indian pilgrims and business travellers than foreign tourists, so you can generally expect poorer value for money than you would get in bigger international tourist centres.

✳ 🏠 **Fortune Riviera** (29 rooms) 9 Gulab Singh Marg; ❧ 01 800 102 2333 (Delhi); e innriviera@fortunehotels.in; w fortunehotels. in. Centrally located, this branch of Indian chain Fortune is a haven of calm & good service. Rooms are well-presented & comfortable & have all the mod cons you'd expect of this class of hotel. There

are 3 good restaurants & a coffee shop & all the staff speak excellent English. Very good value. **$$$$$**

🏠 **Hari Niwas Palace Hotel** (40 rooms) Palace Rd; ❧ 254 3303; e saleshnp@hotmail. com; w hariniwaspalace.in. Atmospheric & historic hotel where the treaty between Lord

Mountbatten & Maharaja Hari Singh was signed in 1948 in room 318. As you sit on manicured lawns drinking tea (or a G&T), you really do feel like a royal guest. Some rooms have river-facing balconies & room 311 has a 4-poster bed. $$$$–$$$$$

🏠 **Jammu Residency** (148 rooms) Behind the tourist office, Residency Rd; ☎247 9554; w hotel-jammu-residency-jktdc.hotelsgds.com. Large, colonial-era hotel run by the govt & in need of love. There's a beautiful painted ceiling in reception. Rooms have fans but no AC. $$$–$$$$

✗ WHERE TO EAT AND DRINK *Map, page 219*

There are numerous places to eat in Jammu, and most types of cuisine are represented. At the upper end of the market, the Fortune Riviera hotel (see opposite) has three excellent restaurants that are open to both guests and non-guests (all $$$$: a multi-cuisine buffet is served in **The Orchid**; there is a delicious Chinese menu and views across Jammu towards the river at the **Oriental Pavilion**; and in **Earthen Oven** you'll find traditional north Indian cuisine, including dishes cooked in the *tandoor*.

If you've been craving American-style pizza, there's a **Domino's Pizza** ($$$–$$) in City Square Mall, where the menu includes a large number of vegetarian options. **Café Coffee Day** – India's answer to Starbucks – is located on Residency Road and is open until late. For fresh juices, try the **Juice Bar** on Old Hospital Road, where a cup of freshly squeezed juice will set you back just Rs30.

ENTERTAINMENT AND NIGHTLIFE As a major city, there are opportunities for evening entertainment in Jammu. **Hari Cinema** (Old Hospital Rd; tickets from Rs80) shows Bollywood flicks in slightly run-down surroundings but in a convenient location. For an evening drink, the **Polo Bar** at the Hari Niwas Palace (see opposite) oozes old-world charm: you can slide back in time with a cocktail in hand. More centrally located and contemporary in style, **Neptune** (at the Fortune Riviera, see opposite) has a good selection of spirits and attracts mostly travelling businessmen, as well as a few well-heeled locals. The Polo Bar opens at around 19.00, while the Neptune opens at 11.00 but doesn't get busy until after 21.00.

SHOPPING Jammu lacks the higher-end craft and souvenir shops of Srinagar and Leh, but wandering in the **Main Bazaar** still provides an hour or so of entertainment. There's an underwhelming but fixed-price selection of handicrafts on sale at the **Kashmir Government Arts Emporium** (Residency Rd; ⊕ 10.00–18.00 daily) and the rather more rewarding **Jay Kay Book House** (Residency Rd; ⊕ 10.00–20.00 Mon–Sat) a few doors along.

For photo printing and camera and phone accessories (including memory cards and chargers), try **Clifton Studios** (Residency Rd; ⊕ 10.00–18.00 daily). You may also find what you need among the general selection of upmarket retail outlets at **City Square Mall** (Exhibition Ground Rd).

OTHER PRACTICALITIES

Communications

🖥 **Internet** All the hotels we've listed have Wi-Fi, but if you do need an internet café then there are still a few around Jewel Chowk offering cheap access. You may need to show your passport or other photo ID to get online.

✉ **Post office** Next door to City Square Mall.

Medical

✚ **Medical Shop** Simple pharmacy on Old Hospital Rd.

✚ **SMGS Hospital** ☎250 4802. Jammu's main hospital is centrally located on Shalimar Rd. It is the city's teaching hospital & all main areas of practice, including A&E, are covered.

Money

All of the major Indian banks are well represented in Jammu & ATMs are commonplace. Most conveniently located are the **J&K Bank** & **PNB**

ATMs at the railway station; the **Axis Bank** & ATM next door to City Square Mall; the **SBI** ATM on Old Hospital Rd; & the **Oriental Bank of Commerce** & **UCO Bank** ATMs on Residency Rd.

WHAT TO SEE AND DO Jammu is home to a vast number of sites of interest to both leisure tourists and pilgrims. The sheer variety of things to see means you can easily fill several days of your itinerary soaking up all that the city has to offer.

Amar Mahal (Palace Rd; ⊕ Apr–Sep 09.00–13.00 & 14.00–18.00 Tue–Sat, Oct–Mar 09.00–13.00 & 14.00–17.00; admission Rs20/100 normal/special; Rs50 camera) Set in an imposing position above the Tawi River, the Amar Mahal is the former royal palace of the 19th-century Dogra king Raja Amar Singh. Designed by a French architect and inhabited by the family until 1967, it now houses the **Amar Mahal Museum**, an eclectic collection of family heirlooms, artworks and photographs.

The wood-panelled **hall** contains family photos and an informative biography of Dr Karan Singh, prince, singer, environmentalist, cabinet minister, diplomat and state governor. From here you move into the **Nala Damyanti Gallery** with its full-length oil portraits of the royal family and a large and well-presented collection of 18th-century Pahari miniatures. There are also two fascinating models: a 1:633,600 scale (1 inch = 10 miles) topographical model of J&K, and a finely made wooden model of the Brihadishwara Temple in Tanjore.

The museum also contains a **contemporary art gallery** with three works by M F Husain; a permanently locked throne room (you can see the throne through the window); and the **Dash Avatar Gallery**, which contains a dozen unremarkable modern oils and a rather more attractive fibreglass Buddha in an antechamber.

Opposite the palace entrance is the impressive **statue of Maharaja Gulab Singh,** founder of J&K state, commissioned by Dr Karan Singh and unveiled by the vice-president of India in 2000.

If you buy the 'special' ticket you can also visit the upstairs floors, which consist of the bedrooms, bathrooms and a large portrait of a not-very-amused-looking Queen Victoria.

Aquarium (Nr Bahu Fort; ☏ 243 5596; ⊕ Apr–Sep 09.00–21.00 daily, Oct–Mar 09.00–20.00 daily; admission Rs30) Guaranteed to make heads turn, the city's aquarium is housed within a giant fish sculpture (enter through its mouth). Run by the Department of Fisheries, most of the aquarium is actually underground, making it rather dark. Its principal function is to educate local schoolchildren, so foreigners who have already seen the sea may wish simply to photograph the outside of the building and, while standing in the driveway, take a look up at the fort.

Bagh-e Bahu (Bahu Rd; ⊕ Apr–Sep 08.00–22.00 daily, Oct–Mar 09.00–21.00; admission Rs24) Probably the most delightful public space in Jammu, Bagh-e Bahu (Bahu Garden) overlooks the river while looking up at the fort. Families picnic in shady patches beneath the trees, and tiny chipmunk-squirrels chase each other across the lawns.

The park is carefully laid out and well maintained. Paved pathways and water channels demarcate the different areas, manmade waterfalls lead the eye, and dark pink and purple flowers add a splash of colour. Sitting in the rose garden is particularly peaceful. The **JKDC Cafeteria** in the centre of the park serves soft drinks and ice creams.

Bahu Fort (Bahu Rd; free) It is claimed there has been a fort on this site for around 3,000 years, though the current structure mostly dates from the 1800s, when it was rebuilt by Jammu's Dogra rulers on top of an earlier (16th-century) structure.

Bahu Fort looks quite a sight from the outside, and this is the best way to appreciate it. If you are determined to get inside to the **Mahakali Temple**, however, you must first fight your way through a parking lot and an arcade of souvenir shops selling all manner of tat for devotees. You'll also need to remove your shoes before entering through the gates, and also leave cameras, mobile phones and any other electronic items outside. There is nothing to see in the fort courtyard and you are not allowed up on to the walls: the monkeys are apparently too aggressive, though the live wires and numerous trip hazards are probably an equal threat. Inside the temple is a small shrine dedicated to the goddess Durga.

Mubarak Mandi (Panjthirthi) The Mubarak Mandi complex was the royal seat of Jammu's Dogra rulers from 1824 to 1925, when Hari Singh relocated to the new Hari Niwas Palace (page 220). The vast site, which includes the Darbar Hall, Sheesh Mahal, Hawa Mahal, Pink Palace and Royal Courts, is a smorgasbord of European Baroque, Mughal and Mewari styles. Sadly, however, the buildings are in extreme danger, already the victims of two earthquakes, more than 30 fires and decades of unforgivable neglect. A conservation programme is under way, but as large sections of the palace have already been gutted or collapsed, conservators are limited in what they can do. The monkeys have taken over, along with the birds.

One of the few operational buildings in the complex is the **Dogra Art Museum** (256 1846; ⊕ 10.00–16.30 Tue–Sun; admission Rs10/50 local/foreigner; Rs280 photography), though this too is in need of damp-proofing, a clean and a lick of paint. The highlights of the collection are displayed in the **Main Hall**, a double-height room with internal balconies. We were particularly taken by the beautiful mural fragments removed from Reasi Fort, four 4th-century terracotta heads excavated at Ambaran near Akhnoor, and the large Kushan coin hoard. Look out also for the 107 12th-century coins found recently by prisoners gardening within the confines of Kot Bhalwal Jail. The rest of the museum is a bit disappointing, and the tour staff do little to bring it to life.

The **Long Gallery** on the first floor has an attractive carved wooden ceiling that is original to the building and a glass cabinet containing what is apparently a piece of elephant fossil, though you'll have to use your imagination. The adjoining room has a display of 19th-century paintings, unremarkable individually but pleasant enough as a group, and two sets of colourful doors salvaged from somewhere else in the Mubarak Mandi complex. The **contemporary art gallery** is best avoided unless you like your art either banal or hideous. A dozen or so pieces of sculpture on plinths are arranged around a sunken bath alongside two truly monstrous larger works and a few unremarkable paintings.

Other temples Jammu is famed for its **Hindu temples** and though you're unlikely to want to visit all of them (there are, by some estimates, more than 300), visiting a few will give you valuable insight into the city, its people and their beliefs. If you are going to Bahu Fort, continue to the neighbouring **Mahamaya Temple** in the forest on the facing ridge. This 19th-century temple contains a *pindi*, said to be the manifestation of the goddess, and offers superb views across both the city and the forest.

Peer Kho Temple (Circular Rd) dates back far earlier than Jammu's other temples, having been a place of prayer since the late 1400s. The holy man Jogi Guru

Garib Nath lived and meditated in this cave (*kho* meaning cave) as it contains a Shiva *lingam*. The cave is also thought to have been visited by Jamwant, the bear figure in the *Ramayana* epic. This temple is particularly busy during the Shivratri festival (February/March).

The most famous of Jammu's temples is the **Shri Raghunathji Temple** (Old Hospital Rd), the largest temple complex in northern India. Built by Maharaja Ranbir Singh in 1857, the main temple's interior walls are covered with sheets of gold, and there are large statues of Rama, Sita and Lakshmana. Bibliophiles may also want to check out the **Sanskrit library**, which contains a number of rare manuscripts.

Also built by Maharaja Ranbir Singh, but several years later, is the temple that bears his name: the **Shri Ranbireshwar Mandir** (Shalimar Rd). It took 15 years to complete and is the largest Shiva temple in northern India. Inside you'll see a large Shiva *lingam* surrounded by nearly a dozen smaller crystal *lingams*, and 125,000 tiny *lingams* brought from the Narmada River in central India.

For details on a far wider selection of Jammu's temples, as well as its *gurudwaras* and churches, pick up the free *Jammu: City of Temples* brochure from the tourist office (page 220).

AROUND JAMMU CITY

AKHNOOR On the banks of the Chenab River, 20km northwest of Jammu, is the town of Akhnoor, over which the impressive **Akhnoor Fort** presides. Though construction of the present buildings began only in 1762 (and was not completed until 1802), archaeological evidence suggests there has been a succession of structures on this site since Harappan times, and some of the finest exhibits in the Dogra Art Museum (page 223) were excavated here. Conservation of the fort is ongoing, so heed the advice of local caretakers about where it is safe to go.

Another archaeological site here of great historical importance is **Ambran** (⊕ dawn to dusk), a series of 2,000-year-old structures including a Buddhist stupa. The Archaeological Survey of India is slowly excavating the site, and has already unearthed decorative terracotta figurines, copper objects, beads made from semi-precious stones, pottery and caskets containing human relics.

Elsewhere in Akhnoor it is possible to visit the **Pandava Gufa**, an ancient cave hidden behind the pink façade of a modern building, which somewhat spoils the atmosphere. It is believed that the five Pandava brothers, heroes of the *Mahabharata*, took refuge here and so pilgrims still come to pray.

SURINSAR-MANSAR LAKES Declared a wildlife sanctuary in 1981 and some 42km east of Jammu, these wetlands are a prime habitat for birdlife and it is possible to see both local and migratory species, including various types of cranes and ducks. The twin lakes are of great religious importance too, and for this reason it is not permitted to swim in the water or attempt to catch the fish. Legend has it that Arjuna, hero of the *Mahabharata*, shot an arrow into the ground at Mansar, and it exited at Surinsar, creating the two lakes. Mansar is also considered to be the home of Sheshnag, a mythical (one would hope) six-headed snake god who is lord of all serpents. The **Sheshnag Shrine** is on the eastern bank of the lake, and it is visited by newlywed couples seeking his blessings.

Should you wish to stay overnight at the lakes, JKTDC operates a **guesthouse complex** (w jktdc.co.in; **$$**) with rooms and bungalows on the shore of Lake Mansar. There is no public transport to the lakes so you would need to hire a taxi from Jammu.

Appendix 1

LANGUAGE

Although English is widely spoken, especially in the state's urban areas and places with a high footfall of tourists, the official language of J&K is Urdu, an Indo-European language closely related in its grammar and vocabulary to Hindi, but which is written from right to left in the Perso-Arabic script. As a spoken language it is relatively straightforward and you will be able to pick up common phrases quickly; learning to read and write it will take more time and, in any case, it is unlikely to be necessary on a short visit as most signage is written in English.

While in Ladakh, you may want to try speaking a few words of Ladakhi too. Ladakhi is rather more difficult: it is a Tibetic language (though not mutually intelligible with Standard Tibetan). Some dialects of Ladakhi are tonal.

See also page 233 for books on learning Urdu and Ladakhi.

URDU
Alphabet

ا	as in apple	ذ	as in that	ق	a k in the throat
ب	as in book	ر	trilled r	ک	as in kilo
پ	as in pool	ڑ	as in rabbit	گ	as in guest
ت	t as in time	ظ، ز	as in zen	ل	as in leaf
ٹ	as in art	ژ	as in pleasure	م	as in much
ث	as in thank	س	as in small	ن	as in not
ج	as in hedge	ش	as in worship	و	varies between
چ	as in catch	ص	as in sue		w and v
ح	as in head	ض	as in those	ه	as in house
خ	as in Bach	ط	as in stable	ی	as in yak
د	as in dove	غ	similar to a French r	ے	as in way and yell
ذ	as in drink	ف	as in food		

Useful phrases

Hello	*salaam aleikum*
How are you?	*aap kaise hain?*
I am fine	*main thik hun*
Where do you come from?	*kahan se aap?*
I come from…	*mai… se hun*
What is your name?	*aapka naam kya hai?*
My name is…	*mera naam… hai*
Goodbye	*khuda haafiz*
Yes	*haan*
No	*nahin*

Thank you	*shukriya*
I understand	*main samajhta/ti hun*
I don't understand	*main nahin samajhta/t*
Do you have…?	*kya aap ke paas…?*
How much is this?	*yah kitna hai?*
May I have…?	*mujhe de dijie… (lit. Please give me…)*
I am hot	*mujhe garam lagta/ti hai*
I am cold	*mujhe thanda lagta/ti hai*
I am tired	*mujhe thaki hui hai*
I am ill	*mujhe bimaar hai*

Urdu numbers

1 *ek*	11 *gyrah*	30 *tees*
2 *do*	12 *baarah*	40 *chalees*
3 *teen*	13 *taraah*	50 *pechchas*
4 *char*	14 *chaudah*	60 *sath*
5 *panch*	15 *pendrah*	70 *sattar*
6 *cheh*	16 *solah*	80 *aasi*
7 *saath*	17 *setrah*	90 *navway*
8 *aath*	18 *aatraah*	100 *ek sau*
9 *noh*	19 *unees*	1,000 *hazaar*
10 *das*	20 *bees*	

LADAKHI
Alphabet

ཀ	ka	ད	da	ཞ	zha
ཁ	kha	ན	na	ཟ	za
ག	ga	པ	pa	འ	'a
ང	nga	ཕ	pha	ཡ	ya
ཙ	ca	བ	ba	ར	ra
ཚ	cha	མ	ma	ལ	la
ཇ	ja	ཙ	tsa	ཤ	sha
ཉ	nya	ཚ	tsha	ས	sa
ཏ	ta	ཛ	dza	ཧ	ha
ཐ	tha	ཝ	wa	ཨ	a

Useful phrases

Hello	*juley*
How are you?	*rdemo ina?*
I am fine	*kasa dju*
Where do you come from?	*nyerang kane in le?*
I come from…	*nga… ne in le*
What is your name?	*nay rangi ming la chi yin?*
My name is…	*nay ming la… yin lay*
Goodbye	*juley*
Yes	*yot*
No	*met*
Thank you	*juley*
I understand	*gnya hago*
I don't understand	*gnya hamago*
Do you have…?	*… yo ta lay?*

How much is this?	*eebowa zrin sam in lay?*
May I have…?	*thobina le…?*
I am hot	*tsante rak*
I am cold	*tangmo mi rak*
I am tired	*ngalte rak*
I am ill	*zumo rak*

Ladakhi numbers

1 *chik*	11 *chug-tzik*	30 *somtchu*
2 *nyis*	12 *chug-nis*	40 *jiptchu*
3 *sum*	13 *chug-sum*	50 *ngaptchu*
4 *jzhe*	14 *chug-jzhe*	60 *tuktchu*
5 *nghra*	15 *chug-nghra*	70 *rduntchu*
6 *tuk*	16 *chu-ruk*	80 *rgyet tchu*
7 *dun*	17 *chub-dun*	90 *rgup tchu*
8 *gyat*	18 *chob-gyat*	100 *rgya*
9 *gyu*	19 *chur-gu*	1,000 *stong*
10 *chu*	20 *nyi-shu*	

Appendix 2

GLOSSARY

afsaras	angel-like figures
amchi	medicine man
arhat	Buddhist missionary
auto	motorised rickshaw
avatar	incarnation of a deity or other holy figure
bagh	garden
baradari	pavilion
Bharat	India
BJP	Bharatiya Janata Party
BSNL	Bharat Sanchar Nigam Limited, a state-owned telecommunications company
Bodhisattva	one who has obtained 'enlightenment' but remains on earth to show others the way
Bollywood	nickname for the Mumbai (formerly Bombay) film industry
Buddha	Prince Gautama Buddha, the first mortal to obtain 'enlightenment'
caste system	Hindu social and religious hierarchy
chadar	blanket
chai	tea
chang	homemade barley beer
char bagh	Persian garden
chorten	*see* stupa
chowk	crossroads or marketplace
Congress	Congress Party of India
dal	lentils
dargah	burial place or shrine of a Muslim saint
Devi	goddess
dhaba	roadside café
dharma	moral or natural code
dhobi	washerman
dudh	milk
dukhang	Tibetan prayer hall
dum aloo	spiced potato curry
dzo	offspring of a yak and a cow
ghee	clarified butter
gompa	Buddhist monastery
guru	teacher or religious leader

Gurudwara	Sikh temple
Guru Granth Sahib	Sikhism's holy book
gushtaba	minced-lamb meatballs with yoghurt gravy
Gypsy	popular 4x4 manufactured by Maruti
hijab	headscarf worn by Muslim women
Hindustan	India
HPTDC	Himachal Pradesh Transport Development Corporation
imam	Muslim religious leader
idli	South Indian snack made from rice flour
J&K	Jammu and Kashmir state
Jama Masjid	Friday mosque
ji	honorific suffix
Jihad	Holy war
jimdak	Korean dish
JKLF	Jammu and Kashmir Liberation Front
JKSRTC	J&K State Road Transport Corporation
kahwah	green tea prepared with saffron and almonds
kanger	pot filled with hot embers
karma	justice for past deeds (good or bad)
kesar	saffron
khanqah	shrine
Koran	Islam's holy book
lama	Buddhist monk
lingam/linga	phallus symbolic of Hindu god Shiva
LoC/LOC	Line of Control
Losar	Tibetan New Year
LTOCL	Ladakh Taxi Operators Cooperative Limited
madrassa	Islamic school
Mahabharata	famous Hindu epic poem
mahal	palace
maharani	queen
maharaja	king
malai kofta	vegetable dumplings in a creamy sauce
mandala	circular artwork symbolising the universe
mandir	temple
mani	stone wall with religious inscriptions
masjid	mosque
minaret	tower on a mosque
momos	steamed dumplings filled with vegetables or minced meat or cheese
muezzin	man who sings the call to prayer
nag	snake, specifically a cobra
namaste	Hindi greeting
NH	National Highway
nirvana	release from the cycle of reincarnation
noon chai	salted green tea served with bread
om	sacred symbol
pagoda	*see* stupa
paisa	money; there are 100 paise (pl) in a rupee
Pali	ancient script in which the Buddhist scriptures were first recorded

paneer	soft, white cheese often used as an ingredient in curries
paratha	flat bread, sometimes stuffed with potato or cheese
Partition	division of British India into the countries of India and Pakistan
pashmina	fine woollen shawl made with wool from a Pashmina goat
photang	place for Buddhist teaching
pindi	stone manifestation of the goddess Shakti
pir	Muslim saint
POK	Pakistan-Occupied Kashmir
prasad	offering of food to the gods
puja	prayers or session of religious teaching
pulao	rice-based dish akin to biryani
qila	fort
Raj	period of British rule
Ramadan	Islamic holy month of fasting that ends with the festival of Eid ul Fitr
rista	mutton meatballs in gravy
rogan josh	slow-cooked lamb in spicy gravy
samosa	deep-fried pastry triangle stuffed with minced lamb or vegetables
Sanskrit	classical language in which Hindu religious texts were written
shahi paneer	cheese curry
Sharia	Islamic law
sheer chai	salted green tea served with bread
shikara	punt-like boat used on the backwaters and lakes of Kashmir
shri	Lord or Mr
shrimati	Mrs
stupa	domed structure covering sacred relics
Sufism	mystical Islam
tank	reservoir
thangka	Tibetan cloth painting
thukpa	soup with noodles
tilak	a red mark on the forehead that denotes a blessing
tso	lake
uttapam	South Indian snack akin to a thick pancake
waazwaan	traditional banquet served on special occasions
yakhni	lamb cooked in yoghurt gravy
yatra	pilgrimage
yatri	pilgrim
zenana	harem

Appendix 3

FURTHER INFORMATION

BOOKS
History and archaeology

Boulnois, Luce *Silk Road: Monks, Warriors and Merchants on the Silk Road* Odyssey Guides, 2012. Detailed history of the people and ideas that spread along the Silk Road. Also available in French.

Dewan, Parvez *A History of Ladakh, Gilgit, Baltistan* Manas Publications, 2007. The founder of the Ladakh Festival brings alive the region's past from pre-history to the present day.

Fewkes, Jacqueline *Trade and Contemporary Society along the Silk Road: An Ethno-history of Ladakh* Routledge, 2011. Fewkes combines archaeology, history and anthropology in this book on Ladakh and its trading links. It can be hard to find, so look in specialist bookshops.

Fouq, Muhammad *A Complete History of Kashmir* Gulshaan, 2009. Translation and reprint of a wordy, 19th-century history written in Urdu. Covers more than 5,000 years of history. Although out of print, it is still fairly easy to come by.

Rai, Mridu *Hindu Rulers, Muslim Subjects: Islam, Community and the History of Kashmir* C Hurst & Co. Publishers Ltd, 2004. Rai looks back to the British policies of the 19th century for the underlying causes of Kashmir's 20th-century problems.

✳ Rizvi, Janet *Ladakh: Crossroads of High Asia* OUP India, 2012. Himalayan specialist Rizvi takes a multi-disciplinary approach to the history of Ladakh, including recent economic and social change. Recently updated, this is the biggest single book dedicated to Ladakh. Easy to read and comprehensive.

Kashmir post-1947

Ali, Tariq *Kashmir: The Case for Freedom* Verso, 2011. Collected writings from Tariq Ali, Arundhati Roy, Hilal Bhatt and others.

Noorani, A G *Article 370: A Constitutional History of Jammu and Kashmir* OUP India, 2011. Collection of White Papers, letters, memorandums and other documents that goes some way to explaining the complex constitutional status of J&K, and the impact of that status since independence. As the 'catchy' title suggests, this isn't the easiest of books to read.

Quraishi, Humra *Kashmir: The Untold Story* Penguin Books India, 2004. A look behind the statistics and propaganda at the human tragedy of the Kashmir conflict.

Schofield, Victoria *Kashmir in Conflict: India, Pakistan and the Unending War* IB Tauris Publishers, 2010. Expert Schofield explores the roots of the modern conflict and how it developed into a possible nuclear war. Schofield is both highly articulate and well informed.

Whitehead, Andrew *A Mission in Kashmir* Penguin Books, 2007. The story of how conflict started in 1947, drawn from oral history, contemporary media and archive materials. Out of print and very hard to find.

Memoirs and travellers' accounts

Boyden, Mark *Travels in Zanskar* Liffey Press, 2013. In 1981 Boyden set out on horseback to explore Ladakh and Zanskar, in doing so becoming one of the first foreigners to visit the Zanskar Valley. Foreword by Dervla Murphy.

Campbell, Iain *From the Lion's Mouth* Bradt Travel Guides, 2019. An engrossing account of a journey following the course of the Indus River from its mouth in the mudflats of Karachi through Ladakh to its source in Tibet.

Hardy, Justine *In the Valley of Mist: Kashmir's Long War* Rider, 2010. Beautifully written, personal account of Hardy's own travels in Kashmir, and the lives of those she's met. Poignant and accomplished.

Harvey, Andrew *A Journey in Ladakh* Rider, 2003. A travel writer and academic, Harvey explores Ladakh's Buddhist culture in a captivating way.

Keenan, Brigid *Travels in Kashmir* Hachette India, 2013. Formerly fashion editor at the *Sunday Times*, Keenan vividly explores the colours and textures of Kashmir, and in particular its cultural heritage.

Omrani, Bijan *Asia Overland: Tales of Travel on the Trans-Siberian and Silk Road* Odyssey Guides, 2010. Beautifully written and heavily illustrated historical travelogue drawing on accounts from Fa Xian to Marco Polo to Francis Younghusband. Full of humour, it is an entertaining and informative read for armchair travellers and modern-day explorers alike.

Peer, Basharat *Curfewed Night: A Frontline Memoir of Life, Love and War in Kashmir* Harper Press, 2011. Passionate account from a Kashmiri journalist. Winner of the Crossroad Prize for non-fiction.

Culture and traditions

Ames, Frank *The Kashmir Shawl and its Indo-French Influence* Antique Collectors' Club Ltd, 1999. Vast coffee-table book exploring the history and influences of Kashmiri shawls, written by a renowned textile dealer.

Isaac, John *The Vale of Kashmir* W W Norton & Company, 2008. Photographic tribute to the people and places of the Kashmir Valley. Coffee-table format.

Jaitly, Jaya *Crafts of Jammu, Kashmir and Ladakh* Grantha Corporation, 1999. General introduction to the region's crafts, with photos from contemporary artisans.

Koch, Ebba *Mughal Architecture* Prestel, 1991. Still the definitive book on the Mughal emperors' mosques, palaces, pleasure gardens and shrines.

Michell, George *Mughal Architecture and Gardens* Antique Collectors' Club Ltd, 2011. Authoritative book with superb photos.

Pritchard-Jones, Sian and Gibbons, Bob *Ladakh: A Land of Mystical Monasteries* Himalayan Travel Guides, 2018. Very detailed but easy-to-read guidebook covering the history and background of almost every major monastery in Ladakh.

Rizvi, Janet *Pashmina: The Kashmir Shawl and Beyond* Marg Publications, 2009. Sumptuous photographic book. A fitting tribute to the most beautiful of products.

Van Ham, Peter *Heavenly Himalayas: The Murals of Mangyu and Other Discoveries in Ladakh* Prestel, 2011. Focusing principally on the Mangyu Monastery, Van Ham explores Mayahana Buddhism in India and its impact on the visual arts.

Walker, Daniel *Flowers Underfoot: Indian Carpets of the Mughal Era* Thames & Hudson, 1998. Published to coincide with an exhibition at the Metropolitan Museum in New York, this is the definitive history of Mughal carpets and their motifs.

Language The website w koshur.org offers a good introduction to the Kashmiri language, with downloadable texts, vocabulary and lessons for beginners.

Delay, Richard *Read and Write Urdu Script* Teach Yourself, 2010. Helpful book for those simply wanting to understand the Urdu script. Ideal for readers with a prior knowledge of Hindi.

Koshal, Sanyukta *Conversational Ladakhi* Hanish & Co., 2005. Weighty hardback tome for those keen to gain a greater understanding of the Ladakhi language.

Koshal, Sanyukta *Guide to Learn Ladakhi Language* Hanish & Co., 2006. A smaller, lighter and generally more accessible version of Koshal's earlier textbook. Includes helpful tips on pronunciation and numerous useful phrases arranged by scenario.

Matthews, David *Complete Urdu* Teach Yourself, 2010. Well-written introduction to the script, vocabulary and grammar of the Urdu language.

Norman, Rebecca *Getting Started in Ladakhi* Melong Publications, 2012. Beginner's language guide with clearly explained sections on grammar and pronunciation. Pocket sized, but not easy to find outside Ladakh.

Literature

Chandra, Vikram *The Srinagar Conspiracy* Penguin India, 2000. Described as 'Great Game meets Bollywood', this modern thriller revolves around two childhood friends, one Muslim and the other Hindu, whose lives are torn apart by war.

Ded, Lal *I, Lalla: The Poems of Lal Ded* Penguin Classics, 2013. Collected poems of the 14th-century Kashmiri mystic Lal Ded. New translation into English.

Ghani, Tahir *The Captured Gazelle: The Poems of Ghani Kashmiri* Penguin Classics, 2013. Translated poems of the 17th-century Persian poet Mulla Tahir Ghani.

Raina, Trilokinath *A History of Kashmiri Literature* Sahitya Akademi, 2002. Very few overviews of Kashmiri literature exist. This title is hard to find and likely to be available only in India.

Singh, Jaspreet *Chef: A Novel* Bloomsbury USA, 2010. Tragic novel about the Kashmir conflict, as seen through the eyes of a young Sikh chef in the Indian army.

Thomas, Rosie *The Kashmir Shawl* Overlook Press, 2013. Evocative novel transporting readers from colonial-era houseboats to modern Wales.

Waheed, Mirza *The Collaborator* Penguin, 2012. Gripping debut novel that paints a devastating picture of Kashmir and the brutality of the conflict.

Trekking guides

Kucharski, Radek *Trekking in Ladakh* Cicerone, 2015. Detailed descriptions of eight of the best trekking routes in Ladakh and Zanskar. Some are well-known classics such as the Markha Valley trek but others blaze a long trail into little-walked valleys. Excellent.

Other Bradt guides For a full list of Bradt's Asia guides, see w bradtguides.com/shop.

Buckley, Michael *Tibet* Bradt Travel Guides, 2018.

NEWSPAPERS Major Indian newspapers are published in English as well as vernacular languages, and their content is usually available online even if the distribution of paper copies does not reach as far as the town you are in. This is frequently the case in J&K, and especially in the remoter areas.

Of the large, English-language newspapers, only the *Indian Express* (w indianexpress.com) is available in Jammu. Smaller, more regionally focused newspapers available in J&K include *Greater Kashmir* (w greaterkashmir.com; Srinagar only) and *Kashmir Times* (w kashmirtimes.in; Jammu only).

MAPS Though it may not be easy to get maps of J&K abroad, once you arrive they are plentiful, though not always of the highest quality, which is an issue if you are planning to trek. Note that some maps published in India do not demarcate the LoC, which would bring you into difficulty if you inadvertently were to cross into areas under the control of Pakistan.

India North & West 1:1,900,000 ITMB International Travel Maps. Large, folding map of northern India that includes the entirety of J&K.

Jammu & Kashmir 1:1,000,000 TTK Maps. Road map of J&K with larger-scale insets of Anantnag, Kargil, Leh and Srinagar. Note that the LoC is not shown on this map.

Ladakh 1:500,000 Hanish & Co., 2013. Widely available in Leh, this trekking map covers Ladakh, Zanskar and Manali and includes information on the most important monasteries.

Ladakh & Zanskar 1:150,000 Editions Olizane, 2013. The most detailed trekking map available is published in three parts (north, central and south). It is printed on non-tear paper and includes a short glossary.

Ladakh Trekking & Road Map HPC Publications, 2012. Small folding map (A4) with laminated surface. Not to scale.

WEBSITES
Travel advice
w **fco.gov.uk/travel** Foreign and Commonwealth Office travel advice.
w **fitfortravel.nhs.uk** NHS travel health advice.
w **travel.state.gov** US State Department travel advice.

Tourist information
w **jksrtc.co.in** J&K State Road Transport Corporation.
w **jktdc.in** J&K Tourism Development Corporation: accommodation booking.

Government sites
w **jammu.nic.in** Jammu district.
w **leh.nic.in** Leh district.
w **srinagar.nic.in** Srinagar district.

News and political analysis
w **bbc.co.uk/news/world/asia/india** BBC news coverage from India, including J&K.
w **greaterkashmir.com** E-paper and online video content.
w **kashmirtimes.com** The oldest English-language paper in J&K.
w **knskashmir.com** The first online news service for J&K.
w **risingkashmir.com** Local news published from Delhi, Jammu and Srinagar.

Culture

w **whc.unesco.org/en/tentativelists/5580** The Mughal Gardens on UNESCO's Tentative List of World Heritage Sites.

w **ladakhstudies.org** The International Association for Ladakh Studies (IALS).

FOLLOW US

Tag us in your posts to share your adventures using this guide with us – we'd love to hear from you.

🔲 BradtGuides
🐦 @BradtGuides
📷 @bradtguides & @stuartbutler1974
𝒫 bradtguides
▶ bradtguides

Index

Page numbers in **bold** indicate main entries; those in *italics* indicate maps.

INDEX OF ADVERTISERS